The Arms Trade and International Law

There are believed to be about 700 million small arms and light weapons (SALW) in the world, often contributing to highly destabilising security and other concerns in international law. SALW are the primary source of violations and abuses of humanitarian and human rights principles by states, rebels, terrorists and criminals. Many consider them the real weapons of mass destruction of our time, causing about half a million deaths annually. The unrestricted international transfer of SALW by states (99 states and 1000 companies involved in manufacturing and supply) is one of the major contributory and aggravating factors of this crisis; another is the illicit traffic in small arms. This book deals with the proliferation of SALW and their unregulated trade and transfer across borders. It addresses questions of definition, manufacturing, trade/transfer, and issues relating to state responsibility. The primary focus is on conventional small arms, in particular military-style weapons. The book tackles the core and most divisive legal problem of whether or not the laws relating to arms control and relevant norms of international law provide substantive restrictions upon the transfer of small arms by states. The application of the norms of international peace and security, non-intervention, humanitarian and human rights laws, and evolved relevant customary rules of arms control relating to these norms are considered particularly carefully. Questions of application and enforcement of relevant rules and institutional responses to the problem are also examined. The UN began considering an arms trade treaty in 2006; the publication of the book at this critical moment in time will make a positive contribution towards shaping the debate and aims to further enhance understanding in an area where close analysis is required.

Volume 15: Studies in International Law

Studies in International Law

Volume 1: Between Light and Shadow: The World Bank, the International Monetary Fund and International Human Rights Law
Mac Darrow

Volume 2: Toxics and Transnational Law: International and European Regulation of Toxic Substances as Legal Symbolism
Marc Pallemaerts

Volume 3: The Chapter VII Powers of the United Nations Security Council
Erika de Wet

Volume 4: Enforcing International Law Norms Against Terrorism
Edited by Andrea Bianchi

Volume 5: The Permanent International Criminal Court
Edited by Dominic McGoldrick, Peter Rowe and Eric Donnelly.

Volume 6: Regional Organisations and the Development of Collective Security
Ademola Abass

Volume 7: Islamic State Practices, International Law and the Threat from Terrorism: A Critique of the 'Clash of Civilizations' in the New World Order
Javaid Rehman

Volume 8: Predictablity and Flexibility in the Law of Maritime Delimitation
Yoshifumi Tanaka

Volume 9: Biotechnology and International Law
Edited by Francesco Francioni and Tullio Scovazzi

Volume 10: The Development of Human Rights Law by the Judges of the International Court of Justice
Shiv Bed

Volume 11: The Environmental Accountability of the World Bank to Third Party Non-State Actors
Alix Gowlland-Gualtieri

Volume 12: Transnational Corporations and Human Rights
Edited by Olivier De Schutter

Volume 13: Biotechnologies and International Human Rights
Edited by Francesco Francioni

Volume 14: Human Security and International Law
Barbara von Tigerstrom

The Arms Trade and International Law

Zeray Yihdego

• HART •
PUBLISHING
OXFORD AND PORTLAND, OREGON
2007

Published in North America (US and Canada) by
Hart Publishing
c/o International Specialized Book Services
920 NE 58th Avenue, Suite 300
Portland, OR 97213-3786
USA
Tel: +1-503-287-3093 or toll-free: (1)-800-944-6190
Fax: +1 503 280 8832
E-mail: orders@isbs.com
Website: www.isbs.com

Hart Publishing, 16C Worcester Place, Oxford, OX1 2JW
Telephone: +44 (0)1865 517530 Fax: +44(0)1865 510710
E-mail: mail@hartpub.co.uk
Website: http://www.hartpub.co.uk

British Library Cataloguing in Publication Data
Data Available

ISBN-13: 978-1-84113- 746-9 (hardback)

Typeset by Hope Services Ltd, Abingdon
Printed and bound in Great Britain by
TJ International Ltd, Padstow, Cornwall

Foreword

Nobody can dispute the damage which small arms (and the trade which makes them available) do. The AK-47 might be the most dangerous device that has ever been invented – but, of course, it has also been employed in the realisation of good causes, too. Few see an easy solution to this situation, controlling 'bad' guns without pulling in 'good'guns – or, indeed, any solution at all. Of course, a treaty might help but, until recently, even getting the treaty process going seemed a distant prospect. It was under the practical shadow of the guns and in the face of remoteness of a comprehensive solution that Dr Yihdego began his research. It was inspired by an idealistic objective, the making of a contribution, however slight, to diminishing the conditions under which the availability of small arms caused such destruction, that he undertook his project. However, he sought to realise it by bringing his technical skills as an international lawyer to bear by examining what constraints there were on their supply and use already in the law. So, he looks at the general principles of international law, international humanitarian law and the law of human rights to see if they may be interpreted to provide some means of regulating the manufacture and trade in small arms. He also looks at the consequences of violations of those limits already in the law he has identified, to see how they might make a difference. He concludes that there are some restraints to be found, if the law is looked at carefully and with his particular objective in view. Those who take a more stringent approach to the technique of international law might have their doubts but, at the very least, Dr Yihdego's work will be valuable to those engaged in the drafting of a small arms treaty. The big questions are for political resolution but, once it has been decided to embark on the process of setting up a regime for control of small arms, a whole series of legal problems arise, many of which have been identified by Dr Yihdego and to which he has some solutions to offer, solutions which have the virtue of drawing on established rules and mechanisms within the international legal system.

This book is the result of a great effort of inquiry and reflection. It is in the tradition which sees international law as having within its existing structures the resources for reform in the interest of projects to increase the common good. The tide of change may be flowing, even if rather limply, in the direction which Dr Yihdego wishes. His book is part of a process which seeks to move the tide into a narrower channel, so that its force may produce real and necessary change in the way States deal with the problem of small arms.

Colin Warbrick
Barber Professor of Jurisprudence
Birmingham Law School

Acknowledgements

First and foremost, I am thankful to and proud of my family, both in Ethiopia and abroad, for their overall backing in my struggle to fulfil this academic ambition; I am particularly grateful to my mother Eteye and my brother Atakility. This book is equally devoted to the memory of my beloved nephew, Elias Girmay, who unfortunately could not witness the success of this publication as a result of his sudden death in winter 2006.

Furthermore, my sincere gratitude goes to my supervisor—Professor Kaiyan Kaikobad, for having painstakingly supervised the doctoral thesis. His thoroughness and devotion to duty including the hard work with which he supervised my research is unparalleled and I am eternally grateful to him. My gratitude would be incomplete if I forgot to acknowledge Professor Colin Warbrick for the exceptional academic support I received from him during the course of this work. His contributions, ranging from the initiation of the topic to advice and guidance on the development of the core ideas and arguments of the project, are highly appreciated and valued.

I owe acknowledgement to my PhD examiners Professor Warbrick and Professor Nigel White, for their willingness to examine the doctoral thesis; I have learned invaluable lessons from their comments, questions, reports and their civility in respect of academic disagreements.

I also particularly thank Dr Gillian Boughton for her dedication, time and energy to proofread this long manuscript; the ideas and criticisms she offered have greatly improved the quality of the book. Equally important were the useful comments I received from General Tony Rogers, Professor Barbara Frey, Ms Holly Cullen and Dr Boughton, on parts of the PhD thesis. I must acknowledge Daniel Bethlehem (QC) for the advice he offered, and Professor James Crawford for clarifying some legal issues discussed in the book.

In any human endeavour, there is usually a time of difficulty. Mine is not an exception. I am therefore extremely grateful for the financial and moral assistance I received during difficult times from the various institutions and individuals who contributed in one way or another. In this regard, I am grateful to Professor Colin Warbrick, Professor Kaiyan Kaikobad, Mrs Theresa McKinven, Dr Catherine Seville, Dr Linton Lewis, Dr Elena Katselli, Mr Robin Shawyer, Dr Getachew Betru, Mrs Rebecca Peters, the Department of Law, Ustinov College, Durham University, the Liche Trust, Churches' Commission, the Sidney Perry Foundation, Gilbert Murray Trust (Oxford), IANSA, the Thessaloniki Institute of International

Law, Shell, the Cambridge Overseas Trust and my family and friends, for their assistance. Specifically too, my gratitude goes to the Department of Law and the University of Durham for offering me a part-time teaching position, invigilation and other appointments. I am equally very thankful to Ms Sarah Williams for being a very good colleague in my teaching of international law within the Department.

In the two years of being a tutor at St Mary's and Grey Colleges of the University of Durham, I have had the opportunity of interacting and relating with both students and college officials. This has been a very rewarding and illuminating experience to me. I am therefore indebted to Miss Jenny Hobbs and Dr Gillian Boughton of St. Mary's, and Mr Tony Cleaver and Professor Martyn Chamberlain of Grey.

Last but not least, my friends in Britain and abroad (to name a few, Michael Assfaw, Dr Tesfay Berhe, Francis Oni, Martin Uriarte, James DiTullio, Dr Shubeur Rahman, Dr Mazviita Chirimuuta, Dr Benjamin Wold, Valentina Asciutti, Ashley Savage), the service providers of the University, in particular the Academic Staff Development Office, SPA and the staff therein and the librarians in the Palace Green Library were all exceptionally compassionate and so deserve my thanks.

Zeray W Yihdego
London, February 2007

Preface

This monograph was initially a PhD thesis undertaken at Durham University from October 2002 to December 2005, which was successfully defended in April 2006. It has been fully revised and updated for the purpose of turning it into a book, 'The Arms Trade and International Law'.

The central question considered here is the proliferation of small arms and light weapons and their unregulated trade and transfer. There are believed to be about 700 million in circulation causing highly destabilising security and other concerns of international law. Small arms and light weapons (SALW) are the primary tools of violations and abuses of humanitarian principles by states, rebels, terrorists and criminals. Many consider them as *the real weapons of mass destruction* (WMD) of our time. Causing about half a million deaths annually. The unrestricted international *transfers* of SALW by states (99 states and 1000 companies involved in manufacturing and supply) is one of the major contributory and aggravating factors of the crises—they are the main source of the illicit trafficking in small arms, and therefore deserve prime attention.

This book deals with questions of definition, manufacturing, trade/transfer, and some issues relating to state responsibility. While a wide approach has been adopted to define SALW, the focus of the research has been on conventional small arms, in particular military-style weapons. There seems no substantive restriction on small arms manufacture, although there are evolving norms. Issues of definition and manufacturing have been examined as a background to the main issue.

This book tackles the core legal problem of whether or not the laws relating to arms control and relevant norms of international law provide *substantive restrictions* on the transfer of small arms by states. As a response to the crisis caused by the proliferation of small arms the book emphasises supply aspects of the issue. Some studies and publicists argue that there are no rules of international law applicable to these transactions, save Security Council arms embargoes. The book will challenge this assertion from the perspective of the application of the norms of international peace and security, non-intervention, humanitarian and human rights laws, and evolved relevant customary rules of arms control relating to these norms.

It will be argued that international law has succeeded in having and applying arms control and other related restrictions and obligations to such transactions. Very recent developments, notably the ECOWAS Convention on small arms of 2006, and UN General Assembly Resolution 61/89 of December 2006 entitled 'Towards an Arms Trade Treaty . . . '

(Voted 153-1-24) reinforces such an assertion. While the application of the aforementioned norms of international law to the problem has been fairly examined, relevant practices of the international community at all levels, including the position of prominent NGOs and publicists since the League of Nations era, have been particularly considered in the light of sources of international law and analogous legal regimes. The details of the legal standards are subject to the progressive development of international law. However, any violations may be regarded as the primary responsibility of the weapons supplier, recipient or other states.

Finally, the findings and recommendations of this book highlight the legal measures that must be taken to arrest illegal small arms transfer with their atrocious consequences as well as the achievements and challenges of the international community.

GA Resolution 61/89 has called on the Secretary-General to establish a Group of Governmental Experts 'to examine the feasibility, scope and draft parameters for a comprehensive, legally binding instrument establishing common international standards for the import, export and transfer of conventional arms, and to transmit the report of the group of experts to the General Assembly for consideration at its sixty-third session', commencing in 2008. The author hopes that the publication of the book at this critical moment will make a positive contribution towards shaping the debate and moving it forward.

Contents

PART II

INTERNATIONAL TRANSFERS OF SALW: SUBSTANTIVE LIMITATIONS AND PROBLEMS

Table of Abbreviations and Acronyms

AECA	Arms Export Control Act (US, 1976)
AJIL	American Journal of International law
AM.C-HRs	American Court of Human Rights
ARMSCOR	Armaments Development and Production Corporation of South Africa
Art.	Article
AU	African Union
BASIC	British-American Security Information Council
BJWA	The Brown Journal of World Affairs
BMS	UN Biennial Meeting of States
British Ybk Intl L	British Yearook of International Law
CCP	Council Common Position
CCW	Convention of Conventional Weapons, 1980
CFE	Conventional Forces Europe Treaty, 1992
CHD	Center for Humanitarian Dialogue
CIA	Central Intelligence Agency
CNG	China North Industries Group Corporation
CSG	China South Industries Group Corporation
CWC	Chemical Weapons Convention, 1993
DC	Disarmament Commission (UN)
DPoA	Draft Programme of Action
DRC	Democratic Republic of the Congo
ECHR	European Court of Human Rights
ECHRs	European Convention on Human Rights
ECOSCO	UN Economic and Social Council
ECOWAS MORATERIUM	West African Arms Moratorium on the Manufacture, Importation and Exportation of Small Arms of 1998
EJIL	European Journal of International Law
EU	European Union
EU CODE	EU Code of Conduct on Arms Exports, May, 1998
EUJA	EU Joint Action on Small Arms, Dec. 1998 (as amended in 2002)
FCIAT	Framework Convention for International Arms Transfers
FIREARMS PROTOCOL	UN Firearms Protocol of 2001
FRY	Federal Republic of Yugoslavia
GA	UN General Assembly

GA Res	General Assembly Resolution
GA.J.INT'L & COPM.L	Georgia Journal of International and Comparative Law
GATT	General Agreement on Tariff and Trade
GC	Geneva Convention (1949)
GCA	The Gun Control Act of 1968 (US)
GCAC	Guidelines on Conventional Arms Control/Limitation and Disarmament
GDR	German Democratic Republic
GGE	Group of Governmental Experts (UN)
GIAT	Guidelines for International Arms Transfers (Disarmament Commission)
GIIS	Graduate Institute of International Studies (Small Arms Survey)
GP	Geneva Protocol
HRC	UN Human Rights Committee
IANSA	International Action Network on Small Arms
ICCAT	International Code of Conduct for Arms Transfer of 1997
ICESCR	International Covenant on Economic, Social and Cultural Rights of 1966
ICJ	International Court of Justice
ICJ Repts	International Court of Justice Reports
ICRC	International Committee of the Red Cross
ICTY	International Criminal Tribunal for Yugoslavia
IGOs	Inter-governmental Organizations
IHL	International Humanitarian Law
IHRL	International Human Rights Law
ILC	International Law Commission
ILM	International Legal Materials
ILR	International Legal Reports
LDCs	Least Developing Countries
LIWL	Yttleton Engineering Works
LRCIL	Lauterpacht Research Centre for International Law
MCW	Major Conventional Weapons
MCWs	Major Conventional Weapons
MINES CONVENTION	Convention on the Prohibition of the Use, Stockpiling, Production and Transfers of Anti-Personnel Mines and their Destruction of 1997
MTCR	Missile Technology Control Regime
NATO	North Atlantic Treaty Organization
NFA	National Firearms Act
NGOs	Non-governmental Organizations

NIROBI PROTOCOL	Nairobi Protocol for the Prevention, Control and Reduction of Small Arms and Light Weapons in the Great Lakes Region and the Horn of Africa of 2004
NLMs	National Liberation Movements
NORNI	The State owned China North Industries Group Corporation
NRA	National Rifle Association
NSAs	Non-state Actors
NSSF	National Shooting Sports Foundation
OAS	Organization of American States
OAS CONVENTION	Organization of American States Convention on the Illicit Trafficking on Small Arms of 1998
OASTS	OAS Treaty Series
OAU	Organization of African Union
OJEC	Official Journal of European Community
OSCE	Organisation for Security Cooperation Europe
PCASED	Programme for Coordination and Assistance for Security and Development (West Africa)
PMP	Pretoria Metal Pressing
PoA	Programme of Action to Prevent, Combat and Eradicate the Illicit Trade in Small Arms and Light Weapons in All Its Aspects, 2001
PRC	People's Republic of China (Mainland)
PrepCOM	Preparatory Committee
RO	Royal Ordnance
ROC	Republic of China (Taiwan)
SAAMI	Sporting Arms and Ammunition Manufacturers Institute
SADC PROTOCOL	SADC Protocol on the Control of Firearms
SADC	Southern African development Community
SALW	Small Arms and Light Weapons
SAS	Small Arms Survey
SC	UN Security Council
SC	Res Security Council Resolution
SIPRI	Stockholm International Peace Research Institute
UAE	United Arab Imarets
UBR	Use-based Rule
UDHR	Universal Declaration on Human Rights
UKMIL	UK Materials on International Law
UNDP	United Nations Development Programme
UNIDR	United Nations Institute for Disarmament Research
VCLT	Vienna Convention on the Law of Treaties of 1969

VJIL	Virginia Journal of International Law
WFSSA	The World Forum on the Future of Sport Shooting Activities
WMD	Weapons of Mass Destruction
WTO	World Trade Organization
YBIHL	Year Book of International Humanitarian Law

Table of Cases

PART I

INTRODUCTION: FEATURES, DEFINITION AND MANUFACTURING OF SALW

1

Introduction

> International law, like all law, is inherently dynamic—developing structurally and systematically, developing substantively, flowing into new areas, embodying and responding to the social development of the world—human rights, . . . , and international public law to control the use and abuse of public power. (Philip Allott, *The Health of Nations*, 14.55).

DISARMAMENT OR ARMS control, as an issue of international law only emerged in the twentieth century, as has been shown in the Covenant of the League of Nations and the UN Charter.[1] Customarily, arms control implies the international regulation of armaments, such as verification measures. Arms control is also described as a measure necessary to ensure a military balance, which might lead to an increase in weapons. It is understood as separate from, but linked with, disarmament. The latter on the other hand refers, inter alia, to the banning and/or reduction of armaments.[2]

In recent times, however, both legal terms appear to be the same. The notion of arms control for instance includes freezing, reducing, and limiting certain weapons or methods of war and military activities. It is often considered as synonymous with 'arms regulation', 'arms limitation' and even 'disarmament'.[3] The UN often uses the word 'disarmament',[4] although it seems to be that both terms were in use in the League era (see chapter four).

Members of the League of Nations accepted unequivocally 'that maintenance of peace requires the reduction of national armaments to the lowest point consistent with national safety and the enforcement by common action of international obligation', as set out in Article 8 of the Covenant. In contrast, the UN Charter does not mention disarmament in its core purposes and principles. The term is only found in Articles 11, 26 and 47 of the Charter. The General Assembly ('GA') is authorised to consider 'principles governing disarmament and the regulation of armaments'. This has to be exercised in the light of the notion of co-operation to

[1] Shi, 'Address Delivered at the Formal Plenary Session', in Dahlitz, below n 7, at 21–22; see also Feldman, 'The Place of Arms Control and Disarmament in the System of International Law' in Dahiltz and Dicke, below n 7, at 38.

[2] Feldman, *ibid*; see, eg Carter, *Success and Failure in Arms Control Negotiations* (Oxford, Oxford University Press, 1989) 4.

maintain peace and security. The Security Council ('SC') has been entrusted with the power to formulate plans 'for the establishment of a system for the regulation of armaments', as will be discussed further in chapter five.

It is the prevailing view that arms control had 'a prominent place', as a universal obligation in the League's Covenant, as opposed to the UN Charter.[5] Even so some consider that the UN Charter has adopted a wider approach to the maintenance of peace and security, which embraces the international regulation of armaments. The prohibition of the use of force under Article 2(4) of the Charter may also provide sufficient legal basis for arms limitations. So the Charter is not weaker than its predecessor on the subject; rather the League was not comprehensive in its approach.[6]

While both arguments are sensible, this gives the impression that arms control was one of the core principles on which the League was built unlike the UN. In the latter, however, arms control has clearly been placed under the law of international peace and security, as a branch of international law. It could also be described as 'a new "branch of the tree" of Public International Law', due to 'the highly specialised nature' of the field.[7] The objectives, scope, types, methods, and sources of this field of law will now be described, as a basis for later discussions.

At least five principal *objectives* of arms control could be said to be evident. First, through removing the kinds and levels of armaments which could cause a war, commonly known as stopping the drift to war, disarmament contributes to the maintenance of international peace and security. Many consider this to be the major goal of arms control. Secondly, weapons are 'economically ruinous or profligate', and so arms control could divert resources into other social, economic and similar channels, also known as the objective of reducing the burden of armaments.[8] Thirdly, arms control helps humanise warfare and reduce the destructiveness of armed conflicts by limiting the use of inhumane weapons and methods of conducting a conflict.[9] Fourthly, it facilitates the proper enforcement of the values of general international law; inter alia,

[3] Goldblat, *Arms Control: A Guide to Negotiations and Agreements* (London, Sage Publications, 1994) 3.

[4] Jasentuliyana, 'The Process of Achieving Effective Arms Control' in Dahlitz and Dicke, below n 7, at 181.

[5] Shi, above n 1, at 22.

[6] Elaraby, 'Practical Problems with Multilateral Arms Control Treaties' in Dahlitz and Dicke, below n 7, at 45; see also Shi, above n 1, at 23.

[7] Feldman, above n 1, at 42; see also Dahlitz and Dicke, *The International Law of Arms Control and Disarmament, Proceedings of the Symposium, Geneva, 28 February–2 March 1991* (New York, Frederick A Praeger, United Nations, 1991) 219.

[8] Bull, *The Control of the Arms Race: Disarmament and Arms Control in the Missile Age*, 2nd edn (New York, 1965) 3–4 and 30; see also Galtung, *There are Alternatives: Four Roads to Peace and Security* (Nottingham, Spokesman Books, 1984) 124–31.

[9] Towle, *Arms Control and East-West Relations* (London, Croom Helm, 1983) 1–2; see also Galtung, *ibid*.

the principle of non-interference, sovereign equality, co-operation among states and the fulfilment of international law obligations in good faith.[10] Lastly, arms control may be essential for the demilitarisation of society, as 'overgrown military establishments are inimical to liberty'; in effect to democracy.[11] This may imply an expansion of the law of arms control to human rights law, as this book will discuss. In all these ways, the approaches and objectives of arms control law are multifaceted and interrelated.

With respect to the scope of arms control, five issues are worth illustrating. The first is that this branch of law is a broad subject, which involves armed forces, military activities and armaments.[12] The focus of this work is on armaments. The second is to consider arms control could be forced or mutual and consensual. Some of the examples of the former are measures against Germany and Japan after the two world wars.[13] This kind, as the older type of disarmament, is usually imposed upon a defeated adversary[14]; yet it may take place without resorting to war, through inspection and verification mechanisms.[15]

Peaceful and consensual methods of disarmament are principal to present-day international law, in accordance with the purposes and principles of the UN Charter. This form of disarmament is a product of negotiation, compromise and mutual agreement between states. As shown earlier, such attempts lead to the adoption of conventions, protocols and other legal and political instruments, at the universal, regional or unilateral echelons. International organisations, notably the UN, play an important role in organising efforts and measures of this type.[16] It has generally been thought 'arms control can occur only if governments want it and can agree on its terms'; its conditions are thus political.[17] This should not, however, defeat applicable principles and norms of international law.

As a third point, arms control embraces quantitative and qualitative restrictions. While the former limits the number of particular armaments such as nuclear warheads of a state, qualitative restrictions prohibit the use, possession and transfer of 'specified items' or weapons such as poisonous gas, bacteriological weapons and anti-personnel landmines.[18]

[10] See, eg Feldman, above n 1, at 40; see also Komatina, 'Address Delivered at the Formal Plenary Session' in Dahlitz and Dicke, above n 7, at 33.

[11] Bull, above n 8, at 4.

[12] Goldblat, above n 3, at 3.

[13] See, eg Towle, above n 9, at 154, 162 and 169.

[14] *Ibid*, at 1.

[15] See, eg on Iraq, SC Res 687/1991, paras 8 (a), (b), and 9 (i), (ii), SC Res 1441/2002, paras 2, 3 and 5.

[16] Galtung, above n 8 at 134–38; see also Towle, above n 9.

[17] Bull, above n 8, at 65; see also Edmonds, 'International Disarmament: the Main Objectives' (1996) 6 *Disarmament Diplomacy*.

[18] Vagts, 'The Hague Conventions and Arms Control' (2000) 94 *AJIL* 31.

In other words, quantitative restrictions usually adopt a non-proliferation approach, with the aim of limiting the use and availability of weapons[19]; whereas qualitative restrictions often forbid the manufacture, use, stockpiling and transfer of certain weapons, in particular those deemed to be illegal by their very nature.[20] Fourthly, while international law is primarily concerned with *macro* disarmament, *micro* disarmament also rests within its domain, in particular, in post-conflict, peace keeping and peace building situations.[21]

Lastly, diverse methods and techniques of application could be deployed to limit armaments, depending on the circumstances, purposes and rules of application of legal regimes relating to weaponry. For reduction of arms, for example, destruction, conversion for non-military purposes, static display in museums or similar sites, limit on use and quantity, and modification (in multi- purpose arms),[22] may well be effective ways to achieve this.

The legal sources of arms control are primarily treaties and custom, similar to other fields of international law. Indeed, since the Second World War, vast developments have been achieved in arms control treaties at different levels,[23] as we shall later see. Subsequent practices of disarmament treaties also constitute an essential part of such agreements.[24] Despite this, substantive rules of arms control usually develop as a custom first. Custom is thus part of the law of arms control, which also includes domestic legal regulations and practices of states on armaments. This is the most overlooked source of law, relating to the field under consideration. Elements and requirements of custom, ie state practice and *opinio juris* remain crucial in establishing such norms[25]; yet some favour restrictive and others loose approaches, in applying the elements of custom to arms control issues (see chapter five). In addition, the use and transfer of armaments, among others, are subject to general principles and rules of international law [26] (see chapter four).

[19] See Komatin, above n 10, at 33.

[20] See Galtung above n 8 and Towle, above n 9.

[21] *Supplement to an Agenda for Peace*, 3 January 1995, paras 57–63; see also, Laurance and Meek, 'The New Filed of Micro Disarmament: Addressing the Proliferation and Build-up of Small Arms and Light Weapons' *BICC Brief 7* (September 1996) 10.

[22] Koulik and Kokoski, *Conventional Arms Control: Perspectives on Verification* (Oxford, Oxford University Press, 1994) 31–35.

[23] *Ibid*, at 157.

[24] Ronzitti, 'Problems of Arms Control Treaty Interpretation' in Dahlitz and Dicke, above n 7, at 115.

[25] Dahlitz, 'The Role of Customary Law in Arms Limitation' in Dahlitz, above n 7, at 158–59 and 165–71.

[26] Feldman, above n 1, at 40; see also Dahlitz and Dicke, above n 7, at 219; see also Falk, 'Nuclear Weapons, International Law and the World Court, A Historic Encounter' (1997) 9 *AJIL* 66; see also *Declaration* of Judge Bedjaowi, Nuclear Weapons Advisory Opinion, *ICJ Repts* 1996, paras 12–16.

Nonetheless, the following problems concerning sources of arms control law are worthy of note. First, due to the sensitive nature of the regulation of armaments, states are generally reluctant to enter into treaties of this kind. Secondly, the emergence of customary rules of disarmament is a gradual process; thus, one has to be aware of the difference between *lex ferenda* and *lex lata* rules of arms control.[27] Thirdly, general principles of international law may not provide detailed prohibitions, standards and exceptions on the use, manufacture and transfer of weapons. Fourthly, judicial decisions, as a source or evidence of rules are virtually non-existent, as states hardly refer their disagreements on those issues to third party dispute resolution; disarmament policies are generally non-justiciable.[28] And lastly, legal problems of this branch of law are not well studied; the area is '*neglected by lawyers*'.[29] Though vagueness of rules of arms control may offer flexibility and further development of such regulations, the negative effects outweigh such an advantage.

Despite these and other challenges, various measures of disarmament have been adopted, both in early and modern-day history. To mention just a few, the use of 'any projectile of a weight below 400 grammes',[30] Dum-Dum bullets, noxious gases, explosives launched from balloons, sub-marine contact mines, poisonous gas and bacteriological weapons,[31] have been outlawed; the ban on the production and stockpiling of bacteriological[32] and chemical weapons,[33] have expanded and reinforced the aforesaid measures. The use[34] and proliferation[35] of nuclear weapons have been placed under some restrictions (see chapter five).

[27] Dahlitz, above n 25 at 174; Jusentuliana, above n 4, at 221–22.

[28] Dahlitz, *ibid* at 159; see also Dahlitz and Dicke, above n 7, at 222.

[29] Komatina, above n 10, at 29; see also Shi, above n 1 at 26–27.

[30] *Declaration Renouncing the Use, in Time of War, of Certain Explosive Projectiles*. St Petersburg, 29 November/11 December 1868; see also Schindler and Toman, *The Law of Armed Conflicts* (Geneva, Martinus Nijhoff, 1988) 102.

[31] See, eg *Protocol for the Prohibition of the Use in War of Asphyxiating, Poisonous or other Gases, and of Bacteriological Method of Warfare*, 17 June 1925, entered into force 8 February 1928; see also *Treaty relating to the Use of Submarines and Noxious Gases in Warfare*, Washington, 25 L.N.T.S.202 (1922). It was never ratified; see also Best, *War and Law Since 1945* (London, Clarendon Press, 1994) 163; see also Vagts, above n 18, at 8.

[32] *Convention on the Prohibition of the Development, Production and Stockpiling of Bacteriological (Biological) and Toxin Weapons and on their Destruction*, see eg Arts I, and II, entered into force 26 March 1975; see also SIPRI, 'Dubious Weapons' below n 128, at 7.

[33] *Convention on the Prohibition of the Development, Production, Stockpiling and Use of Chemical Weapons and on Their Destruction* (CWC), 13 June 1993, entered into force on 29 April 1997, see eg Art III; see also Kenyon, 'The Organisation for the Prohibition of Chemical Weapons: The Birth is Due-are we Ready?' in Brown, *Arms Control Issues for the Twenty-First Century* (New Mexico, Sandia, 2000) 223–38; see also Vagts, above n 18, at 11.

[34] See, eg *Treaty Banning Nuclear Weapons Tests in the Atmosphere, in Outer Space and under Water*, 5 August 1963, USA-UK-USSR, 14 UST 1313,480 *UNTS* 43, effective 1 January 1979. Signed by 108, ratified by 94 and acceded by 23 states.

[35] See, eg *Treaty on Nuclear Non Proliferation*, signed 1 July 1968, entered into force in 5 March 1970, Preamble para 4, Art 1; the International Atomic Energy Agency is responsible for inspecing the application of the treaty; see also *Strategic Arms Reduction Treaty (START II)*,

To some extent, conventional weapons are also in the realm of arms control, in particular, major or strategic conventional weapons (hereafter 'MCWs') and inhumane weapons. Concerning MCWs, some non-binding and voluntary arrangements of restriction,[36] and transparency[37] measures, have been undertaken at the global level (see chapter two). It is noteworthy that the CFE Treaty of 1992 in Europe[38] has imposed quantitative limitations on armaments such as battle tanks, armoured combat vehicles, combat aircraft and artillery pieces which are assumed to be essential for conducting surprise attacks and large scale offensive operations.[39] Such endeavours have been characterised as important co-operative security and confidence building measures among neighbours and other states.[40]

Inhumane weapons could be described as a second aspect of the efforts to control conventional weapons. The CCW of 1980 and its protocols regulate the use and/or manufacture and/or transfers of non-detectable fragments, landmines, booby traps and similar devices, incendiary and blinding laser weapons.[41] In addition, the 1997 Mines Convention outlawed the production, use, stockpiling and transfer of anti-personnel landmines. Essential elements of both conventions will be considered in the book, as a matter of direct or indirect relevance.

Overall, the aforementioned measures signify the initiatives carried by the international community, to regulate, inter alia, chemical, biological, nuclear, and conventional weapons. The first three, also known as weapons of mass destruction, have attracted the primary attention of states, international organisations,[42] and even publicists.

The international community is also challenged with SALW proliferation, which needs to be addressed swiftly. In this work these armaments are defined as 'all those deadly weapons, including their components and ammunition, suitable for personal and/or for group use, employed or to be employed by states and others, for legal and/or illegal purposes and are uncovered in *lex specialis* weaponry legal regimes' (see chapter two). The following core issues explain the challenge of SALW proliferation,

3 January 1993, not yet in force; see also 'Russia and US Agree Arms Cuts', *BBC News*, 13 May 2002; see also *Treaty between the USA and the USSR on the Elimination of their Intermediate-Range and Shorter-Range Missiles*, 8 Decmeber 1987, entered into force 1 June 1988.

36 The 1991 Paris *Communiqué*, UN SC Permanent Five; see also the 1991 London Guidelines; for bilateral US-Russia measures see Goldblat, above n 3, at 182–83; see also the UN Register, below n 37, Preamble, para 12, operative, paras 5, 9, 12, and 18.

37 *UN Register of Conventional Arms*, GA Res 46/36 L/1991.

38 *Conventional Forces In Europe Treaty* (CFE), entered into force 17 November 1992; see also <http://www.defenselink.mil/acq/acic/treaties/cfe/cfe_es.htm>

39 *Ibid*; see also Goldblat, above n 3, at 173–74.

40 Homan, 'The OSCE and Cooperative Security: Conventional Arms Control in Europe' in Brown, above n 33, at 181–85.

41 *Convention on Prohibition or Restriction on the use of Certain Conventional Weapons which may be deemed to be Excessively Injurious or to have Indiscriminate Effects*, 1980.

42 See, eg *Final Document of the Tenth Special Session of the GA*, A/5–s10/2; see also UN PoA.

and provide the reasons for this study of 'The Arms Trade and International Law'.

(A) 'The world is flooded with small arms and light weapons numbering at least 500 million, enough for one of [sic.] every 12 people on earth'.[43] Besides, 99 states and 1000 companies have been involved, in manufacturing and/or supply of SALW (see chapters three and four).

(B) It has been generally accepted that half a million people die every year, as victims of SALW; most of these are *civilian* losses.[44] The UN Secretary-General, in his Millennium Summit rightly observed that:

> The death toll from small arms dwarfs that of all other weapons systems—and in most years greatly exceeds the toll of the atomic bombs that devastated Hiroshima and Nagasaki. In terms of the carnage they cause, small arms, indeed, could well be described as 'weapons of mass destruction'.[45]

(C) SALW aggravate and prolong armed conflict, ignite a sense of insecurity and refugee flows, and hinder humanitarian assistance.[46]

(D) They are the main tools of genocide and repression—including illegal killings, torture and forced disappearances[47] (see chapter eight).

(E) Violence and crimes such as homicides, robberies, rapes and kidnappings usually involve small arms.[48]

(F) In *economic and development* terms, the money involved in this business ranges from $4–12 billion per year[49]; in particular, spending on small arms has a significant impact on the economy and development of LDCs[50]; further, the excessive availability of arms discourage both domestic and foreign investment and investors[51];

[43] See, eg Annan, 'Small Arms, Big Problems', *International Herald Tribune* (10 July 2001) 1 [emphasis added].

[44] See, eg *Report of the Secretary General to the Security Council, 'Small Arms'*, 20 September 2002, p 2.

[45] *Millennium Summit*, 2000, Part IV, 'Freedom From Fear', p 11.

[46] *Report of the SG*, above n 44, at 2; see also Annan, above n 43

[47] See, eg Annan, above n 43.

[48] William, Robert and Camilla, 'Stray Bullets: The Impact of Small Arms Misuse in Central America', *Small Arms Survey, Occasional Paper* (No 5, October 2002) 1, 15 and 26; see also Pirseyedi, United Nations Institute for Disarmament Research (UNIDIR), *The Small Arms Problem in Central Asia: Features and Implications*, (Geneva, United Nations Publications, 2000) 39*ff*; see also Chi Chi Sileo, 'Gun Control War Targets Our Worst Nightmares' *10* (23) *Insight* (June 1994) 12–15, each year over 600,000 Americans are confronted by a criminal with a handgun.

[49] See chs 3 and 4.

[50] Eminent Persons Group, *Humanitarian Challenge of Small Arms Proliferation*, presented to the First PrepCom for the 2001 UN Conference on Small Arms, 28 February–3 March 2000, p 4; see also Mrs Albright (US) on the economic and social effect of arms sale on poor countries, *SC debate on Small Arms*, 24 September 1999, pp 19–20; see also *GGE 1997*, para 77 (c) [for the Panel's background see ch 2, p 26]; see also Annan, above n 43.

[51] *Eminent Persons*, above n 50, at 7; see also Group of Governmental Experts of 1999 on Implementation (A/54/258) p 9 [for details on the Panel see 3.3.1, p 72].

and their destructive feature, particularly of light weapons and explosives is not be undermined [52] (see chapters three and four).

(G) To date, it is not controversial that the main stream of the proliferation is the 'legal trade' of arms by states and their authorised entities; although the black-market in weapons is a real problem, the 'licit' and grey market transfers are the major sources of the crises and diversion to clandestine markets (see chapter four).

(H) Their unrestricted circulation from country-to-country and conflict-to-conflict, mainly by states and their companies have been causing enormous problems (see chapter two).

While most of these problems will be expounded later (see chapter two), some reflections on the cause and effect of small arms versus the aforesaid calamities could be imperative at this point.

The 1997 UN Panel of Governmental Experts on Small Arms (hereafter 'GGE Panel 1997') emphasised that SALW do not cause conflict—rather they 'exacerbate and increase their lethality'.[53] Some countries, especially those that are suppliers emphasise this approach.[54] In contrast, the 1999 UN Panel has considered small arms as a major source of insecurity. The UK, for example, believes that the supply of arms is one of the underlining causes of conflict.[55] Interestingly, the Russian Federation argued that without solving the uncontrolled spread of small arms, settlement of conflict will be impossible in the world.[56] Indeed, small arms and their excessive availability appears to be one of the key causes/factors of conflict, atrocities, violence and tyranny, yet the level and nature of causation may vary from country-to-country.

As one essential factor, inter alia, of conflict and violations of humanitarian principles, therefore, the international law issues attached to the proliferation of small arms generally include, but are not limited to: (1) defining SALW; (2) substantive limitations upon the use, manufacture, transfer, and surplus of small arms; (3) controlling/regulating the aforementioned activities through licence, end-use certificate, marking and tracing and measures of transparency; (4) regulating the persons involved in such activities, in particular dealers of arms; (5) the demarcation between 'licit' transfers versus 'illicit' trafficking of SALW; (6) issues of

[52] The Deputy Secretary-General, *Address to the UN Conference on the Illicit Trade in SALW in All its Aspects*, New York, 9 July 2001, p 1, according to the Inter American Bank, the direct and indirect costs of violence carried out by small arms is estimated at $140–170 billion annually in Latin America alone.

[53] *GGE 1997*, p 15.

[54] See, eg China's position, *SC Debate*, above n 50, at 15.

[55] *SC Debate*, *ibid*, at 2–23.

[56] *Ibid*, at 11; see also '*The ECOWAS Convention on Small Arms of 2006*', p 2, para 2; the Heads of State have unequivocally asserted that: 'the proliferation of SALW constitutes a major destabilising factor in ECOWAS Member States, and poses a serious threat to the peace and stability of our people'.

application and enforcement of relevant rules; and (7) the consequences of violations of such norms by states.

Because of the newly emerging nature of the subject, the uncertainty and confusion over the applicable primary rules of international law, so as to address the most important aspects in-depth, and the fact that all these complex problems could not be addressed in one piece of research, the book will largely be limited to questions of substantive limitations upon SALW transfers by states.

For that reason, the work comprises the following six areas. First, this book is primarily devoted to examining the applicable principles of general international law, and the emergence of relevant primary rules/standards on trans-boundary transfers of SALW. As treaties are scarce on the subject, special attention has been paid to international custom. This approach, supported by treaties of general relevance, is believed to help focus on concrete practices and their legal implications, which may be incorporated in future global arms trade treaty. Mainly, the work challenges the general thesis that contemporary international law offers no rules/norms, which have to be adhered to in the course of arms transfers. The details of possible legal restrictions and issues will be defined further in the appropriate chapters in due course.

Secondly, definition of SALW and the question of substantive limitation upon manufacturing of small arms have been covered to some detail, both as legal problems and as background to the main issue.

Thirdly, taking into consideration the dual-use nature of small arms, the circumstances and the manner of actual and/or potential use of small arms have also constituted the basis for investigating pertinent international law norms.

Fourthly, although the focus is on the 'licit trade', in particular on state-to-state transfers, the 'illicit trade' is covered to the extent that a state is involved in such transactions. This means that the inquiries are essentially into state-to-state and/or state-to-NSA transfers vis-à-vis relevant rules of international law (for types of transfers see chapters four and nine).

Fifthly, although not focused on, the application and associated problems of the rules, including SC and regional organisations' arms embargoes have been examined, so far as they are useful to address the major concerns of the book. Lastly, the nature of responsibility of states vis-à-vis breaches of the rules of arms transfer has been examined to a certain extent.

However, some regulatory aspects have been fully excluded for the reasons discussed above and in the interest of economy; questions of marking and tracing and brokerage, among others, are not thus within the scope of this book.

The book is divided into three parts. Part I deals with features and definition of small arms in chapter two, and questions of manufacturing in chapter three. Part II, the core segment of the book, examines general principles and the particular rules of international law on SALW transfer; it consists of four chapters; chapter four, as an introduction clarifies the use of terms and scope, and identifies relevant fundamental principles of international law and other considerable bases for the rules on transfers; chapters five to eight examine particular rules, which must apply to the small arms trade, namely, peace and security, non-intervention, humanitarian and international human rights limitations. Part III, followed by chapters nine and ten will ask questions over state responsibility, findings and recommendations respectively.

For the most part, chapters are organised to show: (1) problems and the scope to be discussed; (2) relevant facts and figures; (3) applicable rules and efforts at all levels (global, regional and domestic, the position of courts, publicists and NGOs); (4) analysis on particulars of rules (sources, contents, standards, analogies, exceptions and problems); and (5) conclusion.

As explained later, the terms 'small arms', 'small arms and light weapons' or 'SALW', and the terms 'trade', 'import-export' or 'transfers' have been synonymously used throughout. The first step is to establish a cluster of weaponry called SALW, including their salient features.

2

Features and Definition Of SALW: Associated Problems

2.1 FEATURES

IDENTIFYING THE NATURE of small arms may help define and differentiate them from other weaponry regimes. In general, SALW has its own characteristics as one category of armaments. The nature of their consequences, accessibility, suitability, durability, versatility of use and scope are among the issues from which some of the salient features could be set.

2.1.1 Lethal Character

One of the core salient features of SALW is their lethal nature. It is persistently reported that the human cost is half a million peoples' lives on an annual base. The death toll of SALW is higher than the atomic bombs dropped on Japan at the end of the Second World War.[1] Advancements in technology have resulted in greater efficiency in terms of lethality. This means that, presently, it is possible to fire over 700 rounds per minute using small arms. Small arms therefore cause many more causalities than major weapons in contemporary conflicts.[2] The best example of this is the 1994 terrorist attack by the IRA at a Roman Catholic bar in Belfast in which one of the gunmen was able to reload and expend a second magazine of ammunition in less than a minute. The terrorist attack of March 2004, which 'killed scores of commuters on packed trains in Madrid' was committed with explosives that may be classed as SALW. The portability and firepower, particularly of light weapons attracts a high demand.[3] However, the use of SALW may not always result in death; for example,

[1] Secretary-General Annan, 2000, *Millennium Summit*, Pt IV, *Freedom From Fear*, p 11, at <http://www.un.org/millennium/sg/report/ch3.pdf>

[2] Berkol, 'Marking and Tracing Small Arms and Light Weapons, Improving Transparency and Control', *special issue 2002*, p 16, at <http://www.grip.org-pub-rap-rgo2-hs1_alg.pdf>

[3] Smith, 'Light Weapons—The Forgotten Dimension of the International Arms Trade', in Brassey's Defence Studies, (1994) *Brassey's Defence Year Book* 274–75; see, eg *Press Release*, 'SC Condemns Madrid Terrorist Bombings' SC/8022, UN SC Res1530/ 2004.

anti-personnel landmines usually maim human beings.[4] Bereavement or permanent disability also needs to be taken into account. Beyond that, human insecurity, displacement, humanitarian and social crises are also among the consequences that are associated with the potentially lethal nature of the use of these arms.[5]

The GGE Panel 1997 acknowledged them as 'lethal instruments of war'.[6] The Programme of Action of the UN Conference (hereafter 'UN PoA') also underlined that these arms pose a serious threat to the safety and security of an individual, community, nation, region, and the world. It emphatically mentioned the human suffering caused by SALW.[7] Yet, whether all small arms including non-explosive weapons and civilian firearms are said to be fatal remains a divisive question. In the technical and actual use sense, however, all are believed to be dangerous. As lethal weapons, some go to the extent of considering SALW as 'weapons of mass destruction'.[8] Indeed, a massive number of lives have been victimised by small arms for a number of decades. Replicas of guns that do not cause fatalities may not be regarded as small arms despite the fact that they evidently cause psychological insecurity.

However, lethal character does not necessarily entail illegitimate results. Thus, while it is apparent that all small arms are fatal, the outcomes may or may not be justifiable (see 2.1.5).

In our case, 'lethal' basically refers to illegitimate human disasters, as a result of internal or international warfare, crime, violence, suppression of human rights norms, terrorism and so on. For that reason, therefore, the lethal characteristic of small arms and light weapons must be seen in combination with other features; this will equip us with a better understanding on the question as to why SALW is the most lethal group of weaponry.

[4] *Convention on the Prohibition of the Use, Stockpiling, Production and Transfer of Anti-Personnel Mines and on their Destruction*, 1997, entered into force, 1 March 1999, Preamble, para 1.

[5] Canada-EU Statement, *Small Arms and Anti- Personnel Landmines*, p 1, at <http://www.iansa.org/documents/gov/gov6.htm>; *Report of the Secretary-General to the Security Council on Small Arms*, 20 September 2002, p 2, para 4.

[6] *Report of Group of Governmental Experts* (*GGE 1997*), 27 August 1997, p 11, para 24.

[7] *Report of the United Nations Conference on the Illicit Trade in Small Arms and Light Weapons in All its Aspects*, 9–20 July 2001, particularly see–*Programme of Action to Prevent Combat and Eradicate the Illicit Trade in Small Arms and Light Weapons in All its Aspects* (UN PoA), p 7, Preamble, paras 1.2 and 1.3; 'Can Small Arms and Light Weapons Be Controlled?' *United States Department of State, International Information Programmes*, 2 June 2001, p 1, para 2, at <http://usinfo.state.gov/topical/pol/arms/stories/01060243.htm>

[8] UN Deputy Secretary-General, Speech-*UN Conference on Small Arms*, New York, 9 July 2001, p 1.

2.1.2 Accessibility

Overall, SALW are accessible to a wide range of people. Although they are in use by state forces for military and law enforcement needs, the unique characteristic goes to accessibility by, and suitability for armed conflicts, terrorism, and criminality (see 2.1.5). Why and how could they be easily accessible is the first issue that requires an answer. First, they are sold cheaply in black, grey, or legal markets (see further chapter four). For example, a decade ago, in Lomashasha, Swaziland, as a centre of arms trade in the region, an AK-47 assault rifle could be purchased for $6 dollars[9]. In Kenya, until recently, AK-47 automatic rifles could be bought for the price of a chicken and goat.[10] In Mozambique, Angola, and Albania, an AK-47 or FN-FAL assault rifles could be sold for $20.[11] Conversely, the price of some sensitive technologies is said to be very expensive. One aeroplane alone could cost $10 million.

This however, is not evidence that all small arms can be purchased cheaply. Some light weapons, particularly missiles, are expensive armaments. For instance, the US was trying to retrieve stinger surface-to-air missiles from Afghans for $65,000 each in the 1980s.[12]

So, although some weapons may be bought cheaply, one cannot clearly state this is the case for every weapon. It may not be true also that all small arms are obtained through purchase; for example, some small arms could traditionally be made, with insignificant expense in market terms.

Secondly, these arms have been excessively manufactured and distributed. The world stockpile is currently estimated to be 639 million, excluding mines, dispersed all over the world.[13] In 2002, the global military stockpile grew by 700,000 and the insurgent one by 100,000.[14] As stated elsewhere, 100 million mines are in circulation, albeit the US army suggested in the early 1990s that 'there may be as many as 400 million dumb mines sown around the world'.[15]

In addition, 1000 companies in 98 countries are involved in the manufacture of small arms. Eleven of these are in the volatile region of the Middle East.[16]

[9] Smith, above n 3, at 281.

[10] Rocard, Former Prime Minister of France and Co-chair of the Eminent Persons Group, 'The Scourge of Small Arms: Who Supplies, Who Dies?' speech, *Kennedy Political Union at American University*, Washington DC, 28 February 2000, p 1; see, eg Deputy Secretary-General, above n 8, at 1.

[11] Berkol, above n 2, at 16.

[12] Smith, above n 3, at 281.

[13] *Report of the Secretary-General*, above n 5, at 2.

[14] GIIS, *Small Arms Survey 2002: Counting the Human Cost* (Oxford, Oxford Univeristy Press)103–04.

[15] Smith, above n 3, at 276.

[16] *SAS* 2002, above n 14, at 9–10.

These arms have been distributed during and after the Cold War era. The 'superpowers', China, and their allies delivered a large amount of SALW that ranged from landmines to missiles, to combatants in south-east Asia, Africa, and Latin America, during the Cold War.[17] Since then, the manufacture and stockpiling has continued, although it may not be the same as the Cold War era. The Small Arms Survey (hereafter 'SAS') estimated that in the year 2000, 815,000 military-style small arms and 6.9 million commercial firearms have been produced worldwide.[18] Members of Russian armed forces, in collaboration with former KGB members for instance supplied $360 million worth of light arms to the Serbs during the Yugoslav crises.[19] Small arms, as opposed to major weapons, are available both in the civilian and military markets for legal or illegal purchase. As a result, citizens and even minors can easily acquire them.[20]

Thus, the excessive production and dispersion of these arms is significant enough to reach one in every ten people on a global scale. End-users can obtain them through covert and overt transactions and thus through licit or illicit international transactions.

2.1.3 Suitability for Use

SALW are weapons of choice for insurgents, belligerents, criminals, and terrorists for the following reasons. First, they are easy to operate and maintain. Their operation is not as complex as major weapons. For both use and preserving purposes, the demand for technical experience is very little compared with other major weapons, which require elaborate operational and maintenance expertise that can only be provided by professional military organisations. Consequently, insurgents, criminals, even child combatants, could easily use these arms without prior training and special skills.[21] Nevertheless, it is submitted that this feature is not an absolute factor. Some light weapons obviously need proper training for both use, and fixing when they are broken. They could even be more complex than some heavy weapons.

Secondly, SALW are portable. The GGE 1997 Panel on Small Arms stated that an individual, two or more people as a crew, a pack animal, or a light vehicle could carry such arms, and this unique feature makes them

[17] Mathiak and Lumpe, 'Government Gun-Running to Guerrillas' in L Lumpe (ed), *Running Guns: The Global Black Market in Small Arms* (London Zed Books, 2000) 56.

[18] *SAS 2002*, above n 14, at 12, paras 3–4.

[19] Smith, above n 3, at 279.

[20] Berkol, above n 2, at 3.

[21] Klare, 'The Global Trade in Light Weapons and the International System in the Post-Cold War Era' in Boutwell, Klare and Reed (eds), *Lethal Commerce: the Global Trade in Small Arms and Light Weapons* (Cambridge, Mass, American Academy of Arts and Sciences, 1995) 33; see also Berkol, above n 2, at 15.

suitable for mobile operations by irregular forces and others in urban terrains, mountains and jungles unlike heavy and mechanised weapons.[22] Many writers agree on this point. Nevertheless, they also reveal their concern about the probability of an overlap between major and light weapons, since some major weapons such as 107 mm recoilless rifles and 120 mm mortars could be transported by quarter ton trucks.[23]

Finally, these weapons are suitable for irregular warfare or criminality because they are easy to conceal and transfer within and outside a country.[24] SALW are also advantageous for hide-and-use tactics by non-state-actors (hereafter 'NSAs'). This makes them very difficult to control by states, if there is a will to do so.

The aforesaid elements seem to be duly appreciated by states. The 1997 GGE Report (see 2.2) recognised that these arms are portable, suitable to conceal for covert action or transfer objectives, and require less maintenance and logistic support. They are also less expensive than major weapons, ready to use with less training, and therefore they are weapons of choice for irregular warfare and violence. The panel particularly stated that if small arms are used or surplus, NSAs other than states can meet the expense for acquisition.[25] Besides, the PoA explicitly recognised the existence of excessive accumulation of small arms.[26]

2.1.4 Durability

Durability makes SALW hazardous since they last so long. They have few moving parts and need little maintenance. They therefore serve for decades as effective weapons. Many such arms in conflict areas were made during the Second World War and the Cold War.[27] The 1997 GGE Report expounded that the majority of weapons that are in use in conflicts are not newly produced.[28]

The UN Secretary-General reported that 'unlike their victims, small arms survive from conflict to conflict, perpetuating the cycle of violence by

[22] *GGE 1997*, above n 6, at 12, para 27(a).

[23] Karp, 'Small Arms-The New Major Weapons' in Boutwell et al, *Lethal Commerce*, above n 21, at 24.

[24] Dhanapala, Rana, and Lumpe, *Small Arms Control: Old Weapons, New Issues* (Aldershot, Ashgate Publishing, 1999) 5; see, eg 'most guns, grenades and other small arms can be concealed in the clothing or hand luggage of a single individual—making them ideal for assassinations, terrorism and banditry; see also Berkol, above n 2, at 16; see also Smith, above n 3, at 280.

[25] *GGE 1997*, above n 6, at 12–13, para 27(a), (d), (e), (f), and p 9, para 16.

[26] PoA, above n 7, at 7, Preamble, para 1.2.

[27] Newsom, 'Small Arms Use and Proliferation: Strategies for a Global Dilemma', p 1 at <http://www.iansa.org/documents/gov/sept_99/newsom.htm>; see also Berkol, above n 2, at 16.

[28] *GGE 1997*, above n 6, at para 35.

their mere presence'.[29] The hideous feature of these arms is that they survive for generations, and they are recycled from conflict to conflict though their users and targets are incapacitated. However, this factor is additional to the problem of the incessant manufacturing and circulation.

2.1.5 Versatility

The end users of small arms are threefold. Primarily, they are government or public agencies. The law enforcement agencies of a state such as defence forces, police, intelligence and security personnel are authorised to possess and use small arms for public order and self-defence purposes. The global stockpile portion of holdings in 2001, for instance, was estimated to be 37.8 per cent held by government armed forces, and 2.8 per cent by police forces.[30]

Legal and public causes which involve the use of small arms can take human life. The execution of capital punishment by those who are entrusted to do so, actions against rebels, pirates, or terrorists by military or special law enforcement forces, in the course of enforcement of law and order, and proportional actions of UN peacekeepers—constituting state forces-can all be cited as examples. Incidents relating to their use are normally extended to the destruction of public or private property. Beyond such necessary evils, they are often utilised, nevertheless, by state authorities, for violations of humanitarian norms (see Part II). The nature of SALW use by the state or international operations could therefore be legal or illegal.

Civilians and others, in their private capacity may legally own, possess and use SALW for self-protection and other lawful activities like hunting, sport shooting and collection; the number of firearms under such possession is estimated to be 378,300,000 worldwide. This is nearly 59.2 per cent of the global stockpile.[31] The nature of such use poses two contentious issues. First, it is often claimed that small arms are necessary for human pleasure in activities such as sport shooting, and for survival and economic reasons, in the case of hunting. Even so, paramount concerns for the protection of wildlife often impose prohibition or stringent restrictions on such practices.[32] In the US for example, in which there is a vast assertion of the existence of sporting and hunting culture, more than 90 per cent of rifle and shotgun owners 'fall into the 25 to 34 years-old age

[29] *Security Council, Agenda: Small Arms,* 24 September 1999, p 2.

[30] *SAS 2002,* above n 14, at 103, fig 2.5; see also for states' use of SALW, *GGE 1997,* above n 6, at 13, para 25.

[31] *SAS 2002, ibid,* at 80, table 2.9.

[32] Singh, 'National, Regional, and Global Measures for Controlling Light Weapons', in Dhanapala et al, above n 24, at 283.

group, earn between $35,000 and $50,000 annually, and do not need to kill animals for their survival'.[33] Here, the crucial issue is that the firearms useful for such business are too often deployed in civil conflicts and violence, as pointed out by the GGE 1997 (see 2.2). Therefore, while the use of firearms for lawful sporting or hunting might fulfil the pursuit of happiness, its very nature also poses concerns over human security and international law.

Self-defence at the interpersonal level is another problem. Individual members of a society, for the sake of safeguarding legally protected rights and interests, may inflict fatal harms on others and their properties, deploying such weapons. This is commonly subject to legal justification—yet the civilian possession of firearms is highly controversial (see chapter eight).

Finally, NSAs such as insurgents, criminals, drug cartels, and terrorists use these weapons for illegal purposes. For example, these groups were responsible for 0.2 per cent of the world stockpile in 2001.[34] Presently, apart from their grave humanitarian and social consequences, a growing trend has been recorded relating to their close ties with other major problems such as international terrorism, drug trafficking, and trans-national organised crimes. All these are closely linked to the clandestine arms trade.[35] Such wider understanding of the problem seems to have attained global consensus[36] (see chapter five).

Therefore, states, individuals, and NSAs, can have and use SALW for the pursuit of their objectives.[37] This is not normally the case with other weapons. The multifaceted character of the use and users is thus a unique feature which makes the issue of small arms trade more complex.

2.1.6 SALW Comprises a Vast Range of Weapons

Finally, this group of weapons is characterised as an umbrella for an immense number of types of arms and the possible sub-categories. This offers scope to consider traditional, civilian, and military weapons. Commonly, it has been sub-categorised into small, light arms, and ammunition and explosives.[38] Later developments introduced a new category

[33] Bellesiles, *Arming America: the Origins of a National Gun Culture* (New York, Random House, 2000) 5.

[34] *SAS 2002*, above n 14, at 103, fig 2.5.

[35] Dragani, 'Interrelationship between Illicit Trafficking in Small Arms, Drug Trafficking, and Terrorist Groups: African and European Issues, in Alves and Cippollone (eds), *Curbing Illicit Trafficking in Small Arms and Sensitive Technologies: an Action Oriented Agenda* (New York, United Nations, 1998) 77–83.

[36] PoA above n 7, at 7, Preamble 1.7; see also *SC*, above n 29, at 22, para 2.

[37] Berkol, above n 2 at 16; see also *GGE 1997*, above n 6, at 12, para 27.

[38] *GGE 1997*, above n 6, at 11.

called 'parts and components of small arms'.[39] Unlike major weapons, which are identified as seven clear and viable categories, therefore, SALW comprises many categories with varying firepower, size, purpose, and operational set-up. Major controversies on scope and definition are evident as discussed subsequently.

2.2 DEFINITION

It is important to note here that all light weapons may not categorically fulfil all the features discussed above; they nevertheless fit with the majority of the characteristics considered. Besides, in spite of the aforementioned common features, defining SALW as one group of weaponry is one of the contemporary challenges of international law.

2.2.1 Why is Definition Essential?

Definitions of terms and phrases are particularly important in legal science. Due to the diverse cultural, political, and economic influence of states and other legal persons, it has been acknowledged that the formation of legal rules in international law is complex. The norms originate from various sources, such as treaty and custom, purporting to govern the behaviour of states and other persons of international law are subject to interpretation by international tribunals, organisations and states, in the course of application and evolution.[40] Clear definitions are therefore vital for the harmony, development, and enforcement of international law.

Indeed the international community appreciates the consequences of SALW dispersion. Wide-ranging issues arise regarding the regulation of their manufacture, trade, brokering, etc.[41] The issue broaches, inter alia, security and humanitarian concerns.[42] This makes the regulatory regime of SALW diffusion more problematic and the need to have clear definition more desirable.

Defining SALW is, therefore, the first step in establishing a legal regime. It is not possible to discuss legal restrictions on manufacturing or transferring of light weapons, while the weapons remain undetermined. The definition of small arms does not, however, solve the whole problem

[39] *Mines Convention*, above n 4, Art 3.

[40] Dixon and McCorquodale, *Cases and Materials on International Law*, 3rd edn (London, Blackstone Press, 2000) 1, 20.

[41] Klare, 'An Overview of the Global Trade in Small Arms and Light Weapons', in Dhanapala et al (eds), above n 24, at 3–10.

[42] Bring, 'Regulating Conventional Weapons in the Future—Humanitarian Law or Arms Control?' (1987) 24 (3) *Journal of Peace Research* 275–86, see p 1; see also *Report of the Secretary-General*, above n 5.

under discussion and may not be more significant than the real commitment needed to alleviate the danger posed by small arms.[43]

A definition of small arms is therefore essential to establish where we start; what is the upper limit and which are the exceptions in categorising these weapons. Some exclusions may also be necessary as will be seen later. It should hence be treated as part of the remedy of the problem, and not as an ultimate objective of itself.

2.2.2 General Definition—SALW

The fundamental question is whether or not there exists a universally accepted definition and scope of SALW. Global, regional, and domestic efforts, including the understanding of armament industries, NGOs, and writers on the subject, are considered in this section.

2.2.2.1 Global Efforts

Historically, the concept of defining or describing this category of armament has progressed throughout decades. During the League of Nations, for instance, such weapons were divided into three: (1) arms of war, such as machine guns, automatic or self-loading pistols and revolvers or similar nature firearms of a calibre greater than 6.5 mm and length of barrel more than 10 cm, and their ammunition and parts and components; (2) arms and ammunitions capable of use both for military and other purposes such as firearms designed or adapted for non-military purposes but which are capable of firing cartridges of arms of war, all other rifled firearms firing from the shoulder and a calibre of 6 mm or above, and their ammunition and explosives; and (3) arms and explosives having no military value such as rifled weapons of less than 6 mm calibre, single shot pistols, muzzle-loading firearms and guns for whaling or other fishing purposes.[44]

Therefore, it has been claimed that there was only a broad and general understanding rather than a specific definition of these arms. Traditionally, however, firearms had been defined as 'designed primarily to be carried and fired by one person and, commonly, held in the hands, as distinguished from heavy arms, or artillery'.[45] Thus, until the Second

[43] Karp above n 23 at 24.

[44] *Convention for the Control of the Trade in Arms and Ammunition, and Protocol,* signed at Saint-Germain-en-Laye, 10 September 1919, Art 1, paras 1 and 3; see also *Draft Convention for the Control of the International Trade in Arms, Munitions and Implements of War,* League of Nations, 1924, p 17, Art 1, categories i, ii and iii; *ibid, Analysis of the Draft Convention,* p 26; see also *Draft Convention with regard to the Suppression of Private Manufacturers,* League of Nations, 29 August, 1929, Art 1, categories i,ii, iii and v; for details see ch 3.

[45] *The Colombia Electronic Encyclopaedia* (2000) on '*Small Arms*', at <http://www.infoplease.com/ce6/sci/A0845576.html>

World War, small arms were perceived to be the individual weapons of troops, which were restricted to 12.7 mm and less calibre firearms.[46]

The Second World War definition includes man-portable weapons such as rifles, light machine guns, pistols, and grenades.[47] It appears that no major development in definition occurred until the early 1980s, when NATO expanded the definition to 'all crew-portable direct fire weapons of a calibre of less than 50 mm and will include a secondary capability to defeat light armour and helicopters'. Weapons which could attack light armour and helicopters, automatic assault rifles such as Kalashnikov, M16, and Uzi were considered as small arms. Shoulder held launchers and surface-to-air missiles, and machine and sub-machine guns were incorporated too.[48] These provide some of the origins for later developments in definition.

The UN has been at the forefront of contemporary efforts to define SALW. In Resolution 50/70 B of 12 December 1995, the GA requested the Secretary-General to establish GGE to study the subject, including the definitional aspect of small arms.[49]

The panel examined the types of SALW practically useful in conflicts which the UN is anxious to respond to as a matter of institutional duty, and the scope and distinct features of SALW.[50] The possible definitions could be inferred from the descriptions made in the report. Under paragraph 11 of the report the GGE set out:

> Broadly speaking, small arms are those weapons designed for personal use, and light weapons are those designed for use by several persons serving as a crew.[51]

Likewise, the panel has clearly adopted both broad and exclusionary approaches and assured that SALW:

> Range from clubs, knives and machetes to those weapons just below those covered by the United Nations Register of Conventional Arms.

Even so it is also made clear that:

> The small arms and light weapons, which are of main concern for the present report, are those which are manufactured to military specifications for use as lethal instruments of war.[52]

Then again, the panel, under paragraph 28 considered non-military weapons 'such as hunting firearms and home made weapons' relevant to

[46] Singh, 'Illicit Trafficking in Small Arms: Some Issues and Aspects' in Alves and Cippollone (eds), *Curbing Illicit Trafficking*, above n 35 at 10.

[47] *Ibid.*

[48] *Ibid.*

[49] *GGE 1997*, above n 6, at 7, 11.

[50] For basic facts and issues see *ibid*, paras 1, 14, 15, 16, 22, and 23.

[51] *Ibid*, p 11, para 25.

[52] *Ibid*, p 11, para 24.

the report when they are 'accumulated in numbers that endanger the security of a state' and when they are used in conflicts, terrorism and violence.[53] This could be considered as an analytical approach, which took into account the use, users and other features of small arms.

Finally, working towards a broad definition the panel came up with a list of weapons that they considered to be among the small arms and light weapons often employed in conflicts. The list appears as follows:

> Small arms: (i) revolvers and self-loading pistols; (ii) rifles and carbines; (iii) sub machine guns; (iv) assault rifles; (v) light machine guns. (b) Light weapons: (i) heavy machine guns; (ii) hand-held under-barrel and, mounted grenade launchers; (iii) portable anti-aircraft guns; (iv) portable anti-tank guns, recoilless rifles; (v) portable launcher of anti-tank missiles and rocket systems; (vi) portable launchers of anti-aircraft missile systems; (vii) mortars of calibres of less than 100 mm. (c) Ammunition and explosives: (i) cartridges (round) for small arms; (ii) shells and missiles for light weapons; (iii) mobile containers with missiles or shells for single-action anti-aircraft and anti-tank missiles; (iv) anti-personnel and anti-tank hand grenades; (v) landmines; (vi) explosives. [54]

At this stage, the panel has promoted an enumerative approach to definition.

At least three problems arise from such a description. The inclusion or otherwise of traditional and civilian weapons, as to what is meant by 'manufacture to military specifications', and as to what and what is not excluded from such a cluster of arms.

First, the panel has not elaborated the notion of traditional weapons, except the inclusion of machetes and other similar weapons in the ambit of small arms. Writers seem to have different views on the role of traditional weapons on conflict and crime. Klare and Boutwell believe that conventional weapons have been in use in civil conflicts. For instance, the assertion of the use of ordinary tools in the Rwandan genocide is incorrect. Automatic rifles were distributed to militias and gangs before the start of killings. 'It was this firepower that made the genocide possible'. For Klare in particular it seems to be that such tools are not SALW.[55]

However, taking into account the sophistication of the violence which occurred in Rwanda and Burundi, Rana asserted that anything including non-conventional tools can be used in such violence, and thus state control over such tools is necessary. Although they are not weapons until the moment they are in use as weapons of violence, they are one category of small arms.[56] In addition, Berkol deems these tools as human muscle

[53] *Ibid*, p 13, para 28.

[54] *Ibid*, pp 11–13, para 26; see, eg the weapons with hash are some times mounted.

[55] Boutwell and Klare, 'A Scourge of Small Arms' *Scientific American* (*2000*) p 1, at <http://www.pugwash.org/reports/pim/pim21.htm>; see also Klare, 'The Global Trade' above n 21, at 33.

[56] Rana, 'The Role of State' in Alves and Cippollone (eds), *Curbing Illicit Trafficking*, above n 35, at 118–19.

dependent, in use through a direct contact with an enemy. This is one sub-group of small arms.[57] So, there is no settled view on the subject, as will be discussed later.

Secondly, a discussion on weapons for 'military specification' could help distinguish civilian firearms from military weapons, if feasible. Here too, the panel gives no explanation. The term 'military' often implies 'soldiers, arms or war'. Specification is understood to mean, inter alia, 'a written description of an invention for which a patent is sought' or a 'statement of legal particulars'. As a result, therefore, military firearms include assault rifles such as M16, AK-47, G3, FAL and FNC, which are 'chambered for ammunition or reduced size or propellant charge and has the capacity to switch between semiautomatic and fully automatic fire'. On the contrary, guns such as the shotgun are non-military small arms. 'Bolt-action rifles, which use a manually operated cylinder to drive the cartridge into the rifle's chamber' are also used for hunting[58] and similar activities as civilian weapons.

So, the distinction between military and non-military small arms centres, among others, on the firepower of particular weapons, the intention of weapon designers or the specification and end use and users of such arms. However, the circumstances of their use affirm that both groups serve militaries, combatants and civilians. They are also in use in civil conflicts, violence, etc (see 2.1).

In the light of such technical and other parameters of distinction, the impact of the panel's reference to weapons designed for military specifications is worth further consideration. In principle, the panel has included both sub-categories as SALW. In the end, however, its main emphasis lay on the military-type weapons. The reason for this can be inferred from the indications given in the report and subsequent statements. First, the panel was assigned 'to consider the type of small arms and light weapons actually being used in conflicts'.[59] It also referred to civil or interstate conflicts. Secondly, it has been stated at the outset that they decided to focus their attention on military weapons so as to avoid 'duplication of UN efforts'. The UN Commission on Crime Prevention and Criminal Justice was undertaking a work on firearms regulation for the purpose of crime prevention and public health concerns.[60]

Thirdly, in 1999 the chair of the panel, ambassador Donowaki commented that 'prior to World War II small arms made to military specifications were not readily accessible to ordinary citizens'. Referring to the proliferation of such arms during the Cold War, he further suggested that

[57] Berkol above n 2, at 15.

[58] Bosco, Braucher and Kessler, *Encyclopedia Britannica Ready Reference* (deluxe edn, CD-Rom, 2003) words: military, specification, rifle, assault-rifle, and gun.

[59] *GGE 1997*, above n 6, p 11, para 23.

[60] *Ibid*, p 8, para 8.

it is impossible to 'ignore the serious problems posed by the unchecked spread of military-style small arms'.[61] Therefore, the belief and the mandate of the panel may be interpreted as having given a strong emphasis to military weaponry.

There is no unanimity on the way the report has been interpreted by states and writers. Canada, for example, believes that civilian weapons such as pistols, rifles and carbines are excluded from the GGE Panel's definition of small arms.[62] Conversely, the US understood that the definition, as its now stands, includes many weapons, which ranges from handguns to portable air defence systems, in other words, from hunting rifles to crew–served mortars.[63] This will be discussed in-depth in domestic practice later.

Lansu, for instance, exactly repeated the words of the report on light weapons without a comment except paraphrasing the listing, in his definition of SALW.[64] In contrast, Berkol presumed that the GGE excluded arms like shooting for sport and hunting by saying that small arms should be 'manufactured for use as lethal instruments of war'; he found, however, the distinction between military and non-military weapons confusing; this is because some military–type arms are in fact authorised for use in sports shooting, and for hunting; moreover, hunting rifles (not traditionally classified as military) are in fact in military use in some internal conflicts. In addition, these arms are often the cause of accidents and suicides and their possession often provokes aggression on the part of the human user.[65]

Finally, the panel has excluded arms, which are regulated by the UN Conventional Weapons Register, as an upper limit to SALW. It is thus essential to explain the essence, scope, legal standing and problems of the register. It is a voluntary arrangement, established in 1991, through Resolution 46/36L of the UN GA, intended to address major conventional weapons (hereafter 'MCW') with a proven capacity for large-scale cross-border offensive action and surprise attack. The philosophy behind it is to promote transparency in major weapons for confidence building among states. When the register celebrated its tenth anniversary in August 2002 it was noted that 162 states were taking part in the process.[66]

[61] Dhanapala, above n 24, Prologue, xv, paras 1and 4.

[62] *A Proposed Global Convention Prohibiting the International Transfer of Military Small Arms and Light Weapons to Non-State Actors,* Canadian Mission to the UN, New York, December 1998, discussion paper, pp 2–3, see eg, para 10.

[63] Bolton, *United States Press Briefing on Small Arms Conference,* 9 July 2001, UN Headquarters, New York, p 1, at <http://www.un.org/news/briefings/docs/2001/usarmsbrf.Dochtm>

[64] Lansu, 'Light Weapons—The Questions of International Regulation and the Role of both Global and Regional Institutions' in 'Towards a more Effective and Legitimate Global Multilateral System' (The School of Sociology, Politics and Anthropology of the La Trobe University, November 1998) 3.

[65] Berkol, above n 2, at 15.

[66] See Hendrik (Ambassador) speech, *'The Coming into Being of the UN Register',* Symposium, the 10th anniversary of the UN Register of Conventional Arms, 15 October 2002, New York, pp 1–2, at <http://disarmament.un.org/cab/reg-10thanniv.html>.

According to Resolution 46/36L section 2 of the annex, Member States are requested to register seven categories of MCW. These are battle tanks, armoured vehicles, large calibre artillery systems, combat aircraft, attack helicopters, warships and missile/missile launchers.[67]

Theoretically, states might include others and in the course of continuous negotiations the coverage of weapons in the register has been widened. It is thus an open system for further expansion (see Part III). The drafting history of the register shows that small arms and light weapons are not included, although there was some pressure to do so[68] (for recent developments see chapter ten).

The UN system of MCW register could not escape criticism for having enormous gaps and for being limited to only seven systems. The register only focused on weapons that are basically challenging to hide. It has not addressed any surface-to-air missiles, any missiles under 25 km range, ships less than 750 tons, unarmed helicopters, and military transport aircraft. In addition, nuclear and biological weapons are not within the scope of these categories,[69] although they can be deployed in combination with and through combat aircraft.

The legal standing of the register in the international order is not insignificant. More than 160 states are participating in the process. The willingness of states to become participants drastically increased during 2000–01, as the UN Secretary-General recently confirmed.[70] The Inter-American Convention on Transparency of Conventional Weapons Transfer fully adopted the seven categories of the weapons in the register. The South African State recently adopted legislation, which obliges the country's government to report the movement of conventional weapons, that is, exports from or imports to the country, as a matter of international obligation. The one-decade experience and the increasing commitment of states in reporting, suggests confusion over whether this arrangement is still voluntary or has been transformed into an international norm.[71]

[67] Res titled *Transparency in Armaments,* see Preamble para 15, for the concerns of the GA Preamble (2), and for the establishment of the Resister see Preamble (7), and the Annex (*Register of Conventional Arms*); see also SIPRI, *Sources and Methods of Arms Transfers Project'*, 15 January 2003; see, eg the definition and exclusion from MCW, at <http://projects.sipri.se/armstrade/atmethods.html>; for similar scope adopted in the *Conventional Armed Forces in Europe Treaty of 1990* see Koulik and Kokoski, *Conventional Arms Control: Perspective on Verification* (Oxford, Oxford University Press, 1994) 23.

[68] See the speech of Ambassador Hendrik, above n 66, at 1–3.

[69] See Symposium, *UN Register*, above n 66, at 1–2.

[70] Annan, '*If Effectiveness of the UN Arms Register is Strengthened, it can Serve as Significant Early Warning Mechanism*', 30 August 2002, at <http://www.un.org/News/Press/docs/2002/sgsm8355.Dochtm>

[71] See, eg Art 1, and Annex 1, *Inter-American Convention on Transparency in Conventional Weapons Acquisition* (Resolution adopted at the first plenary session, held on 7 June 1999); for the status and related issues of the Registry see, eg Symposium, *UN Register*, above 66, at 1–3 and the statement of Dhanapala, the Under-Secretary-General for Disarmament Department, p 1.

However, our focus has to be on whether the aforesaid major weapons can serve as an upper limit for SALW. Many considerations, inter alia, affordability, sophistication, actual use against civilians and the weight and ease of transportability caused the GGE to distinguish SALW from MCW in 1997.[72] Similarly, the 1999 UN Panel on Explosives underlined that the register excluded small arms and light weapons with their ammunition and explosives.[73] In these ways, the register's major weapons are an important general threshold for SALW. As a result, it is now accepted in general terms that light weapons are those below the seven categories of conventional weapons.

The UN Panel's definition of SALW is important for two main reasons. First, the group which was constituted from sixteen UN Member States unanimously endorsed the definition(s). The appointment of the panel by the Secretary-General considered 'equitable geographical representation'. The majority of the experts were chosen from small arms manufacturing states (see chapter three).[74] Secondly, these descriptions supported the UN's position; they laid down the parameters for the definition, scope, and features of SALW.

The work of the panel gave rise to some problems as well as positive aspects. The encouraging aspects include the fact that the UN Panel has to a great extent contributed to the development of a uniform global definition of small arms. A number of aspects have been considered in the document—ease of transport, users and end uses, lethality, durability, simplicity, accessibility due to extreme factors and comparison with major weapons of SALW all go to define this group of arms. A list of armaments in three major sections was successfully developed. Most importantly, the report, which comprises definition and additional recommendations on this global concern, was unanimously agreed by the panel. The GA also adopted the report. Even so, whether all states actively agree with the definition and its interpretation is doubtful including even those who took part in the work through their expert representatives. Nevertheless, it was a major breakthrough at the international level and a progressive development of the SALW legal regime.

In order to make further progress, the following issues need to be addressed. First, it's not yet clear whether the list is exhaustive or open ended for further development. It could be said the list is indicative, taking into consideration the complexity of the matter and the advancement of technology. Secondly, the focus is on those arms manufactured to military

[72] *GGE 1997*, above n 6, at p 9 para 16, and p 11, para 24.

[73] *Report of the Group of Experts on the Problem of Ammunition and Explosives*, 29 June 1999, p 12, para 71.

[74] *GGE 1997*, above n 6, at p 5 and p 3. Experts were chosen from Malaysia, the US, Canada, Japan, Egypt, El Salvador, Sri Lanka, Russian Federation, South Africa, Switzerland, Islamic Republic of Iran, Finland, Belarus, Germany, Mali and Colombia.

specifications. In other parts of the paper, however, it is acknowledged that civilian firearms are considered as part of the difficulty. Non-barrel weapons such as machetes are mentioned as part of small arms. This is confusing and has led to varied interpretations of the work of the panel. Furthermore, they did not elaborate the phrase 'weapons designed to military specification', which added ambiguity to the civilian-military weapons distinction.

Thirdly, under the phrase 'weapons used in conflicts being dealt with by the UN', the panel listed what they have considered as SALW. In accordance with this formula the question arises whether we can anticipate a separate list of small arms that are in use in non-conflict zones of the world. Fourthly, whether they intended to include all weapons which are not covered under the UN Conventional Weapons Register is rather unclear. Fifthly, the consideration of the firepower of arms or their operational set up for definitional purposes is unclear. Finally, it would have been more convenient for further development, if features and definition had been clearly distinguished.

There are general indications that the lower limit of SALW includes non-barrel weapons such as machetes and clubs; military and civilian weapons are also included, though the former is much more emphasised than the latter; MCW are excluded from the scope of small arms; all these give rise to controversy. Other efforts might help rectify such problems.

The UN Protocol of 2001 on illicit firearms, which supplements the 2000 UN Convention against Trans-national Organised Crime, is the first 'legal instrument' on small arms at the global level. States have declared their awareness of the harmful effects of illicit firearms on the security of states, regions and individuals. It entered into force on 4 April 2005. It was also adopted by the UN GA (see further chapters three and four).[75]

Article 3(a) of the Protocol expounds: 'firearms shall mean any portable barrelled weapon that expels, is designed to expel or may be readily converted to expel a shot, bullet or projectile by the action of an explosive'.[76] The approach and criteria adopted here are different from those of the UN Panel, except the consideration of portability in both cases. It seems to be that non-explosive/barrel weapons are not considered in the instrument. However, a distinction is not made between military and civilian firearms. Its features will be elaborated later with other developments, in particular, the OAS Convention.

At the global level, the most important development on the issue appears to be attached to the detailed analysis of the 1997 UN Panel, as

[75] *Protocol against the Illicit Manufacturing of and Trafficking in Firearms, their Parts and Components and Ammunition, Supplementing the UN Convention against Trans-national Organised Crime*, 31 May 2001, Preamble, para 1. It has been ratified by 41 states as of 24 April 2005.

[76] *Ibid.*

demonstrated before—the result is not, however, unambiguous. Pertinent regional practice may be of help to clarify problems.

2.2.2.2 *Regional Efforts*

The OAS, OSCE and African approaches are believed to show the input of regional efforts on defining this group of weapons; as opposed to the panel's report, the Inter-American (OAS) Convention against illicit firearms, as a first regional Convention on the matter, under Article 1(3) defined the word 'firearms' as:

> Any barrel weapon which will or is designed to or may be readily converted to expel a bullet or projectile by the action of an explosive.., or any other weapon or destructive device such as any explosive, incendiary or gas bomb, grenade rocket, rocket launcher ,missile, missile system, or mine.[77]

Canada, in its proposed Convention of 1998 on small arms transfer to NSAs, for instance, viewed the OAS definition as too broad for a legal instrument that seeks to prohibit illicit aspect of the problem. This was because of its inclusion of both military and non-military weapons; while it was one of the signatories, it has not ratified the Convention.[78] The definition is thus very broad in scope and not limited in regard to purpose of use, list, exclusion and similar factors.

In contrast to this, the Organisation for Security and Co-operation in Europe (OSCE) preferred the terms 'small arms' and 'light weapons', and defined 'small arms' as: 'man–portable weapons made or modified to military specifications for use as lethal instruments of war'.[79] The distinct element here seems to be the clear-cut division between military and non-military weapons. Essentially, it complies with the definition of the GGE except that non-military weapons are clearly excluded. The definition in this document is made with an open mind for prospective negotiation on defining the terms.

The African position is along the lines of the UN Panel in respect of definition. African experts clearly adopted the UN GGE definition of 1997. They underlined: 'deviation from the commonly accepted UN definition may not be constructive'. They emphasised the need for a common perspective to define and understand small arms.[80]

[77] *Inter-American Convention against the Illicit Manufacturing of and Trafficking in Firearms, Ammunition, Explosives, and other Related Materials*, 1997 (OAS Convention) Art 1(3).

[78] Above n 62, at 3; see also Canada's position on the OAS Convention, at <http://www.oas.org/juridico/english/Sigs/a-63.html>.

[79] *OSEC Document on Small Arms and Light Weapons,* Forum for Security Co-operation, adopted at the 308th Plenary Meeting, 24 November 2000, Vienna, p 2; see also O'Callaghhan et al, 'NATO and Small Arms: From Words to Deeds' *BASIC Research Report 2000*, 4 October, 2000, p 2, para 1.1, and p 11, para 5.

[80] *First Continental Meeting of African Experts on Small Arms and Light Weapons, Report of the Meeting of Experts*, May 2000, Addis Ababa, Ethiopia, p 11, para 34.

The southern African (SADC) countries have nonetheless introduced a different approach. The Protocol on the Control of Firearms, Ammunition and Other related Materials in the Southern African Development Community Region of 2001 defined a 'firearm' under Article 1(2) to mean:

> (a) Any portable lethal weapon that expels, or is designed to expel, a shot, bullet or projectile by the action of burning propellant. . .; (b) any device which may be readily converted into a weapon referred to in paragraph (a); (c) any small arms defined in this article; or (d) any light weapon as defined in this article.[81]

And, it went on to separately define the terms 'small arms' and 'light weapons' as below:

> Small arms include light machineguns, sub-machineguns, including machine pistols, fully automatic rifles and assault rifles and semi-automatic rifles.[82]
>
> Light weapons include the following portable weapons designed for use by several persons serving as a crew: heavy machine guns, automatic canons, howitzers, mortars of less than 100 mm calibre, grenade launchers, antitank weapons and launchers, recoilless guns, shoulder fired rockets, antiaircraft weapons and launchers and air defence weapons.[83]

It is useful to compare and contrast the regional approaches both within themselves and with international ones. Generally, regional efforts seem to have been divided into three. Africa and the OSCE countries, with certain controversies, follow the UN Panel's line of thinking and speak about SALW. The UN Firearms Protocol of 2001 follows from the OAS definition of 1997. Except the word 'portable', which was mentioned in the latter but not in the Convention, one might find both instruments sharing identical terms. The third approach is a combination of the two terms 'SALW' and 'firearms', as has been seen in the SADC definition. The difference ranges from the use of terms to elements of definition.

As in the UN Protocol, with respect to the wording, the terms 'small arms' or 'light weapons' do not appear in the entire treaty of the OAS. Rather, the term 'firearms' is adopted. In a different way, the OSCE and majority of African countries tend to use the term SALW. The SADC states have incorporated both the terms 'small arms and light weapons' and 'firearms' in defining this group of weaponry. Here, the issue is shall we use the terms 'SALW' (small arms) or 'firearms'? One may envisage that this could mean the same as the synonymous use of the terms 'crime' and 'offence' in criminal law; unfortunately, it does not seem to be as simple as

[81] *Protocol on the Control of Firearms, Ammunition and Other related Materials in the Southern African Development Community (SADC) Region*, Blantyre, Malawi, 14 August 2001, Art 1(2); see, eg the negotiating states: Angola, Botswana, the DRC, Lesotho, Malawi, Mauritius, Mozambique, Namibia, Seychelles, South Africa, Swaziland, Tanzania, Zambia, Zimbabwe. All except Angola have signed the Protocol. <http://www.iss.co.za/AF/RegOrg/unity_to_union/pdfs/sadc/3Protocol_on_Firearms.pdf>

[82] *Ibid*, Art 1 (2).

[83] *Ibid*, Art 1(2).

that. The issue is whether we rely on 'technical definition', 'descriptive definition', or a combination of the two.

The UN Protocol and the OAS on the one hand, and the GGE Panel, OSCE, and the dominant African position on the other, have incorporated different parameters in their definitions. The former definitions have not stated anything about other elements, which were used by the GGE and writers, such as the purpose of use and users, listing and exclusion. Military use and lethal features are not found in the definition. Consideration of all these elements could be understood as a descriptive definition. The technical set-up and operation of the weapons seems to be the main factor for defining firearms in the Protocol and the Convention, which was not considered by the GGE and others.

This may appear to be an academic hair-split. The whole question is related to the scope of small arms. If we use the OAS's line, the traditional weapons such as machetes would not be small arms since they are not barrel weapons; however, civilian and military weapons are both considered and therefore constitute a broader definition. The unique character of the OAS Convention is that an attempt has been made to define 'ammunitions', 'explosives', and 'parts and components' of firearms separately as we shall later see.[84]

Taking the nature and technical set-up of small arms and light weapons, it may be argued that the term 'firearms' is an abridgment of the terms 'civilian and military small arms' and 'light weapons' in the OAS Convention and the Protocol. This has plainly been adopted in the SADC firearms Protocol. Of course SALW are barrelled weapons, with the capability of expelling a bullet or an explosive, although the technical sense of the terms could be left to military engineers. Yet the constituent portability is evident in the GGE and the UN Protocol.

There remains an unresolved problem, therefore, the difference between the two major approaches, that is to say, the technical and descriptive aspects of SALW.

The third approach, which seems a good point of compromise, is the SADC approach. It has incorporated in its definition the technical aspect and other features of SALW. The lethal character, portability, the method of enumeration, and the technical definition are combined together to define a firearm. The problem is that traditional and civilian weapons such as shotguns or other non-semi or non-fully automatic firearms are excluded. State practice at a national level could help clarify the problem.

[84] Above n 77, Art 1(4), (5) and (6); see also <http://www.state.gov/t/pm/rls/othr/rd/1997/4366.htm>

2.2.2.3 Domestic Legislation

State practice varies greatly. The US, France, South Africa, Jamaica and Canada's domestic laws on SALW definition will briefly be discussed. The South African definition is as follows:

Section 1, (xii) states:

> Firearms' means any-(a) device manufactured or designed to propel and bullet or projectile through a barrel of cylinder by means of burning propellant, at a muzzle energy exceeding 8 joules (6 ft-lbs); (b) device manufactured or designed to discharge rim-fire, centre-fire, or pin-fire ammunition; (c) device which is not at the time capable of discharging any bullet or projectile, but which can be readily altered to be a firearm within the meaning of paragraph (a), or (b); (d) device manufactured to discharge a bullet or any other projectile of .22 calibre or higher at a muzzle energy of more than 8 joules (6 ft-lbs), by means of compressed gas and not by means of burning propellant; or (e) barrel, frame or receiver of a device referred to in paragraphs (a), (b), (c), or (d), but does not include any device contemplated in section 5.[85]

Section 5 excludes, inter alia, explosives manufactured *specifically* for use in the mining and steel industry and construction works, from the definition of a firearm.[86]

At least, four elements can be identified. First, the base for the law is the technical characteristics of a weapon. Secondly, minimum firepower is set out; muzzle energy of more than 8 joules or .22 calibres is required. Thirdly, some exclusions have been made. Finally, a ceiling of firearms vis-à-vis MCW is not given in the definition. It is also explicitly stated that both military and civilian arms are included in the definition.

In a similar approach but a different outcome, Canadian law defines a firearm to mean 'any barrelled weapon (including the frame or receiver) that fires projectiles, shot or bullets and that is capable of causing serious injury or death to an individual'.[87] The technical approach has been adopted similar to that of South Africa. The distinctive feature of this definition, as a domestic law, is however its reference to harmful consequences. This is a linking constituent between the Canadian law and the GGE 1997 and the SADC Protocol definitions. It is simple to understand and is broad in scope.

Nonetheless, in the earlier mentioned proposed Convention of 1998, Canada suggested that pistols, rifles, and carbines should be excluded from military SALW. It has been admitted as a possible criticism of such a definition that it excludes 'whole categories of deadly weapons which

[85] Republic of South Africa, *Firearms Control Act No 60 2000*, ch 1, s 1 (xii).

[86] *Ibid*, ch 3, 3.5.

[87] '*Understanding Canadian Firearms Law, A Guide to Key Information in the Firearms Act, Regulations and Support Material*', Revised March 2001, at <http://www.cfc-ccaf.gc.ca/en/owners_users/guide/default.asp>

have a "non-military identity" '. Reliance had been made on the findings of the GGE 1997 to justify the point that it is military rather than non-military small arms which cause instability. Paradoxically, the use of non-military weapons in violence and crime all over the world is not disputed.[88]

Likewise, US laws have defined the word firearm. The National Firearms Act (NFA) in section 5845(a) sets out:

> The term 'firearm' means (1) a shotgun having a barrel or barrels of less than 18 inches in length; (2) a weapon made from a shotgun if such weapon as modified has an overall length of less than 26 inches . . .; (3) a rifle having a barrel or barrels of less than 16 inches in length; (4) a weapon made from a rifle . . . a barrel. . .of less than 16 inches in length; (5) any other weapon, as defined in subsection (e); (6) a machinegun; (7) any silencer . . .; and (8) a destructive device.[89]

In addition, the Gun Control Act (GCA), under section 921 (a), (3) defined:

> The term 'firearm' means (A) any weapon (including a starter gun) which will or is designed to or may readily be converted to expel a projectile by the action of an explosive; (B) the frame or receiver of any such weapon; (C) any firearm muffler or firearm silencer; or (D) any destructive device.[90]

A bomb, grenade, incendiary and similar weapons have been regarded as destructive devices.[91]

The US laws have focused on the barrel length of a weapon. Further, any weapon with a capability of expelling a projectile is a firearm—shotguns, rifles, machine guns, and bombs have been included. A civilian-military distinction has not been made.

As stated earlier, the US understood the definition of the GGE broadly, and objects accordingly. To the extreme, John Bolton stated in the 2001 UN Conference on Small Arms, 'specific definition on small arms and light weapons is impossible to achieve'. He underlined that definition shall be 'up to each nation to interpret according to its national laws'. However the US was very concerned with numbers of weapons, which might have both military and civilian aspects, such as the automatic M-16 as a US army weapon, and its civilian counterpart of the AR-15, a single shot weapon, which with certain adjustment can be changed into an M-16. The ambiguity between civilian and military weapons is therefore a great concern to the United States.[92]

[88] See *Canadian Proposal* (not 62) pp 2–3, see also, <http://www.nisat.org/export_lawsregs%20linked/canada/discussion_papera_proposed.htm20/12/2002>.

[89] *National Firearms Act* (NFA), 1934, U.S.C. 26, Ch 53, s 5845(a), see also <http://www.atf.gov/pub/fire-explo_pub/nfa.htm>

[90] *The Gun Control Act* 1968 (GCA), Public Law 90–618, 18 U.S.C. Ch 44, s 921 (a), (3) at <http://www.atf.gov/pub/fire-explo_pub/gca.htm>.

[91] *Ibid*, (a), (4).

[92] Bolton, above n 63; see also <http://usinfo.state.gov/topical/pol/arms/stories/01071203.htm, p 2 >

Despite that, the Department of State has later disclosed that the term SALW is 'commonly viewed as encompassing man-portable firearms and their ammunition primarily designed for individual use by military forces as lethal weapons'. On the basis of this definition, weapons such as civilian handguns are excluded and rifles and carbines are included. Light weapons are described as heavier than small arms but below the seven categories of the UN Register of Conventional Arms.[93] Except for the distinction between military and civilian weapons, it resembles the UN Panel's definition.

Consider also that only the US has been contemplating the inclusion of weapons 'primarily designed' for military use, a phrase which was also contentious but not finally regarded in the Mines Convention.[94] Therefore, it is not difficult to perceive that the US attitude in defining firearms is broad in scope in the domestic domain, but narrow for international law purposes. It also entertains the view that the definition and its interpretation of these weapons should be left to each domestic jurisdiction. Other states may also uphold this interpretation.

Jamaican law defines firearms as: 'any lethal barrelled weapon from which any shot, bullet or other missile can be discharged. . .and includes any component part of such weapon and accessory to any such weapon'.[95] This definition stresses the fatal salient feature like that of Canada. It incorporates all parts and components such as silencer devices. The Chinese law expounds further the lethal effect doctrine stating 'a firearm in this law refers to all kinds of firearms. . . powerful enough to hurt or kill people or make people lose consciousness'.[96] Harmful consequences other than death are also underlined.

French law has divided all weapons into two main categories. The first one comprises weapons designed for terrestrial, naval or air war. Not only all major conventional, chemical and gas weaponry, but every gun, mortars of all gauges, mines of all species and grenades are classified under this cluster. The second has included, inter alia, weapons and ammunition for defence uses, weapons of fist with a total length greater than 28 cm, guns and revolvers of choke and alarm, semi-automatic weapons of

[93] 'Can Small Arms and Light Weapons Be Controlled?' *US Department of State*, 2 June 2001, at <http://usinfo.state.gov/topical/pol/arms/stories/01060243.htm>

[94] Maresca and Maslen, 'History and Negotiation of the Ottawa Treaty' in Maresca and Maslen (eds), *The Banning of Anti-Personnel Landmines: the Legal Contribution of the International Committee of the Red Cross* (Cambridge, Cambridge University Press, 2000) 611–12.

[95] *Jamaica Firearms Act*: Acts 1 of 1967/ 29 of 1973/38 of 1973/ 8 of 1974 S.19/ 17 of 1974/ 1 of 1983 ss 10/12 of 1985 sch, s 2(1)(b), at <http://disarmament.un.org/cab/salw-legislation.htm>; see for eg *UK Firearms Act 1968*, ch 27, *Public General Acts and Measures* 1968, Pt I, p 611, London, s 57(1).

[96] *Law of the Republic of China on the Control of Firearms*, twentieth session of the standing committee of the Eighth National People's Congress, 5 July 1996, Presidential order No 72, effective as of January 1996, Art 46.

shoulder with a storage capacity to contain more than ten cartridges, and hunting weapons and their ammunition.[97]

Moreover, the second category, in Article 2 (sixth category), emphatically stated: 'all objects likely to constitute a dangerous weapon for public safety' as weapons and elements of weapons. Bayonets, daggers, bowie knives, canes with swords, canes leaded and shoed except those shoed only with one end, Japanese plagues, stars of jets, American blows of fist, etc are enumerated in the law.[98]

Berkol grouped small arms under French law into three and defined them accordingly; 'hand weapons' are defined as: 'arms that injure an adversary through direct contact using muscle power alone'. Differently, '*Arms de ffense*' are to include short-range firearms with a barrel length of less than 30 mm and possible to fire at a one shot but with automatic reloading capability. '*Arms de guerre*' are different from the first two—they include mainly automatic firearms that are 'able to fire various projectiles during one sustained pressure on the trigger' and are used by civilians. Arms that do not fall into any other category are called 'hunting and sporting shotguns' which are said to be single action guns.[99] The definition is focused on the fire and loading speed capabilities of weapons, which was not considered, either by the UN panels and the Protocol or the OAS Convention.

The French law is thus exceptional for a number of reasons. Instead of defining the whole range of weapons in one term like others do, the legislators preferred to have categories of arms on the ground of the general purpose of use of the firearms. In addition, a range of elements like fire loading, mode of use, and operational aspects have been taken into consideration. The purpose and use of weapons standards, as a broad method helps demarcate categories of weapons. Even so, the law mixes SALW up with that of MCW and even chemical weapons, as all of them are grouped in one cluster. It is interesting that dangerous weapons, such as knives, have been defined as elements of weapons in this law, which applies to non-barrel or bullet weapons.

This is not the case in the French legislation alone. The Indian 1959 Act regulates any article including 'sharp-edged and other deadly weapons'. Even so, articles designed for non-violent purposes such as a lathe or an ordinary walking stick are excluded from the law.[100]

[97] *Order in Council Fixing the Mode of Weaponries, Weapons and Ammunition*, French Order in Council of 18 April 1939, Art 1; further see Decree No 95–589 of 6 May 1995 Relating to the Application of the Decree of 18 April 1939, Fixing the Mode of the Weaponries, Weapons and Ammunition, *Journal No 108 of May 7,1995*, p 7458, Art 2, also at <http://fal-2001.virtualave.net/droit.html>

[98] *Ibid*, Decree No 95–589 of 6 May 1995, Art 2, 6th category, para 1.

[99] Berkol, above n 2 at 15.

[100] *Indian Arms Act* No 54, 1959, s 2(c).

The Australian legal system has some common features with the French law. Small arms refers to any weapon 'that is .50 calibre (Browning machinegun or similar) or less'. By doing so, it has established a distinction between small arms and weapons of warfare. A list of small arms has been attached too.[101] It resembles the French law since the purposes of use and firepower have been used for definitional needs. However, small arms have been serving as weapons of warfare for decades.

In sum, state practice demonstrates divergent approaches and elements. More or less, all states define firearms in a broader sense in their respective jurisdictions. They make general exclusions from firearms like explosives for peaceful or industrial uses. They establish definitions including different kinds of SALW within such a broad meaning. Many states considered the technical components such as the length of a weapon. Others have also emphasised the lethal consequences and purpose of their use. Still, there is no uniform and straightforward definition of small arms in state practice. As appreciated during the League of Nations, some states also recognise the problem of distinction between military and non-military firearms. Some of them also showed their desire to exclude civilian firearms from SALW. Yet, the recent attitude of a few states, particularly the developed ones, to confine the definition of small arms to 'military-type weapons', does not seem to be well founded, as far as domestic state practice is concerned. The implications for international law of these findings will be analysed later (see 2.2.5). The views of weapon traders, NGOs and writers on the definition of SALW could also be an asset in resolving the controversy over definition.

2.2.2.4 Firearms Industries, NGOs and Writers

First, the views of firearms industries on definition/description of small arms may reflect the perception of weapon designers and their clients on the issue. Manufacturing industries often resort to a specific description of particular weapons other than general definition. Descriptions of two sample weapons are believed to illustrate certain typical features.

Heckler and Koch describe a particular machine gun, considering the perception and experience gained from national and international weapon testing, as follows:

> For these reasons the improved HK21E and HK23E feature an excellent performance and durability and represent today's most advanced machine gun technology. Their modular construction permits the easy conversion from a belt feed to a magazine feed gun and vice versa. Weight and exterior dimensions make them real one-man-weapons even in the belt fed configuration, where one

[101] Mouzos, 'International Traffic in Small Arms: an Australian Perspective', Australian Institute of Criminology, *Trends and Issues in Crime and Criminal Justice* (Canberra, No 104, February 1999) 1.

> man can carry and handle the weapon and a full load of ammunition. Firing is possible from all positions, even from the hip.[102]

And for a rifle weapon:

> The new Assault Rifle G36/G36E is a true modular weapon system in calibre 5.56mm × 45. Constructed almost entirely of a tough, fibre reinforced polymer material and using a simple, self-regulating gas system, the G36/G36E provides the user with a lightweight weapon that delivers high performance with extremely low maintenance. . .[103]

The assertions are made for market uses. We can infer various elements from them. Producers consider the durability, portability, ease of use, transportability and technical components of a weapon in describing a particular armament. Also, firepower, technological manipulability, the body set-up, and performance of armaments have been emphasised. Factors such as economic viability are taken into account in the description of other similar firearms. Thus, the definition of a weapon is both economically and technically driven.

Secondly, NGOs have attempted to address definitional issues to SALW. Following the definition of the panel, the SAS defined SALW as 'both military style weapons and commercial firearms (handguns and long guns)'. They also used the terms 'small arms', 'firearms', and 'weapons' interchangeably, to describe SALW.[104]

The Draft Framework Convention on International Arms Transfers (hereafter 'FCIAT') states that:

> 'Arms' means small arms and light weapons within the meaning of these terms in the Report of the Panel of Government Experts on Small Arms (A/RES/52/298) save that the enumerated categories therein are not to be regarded as restrictive of the definition.[105]

All principal elements of the UN Panel's definition have been adopted in the proposed treaty.[106] The non-exhaustive nature of the panel's list of SALW has to be emphasised here. The trend of NGOs has been thus in favour of a broad definition of SALW.

Nonetheless, the World Forum on the Future of Sport Shooting (hereafter 'WFSA') and its affiliate NGOs fundamentally differed from the views of the SAS and the FCIAT. For instance, Keith Tidswell, on behalf of the WFSA, has presented his view on the issue to the UN BMS of 2003. He highlighted that: first, 'there are at least five definitions for small arms and

[102] Heckler and Koch, at <http://www.heckler-koch.de/html/index.html>; for the details on the industry see 3.1.

[103] *Ibid*.

[104] *SAS 2002*, above n 14, at 10, box. 1.1.

[105] Working Draft of 21 December 2003, Art 7 (1), it was also circulated at the UN BMS of July 2003; for details see Part II.

[106] *Ibid*, commentary, para 19.

firearms found in the UN reports'; yet, 'we have been constantly assured that UN efforts are not focused on sporting arms. . . But, . . .this does not seem the case'; secondly, sporting arms are not considered 'arms' and the concern shall be on weapons of war that could be defined 'as those capable of fully-automatic fire'; and finally, 'if the definition issue were to be effectively resolved to exclude sporting arms it would help with the whole effort to implement the Programme of Action' (see Part II). [107]

This offers the impression that sporting arms are included in the UN definition and the efforts therein. It has also signified the basic division among NGOs on definition. So, differences of proponents and opponents of gun-control NGOs encompass definitional matters too.

Finally, writers have also attempted to formulate various approaches and definitions of this cluster of arms, even before the GGE 1997 Report. To Klare and Karp, the contemporary endeavours of defining SALW have laid down the following approaches. The first one is definition of small arms by exclusion from the UN Register of MCW, as considered in section 2.2.2.1. Weapons that are not covered in the register and similar arrangements, as heavy/major weapons, would be considered as SALW.[108] In addition, others tend to adopt tremendously broad exclusionary standards to define light weapons. Anything heavy such as tanks, heavy artillery, planes and ships and weapons of mass destruction are not light weapons.[109]

While this approach is essential for both the definition and scope of small arms, it may not provide us with a clear demarcation between major and light weapons.

The second approach entirely depends on the weapons of an individual soldier and defines small arms as 'those, which can be carried by a normal infantry soldier'. This includes pistols, grenades, medium machine guns, grenade launchers, light mortars, hand held rocket launchers, and some often considered as major weapons like shoulder fired surface to air missile systems and some anti-tank weapons. From this definition, all heavy machine guns including light anti-aircraft artillery, which are commonly in use in civil conflicts have been taken out of the category of SALW.[110] What is not clear in this approach is whether the criterion is fully dependent on an individual infantry solider; some of the weapons listed under this definition might not be carried and operated by an individual alone.

[107] Tidswell, representative of Sport Shooter Association of Australia, *Definition, Reliable Facts and Human Rights Concerns*, 1st BMS, 7–11 July 2003, New York, paras 3, 4; for the PoA see chs 3 and 5.

[108] Karp, above n 23, at 23; see also Klare, 'The Global Trade', above n 21, at 33. Additionally, the Military Balance of the International Institute for Strategic Studies does have a list of heavy weapons.

[109] Klare, *ibid*.

[110] Karp, above n 23, at 23–24.

Thirdly, arms 'that can be transported by pack animals and light vehicles (eg, quarter-ton trucks)' are small arms and light weapons. This comprises heavy machine guns, light artillery, 107 mm recoilless rifles, and 120 mm mortars. It overlaps the above-mentioned two approaches and particularly the UN Register of MCW. Hence, it is not helpful for establishing clear-cut differences between heavy and small arms.[111]

Fourthly, some writers define light weapons 'as all those conventional munitions that can be carried by an individual combatant or by a light vehicle operating on back-country roads'. Light weapons would include, according to this definition, small arms such as handguns, and light weapons such as light anti-tank and shoulder-fired anti-aircraft missiles.[112] To some degree, noteworthy elements that are useful in later developments have been incorporated in this definition. Conventional munitions, the use of the terms 'small' and 'light', the reference made to both individual combatant and a light vehicle can be acclaimed. It has widened the easy transportability standard. This appears to be a combination of the aforesaid two approaches.

Finally, an actual use-oriented approach asserts that small arms are those in real use in civil warfare. The premise of this standard is that such arms carry the burden of armed conflicts in history.[113] A list of small arms has to be established out of the use of each particular weapon. This utility-oriented parameter may pose some difficulties. If the definition is to be determined by a list of weapons in empirical terms on the ground of their utility in civil conflicts, does everything deployed in civil wars constitute small arms? It is obvious that heavy weapons are also used in civil conflicts.

Also, why we restrict the definition to ethnic and internal conflict, or whether we could have another definition of this category in the case of hideous organised crimes in non-conflict zones and countries is not elaborated. It seems to be that this approach has been influenced greatly by the civil conflicts of the post-Cold War era.

Among recent writers, Faltas and Paes regard the GGE 1997 Report as a UN definition and interpret it to mean that small arms are those manufactured to military specifications. As stated earlier, however, Berkol is not at ease with such a distinction as civilian and military weapons are both lethal tools.[114]

[111] *Ibid.*

[112] Klare, 'The Globa Trade', above n 21, at 33, described: 'small arms'—handguns, carbines, assault rifles, and submachine guns, and 'light weapons'—such as machine guns, bazookas, rocket-propelled grenades, light anti-tank missiles, light mortars, shoulder-fired anti-aircraft missiles, and hand placed landmines; Berkol, above n 2, at 15.

[113] Karp, above n 23, at 24.

[114] Faltas and Paes, 'The Problem of Small Arms in Developing Countries: the Current International Debate and Recommendations for Development Cooperation, in Particular Technical Cooperation' *Division* (No 43/2001) 10; see also Berkol, *ibid.*

The approaches are fundamental to the *evolution* of a definition of SALW. They show the efforts that have been made to rectify the terms 'small arms' and 'light weapons'; some conditions such as transportation, lightness, use environment and users, and the verge of 'light' and 'heavy' weapons, as an exclusive or combined factors, were considered to define small arms. Publicists do not seem to adopt the technical approach, which is popular in domestic firearms laws. Their implications for the development of appropriate definition of SALW will later be analysed (see 2.2.5).

2.2.2.5 Conclusion on a General Definition

These definitions and approaches give a threefold impression. First, while there is no uniform definition on SALW, they generally range from non-barrel, small and lethal articles to that of light weapons below those specified in the UN Register. Secondly, a number of problems exist, among others, the dual use of weapons, the easy adaptability from civilian weapons to military and vice versa, a mix-up in the circumstances of use and the absence of a common perspective. Further analysis of the problems and a recommended definition will be offered later. The difficulty is greater than the broad definition, as fragments of definitions within this category overlap other weaponry legal regimes. Two key sub-categories and a discussion of the challenges therein will be considered.

2.2.3 Ammunition and Explosives

Clarification is desirable at this stage as issues of overlaps and exclusion arise with respect to this sub-category. The GGE 1997 Report put ammunition and explosives as a third sub-category in SALW. This was understood to take in cartridges, shells and missiles, for small arms and light weapons, and mobile containers with missiles for anti-aircraft or tank systems, hand grenades, landmines, and explosives.[115] This was not explained thoroughly.

Later, the second GGE expounded the concept of ammunition and explosives in its report to the GA in 1999. They defined both terms separately. The first: 'refers to the complete round / cartridge or its components, including bullets and projectiles, cartridge cases, primers / caps and propellants that are used in any small arms and light weapons'. Ammunition was described as a by-product of both explosive and non-explosive ingredients and serves as a generic name for all devices and missiles useful in both offences and defences. The panel declared from the outset that the type of ammunitions and explosives are those needed

[115] *GGE 1997*, above n 6, at 12.

for the small arms and light weapons listed by the previous panel. Accordingly, they produced a list of ammunition. They described explosives also as they belong to 'the general definition of ammunition' even if some ammunition may not have explosive components.[116]

Without a need to mention exclusions, the panel disclosed its main focus on 'military high explosives (in particular, plastic explosives), industrial explosives such as those used in the mining industry, improvised or "home-made" explosives and particularly explosive initiators, namely detonators (blasting caps)'. These are taken as ammunition and explosives in the sense of SALW. It was underlined that bulk military and industrial explosives, dud shells, and recycled landmines have been used as part of explosives so as to cause mass destruction and death.[117]

The OAS Convention defined ammunition in the same way as the 1999 Panel but stated that they 'are used in any firearms'. The definition of the 1999 Panel is similar, but slightly different in scope due to the possible difference between the terms of definitions in the weapons themselves. It brought about rather a new definition on explosives. 'Any substance, or article that is made, manufactured, or used to produce an explosion, detonation, or propulsive or pyrotechnic effect' is to be an explosive. It explicitly excluded substances that do not constitute explosives by themselves and the articles and substances annexed therein. The annex takes account of compressed gases, air bags and fire extinguishers, fireworks designed for public use, signal flares, among others.[118] The UN Protocol defines ammunition only; repeating the words of the OAS Convention.[119]

It is common practice to define ammunition and explosives in domestic legislation, though the approach varies. South African law, for example, defined ammunition separately from a firearm as 'a primer or complete cartridge' and did not address explosives. Although explosives for construction, industrial and mining uses are not firearms.[120] Similarly, the US defines ammunition as the same as South Africa. Destructive devices (see 2.2.3) are incorporated in the definition of a firearm itself.[121] The UK's law resembles the findings of the 1999 Panel, it defines 'ammunition for any firearm includes grenades, bombs, and other like missiles, whether capable of use with a firearm or not'.[122] The term 'ammunition' embraces explosives. In contrast, the French adopted a different approach, with each

116 *GGE 1999 on Ammunition*, above n 73, at 5; see, eg their focus: the type of ammunition most commonly encountered in conflict areas and illicit activities is small arms ammunition (ie, ammunition for weapons such as pistols, rifles and machine guns below 20mm in calibre), rocket-propelled grenades, light mortar rounds, and improvised explosive devices.

117 *Ibid*, p 5; see in particular paras 15 and 12.

118 *OAS Convention*, above n 77, at Art 1(4), (5) (a)–(b), Annex, p 10.

119 Above, n 75, Art 3(c).

120 *Firearms Control Act*, above n 85, s 1(iii), s 5(b), and (c).

121 *GCA*, 18 U.S.C, above n 90, ss 921 (17(a) and (4) (i), (ii), (iii), (iv), (v), (vi).

122 *Firearms Act*, above n 95, s 57(2).

grouping of weapons held to include its ammunitions.[123] For the French, therefore, there exist no separate definitions for the terms in issue.

The definitions of ammunition and explosives are not uniform in national jurisdictions. The trend appears to identify them closely with the weapons themselves. There is also a prevalent view that ammunition incorporates explosives.

'Ammunition' is defined as any bullet or projectile without which a weapon is inoperative. It embraces explosives as a component thereof. In principle, the definition follows the weapons, though explosives can stand by themselves as weapons. In our case, all these are SALW or firearms. However, certain explosives designed for public use such as fireworks are not regarded as SALW. The dual-use of fireworks could remain a challenge. Three matters are of note in respect of the omissions of certain explosives and ammunitions from the ambit of SALW.

First, sensitive technologies which comprise nuclear materials and chemical substances/technologies do not fall in the category of SALW, although they might be used in conflicts, terrorism and criminality.[124] In addition, chemical agents and similar technologies have been addressed in the 1987 agreement in which 28 states, most of which are developed, agreed to the effect of export control on sensitive technologies related to missile development and manufacture. The operative legal instrument commonly referred to is the Missile Technology Control Regime (MTCR).[125] These technologies may not fall under the definition of explosives in SALW due, inter alia, to the sensitive nature of such components and for the purpose of the avoidance of duplication of laws. Some could also be addressed in other well-developed conventions such as the CWC.[126]

Secondly, certain exceptional explosives and ammunition need to be looked at as a matter of exclusion. They could be divided into four:

(1) the St Petersburg Declaration outlawed the use of projectiles less than 400 grammes weight. It applies to all cases of undetectable x-ray fragments. Protocol I of the CCW also prohibited, in absolute terms, the use of any weapon with the effect of leaving plastic, wood, or glass etc fragments that cannot be detected by x-rays in the human body.[127]

[123] Decree No 95–589, above n 97, Art 2(b) (1), see, eg categories 4, and 5.

[124] Alves and Cippollone, above n 35, at 1.

[125] Sociola, 'Illicit Trafficking in Delivery System Technologies and Components: an Assessment' in Alves and Cippollone (eds), *Curbing Illicit Trafficking*, above n 35, at 23–24; for details of this regime see *US State Department*, at <http://www.state.gov/www/global/arms/treaties/mtcr_anx.html>

[126] Duarte, 'Chemical and Biological Agents' in Alves and Cippollone (eds), *ibid*, at 233.

[127] *Declaration Renouncing the Use, in Time of War, of Certain Explosive Projectiles*, St Petersburg, 29 November–11 December 1868; see also Roberts and Guelff, *Documents on the Laws of War*, 3rd edn (Oxford, Oxford University Press, 2001) 53–54, 516–17, prefatory note; see also *The 1980 UN Convention on the Prohibitions or Restrictions on the Use of Certain Conventional Weapons which may be Deemed to be Excessively Injurious or to have Indiscriminate Effects*, entered into force on 2 December 1983 (1980) 19 *ILM* 1523–36.

(2) Protocol III of the Convention broadly defined incendiary beyond those made up of hydro carbonate substances like napalms; these involve substances that attack targets through the action of flame derived from exothermic chemical reactions. They can be metal, pyrotechnic, and oil-based. Nevertheless, the law only places an obligation not to use them against civilians. Lazar blinding weapons have however been banned. [128]

(3) Protocol II of the CCW along with its amendment addresses land-mines and booby traps. We shall concentrate on the former. Mines are broadly defined as those designed to be exploded by the presence of a person or a vehicle, which may be mined in beaches, waterway, or river crossings. The only exclusion made from the scope of the Protocol is anti-ship mines at seas.[129] Recent negotiations on the CCW, however, reveal that the use and circulation of anti-vehicle mines are not restricted in the CCW. At the Geneva negotiations of December 2000, for instance, there was an attempt to introduce a binding instrument on this type of mine. However, agreement was not reached and it has been left for future study.[130] This shows that states have been attempting to address the problem within the range of the CCW. Also, the Mines Convention of 1997 regulated anti-personnel land-mines. Anti-vehicle mines have also been excluded. [131]

(4) The Protocol on Explosive Remnants of War (Protocol V) to the 1980 CCW, which was adopted by States' Parties on 28 November 2003, obliges a State Party, inter alia, to 'clear, remove or destroy' such explosives 'in affected territories under its control'.[132] Unexploded ordinance and abandoned explosive ordnance are considered explosive remnants of war; mines etc are excluded.[133] This affirms that the CCW is progressively developing.

Clearly, there are significant overlaps between various legal instruments and the newly emerging SALW legal regime in respect to explosives and mines. The UN Panels' inclusion of explosives and mines in general, and the OAS Convention's reference to all mines and incendiaries[134] obviously overlaps the 1980 CCW and its subsidiary protocols. For instance, while negotiations are underway on anti-vehicle mines within

[128] Roberts and Guelff, *ibid*, at 517; see also SIPRI, *The Law of War and Dubious Weapons* (Stockholm, 1976) 63–64.

[129] Roberts and Guelff, *ibid*; see in particular prefatory notes, pp 517, 518, 519 and 536.

[130] 'Countries Agree to Negotiate on Explosive Remnants of War' *Arms Control Today* (January / February 2003).

[131] *Mines Convention*, above n 4, Art 2(1), for the exception see Art 3.

[132] *The Protocol on Explosive Remnants of War (Protocol V) to the 1980 CCW*, 28 November 2003, Art 3(2); not yet in force.

[133] *Ibid*, Art 2(4).

[134] *GGE 1997*, above n 6, para 26; *OAS Convention*, above n 77, Arts 1(3 b, (5)(a), and (b).

the framework of the CCW, the 1999 GGE have exhaustively discussed such improvised explosive devices as SALW.[135]

States and drafters of these humanitarian conventions and related efforts seem to be aware of this overlapping problem between different legal norms and negotiations. The Mines Convention, for instance, calls states to ratify Protocol II, and also refers to some of the obligations therein.[136] The 1997 panel has made it clear that the international community is addressing anti-personnel landmines in other forums and 'agreed to avoid duplication of effort and different approaches' by excluding it from deliberations.[137]

Therefore, ammunition and explosives such as sensitive technologies, exceptional fragments, incendiaries, landmines and booby traps and laser blinding weapons shall be excluded from SALW. One of the major reasons for this is, on the one hand, the indiscriminate, unnecessary and superfluous injury arising from the use of such armaments.[138] Alternatively, peace and security concerns relating to international terrorism and non-proliferation concerns could be the case behind the exclusion of sensitive technologies.[139] All are thus subject to *lex specialis* legal regimes such as the CCW. The second obvious reason is the need to avoid the duplication of measures within the international community.

The last reason is that, in terms of lightness and lethality, the exceptional weapons in consideration could be held to be generally similar to those known as SALW. Due to their peculiar character, however, they might not predominantly fulfil other basic features of SALW, such as accessibility, suitability and versatility of use.[140] For example, nuclear substances and explosives might be used by skilful terrorists and not by ordinary combatants and civilians. The know-how they require for operation, and the expense they involve for possession, seem to be considerable.

Four points could recap the discussion on exclusion. First, although it is not easy to draw demarcations, and although the overlap of laws and efforts to restrict weapons are evident, adequate attention must be paid to avoid and minimise such problems. Consequently, some conventional weapons and explosives, as illustrated above, should not be regarded as SALW. Secondly, the circumstances of each weapon have to be considered to determine its inclusion within, or exclusion from, the scope of SALW, on a case-by-case basis, as drawing a complete list of SALW is almost impossible to do. Thirdly, despite the fact that anti-personnel landmines have been addressed in the UN CCW and the Mines Convention, states

[135] *GGE 1999 on Explosives*, above n 73, at 5, paras 15, and 16.

[136] *Mines Convention*, above n 4. See, eg the Preamble, para 5, see also Art 5(2); see also Roberts and Guelff, above n 127, at 647.

[137] *GGE 1997*, above n 6, para 31.

[138] Roberts and Guelff, above n 127, at 517; see also SIPRI, above n 128, at 63–64.

[139] Alves and Cippollone, above n 35, at 1.

[140] See 2.1.

and writers still consider this to be an essential aspect of SALW, due to the continuing grave effects of such mines in conflicts.[141] It appears to be an exceptional departure from the exclusions. Clarity on this would help the international community to focus on the difficulty of the unrestricted nature of SALW.

2.2.4 Parts and Components

The parts and components of weapons are essential aspects of SALW—they cause them to survive for a long period of time. The OAS Convention defined the phrase 'other related material', as 'any component, part, or replacement, part of a firearm, or an accessory which can be attached to a firearm'.[142] The Firearms Protocol also broadly defined the term 'parts and components' as 'any element or replacement element specifically designed for a firearm and essential to its operation'.[143] Silencer devices that can be attached to a firearm to diminish the possible blast are all included. National legal systems usually consider parts and components as constituent elements of a weapon.[144] Separate definition is not therefore the prevailing exercise.

All components and accessories of SALW are hence part of small arms. For various reasons, however, they could be defined as a sub-category of SALW.

2.2.5 Conclusions

2.2.5.1 Problems

Four points explain the definitional dilemma presented by SALW. The first regards the use of the various terms: some writers and studies favour the term 'small arms and light weapons'. The two UN Panels, the OSCE and writers such as Karp and Klare are precise examples of such a position. On the other hand, the OAS Convention and the UN Protocol rely on the term 'firearms'. Even if the latter appears to comprise both small arms and light weapons, there are considerable disagreements in the interpretation of the terms themselves, as discussed above.

141 *GGE 1997*, above n 6, para 31, first sentence.
142 See also UN *Protocol*, above n 75, Art 1(6).
143 *Ibid*, Art 3(b).
144 See, eg *Jamaica Firearms Act*, s 2(1)(b), the main paragraph of the definition on a firearm expressly included parts and components; *UK Firearms Act*, s 57(1)(b) and (c), components and accessories are explicitly mentioned; *French Decree No 95–589*, Art 2(b), the law incorporates 'weapons and elements of weapons'.

The second difficulty is with respect to the perspectives defining these types of weapons. Some make lightness and others the function and technical set-up of the firearms a key criterion. Some are persistent in pursuing an exclusionary approach, that is, small arms vis-à-vis major weapons or military versus civilian firearms; others tend to consider the effect and purpose of use of these weapons, such as lethality. However, some writers attempted to combine both approaches.

The third confusion concerns fragmented definitions. While the 1997 GGE study described ammunition and mines as one category within SALW, the OAS Convention and the UN Protocol defined them separately. In addition, there is no uniformity in state practice. Some states adopt a wide-ranging but others a fragmented method. In some jurisdictions, different definitions are given for domestic and international relations uses. The same is true in the case of the parts and components of small arms. They have been treated as a different category. However, this does not lead one to conclude that defining sub-categories of SALW is undesirable.

Finally, the source of all these problems could be: (a) the lack of understanding and common perspective on the complex nature and consequences of such weapons; and (b) the conflict between national interest and international norms, since the dispute in definition is with narrowing or widening the effect of possible restrictions on the range of SALW.

2.2.5.2 Perspectives

Undeniably, definitions may vary from perspective to perspective. From a military effectiveness viewpoint, a military strategist or an armament industry might categorise weapons from the point of view of the efficacy of the weapons in destroying enemy forces, supply lines, or other military and economic targets. Suppliers of arms may also resort to cost factors to describe small arms. For a general who heads a high-tech war, an assault rifle could be nothing other than a means of policing activities; for a guerrilla fighter on the other hand a machine gun could be a major weapon, though this might depend on the level of military and organisational strength of the non-state actor. For the actual victims of conflicts and violent crimes, any weapon with a horrifying blast and injury could be a major weapon.

Although it is essential to consider the competing viewpoints of military professionals, combatants and arms industries, etc in defining small arms, the priority should be to ensure common values within the international order.

In short, while the definition of small arms is in progressive development, there seems to be no common perspective which could lead to a globally agreed definition of such weaponry at present. The considerations below are offered as support for future efforts, in the vital work of definition.

2.2.6 Appropriate Definition

(A) The core tests for defining SALW under international law should include humanitarian principles, and the peace and security of states, communities and the human person (see Part II). The whole reasoning behind the dialogue has to be based on these and not on the use of terms or technical considerations. Yet emphasising 'military-style' small arms could be an important step in setting the priority of tackling the most diffused and lethal weapons.

(B) The approaches adopted by different writers and forums are essential if they are taken together to develop a uniform definition. In view of that, the lightness and the transportation approach, the technical features of weapons, the exclusionary and enumerative methods and the actual effect of such arms are all relevant for a multi-use definition on SALW which might be accepted by all parties.

(C) We have to seek out a definition which underlines general principles and guidelines, but not precise terms and a universally accepted definition applying to all types of small arms since legal norms can develop later in reference to a specific type of weapon in due course in accordance with the nature and effect of the instruments and the progression of technologies. Hence, laying down general principles opens the door for further development at all levels. It also helps adopt a wider scope for the regulation of firearms.

(D) For international law purposes, it is crucial to address the problem of SALW as a package and not as pieces of fragmented definition. For instance, weapons are useless in most cases without ammunition, parts and components. Technically speaking, explosives are, for example, constituent parts of ammunition. Even so, due to the peculiar nature of some specific weapons such as landmines, we can arrive at some particular definitions, which are to be inferred from the principal definition.

(E) Bearing in mind the nature and circumstances of use of small arms, in particular the features of SALW as reflected earlier under (B), therefore, sensible inclusions to and exclusions from SALW have to be made so as to avoid overlaps of regulations and duplication of definition. For this reason, weapons which belong to *lex specialis* regimes need to be excluded from SALW, despite the fact that they might share certain common features with them.

Having taken these elements into consideration, my definition is: SALW are all those deadly weapons, including their components and ammunition, suitable for personal and/or for group use, employed or to be employed by states and others, for legal and/or illegal purposes and are uncovered in *lex specialis* weaponry legal regimes.

This definition has taken at least seven core elements into consideration. First, the lethal nature of a weapon/tool has to be apparent. It should be so perceived by states, weapon designers, lawyers and/or by the public at large. Secondly, all types of weapons with their parts and ammunition, including those to be invented in the future are all covered. Article 1 of the ECOWAS Convention on Small Ams of 2006 (has not yet entered into force) has been compatible with this approach. However, semi or fully automatic firearms attract special attention from the international community, due to the magnitude of the damage they bring about and their scale of diffusion. Thirdly, SALW attract individuals or small groups of people due to their lightness, accessibility and suitability for use and transit; all these are in comparison with major conventional, exceptional and other weapons.

Fourthly, SALW are versatile. One might argue that law enforcers, NSAs and individuals typically use SALW as weapons of defence and/or offence. However, some of them are dual-use as they can also be deployed for industrial, mining, sporting and hunting purposes. Fifthly, the end-uses could be in-conformity with international and/or domestic legal norms or otherwise. The interest in this work is albeit on the latter (see Part II).

Sixthly, weapons, ammunition and explosives, already regulated or to be regulated by well-established legal frameworks, ie, the CCW, the UN Register (MCW) and the MTCR are omitted, with the exception of anti-personnel landmines. This exclusion is neither to suggest that MCWs and their use are not global concerns, nor is it to deny the immeasurable human misery they have been causing as observed in the Hezbollah-Israel major armed conflict of the summer 2006. Nevertheless, we still need to define and address SALW as a distinct group of weaponry and a chronic threat to human security—Iraq, Somalia, and Sudan are, for example, typical on-going cases of human suffering, in which small arms and explosives, and not tanks and fighter planes, have been taking a major part (see further chapter ten).

Finally, as the treaties, resolutions, declarations, and legislation are, in total, in favour of a wider approach, it appears that the definition may represent the interests of the international community as a whole. This definition is not intended to answer all possible questions and to some extent is vague; yet future developments have to be considered to strengthen it further. The primary focus of study from now on will be on conventional SALW, in particular on fully or semi-automatic assault weapons. And so, as the initial stage is making SALW, we now turn to the question of manufacturing.

3

Manufacturing of SALW: Associated Problems

3.1 DEFINITIONAL, FACTUAL AND MORAL ISSUES

THERE EXISTS NO uniform definition to cover SALW manufacturing. In the *English Law Dictionary*, the term 'manufacture' is held to mean 'any thing made by art'.[1] Ironsmiths, for example are likely to be included. Some also claim that today the term in use is 'manufacturers of defence equipment' other than arms manufacturers. This widens the scope to include bulldozers and international bombers. In effect, in Britain, 500 firms might be considered as producers of instruments of war.[2]

Yet a study group established by the UN GA described arms 'manufacturers' as those that 'develop, make, assemble, repair or convert small arms and light weapons and ammunition (and components').[3] It seems to be a workable definition, albeit its expansion to repairing activities may be open to criticism. Domestic legislation treats manufacturing of firearms as a business and more often defines the individuals than the task. In US law for example, 'manufacturer means any person engaged in the business of manufacturing firearms or ammunition for purposes of sale or distribution'.[4]

Furthermore, the UN Protocol on Firearms has defined 'illicit manufacturing' as the 'manufacture or assembly of firearms and their parts and components and ammunition'.[5] The OAS Convention[6] has adopted the same words. Although they discuss illicit manufacturing, however, they define the general process of producing weapons.

[1] Jowitt, *The Dictionary of English Law* (London, Sweet & Maxwell, 1959) 1139.

[2] Collier, *Arms and the Men: The Arms Trade and Governments* (London, Hamish Hamilton, 1980) 2.

[3] *Report of a Consultative Meeting of Experts on the Feasibility of Undertaking a Study for Restricting the Manufacture and Trade of Small Arms to Manufacturers and Dealers Authorised by a State*, 6 July 1999, UN Doc Supp No A/45/160, entitled 'General and Complete Disarmament: Small Arms', Annex, p 3, para 4 [emphasis original].

[4] *NFA*, 26 U.S.C. Ch 44, 1968, s 921(10); see also *Canadian Firearms Act* 1995, Ch 39, s 2(1).

[5] *UN Firearms Protocol*, Art 3(d), status: signatories 52, parties 33.

[6] *OAS Convention on Firearms*, Art 1(1), as of February 2002, 16 OAS Member States ratified the Convention.

The SADC Protocol on Firearms has, however, added some new elements to the stated definition. Illicit manufacture is carried on when devoid of a permit from state authorities, among others.[7] By analogy, therefore, the definition of licit SALW manufacturing could be described as a manufacture or assembly of SALW, by states or authorised private or public entities. The lawfulness of this should refer to both international and domestic relevant norms. Taking into account the definitions which have already been covered, two matters deserve clarification. First, this chapter focuses on any manufacture of small arms in which states are involved; the involvement could be direct and / or indirect. By implication, therefore, we will be dealing with the licit manufacturing aspect of the matter. Secondly, the industrial side is considered, although craft production designed for commercial gain is also a problem.

Ninety-eight states and one thousand companies are currently involved in the manufacture of small weapons. This means that it takes place in more than half of all states, for domestic and foreign, or military and civilian markets. Few states claim that their manufacture is only for domestic markets. Nevertheless, most of the producing states make firearms for foreign markets. It is apparent that since the middle of the nineteenth century, all the major firms of armaments of the world seek foreign business, even in peace time, and they are highly encouraged by their governments to do so, in addition to the legal authorisation granted to make arms by state organs.[8]

In the year 2000 alone, 720,000 military type and 7 million commercial firearms were produced worldwide. The total cost of production of the same year was globally estimated to be $7.4 billion. China, the Russian Federation, the US, Austria, Belgium, Brazil, France, Germany, Israel, Italy, Spain, Switzerland, and the UK are the most important SALW producers worldwide; the first three are cited as major producers. The 33 most advanced arms industries in the world exist in the aforesaid states alone.[9]

The extended dimension of manufacturing is called licensed-production. In 1995 alone, this took place in 26 developing countries; as a result, 16 of these were able to export small arms. Even if it is not a major problem internationally, the craft production also operates in a number of countries, including in the Middle East.[10]

[7] *Protocol on the Control of Firearms, Ammunition and Other Related Materials, in the SADC Region*, Blantyre, 14 August 2001, Art 1(2); it is signed by 13 states.

[8] UN Commission on Crime Prevention and Criminal Justice 1998, *United Nations International Study on Firearm Regulation*, New York, p 64, para 1 and Table 4.1, and p 168, para 5, the survey involved 69 states, and it was reported that manufacturers in Burkina Faso, Guinea, India, and Papua New Guinea supply arms only to domestic market; see also *SAS 2002*, below n 17, at 11; see also Collier, above n 2, at 4.

[9] See, eg *SAS 2002*, *ibid*, at 13, 15 and 20.

[10] *Ibid*, at 16, 40.

In a nutshell, states and business groups have widely been engaged in small arms manufacturing. Such activities have also been expanding through licence transfers. The question is what people think about SALW manufacturers and their business.

The moral values of societies normally serve as a background for legal norms, which is why it is essential to discuss this. The following three aspects may give some hints on the question. First, in the past, the attitude of the public toward arms manufacturers resembled the feeling of people towards the East African Masai. The Masai were/are said to be a warlike people. Their ironsmiths make swords and spears for their ordinary business such as cattle raiding. These instruments are potential tools of bloodshed, therefore the non-Masai community neglects them to the extent that marriage with them is regarded as dangerous. Arms manufacturers in the West have likewise been criticised by pacifists as merchants of death. This idea was also common in the 1930s and was expressed by some prominent state leaders, such as President Roosevelt of the US. Others consider their activity as an inherently dirty business. Phrases of opprobrium include 'international dealers in death'. Manufacturers are often exporters and dealers at the same time. Despite this, manufacturers can be publicly praised for their contribution to national defence and the maintenance of peace and order.[11] People's response to this matter is often more cynical than positive.

Secondly, some argue that taking for granted the social and political evil outcomes of such activities are the results of the active approval and involvement of governments.[12] In all arms producing states, the ultimate blame including any responsibility should thus be directed to those governments. Finally, in modern times, as it was seen in the US, civil rights advocates blamed firearms industries for murders and other crimes committed with weapons they made and supplied. For example, a lawsuit which was heard by the Federal District Court in Brooklyn blamed gun makers for violence among ethnic groups in the city of New York[13]; the plaintiffs added that: 'the practices of the gun industry amount to a public nuisance, a widespread intrusion on public health and safety'.[14] The suspicion extends to small arms manufacturers who are involved in

[11] Collier, above n 2, at 1–2; see also Noel-Backer, , *The Private Manufacturer of Armaments* (London, Victor Gollanz, vol 1, 1936) 97. In May 1934, the President revealed that arms manufacturers are 'merchants of engines of destruction'; see also Naylor, 'The Structure and Operation of the Modern Arms Black Market' in Boutwell et al, *Lethal Commerce: the Global Trade in Small Arms and Light Weapons* (Cambridge, Mass, American Academy of Arts and Sciences, 1995) 45. He pointed out that inherently the arm business is dirty; see also 'The International Dealers in Death' *Guardian Unlimited* (9 July 2001).

[12] See, eg Noel-Backer, *ibid* at 15 and 58-62.

[13] 'Court Clears US Gun Makers' *BBC News*, 15 May 2003, para 6.

[14] Glaberson, 'Suit against Gun Makers is Dismissed on Technical Grounds' *New York Times*, 27 July 2003; see also, *China North v Ileto et al*, US S.C. 04-423.

transfers of arms to conflicts, being both traffickers and manufacturers for purposes of market access.[15]

Therefore, in moral terms, the attitude of ordinary citizens towards arms manufacturers has not altered from time immemorial, although advocates of gun culture would not share this ever-growing attitude. A reasonable approach is hence to take an objective look at the manufacturing of small arms as a social and economic phenomenon that exists within societies. By doing this, the evils or strengths, if any, may come to light.

3.2 CONCERNS AND LEGAL ISSUES

At least, four main concerns have to be mentioned here: (1) the most proliferated assault rifles, such as Kalashnikovs-Russia (70-100 million), Israeli Uzi (10 million), M-16s–USA (7 million), G3s–Germany (7 million) and FALs-Belgium (5-7 million), are serving as tools of conflict, violence, crime and repression (see chapter eight); (2) their indiscriminate use against civilians has been a serious problem (see Part II); (3) the widespread use of such weapons has brought a high demand for manufacturing and sale of such types of arms in the world[16]; and (4) under-licence arms manufacture has been a serious concern. Arms industries have been resorting to licence manufacture, as a method of market penetration. Some also argue that it is an easy way to evade export controls. It may include co-operation, technology transfer agreements, and offsets. It is one of the contentious issues in the proliferation of SALW. Nevertheless, we cannot address it due to limits in scope.[17] What is clear is that these issues have not gained appropriate attention by states.

On this basis, legal problems which should be assessed are: (a) substantive restrictions that are imposed on such practices, if there are any; (b) emerging norms on manufacturing; and (c) associated challenges. We shall now consider the question of substantive limitation on the manufacturing of small arms.

[15] Ruben, 'The Role of Arms Manufacturers and Traffickers' in Alves and Cippollone (eds), *Curbing Illicit Trafficking in Small Arms and Sensitive Technologies: an Action Oriented Agenda*, New York/Geneva, United Nations, 1998) 94.

[16] *GGE 1997*, 27 August 1997, para 35; see also Klare, 'The Kalashnikov Age', 55 *Bulletin of Atomic Scientists* (January/February 1999) 3; see also Oxfam, Amnesty International, *Shattered Lives: The Case for Tough International Arms Control*, AI Index: ACT 30/001/2003, below n 89, at 21.

[17] GIIS, *Small Arms Survey 2002: Counting the Human Cost* (Oxford, Oxford University Press) 40, 41 and 42.

3.3 SUBSTANTIVE LIMITATIONS ON SALW MANUFACTURING

Substantive limitation can refer to both quantitative and qualitative restrictions. Whether international law in an implicit or explicit manner imposes any such legal obligation on states, is one of the exigent questions of small arms proliferation. The position of international law and the newly emerging norms will therefore be examined. Relevant global practices and treaties are considered first.

3.3.1 The League of Nations and the United Nations

The League of Nations undertook significant efforts to put in place substantive limitations on the manufacturing of weapons, including on SALW. Of course, members of the League were engaged in such activities as a result of their commitment to reduce and limit their national armaments, as predetermined in the Covenant and the Kellogg Pact. For example, the Assembly of the League, in its Resolution of September 1926 decided to consider the issue of the private manufacturing of arms as a concern of the global order, in particular of international peace and disarmament.[18] The solutions which used to be raised on the matter range from the need for the strictest supervision on their work, to their abolition as a business. Several state delegates were in favour of the idea of abolishing such private business; although there was no consensus on this. Some were also of the opinion that any manufacture of arms should be centralised globally. The latter two ideas did not and could not attain agreement.[19]

Subsequent efforts have combined both the private and state manufacture of arms as one issue. The Committee for the Regulation of the Trade in, and Private and State Manufacture of Arms, which was constituted of twenty countries, had for instance, unanimously adopted a draft Convention on the problem. The following had, inter alia, been agreed in the instrument: first, that the issue is a matter of 'public international order'; thus, contracting parties assume full responsibility in their respective jurisdictions; secondly, states undertake to prohibit the manufacture of arms 'forbidden either for their use or for manufacture, or exceeding the qualitative limits laid down in the Convention'; last but not least, they undertake 'neither to manufacture nor to permit to be manufactured,

[18] Noel-Backer, above n 11, at 198; see, eg *Supervision of the Private Manufacturers of Arms and Ammunitions and of Implements of War*, League of Nations (LN), Res of 21 September 1926; see also 7.2.2.

[19] *Committee for the Regulation of the Trade in, and Private and State Manufacture of, Arms and Implements of War*, 12 November 1932, p 3, paras 9–10.

. . . arms . . . in excess of the quantitative limitations laid down in the present Convention'.[20] The US delegate's proposal, in support of the draft, is notable among others. He stated that qualitative and quantitative limitations shall be the primary basis for restriction and control measures on arms manufacturing. Even so, neither the draft Convention itself nor the weapons and limitations, which were envisaged to be determined, became a reality.[21]

There were also endeavours to analogise the principles and substantive limitations on the manufacture of narcotic drugs, together with that of arms manufacture. For instance, a memorandum communicated to delegates of states by the Secretary-General of the League reflects, inter alia, two essential matters of interest. First, in accordance with the 1912, 1925 and 1931 Conventions on the licit traffic in narcotic drugs, 'satisfying the world's legitimate requirements of manufactured narcotics' was the whole objective. This was meant 'to provide it with narcotics in quantities and qualities corresponding solely to medical and scientific requirements'. And secondly, with respect to the possibilities of adapting this system to arms manufacture, it has been said that 'limitation of manufacture of armaments' could only be practical with the 'introduction of a quota system', that has to be issued on the licences of such activities. Yet the differences in nature of both industries have duly been appreciated. Among others issues, the political complexity of arms manufacture was referred to.[22]

Later developments in the League demonstrate that regulatory measures such as licensing, transparency, supervision and domestic control issues of manufacturing have dominated, as top priorities, rather than concerns of substantive limitation.[23]

Briefly, in the League era, positive endeavours had been shown to place substantive limitations on the manufacturing of arms; the League had also made remarkable efforts to learn lessons from the narcotic drugs control regime; although efforts to limit arms manufacturing failed in the end. The question of whether the UN will evaluate the issue of substantive restriction on arms manufacturing, in terms of its predecessor, remains.

The UN efforts towards addressing this problem could be grouped into two aspects the institutional and declaratory. As regards the former, the

[20] *Ibid, Committee*, 23 July 1934, pp 3–4, Annex B, *Draft Articles* (a) and (c).

[21] *Ibid*, Annex A, *Memorandum by the US Delegate*, No 2.

[22] *Analogies Between the Problem of the Traffic in Narcotic Drugs and that of the Trade in and Manufacture of Arms*, LN, 4 May 1933, pp 4, 7 (I) 2b; see also the *1912 International Opium Convention (the Hague Convention)*, Art 9; the *1925 Convention*, Art 5; the *International Convention for Limiting the Manufacture and regulating the Distribution of Narcotic Drugs 1931*, Preamble and Art 4.

[23] *National Control of the Manufacture of and Trade in Arms* (LN), 14 April 1938, pp 18–20; see, eg *Draft Convention with Regard to the Supervision of The Private Manufacture and Publicity of the Manufacture of Arms and Ammunition and of Implements of War* (LN), 29 August 1929.

work of five UN Panels and/or committees and the Disarmament Commission (hereafter 'DC'), which were carried under the direction of the GA, have now been assessed.

(A) The GGE of 1997 on Small Arms has exhaustively examined the nature and causes of the excessive accumulation of small arms, and discovered some relevant findings. First, the proliferation of legitimate producers of small arms in the world, as a result of the rise in licence production and technology transfer during the Cold War, which had led to foreign market searches, has been identified as one factor for the excessive diffusion of SALW today. This has accordingly signified the need for a study on the feasibility of restricting the manufacture and trade of such weapons as a preliminary solution. Finally, it has emphatically suggested that a regional or sub-regional moratorium on manufacturing and transfer of small arms, 'as agreed by the states concerned', needs to be encouraged by the UN.[24] It appears that the recommendations emphasised solutions of a political nature.

(B) The 1999 GGE on Ammunitions and Explosives (hereafter 'GGE 1999 on Ammunitions') emphasised that the number of companies involved in ammunition manufacture is rapidly changing because of market factors and technology transfer; the industries which can produce ammunition separately from weapons are widespread, both in the developed and developing world. It has been suggested in the end that the efforts to control the accumulation of small arms need to take into account technology transfer.[25]

(C) In accordance with the first panel's proposal and subsequent General Assembly's request, the UN Disarmament Commission organised a 'consultative meeting of experts on the feasibility of undertaking a study for restricting the manufacture and trade of small arms to manufacturers and dealers authorised by states'. The report produced on 6 July 1999 fully acknowledged the feasibility of a study on the subject as follows[26]:

> The consultative meeting of experts concluded that a study for restricting the manufacturers and dealers authorised by states is both feasible and desirable, and could help member states and the international community to promote national and international efforts in addressing the proliferation of small arms and light weapons.

(D) The GGE 1999, which was established to oversee the implementation of the recommendations of the first panel of 1997 (hereafter 'the 1999

[24] *GGE 1997*, above n 16, at paras 47, and 80(L)(ii) and (I).

[25] *Report of the Group of Experts on the Problem of Ammunition and Explosives*, 5 June 1999, *Disarmament Study Series No 28*, United Nations Publication, p. 98, para 23.

[26] *Report of a Consultative Meeting of Experts*, above n 3, at 5, para 23; see also GA Res 53/77 E/1998.

Reviewing Panel'), in its report to the GA, has acknowledged increased manufacturing as one element of the proliferation and referred to the efforts of the consultative meeting made by the Disarmament Commission. The panel further highlighted that in line with previous recommendations, UN agencies have played a vital role 'in promoting and supporting the efforts to establish a moratorium on the . . . manufacturing of light weapons in West Africa'.[27] Having reviewed the application of the proposals of its predecessor, the panel further suggested that: 'states should ensure that they have in place laws, regulations and administrative procedures to exercise effective control over the production of small arms and light weapons within their areas of jurisdiction'.[28] The GA adopted the report in 1999.

(E) The fourth UN GGE Panel of 2001 on Small Arms, produced a report on the 'feasibility of restricting the manufacture and trade and dealers authorised by states', in accordance with previous recommendations and paragraph 14(a) of GA Resolution 54/54 V. The details of the latter will be seen after a while. Initially, the panel agreed with the thesis that past panels formulated, in that the increasing proportion of legitimate manufacturing is among the major causes for the availability of small arms across the globe. It has also repeated the words of the Reviewing Panel of 1999 by reaffirming that 'states are responsible for ensuring effective control over the manufacture of small arms and light weapons' in their respective territories. Yet the panel has in principle recognised that SALW manufacture is not illegal per se, as it enables states to deal with lawful functions, in line with the UN Charter.[29]

Some pertinent findings and proposals of the panels are summarised as follows: first, almost all appreciate that the state and/or state authorised manufacture of small arms is one major cause for the excessive accumulation of these weapons worldwide. Factors such as market search and technology transfers have been reiterated as aggravating factors. Secondly, effective national control has been emphasised as a remedy to the problem; states are therefore responsible for ensuring this control under their respective jurisdictions. Thirdly, the need for restraint on technology transfers has also been suggested. Fourthly, states' voluntary moratorium on manufacture of SALW has generally been encouraged; arms manufacture has been regarded as a lawful and useful practice for states. Finally, almost all panels mention that further action is necessary.

[27] *Report of the Group of Governmental Experts on Small Arms*, UN Doc Supp A/54/258, 1999, *Disarmament Study Series No 28*, 1999, p 43, see paras 18, 73 and 87, the panel was established according to UN Res 52/38 J/ 1997.

[28] *Ibid*, para 113.

[29] *Report of the Group of Governmental Experts Established Pursuant to General Assembly Resolution 54/54 V of 15 December, 1999*, entitled *'Small Arms'* 12 March 2001, paras 36 and 15.

Briefly, the approaches shown above reflect the position of the UN and Member States, as the activities were directed and endorsed by the GA. While the contribution of manufacturing to the crises has duly been accepted, solutions have focused on domestic regulatory measures. Despite this, UN efforts are not limited to studying the subject through expert panels.

The UN has been making declaratory efforts on the issue. The UN GA, in its Resolution 54/54 V of December 1999,[30] which considered, inter alia, 'the need for comprehensive approach to promote . . . the control and reduction'[31] of SALW and the importance of the aforesaid panel reports and studies,[32] decided to convene a global UN conference on the Illicit Small Arms Trade in All Its Aspects in June/July 2001.[33] The conference assembled at New York had adopted a Programme of Action (hereafter 'UN PoA') to combat the illicit trade in all its aspects by consensus. The UN GA without vote adopted the PoA on 24 December 2001 by its Resolution 56/24 V[34] (see Part II). It is essential to look at the salient features of the PoA relating to the manufacturing of small arms and commentaries thereon.

The PoA reaffirmed, inter alia: 'the right of each state to manufacture . . . small arms and light weapons for its self-defence and security needs, as well as for its capacity to participate in peacekeeping operations in accordance with the Charter of the United Nations'. They also underlined that states are primarily responsible for preventing the illicit arms trade and associated problems.[35] In order to prevent the illicit trade in its all aspects, taking into consideration the different situations, capacities, and priorities of regions and states, the participating states agreed to undertake a number of measures. One of these, sought at a national level was, 'to put in place. . .adequate laws and regulations. . ., to exercise effective control over the *production* of small arms and light weapons within their areas of jurisdiction'[36] [emphasis added].

The conference and the PoA did not escape criticism. Karp reflected its desperation on the PoA, saying that powerful proposals which could have forced countries to cut back production and other measures were 'systematically killed off'.[37] Conversely, viewing this as cornerstone of a

[30] Res 54/54 V/1999 entitled '*General and Complete disarmament: Small Arms*'—adopted 119 votes in favour, 2 abstentions, 0 negative, and 0 absent count.

[31] *Ibid*, Preamble, para 4.

[32] *Ibid*, see paras 12 and 13.

[33] *Ibid*, para 1.

[34] *Report of the UN Conference on the Illicit Trade in Small Arms and Light Weapons in All Its Aspects*, 9–20 July 2001, New York, p 1.

[35] *Ibid*. See, eg the PoA, p 7, Preamble, para 10, p 8, para 13.

[36] *Ibid*, PoA, p 10, Pt II, para 2 [emphasis added].

[37] Karp, 'Small Arms: Back to the Future' 9(1) *The Brown Journal of World Affairs* (Spring 2002) 179–80.

partnership for future endeavours by states, some activists on the problem reflect optimistic views, but with certain grievances. The SAS for example propounded:

> Continued disappointment with omissions in or the implementation of the PoA by states may produce a version of the Ottawa process outside of the UN auspices and focusing on the humanitarian and economic costs associated with the proliferation and use of small arms.[38]

Whether such reluctance in the UN will facilitate a process similar to the Mines Convention will be discussed later (see Part II). The first UN conference on small arms produced a non-binding instrument, which also touches, at least, on the problem of SALW proliferation vis-à-vis manufacturing. However, licit manufacture is excluded from the reach of the PoA. The matter is also left to domestic regulation. Does this represent the beliefs of all states on the problem? The views of individual states and some developments thereafter might give some clarity on the issue.

Several states have expressed their concern on the excessive circulation of SALW in various instances. The UN conference and its aftermath is a good example. Many states including some major manufacturers of arms have submitted reports on the national implementation process of the PoA, in their respective jurisdictions in the years 2001 and 2002, to the UN DC. For example, Australia's report has emphasised that the country manufactures few firearms. Bans of certain weapons were also agreed among the states in 1996. By implication the message on, and the need for, substantive limitations on licit manufacturing seem to be conveyed to the DC. Conversely, the Russian Federation and the US focused on the regulation aspect of manufacturing as will be seen.[39] The Tokyo follow-up meeting of the UN conference on the implementation of the PoA, in which 32 governments had participated, did not address the problem.[40]

Similarly, the July 2003 Biennial Meeting of States (hereafter 'UN BMS') on the implementation of the PoA has shown a division of view. Apart from appreciating the ECOWAS Moratorium on SALW, manufacturing was not discussed as a topic on its own.[41] Yet countries such as Turkey, Botswana, Croatia, Namibia, Cambodia, and Lithuania have adopted a comprehensive approach to the SALW issue in their national reports to the BMS. The UK further went on to state that a start should have to be made at the international, regional and national levels towards reducing the

[38] *SAS 2002*, above n 17, at 230–31.

[39] *National Reports on the Implementation of the PoA*. See, eg Australia's 2002 Report, p 1, para 6, and 2001 Report, p 1, para 5; Russian Federation's Report of 2001, p 1, para 2; US 2001 Report, p 1, at <http://disarmament.un.org/cab/salw-undc.htm>

[40] UN Doc Supp No A/56/810-S/2002/145, pp 1–14.

[41] *Report of the UN First Biennial Meeting of States to Consider the Implementation of the Programme of Action to Prevent, Combat and Eradicate the illicit Trade in Small Arms and Light Weapons in All Its Aspects*, 18 July 2003, p 7, para 11.

availability of small arms. The Holy See, as a permanent observer of the UN, has also stressed the need for a binding international instrument and the responsibility of states to reduce the availability and use of SALW.[42] In contrast, states like Thailand, Colombia, Israel and the US have focused on the illicit aspect of manufacturing. It was underscored by the US that 'the illicit trade in small arms' is the focus and mandate of the conference.[43]

Two elements could be inferred from the views of states as presented in the BMS. First, several states appear to be interested in adopting a wider approach to the problem, which might embrace issues of manufacturing of SALW by states and authorised entities. Secondly, some states do not want to even mention authorised manufacturing. It appears that they have chosen to be silent on the controversy over the licit manufacturing as one cause for the proliferation. They merely talked about the illicit aspect. Whether the latter attitude is the case in domestic jurisdictions is something that needs to be addressed later.

In summary, the UN's position on state and/or state authorised manufacture of small arms seems to be full of discrepancies. It has been recognised that legal manufacture has needlessly been filling the world with a stockpile of SALW. Also, reference was only made to self-defence, security needs and peacekeeping, relative to the right of states to manufacture SALW. In contrast, the licit manufacturing is not at the forefront of UN negotiations. What if a state manufactures or authorises to manufacture beyond the stated purposes? The UN has not yet given an answer to the problem. States' views are also enormously divided on the question. Hence, questions of substantive reduction appear to be deliberately ignored by the UN and the latter does not seem to consider some positive lessons from its predecessor on the manufacturing of weapons. The efforts of the international community are not confined to the UN organisation.

[42] See, eg Statements made at the *Biennial Meeting of States on the Implementation of the PoA of the 2001 UN Conference*, New York, 7–11 July 2003: Jerry Ekandjo, *Minister of Home Affairs of the Republic of Namibia*, p1, para 4; Vaclovas Semaskevicius, *Head, Department for International Co-Operation Lithuanian Weaponry Fund*, p 1, para 2; Borith, *Ambassador* of *the Kingdom of Cambodia to the UN*, p 1, para 3; Pamir, *Ambassador of Turkey to the UN*, p 1, para 3; Vice Skracic, *Head of Department for the UN, Ministry of Foreign Affairs of the Republic of Croatia*, p 1, para 3; EJ Batshu, *Botswana, Deputy Commissioner of Police*, p 1, para 2; Broucher, *Ambassador* of the *UK to the UN*, p 1, para 4; and Migliore (Archbishop), *Permanent Observer of the Holy See to the UN*, p 2, para 3.

[43] *Ibid*, (Statements): Kasemsara, *Ambassador of Thailand to the UN*, p 1, para 2; Giraldo, *Ambassador of Colombia to the UN*, p 1, para 1; *Statement of the State of Israel*, p 1, para 2, it was referred for instance to 'illicit proliferation'; LP Bloomfield, *Assistant Secretary of State for Political-Military Affairs*, US, p 2, para 1.

3.3.2 Treaties

The Mines Convention outlawed any manufacture of anti-personnel landmines as a matter of a total ban.[44] Beyond such mines, no global treaty exists in international law with the effect of restraining small arms manufacture, either in quantitative or qualitative terms. Although excluded from the SALW category, as has been reviewed in chapter two, the UN CCW prohibits the manufacture of certain inhumane conventional weapons. Unfortunately, the first international treaty, the UN Firearms Protocol, restricted its scope to illicit firearms manufacturing.[45] It is thus essential to turn our attention to regional efforts.

3.3.3 Regional Efforts

Diverse regions and sub-regions have made profound efforts to tackle this deadly problem. Treaties, moratorium, codes of conduct and programmes of action, declarations and other moves have been achieved within the last ten years. We will be assessing the position of some representative organisations from Africa, Latin America and Europe, on small arms manufacturing.

3.3.3.1 The West African Moratorium

Manufacturing practice is not to be ignored in the sub-region, even if it is not a source of significant supply in the area. For instance, as one Ghanaian states: 'in Ghana today, the manufacture of small arms is one of the leading industrial activities by blacksmiths'.[46] This part of Africa is also best known for civil conflicts. The efforts made by ECOWAS have a unique place in the fight against the proliferation of small arms. The sixteen heads of state and governments of ECOWAS, taking into consideration the consequences of small arms proliferation to peace and security within and outside the region, signed a declaration in 1998 that reads:

> Hereby solemnly declare a moratorium on the . . .*manufacture* of light weapons in ECOWAS member states which shall take effect from the first day of November, 1998 for a renewal period of three (3) years[47] [emphasis added].

[44] *Mines Convention*, Art 1(b).

[45] *UN Protocol*, above n 5, Art 4; see also *SAS 2002*, above n 17, at 238, para 3.

[46] *Ghana Broadcasting Corporation, Radio-1*, 'Commentary suggests ways of curbing menace of small arms trade', 20 June 2001, para 1.

[47] *West African Arms Moratorium*, Abuja, 31 October 1998, para 11, [emphasis added]; the Member States are: Benin, Burkina Faso, Cabo Verde, Cote d'voire, Gambia, Ghana, Guinea, Guinea-Bissau, Liberia, Mali, Mauritania, Niger, Nigeria, Senegal, Sierra Leon, Togo Lese, at <http://www.nisat.org/west%20africa/african.htm>

The Moratorium has proscribed the production of small and light weapons, as a matter of rule. The ban is total but temporary (see 5.4). Even so, exemption mechanisms have also been set out for national or international legitimate security needs. A member state seeking such a demand may apply to the ECOWAS Secretariat for a release of obligation. Such an application is treated according to the standard criteria and with technical support of the Bamako based Programme for Coordination and Assistance for Security and Development (hereafter 'PCASED'). The latter is a UN programme, explained shortly. The request must be circulated to Member States, and if all consent, a certificate of confirmation is issued by the secretariat.[48] However, what would happen if a single state objects to a 'legitimate' request from a Member State remains unknown. An answer is not provided in the working Code which supplements the Moratorium; the Code's draft purports to resolve such potential objections through ECOWAS mediation and Security Council mechanisms.[49]

The Moratorium has been accompanied by implementation mechanisms. The ECOWAS Executive Secretariat, UNDP through PCASED administered by the UN and designated as a mechanism for the implementation and the Lome Centre as a representative of the UN are the three organisations responsible for the implementation of the Moratorium.[50]

The ECOWAS Code of Conduct and the Plan of Action have duly supplemented the process. The ECOWAS July 1999 Code of Conduct is a binding instrument. The Moratorium is, however, a shared political commitment. Manufacturing is placed within its scope, with the expressed inclusion of ammunitions and explosives. The ECOWAS Executive Secretariat has been entrusted with the responsibility of assisting, monitoring, and reporting the progress to the heads of state of the Community. One of the structures and procedures stipulated under the executive is the formation of missions in Member States to ascertain that: 'national arms production is brought to halt in conformity with the spirit of the Moratorium'.[51]

The remarkable aspect of the Code and the Moratorium is that it has been intended to embrace other states within or outside the continent, be it in the form of co-operation, or dynamic membership. Further, it has

48 *Code of Conduct for the Implementation of the Moratorium on the Importation, Exportation and Manufacture of Light Weapons*, Lome, 10 December 1999, Annex 5, in *UNIDR, 2002/2*, below n 50, Art 9(1), (2).

49 *Code of Conduct for the Implementation of the Moratorium on the Importation, Exportation and Manufacture of Light Weapons*, (Draft), Bamako, 25 March 1999, Annex 4, in *UNIDR, 2002/2*, below n 50, pp 47–52, see eg Art 10.

50 *West Africa Small Arms Moratorium: High-level Consultations on the Modalities for the Implementation of PCASED*, Workshop Report, *UNIDR, 2002/2*, United Nations, Geneva, p 3, para 3.

51 *Code of Conduct*, above n 48, Annex 5, pp 53–62; see, eg Arts 1, 2, 5(2)(b); see also Mubiala, 'The ECOWAS Moratorium on Small Arms in West Africa' (2000) 3 *YBIHL* 249.

been stated with emphasis that the ECOWAS Secretariat shall take all necessary measures to encourage other African states to join the Moratorium. The Community is determined to have dialogue with other small arms producing states as well as relevant international organisations for the purpose of securing compliance with 'the spirit and letter of the moratorium' and cooperation.[52]

A 'Plan of Action' for detail implementation is designed for PCASED so as to implement the Moratorium. Facilitating dialogue with manufacturers particularly with Wassenaar has been categorically referred to in the action plan.[53] The Heads of State of the Community have renewed the Moratorium for another three years effective from 5 July 2001.[54]

The ECOWAS Convention on Small Arms and Light Weapons, their Ammunition and Other Related Materials of June 2006, has not transformed the Moratorium's ban on manufacturing into a binding norm—Article 7(1) states: 'Member States shall undetake to control the manufacture' of SALW 'in their national territories'. Sub-paragraph (2) of the Article albeit emphasised that: 'Each Member State. . .shall undertake to adopt strategies and policies to the *reduction and/or limitation* of the manufacture of SALW' [emphasis and abbreviation added]. Clearly there is a retreat, but the ambition of restricting small arms manufacture is still there. (For implications and further analysis see chapter ten.) Both the Moratorium and the Convention will be considered further in Part II, since the African problem is highly associated with the importation and aspects other than manufacturing.

Similar initiatives exist on the African continent. The Southern African Development Community (hereafter 'SADC') is for instance undertaking encouraging measures on the small arms problem in general. Nonetheless, the Protocol on the Control of Firearms only speaks about the illicit trade side of the challenge. It has been recognised, nevertheless, that proper control is needed on manufacturing.[55] It seems to be that the SADC states and others in Africa have not learnt the positive lessons from the ECOWAS Moratorium.

Yet the ECOWAS practice has attracted the international community to a great extent. As stated above, the UN is highly involved in its operation and implementation. PCASED is funded by a number of donors from the developed world.[56] Some supplier states have for instance reported certain requests of imports of arms made by dealers and ECOWAS

[52] *Ibid*, *Code of Conduct*, Arts 17 and 16.

[53] *Plan of Action for the Implementation of PCASED*, Annex 3, pp 31–45; see, eg p 39, VI, above n 50.

[54] *Press Release*, ECOWAS No 63/2001, Lusaka, 6 July 2001, para 1 <http://www.nisat.org/west%20africa/african.htm>

[55] *SADC Protocol*, above n 7, Art 5(3)(e).

[56] Above n 50, at 18; see, eg Belgium, Canada, France, Norway, the UK, and the US have agreed to fund the process.

Member States to the Executive Secretariat for clarification as will be discussed further in Part II. Civil societies have been involved in the implementation process. The high level consultation of 23–24 March 1999 of West African small arms experts and civil societies on the implementation of PCASED, is a proof of such an assertion.[57]

In total, international and regional organisations such as the UN and the EU have welcomed the Moratorium. The practical significance of this model arrangement, in terms of both the quantitative and qualitative bans of the production of small arms has been essential. The ECOWAS Convention has also covered substantive limits on manufacturing. Harmony between the ambition and the reality remains to be proved. Questions of norms, realism and their extra sub-regional effects will be assessed in Part II.

3.3.3.2 *The OSCE and the EU*

In response to the excessive accumulation of small arms, the OSCE Member States have agreed to develop relevant norms and principles on the problem, including manufacturing. The participating states decided in November 1999 to exercise[58]:

> Due restraint and ensuring that small arms are produced . . . only in accordance with legitimate defence and security needs.

Such a commitment to reduce and prevent the accumulation except for legitimate national and collective defence, internal security and participation in peacekeeping, under the UN Charter and OSCE framework, has been reiterated in the year 2000.[59] The need for national control over manufacture has also been emphasised.

In addition, the EU has adopted two relevant instruments, the EU Code of Conduct on arms exports and the Joint Action on small arms, as we shall later explain further (see pp 122*ff*). The EU Joint Action (hereafter 'EUJA') mirrored 'the wish of EU Member States to maintain a defence industry as part of their industrial base as well as their defence effort', and underlined the need for restraining conventional weapons transfer.[60] The EUJA laid two essential foundations; first, it has been clearly exhibited that 'excessive and uncontrollable accumulation' of SALW shall be tackled appropriately; and secondly, contributing 'to the reduction of existing accumulations . . . consistent with countries' legitimate security needs' has been adopted

[57] *Ibid*, at 18–19; see also Mubiala, above n 51, at 250.

[58] *'Weapons Trade: OSCE 1999 Small Arms Decision'*, 269th Plenary Meeting, Decision No 6/99, 16 November 1999, *FSC Journal No 275*, p 3, para 1.

[59] *OSCE Document*, 24 November 2000, *FSC Journal No 314*, p 3, s I, 3(ii), (iii), and s II, 1, 2(a).

[60] *EU Code of Conduct on Arms Exports*, Council of Europe, May 1998; see, eg Preamble, paras 3 and 7.

as an objective of Member States on the small arms problem.[61] As will be seen in subsequent topics, these legal and political instruments are accompanied by implementation and control mechanisms, such as the obligation of reporting of a Member State to the EU Commission.

Prominent civil societies and activists have criticised the Code, arguing that a high common standard of restraining arms could not be gained without addressing problems such as the licensed-production agreement.[62]

In sum, while the EU has acknowledged the necessity of reducing the proliferation of small arms, the direction of the steps forward is regulatory and not a substantive limitation at the manufacture level.

3.3.3.3 Conclusion

Regional efforts, especially the West African experience, have shown a real concern over restraining the manufacturing of small arms. The OSCE countries have also shown some commitment to restrict the manufacture of small arms. The EU supports the need for reducing the proliferation of SALW. Almost all recognise the fact that licit manufacturing is one of the grounds of the rise in world stockpile despite their focus on the control spectrum. Some regions such as the OAS appear to have entirely ignored legal manufacturing and have limited their endeavours to the illicit side. In general, the manufacturing of small arms for legitimate national and international security needs is thus accepted as the legal right of states. To what extent this might restrict manufacturing is as yet a critical issue which remains unconsidered. State practice at the domestic level might help clarify various questions regarding limitations on manufacturing.

3.3.4 Domestic Legal Systems on SALW Manufacturing

Here, domestic legislation and relevant surveys are of great interest. Concerning national laws, the US, China, the UK, India and South Africa have been chosen for discussion, with the belief that they represent both developed and developing states and different regions' positions on the issue.

[61] *Joint Action of 17 Dec 1998, OJEC, 15/1/1999, L/9/1*; see, eg Art 1(1) (2); see also *Council Joint Action on the European Union's Contribution on Combating the Destabilising Accumulation and Spread of Small Arms and Light Weapons* and Repealing Joint Action 1999/34/CFsP, 12 July 2002, *OJEC, No 2002/589/CFSP*, 19/07/2002, this repeal was made to extend the scope to ammunition. See also Annex (a) and (b), the scope of the Joint Action is limited to military type SALW.

[62] Amnesty, BASIC, Christian Aid, Oxfam, Saferworld and World Development Movement, 'Final Analysis: Code of Conduct of the Arms Trade', see eg the introduction, para 3, at <http://www.basicint.org/WT/armsexp/EUcode-final.htm#Introduction>

First, more than 300 US companies have been engaged in manufacturing small arms and ammunition. In 1997, the total value of the manufacture of these weapons was $2.056 billion, according to US official sources. US small arms industries are dominated by private entities as opposed, for example, to that of China. Some of the top firms in the US are Stum, Ruger & Co, Smith & Wesson and Remington Arm Co.[63] The 2001 official manufacture Report of the Bureau of Alcohol shows a total of 3,014,546 small arms that range from pistols to machine guns.[64] The volume of manufacturing is thus immense in the US. Considering these, relevant laws of the country on the manufacturing of guns must be analysed.

The federal government and individual states together exercise jurisdiction over the arms business. The principal tasks pertinent to international law rest on the former. Licensing, prohibitions, conditions, permission, etc are set out for manufacturing activity. The most pertinent laws are: the Gun Control Act (GCA) 1968, which purports to keep arms out of illegal hands and to make state laws more effective, through a federal licensing mechanism which facilitates inter-state commerce; the Arms Export Control Act (AECA) 1976, which regulates the import and export of defence articles. The National Firearms Act (NFA) 1988, which was designed to regulate certain weapons such as machine guns and silencers, imposes stringent requirements and various taxes upon manufacturers and others.[65] Finally, other regulations supplement the application of the aforementioned acts. Substantive restrictions on, and requirements for, SALW manufacturing are put in place in the legal system.

Qualitative restrictions have been obligatory for manufacturers in the US. Three areas of small arms could be shown here. First and most importantly, the making of semi-automatic assault weapons or assemblage of imported parts for non-sporting semi-automatic rifles and shotguns is generally prohibited. Semi-automatic rifle weapons have subsequently been elaborated in the 1994 Violent Crime Control and Law Enforcement Act. Some of the prohibited nineteen semi-automatic rifle weapons are[66]:

> Any of the firearms, or copies or duplicates of the firearms in any calibre, known as (i)Norinco, Mitchell, and Poly Technologies Avtomat Kalashnikovs (all models); (ii) Action Arms Israeli Military Industries UZI and Galil; (iii) Beretta Ar70 (SC70); (iv) Colt AR-15; (v) Fabrique National FN/FAL, FN/LAR,

63 *SAS 2002*, above n 17, at 27 and 29, table 1.10.

64 *Annual Firearms Manufacturing and Export Report*, Year 2001, (AMER), at <http://www.atf.gov/firearms/stats/afmer/afmer2001.pdf>

65 See, eg *The Gun Control Act 1968* (*GCA*), as amended 18 U.S.C. Ch 44; *The National Firearms Act 1988* (*NFA*), 26 U.S.C. Ch 53; *The Arms Export Control Act 1976* (AECA), 22 U.S.C. 2778, at <http://www.atf.gov/firearms/legal/index.htm>

66 18 U.S.C. Ch 44, as amended by Public Law 103–322 *The Violent Crime Control and Law Enforcement Act* of 13 September 1994, s 921(a) (30).

and FNC; (vi) SWD M-10, M-11, M-11/9, and M-12; (vii) Steyr AUG; (viii) INTRATEC TEC-9, TEC DC-9, and TEC-22; and (ix) revolving cylinder shotguns, such as (or similar to) the Street Sweeper and Striker 12; etc.

As an exception, permission can be issued to manufacture such weapons by providing a document that shows they are being made for a federal or state agency or political division of government, for an official use.[67] Such an exception might embrace manufacturing for covert transfers by the CIA or others to foreign jurisdictions.

Secondly, it is unlawful to manufacture large capacity ammunition feeding devices since 13 September 1994. These magazines, belts, and so forth can readily be restored to accept more than ten rounds of ammunition. The exception to this is similar to that of semi-automatic rifle weapons.[68] Lastly, manufacturing of a firearm not detectable by airport security devices is outlawed.[69]

Accordingly, the major features of the US laws are the following: (1) Qualitative restriction on the manufacture of automatic and semi-automatic weapons, machine guns, and large ammunition devices has been introduced. The exception is that manufacture is legal for a government agency and/or authorised export purposes. Although nothing has been said about quantitative restrictions, the existing limitations and its exceptions might have such an implication. (2) The most astonishing aspect of this domestic practice is that the prohibition has been targeted at the most dispersed weapons in the globe; Kalashnikovs and the Norinco group which includes M16 are notable, among other SALW. (3) The GCA does not restrict gun making, so long as it is not designed for sale and is not a machine gun or semi-automatic firearm. Finally, the laws and policies that permit manufacture for exports are unknown. Regarding the letters and the spirit of the law, such permits are more of an exception than the rule, so far as domestic control is concerned.

Secondly, China is one of the major arms producers in the world. The defence industry including small arms is entirely state controlled. The state owned China North Industries Group Corporation (Norinco) established in 1980, operates under the Ministry of Machinery and Electronics, incorporating 160 enterprises and more than 700,000 employees. Between 1980-90, the corporation earned about $12 billion from arms sales. In 1999, Norinco divided into two, China South Industries Group Corporation (CSG) and China North Industries Group Corporation (CNGN). The latter, with 131 companies and 83 industrial enterprises is now covering almost all small arms production by the state.[70]

[67] 18 U.S.C. 922 (o), (r), (v), and 923, 27 CFR 178.39, 178.40, 178.41 and 179.105.
[68] 18 U.S.C. 921(a) (31).
[69] 18 U.S.C. 922 (p).
[70] *SAS 2002*, above n 17, at 22–23.

'Factories designated by the state' shall only manufacture firearms for official use.[71] Whether these are only state factories is not clear. In practice, it implies state owned industries. It also appears that an official use refers to both the use by law enforcement and defence forces and government transfers to outsiders, although not clearly stated in the order. It seems clear that not just any manufacturing firm can deal with military types of small arms.[72]

Moreover, quantitative restrictions are in place in the country. The forestry and sports authorities of a state council at the provincial level along with public security organs determine a quota of annual production for an enterprise. This is a remarkable rule for the control of civilian firearms. Security authorities allot serial numbers for tracing purposes. It is thus illegal to manufacture exceeding this quota, which is fixed for each factory.[73] This law seems to be the most preferable if we compare it with the US laws, as regards civilian firearms manufacture.

China also has other regulations in this field. The 1981 Control of Firearms Measure, which basically addresses the ownership aspect, a Regulation on the Administration of Arms Export, a Regulation on the Administration of Militia Equipment and a Regulation on the Administration of Civilian Explosives are mentioned as the main ones. For example, the second contains nothing with regard to manufacturing. None of the other regulations assure any substantive restriction on gun making either.[74]

In sum, the quota system of China affirms the necessity of quantitative limitation on the manufacture of civilian weapons. Yet whether such decision making takes extra-territorial circumstances into account is unknown. Also, except from the remark made that manufacturing of military style small arms is reserved to state designated factories, and not for any Chinese firearms firms, the laws and regulations state nothing about the restriction under consideration. Whether China imposes substantive restrictions on automatic and semi-automatic arms manufacturing is unclear.

Thirdly, from 1993–2000 the UK was the fourth largest conventional weapons supplier to the developing world, with sales of $8.9 billion, that is an average $1.1 billion, a year. However, in terms of the quantity and sales value of SALW production, some European countries such as Belgium, Germany, and Italy substantially exceed this figure. Among the

[71] *Law of the Republic of China on the Control of Firearms*, Twentieth Session of the Standing Committee of the Eighth National People's Congress, 5 July 5 1996, Presidential Order No 72, effective as of 1 October 1996, Art 14.

[72] Nay, *Firearms Regulations in Various Foreign Countries* (Law Library of Congress, Washington DC 20540, 1990) 35.

[73] Above n 71, Arts 16 and 17.

[74] See, eg *The Law on the Control of Firearms*, above n 71.

major UK small arms producers is the Royal Ordnance (RO), as a small arms division of the arms firm called BAE Systems Plc, which was rated as the third major arms producer in the OECD and developing countries in 1999, as per the SIPRI. Sterling Armaments Company and Heckler & Koch GMBH were also bought by RO. The buying of the latter two producers of small arms, particularly of the second, enabled RO to control more than 70 per cent of European, and a significant share of the world market in small arms, according to up-to-date research. In addition, Accuracy International (sniper rifles), Armalon (sniper rifles), Conjay Arms (small arms ammunitions), Manroy Engineering (machine guns), FR Ordnance (sub-machine guns), and Parker Hale (sniper rifles) are some of the essential manufacturers with few employees but focused products.[75]

The Firearms Act 1968, and subsequent amendment Acts of 1988, 1992, 1994, and 1997 regulate the small arms business and manufacturing. Qualitative restrictions are administered on SALW manufacture in the legal system. It is an offence to manufacture and sell generally prohibited weapons and ammunitions without the authorisation of the government body, the Defence Council.[76] Prohibited weapons include[77]:

> Any firearm which is designed or adopted that two or more missiles can be successively discharged without repeated pressure in the trigger; any self-loading pump action rifle other than one which is chambered for .22 rim-fire cartridge;. . .; any rocket launcher, or any mortar, for projecting a stabilising missile, etc.

Automatic and semi-automatic assault rifles and light weapons are incorporated into this category. It appears that it includes weapons other than SALW. The Defence Council is the body authorised to give permission for the manufacture or transfer of prohibited weapons. The authority must be in writing. The conditions are left open in each particular case. Public safety and/or peace are, however, important conditions for such a permit. After permission is granted, the manufacturer/dealer is expected to comply with any condition set by the Council. Failure to do so is an offence. 'If they see fit', the permit can be revoked at any time; however, notice in writing has to be given by the Defence Council. The revocation automatically results in the cancellation of the original certificate. The person is obliged by law to obey the decision within twenty-one days. If an order is given to surrender a permit, it should be complied with; it is a serious offence otherwise.[78] The details on which the Council operates are not demonstrated in the Act.

[75] *SAS 2002*, above n 17, at 39–40.

[76] *Firearms Act 1968*, s 5(1), *1988*, s 1.

[77] *Firearms Amendment Act 1988*, ss 1(1) (2)(a), a(b), a(e); *1988 Act*, s 18, expanded the prohibited weapons; all automatic firearms, any self-loading pump-action rifle, a smooth-bore revolver gun, etc; see also Nay, above n 72, at 70.

[78] *Firearms Act 1968*, ss 5(1), 5(3), (4), (5), and (6).

Overall, the UK is therefore one of the countries which, in principle, prohibits dangerous weapons including SALW manufacture. Permits are an exception. It is noteworthy that the policy of permit or denial considers, inter alia, public safety and/or peace. It appears to be a confidential process.

Fourthly, India is regarded as one of the newly-emerged producers of arms, along with Pakistan, Singapore, South Africa and Taiwan.[79] The Arms Act 1959 and the Arms Rules 1962 regulate the manufacturing and related business. Various categories of weapons are administered in accordance with the Act and the rules.

Qualitative restrictions have been imposed on prohibited arms and ammunitions, unless it has been specifically authorised by authorities. Prohibited arms are those able to discharge noxious liquid, gas, artilleries, anti-tank missiles and other similar weapons that could subsequently be notified by government in the official gazette. This is almost identical to the UK prohibited weapons definition, under the 1968 Firearms Act. Prohibited ammunitions are those used for noxious or gas uses. Some of them can, however, be manufactured under a specified authorisation.[80] The category appears to be inclusive of light and major weapons and other outlawed arms in international law.

Fifthly, in the 1960s, South Africa began domestic arms assembly and the licensed production of weapons to satisfy its domestic needs. The 1977 mandatory UN arms embargo was said to provide the dynamics for the growth of the arms industry. The state-owned commercial company Denel, which is constituted of ARMSCOR, LIW and Vektor run the business of manufacturing. The Armaments Development and Production Corporation of South Africa (ARMSCOR) is the commercial wing of Denel. Lyttleton Engineering Works (LIW) and Vektor are subsidiary companies, on which the task of small arms manufacture rests. Small arms and ammunitions manufacture have been taking place at Pretoria Metal Pressing (PMP), providing small arms for both defence and civilian markets.[81]

South Africa is one of the best examples of the manufacture of small arms under licence. FN FAL rifle and the R3 weapons were produced as a result of licence production in the country. Acknowledging the re-engineering capacity of the country, it was stated that the FN type weapon became a background for the invention of Vektor 7.62 mm SS77 general-purpose machine gun in the country, which is the principal weapon of the South African army and the armies of countries like Kuwait today.[82]

[79] *SAS 2002*, above n 17, at 20.

[80] *The Indian Arms Act*, No 54, 1959; see also *The Arms Rules*, 1962, Art 7, ch 1, Art 2, I(i) and (ii) on prohibited arms.

[81] *SAS 2002*, above n 17, at 47–48.

[82] *Ibid*, at 48.

With respect to substantive restrictions on manufacturing, 'any fully automatic firearm, any gun, cannon, recoilless gun, mortar or launcher manufactured to fire a rocket, grenade . . ., body or barrel of such a fully automatic firearm . . . and projectile . . . etc.' cannot be possessed or licensed, and in effect their manufacture is prohibited.[83] Aside from some regulatory and inspection provisions of the Act, this prohibition and the entire Act does not regulate the armed forces, police service, the department of correctional services, any intelligence services, the armament acquisition agency of the state or any institution accredited by the Registrar as an Official Institution. These are thus excluded from the restrictions set out on manufacture of arms.[84] By implication, therefore, the state-owned firearms factories do not seem to be subject to substantive restriction.

Furthermore, the global study on firearms conducted in 1998 by the UN, which considered 69 states, highlighted this regard. Generally, almost all states regulate their manufacturing industries. The main findings are summarised as below:

> The majority of responding states restrict the manufacture of firearms, firearm components, and ammunition. A number of responding states totally prohibit the manufacture of firearms, firearm components, and ammunition. The following ten countries totally prohibit the manufacture of both long guns and hand guns; Cuba, Greece, Luxembourg, Papua New Guinea, Peru, Singapore, Trinidad and Tobago, Tunisia, Uganda and Vietnam. Only the Republic of Moldova, Romania, Samoa and Sudan have no restrictions on manufacturing firearms.[85]

The study clearly shows that quantitative and qualitative restrictions exist as a matter of rule in state practice. The priority of the majority of states is albeit on restriction/ quantitative measures. In addition, it has also been proved that there exists no uniform practice and intent to cover such rules, be it on the types of weapons, or the degree of devotion to the problem.

In a nutshell, the practice that has been examined so far could be summarised in three points. First, manufacturing countries strictly regulate SALW manufacturing, with special attention to certain types, commonly known as prohibited or military-style weapons. For some of them, it is intended to regulate the private sector. For others, it is to affirm that certain categories of weapons must only be manufactured by state firms. In both cases, it seems that the manufacture of automatic machine guns, semi-automatic and other similar armaments is forbidden in principle. It is notable that the most troublesome SALW have been classified as illegal to manufacture. Therefore, such small arms can only be

[83] *Firearms Act 2000*, s 4(1)(a), (b), (c), (d), (e) and (f); see also Nay, above n 72, at 174, even civilian weapon manufacture is subject to stringent controls.

[84] *Firearms Act 2000*, ss 96 and 95.

[85] *United Nations International Study on Firearm Regulation*, above n 8, at 11, para 1–2.

manufactured under particular government permits, under a number of conditions. Authorisations often consider, inter alia, the needs of government agencies and state officials, either for domestic or foreign end uses, and public peace and safety. These may be regarded as exceptions to the principle. The second point is that the quantitative restrictions put in place on hunting, sporting, and other similar civilian firearms manufacture could offer an instructive way forward, although it is difficult to deduce a settled practice. The last is that orders or policies which dictate the permit or otherwise are usually kept confidential. This makes the examination of state practice and *opinion juris* of states on the problem much more difficult (see 3.4). NGOs may offer a way forward.

3.3.5 NGOs

NGOs have been playing a vital role in promoting the fight against small arms proliferation (see further Part II); whether their useful efforts in the field have duly been extended to the manufacture issue is a question that needs to be considered. The ICRC, in1999, in its extensive study on small arms availability and their impact on violations of IHL assured that[86]:

> While the primary responsibility for compliance with IHL falls upon users of weapons, states and enterprises engaged in production . . . bear a degree of political, moral and, in some cases, legal responsibility to the international community for the use made of their weapons and ammunition.

It has also suggested that states are under obligation to review their policies on manufacturing of arms and ammunition 'in light of their responsibility to respect and ensure respect for international humanitarian law'. It went on further to remind that weapons shall never be considered as simple as other mercantile goods. Nevertheless, the proposals put forward to halt the problem of the diffusion of small arms were import-export oriented, as discussed in chapter seven of the book.[87] While it has suggested valuable clarifications and policy options on other aspects of the problem, nothing was done to elaborate the moral, political and legal responsibilities of manufacturing states. This leading humanitarian organisation, in its report presented to the BMS in July 2003, reiterated the transfers' focused approach towards the challenge.[88]

NGOs such as Oxfam and Amnesty International have made comprehensive recommendations on the problem of small arms proliferation.

[86] *Arms Availability and the Situation of Civilians in Armed Conflict*: a study presented by the ICRC, 1 June 1999, ICRC publication, p 25, para 2.

[87] *Ibid*, para 3 and pp 20–24.

[88] ICRC, *Report to the BMS to Consider the implementation of the UN PoA to Prevent Combat and Eradicate the Illicit Trade in Small Arms and Light Weapons in All Its Aspects*, New York, 7–11 July 2003, p 2, para 5.

Some of these are adopting the FCIAT (see Part II); creating a legal instrument on brokering; and providing more funding for the practical assistance and responsible use of arms by security forces. This shows the current state of mind of almost all civil societies on how to tackle this deadly challenge. The need for a new legal instrument to address the foreign under licence manufacture has also been discussed. Moreover, many other NGOs such as the American Working Group, European NGOs, IANSA and the Prominent Persons Group have shared the common view that governments have foremost responsibility for controlling arms manufacturing. Some civil societies also make it clear that one of their objectives as NGOs is to seek 'a universal, comprehensive, and non-discriminatory small arms control regime' in the fight against excessive accumulation. Almost all have been emphasising transfers and measures such as collection and destruction, at the macro and micro levels rather than issues of substantive restrictions at the manufacture stage.[89]

In contrast, NGOs such as the WFSSA, which is also linked to manufacturers of firearms, in its presentation to the UN BMS, affirmed that the small arms problem has nothing to do with licit business of weapons in general. They have also declared their readiness to help solve problems on marking and brokering. Mention has not been made of manufacturing.[90]

Opponents of the diffusion of small arms therefore emphasise controls of transfers rather than substantive restrictions on manufacturing. While arms control may refer to a ban of certain weapons, it seems that their focus is the physical restraint of circulation (see Part II). The ICRC and others have given some clues as to the need for regulating manufacturing; the rules of, and responsibilities arising from such activities have not yet been dealt with. In fact, proponents of the legal manufacture appear to have entirely avoided this matter. Briefly, substantive restriction on the manufacturing of small arms does not seem to be the focus of civil societies as things stand now.

3.3.6 Conclusions

First, with the exception of the Mines Convention, there has been no treaty on the subject. The UN generally considers manufacturing as a part of the

[89] Oxfam, Amnesty International, *Shattered Lives: The Case for Tough International Arms Control*, AI Index: ACT 30/001/2003, pp 86–88; see also *The Humanitarian Challenge of Small Arms Proliferation*, presented to the First Precom—2001 UN Conference on Small Arms, by the Delegation of the Republic of Mali—on behalf of the Eminent Person Group, New York, 28 February–3 March 2000, pp 3 and 7; see also Small Arms Working Group (SAWG), *Seek a Broad and Comprehensive Agenda for 2001 Conference*, pp 1–2, at <http://fas.org/asmp/campaigns/smallarms/sawg/2001onepager.htm>.

[90] See, eg Rowe, Chairman Manufacturers Advisory Group (WFFSSA), *Report on Firearms Industry Efforts to Fight Illicit Trafficking in Firearms* UN BMS, New York 7–11 July 2003, p 3, para 6.

problem of the contemporary accumulation of SALW. Unlike its predecessor, however, solid measures have not yet been taken to address problems associated with licit manufacture, even at the political level of its endeavours. Secondly, regional organisations have demonstrated essential commitments. The ECOWAS Moratorium is a unique example. The ECOWAS Convention is still a positive commitment. Others stress the regulatory aspect rather than substantive limitations. Thirdly, domestic legal systems prohibit the manufacture of non-civilian firearms in general. Yet governments enjoy the freedom of granting a permit for or dealing with manufacturing. Fourthly, either at the global or regional level, the manufacturing of SALW is understood as a right of states, pertaining to self-defence, domestic security and participating in peace keeping. Finally, a majority of NGOs have generally been targeting the transfer aspect of the crisis. Does the practice we have seen assure the existence of customary rule on the issue?

3.4 IS THERE A RULE OF SUBSTANTIVE LIMITATION?

Evolving or evolved rules of customary law regarding substantive limitations on the small arms manufacture will now be assessed in the light of the sources of international law. This will begin with a brief description of sources.

As a complete statement of the sources of international law, Article 38(1) of the ICJ Statute incorporated treaties, international custom, general principles of law, judicial decisions and the works of publicists.[91] The first three are generally regarded as formal and the last two as subsidiary sources. While the former can stand on their own, the latter are material sources, which help determine the formal sources.[92] The details of the relevant sources of law in this case will be discussed in combination with the facts at hand.

The regional or global treaties, signed or ratified, so far did not impose such restrictions, save the recent ECOWAS Convention. Some mention the right of states to manufacture and acquire weapons, yet are silent on many other issues relating to small arms.[93] One must resort to the remaining sources of international law and international custom in particular.

It is essential to look briefly at the elements and evidences of customary law. 'International custom' is described in the Statute of the ICJ 'as evidence of a general practice accepted as law'.[94] It embraces two key

[91] *Statute of the International Court of Justice (1945)*, Art 38 I, (a) (b), (c) and (d).

[92] Brownlie, *Principles of Public International Law*, 5th edn (Oxford, Clarendon Press, 1998) 1–6; see also Akehurst, 'Custom as a Source of International Law' (1974–75) 47 *BYBIL*) 53, 1.

[93] See, eg *UN Firearms Protocol*, above n 5, Preamble, para 4.

[94] Above n 91, Art 38 I (b).

factors, state practice and *opinio juris*. The former refers to a reasonable duration, uniformity, consistency and generality of a practice as elements of a certain custom, depending on the circumstances of the practice and the rule in issue. These are normally 'a matter of appreciation'. Material sources, such as diplomatic correspondences, policy statements, state legislation, international and judicial decisions and UN GA resolutions are generally said to be evidences of state practice. The phrase 'accepted as law' on the other hand refers to '*opinio juris et necessitates*'. This is the psychological element, which requires the acceptance of a certain practice as legally binding upon concerned states.[95] Is there uniform, consistent and general state practice, which also exists for a reasonable duration, on the issue under consideration?

First, the uniformity and consistency of the practice on substantive limitations have to be considered. As the ICJ in the *Fisheries* case[96] pointed out, substantial but not complete uniformity is required. Also, minor contradictions or inconsistencies are not generally a barrier for the invocation of a custom.[97] Practice at global, regional and domestic levels is discussed in this sense subsequently. During the League of Nations, almost all states, particularly of manufacturers, were entertaining the view that qualitative and quantitative limitations on arms manufacturing is essential for international peace and security. Extensive studies and draft treaties had been carried out to that effect. Major manufacturers of today such as the US used to back such efforts. The practice made uniform and consistent progress for some time.[98]

By contrast, UN Member States have been expressing their concerns on small arms manufacturing. The studies and recommendations made on the subject clearly accept that restriction on manufacturing is desirable. Though complex in nature, the significance of limits on the expansion of the industry itself, in particular the unrestricted licence transfer has attracted some attention.[99] Among regional organisations, ECOWAS have taken measures to halt manufacturing. The SC, the GA, the OSCE, the EU and others welcomed the Moratorium. Many organisations and states have been assisting the implementation process, in various respects, including financial co-operation. Lately the 'banning' approach of ECOWAS has been replaced by a 'reduction' approach, which has been

[95] Brownlie, above n 92, at 4–7; see also Shaw, *International Law*, 4th edn (Cambridge, Cambridge University Press, 1997) 56–66.

[96] *Fisheries* case, *ICJ Repts* 1951, pp 116–31 and 138, the Court required a substantial uniformity if not universality, and refused to recognise the ten-mile rule for territorial waters.

[97] Brownlie, above n 92, at 5; see also Shaw, above n 95, at 60; see also *Asylum* case, *ICJ Repts* 1950, pp 276–77, the Court stated: 'the party which relies on a custom . . . must prove that . . . the rule invoked . . . is in accordance with a constant and uniform usage practiced by the States in question, and that this usage is the expression of a right appertaining to the state granting asylum and a duty incumbent on the territorial State'.

[98] See, eg above, nn 18 and 19.

[99] See above, nn 24–28.

incorporated in a formal treaty. Other international organisations such as the EU have expressed the need to regulate manufacturing in accordance with the legitimate security needs of states in general (see 3.3.3). In addition, the ICRC has shown its concern about manufacturing. It has affirmed states' legal responsibility to respect and ensure respect for IHL corresponding to weapon manufacturing (see 3.3.1).[100] There cannot be any doubt that these are positive achievements of the international community.

The UN has not pursued the positive deeds of the League on manufacturing. With the exception of the ECOWAS Moratorium, states have often referred to domestic regulatory measures as a solution to the problem. All agree that the licit manufacture is one of the causes of the proliferation of small arms, existing practice emphasises the rights of states to manufacture SALW for their defence, security and peacekeeping activities. The need for substantive limitation has never been considered as an agenda of its own. The attitude of states, particularly of the manufacturers, seems to be confined to the illicit manufacturing aspect (see 3.3.1). Under such circumstances, one may also argue that ECOWAS's retreat from the banning of manufacturing of SALW is understandable. For these reasons, therefore, a uniform and consistent practice by states, with respect to substantive limitations on manufacturing of SALW, appears to be unreal. This should not, however, be the end of the matter.

Domestic legislation by a majority of states, including manufacturers, prohibit the manufacture of certain categories of weapons, often military-style SALW.[101] While restriction is the principle, permit is an exception. This is evident in the relevant laws of major manufacturing countries, such as the UK and the US. This shows substantial state practice in qualitative restriction. Certain major manufacturers such as China impose a quota on the manufacture of civilian firearms. There appears to be no limit when a state undertakes or authorises manufacture of SALW. Despite this situation, uniform and consistent substantive prohibitions have been adopted in domestic firearms laws, unlike the practice in international organisations.

Secondly, in respect of generality element of custom, universality of a practice is not necessary; as the ICJ stated in the *Fisheries* case, however, a practice needs to be 'generally accepted' by interested states.[102] Manufacturer states are the interested states, if not the only ones, in our case. During the League there was a general consensus of states on the subject. Throughout the UN era there has been no widely accepted

[100] See in particular the *UN PoA*, above n 34.

[101] Nay, above n 72, at 136, in the Netherlands, manufacturing is restricted by law, but not applicable to the military; see also China's Legislation, above n 74.

[102] *Fisheries Jurisdiction* case, *ICJ Repts* 1974 3, pp 23–26; see also *North Sea Continental Shelf* case, *ICJ Repts* 1969, p 42; see also Brownlie, above n 92, at 6.

practice other than certain concerns and limited bans on manufacturing. Regional bans have been understood as a voluntary measure, and the newly introduced reduction commitment of ECOWAS is indeed in its early stage. While it is accepted that domestic laws have broadly adopted substantive restriction in some respects, ie to regulate private manufacture only, it appears that there exists no general practice of qualitative and/or quantitative limitation, on the small arms manufacture, as an international law issue.

International custom requires the long duration of a practice although some norms can emerge within a short period. The ICJ for instance does not focus on this requirement in its decisions. Even so, 'the passage of time will of course be a part of the evidence of generality and consistency'.[103] The League's practice continued from the early 1920s until the late 1930s, it did not continue after that. UN and regional efforts have been taking place since the end of the Cold War. The ECOWAS Moratorium came into force in 1998, and remained in operation until the adoption of the 2006 Convention. In contrast, most domestic restrictions have existed for decades. Some are recent. For instance, the UK Firearms Act 1968 and the South African Firearms Act 2000 are cases in point. Thus, in a multilateral sense, the practice started 70-80 years ago. After being ignored for long period of time, it has attracted attention since the middle of the 1990s.

To sum up, at the global echelon, there seems to be no uniformity, consistency, and generality of state practice pertaining to restricting small arms manufacture. There have been major interruptions. Despite the restrictions brought about by national laws, no limit is placed either on state authorised manufacture or state manufacture. Nonetheless, international custom is more than state practice.

As a second key factor, satisfying the *opinio juris* element is a prerequisite for the invocation of a customary rule. The ICJ generally assumes 'the existence of an *opinio juris* on the bases of evidence of a general practice, or a consensus in the literature'. Although in some cases the Court demands more positive evidence of practice.[104] Do states consider substantive limitations on manufacturing as their legal obligation? First, states put more emphasis on their right to manufacture than to restrict small arms manufacturing. Almost all GGE panels and the UN PoA have affirmed this. Even so it could be argued that the right is limited to certain purposes.[105] Does this mean that manufacturing beyond that is illegal under international law? No answer to this question has been found in state practice and in effect *opinio juris*. Secondly, states including manufacturers of SALW have strongly supported the ECOWAS

[103] Brownlie, above n 92, at 5; see also Shaw, above n 95.

[104] *Ibid*, Brownlie, p 7; see also Brownlie, *Principles of Public International Law*, 6th edn (Oxford, Oxford University Press, 2003) 8; see, eg *Asylum case*, above n 97.

[105] See, eg *UN PoA*, above n 100.

Moratorium. Some also consult ECOWAS Member States before they authorise export of arms to the region. This may be interpreted as *opinio juris*, concerning the restrictions placed upon manufacturing, by the West African Community. The adoption of a Convention by the same Community, which is intended to legally bind States' Parties to reduce/limit small arms manufacture, underpins such an assertion. However, declarations, reports and recommendations at the UN or regional levels have clearly stated that such commitment is a voluntary matter, provided there is consent from the state. In this sense therefore a claim of *opinio juris* on the matter would be weaker.[106]

Finally, domestic laws denied freedom to SALW manufacture. Could this show the intent of states to have binding rule of international law on the problem? As the policies of states vis-à-vis international obligations are only known by the committees, councils or other agencies of states, which are entrusted with a power to approve permits of gun manufacture (see 3.3.4), it would be unrealistic to predict whether the general prohibition on the manufacture of certain weapons is meant to create legal obligations of an international nature; it appears to be obvious that states are not generally keen to respond to the challenge of the licit manufacture at the international level.[107]

In the absence of explicit or implied consent of interested states on the problem, can a question of the incorporation of domestic legislation into international law arise? Generally, such incorporation is unproven in international law, unless the laws in question satisfy elements of custom or other sources of law. For instance, the ICJ in the *Nicaragua* case propounded that[108]:

> In international law there are no rules, other than such rules as may be accepted by the state concerned, by treaty or otherwise, whereby the level of armaments of a sovereign state can be limited, and this principle is valid for all States without exception.

As indicated by the Court, acceptance of a rule by manufacturer states is therefore an essential element, which seems to be lacking in this case. So, at the global echelon, neither general practice accepted as law, nor an agreement in academic writings, known as *opinio juris*, exist on the 'rule' at issue. In conclusion, it appears that there has been no *lex lata* rule on substantive restrictions to SALW manufacturing.

Nonetheless, care ought to be taken to appreciate positive achievements. In recent times, along with growing concern about the excessive

[106] See, eg *GGE 1997*, above n 24.

[107] See 2.1.13, 2.1.15; see also GA Res 61/89 of 2006 (UN Doc Supp No A/61/394-XXXI) entitled: '*Towards an Arms Trade Treaty*' Preamble, para 5, and operative, para 2.

[108] *Case Concerning Military Activities in and against Nicaragua, ICJ Repts* 1986, p 135, para 269.

accumulation of small arms and their severe consequences, developments at global and regional levels must be considered. States are urged to effectively control their manufacturing. This could be seen in the light of the inherent domestic regulations of states, which substantially restrict manufacturing. Cumulatively, they give the impression that a customary law of substantive limitation upon SALW manufacture is evolving, although the pace might not be as fast as it should be to cope with the magnitude of the challenge.

The crucial problem with SALW manufacturing is that the products are normally suitable for legal and/or illegal end uses. This is not, however, unique to arms manufacturing. As has been attempted in the League era, some analogy might help elucidate the *lex ferenda* of substantive limitations on the manufacture of small arms. For example, narcotic drugs cure or kill human beings, depending on the manner and purpose of their use. With the aim of circumventing the negative consequences of such drugs, and also to maintain their useful aspects, the 1961 and 1971 Conventions have prohibited any production of certain types of substances 'except when exclusively intended for "medical and scientific purposes"'. As such dangerous drugs are only permitted for the 'relief of pain and suffering'. SALW manufacturing could also be limited in such a way.[109] Obviously, the political will of states is vital for achieving this.

The international community has achieved the ECOWAS practice, which showed the fact that the 'rule' under discussion is not absurd. Member States have concluded a binding instrument. Their commitment to make it part of their domestic law, the mechanism of application they have set out, the binding Code of Conduct, the renewal of the undertaking and the anticipated restrictions incorporated in the new Convention, altogether might suffice to raise the question of regional custom,[110] on substantive restrictions of the activity in issue. The OSCE's commitment to reduce the manufacturing of weapons is also essential. Such regional arrangements, particularly of the OSCE instruments, 'though not legally binding per se (and recognised as soft law), are important expressions of state practice'.[111] In brief, the mere fact that there is not customary rule does not spell a closure of the chapter on the issue of substantive limitations on SALW manufacture.

[109] *Single Convention on Narcotic Drugs*, New York 1961, as amended by the Protocol of 25 March 1972, *Australian Treaty Series* (ATS) 1967 No 31, Art 4 (c); *Convention on Psychotropic Substances*, New York, 1971, *ATS* 1975, No 33, Art 5 (2); see also *Reviewing Legal Aspects of Substitution Treatment at International Level*, p 2 at, <http//:eldd.emcdda.org>; see also the *League's* analogy, above n 22.

[110] Shaw, above n 95, at 62.

[111] Rehman, *International Human Rights Law: A Practical Approach* (Aldershot, Pearson Education, 2003) 22.

3.5 CONCLUSIONS AND PROBLEMS

Four remarks are noteworthy. First, it is not disputed that the UN, regional organisations and civil societies have revealed their discomfort with manufacturing, relative to the proliferation of small arms. Concerns vary greatly from state-to-state and region-to-region. For instance, the West African countries went to the extent of a total ban on manufacturing, while others emphasised their inherent right to engage in this business. However, in most domestic systems, states place stringent substantive limitations on the manufacturing of certain weapons. Regrettably, international rules have not emerged with the effect of substantive reduction. This leads one to raise some problem questions. How can it be possible to address the problem of the excessive accumulation of small arms, without having a real commitment to reasonable cutbacks on this business? Is it justifiable and productive to emphasise destruction of surplus or illicit weapons, while ignoring the issue of millions of new arms which continuously fill up the world stockpile? It is doubtful.[112]

Secondly, the embryonic efforts to address the problem, which have been made so far, should not be forgotten. Most notably, inter alia, the ECOWAS experience and the reaction of the international community to it, the OSCE's commitment and the UN panels' suggestions should be noted. Lessons have to be learned from history, other legal regimes, and domestic legal systems. Thirdly, it is true that more attention has been paid to regulatory norms than to substantive limitations on manufacturing. This might include licensing, marking, transparency, etc. Although excluded from the scope of this book, it is noteworthy that they should be considered as part of the solution, as they could result in an indirect substantive restriction on the manufacturing of such weapons.

Lastly, one of the critical challenges of humanity and security, which has confronted the world community, relating to the subject under scrutiny, is the lack of substantive legal norms on manufacturing. Could this mean that the continuously manufactured SALW are not subject to any substantive limitations, in the course of their trade and transfer? The next part of the book will address the issue.

112 See, eg Goldblat, *Arms Control: A Guide to Negotiations and Agreements* (London, Sage Publications, 1994) 187.

PART II

INTERNATIONAL TRANSFERS OF SALW: SUBSTANTIVE LIMITATIONS AND PROBLEMS

4

International Transfers of SALW: Introduction

4.1 USE OF TERMS, SCOPE, FACTS AND ISSUES

4.1.1 Use of Terms and Scope

THE TERMS 'import-export' or 'transfers', 'legal', 'illegal' and the scope of transactions are full of controversy in the small arms legal regime. It is crucial therefore to evolve clear definitions.

According to the *Oxford English Dictionary*, the term 'export' implies 'sending out goods or services especially for sale in another country'; and the term 'import' is 'bringing in especially foreign goods to a country'. It appears to be restricted to commercial sales. The term 'transfer' is usually in use in the UN with respect to SALW. For example, although undefined, the UN Disarmament Commission Guidelines of 1996 and the 1997 GGE have used the term 'transfers', as appeared in paragraph 13 of the principles and paragraph 37 of the Report respectively. Article 2(4) of the Mines Convention by the same token speaks about the term 'transfer' instead of import-export. Transfer involves the physical movement of mines 'into or from national territory' and the transfer of title and control over the mines.[1]

Similarly, some legal experts and NGOs have shown their support for the word transfer rather than import-export. Article 7(2) of the 2003 Draft of the FCIAT defined 'international transfers' as 'the transfer, shipment or other movement, of whatever form, of arms from or across the territory of a Contracting Party'. It resembles the Mines Convention.[2]

Furthermore, even though the International Code of Conduct on Arms Transfer (hereafter 'ICCAT') is not yet endorsed by governments, it will be appropriate to refer to its relevant provisions as a work of pacifists and

[1] See Annex 1, DC *Guidelines* of 1996.

[2] *Draft Framework Convention on International Arms Transfers* (FCIAT), Working Draft of 21 November 2003.

NGOs. Article 2(a) and (b) of the Code has defined 'international transfers' more widely than the Framework Convention as[3]:

> Any transaction resulting in a change of title to, and/or control over, any arms defined in Article 1, and any physical movement of any arms defined in Article 1 from one jurisdiction to another . . . They also include transfers of expertise, information, designs, technology . . .

Alternatively, the SAS has defined a transfer as 'the reallocation of small arms from the possession, either de facto or de jure, of one actor to another'. It has also added that in SALW transactions, 'there are always two actors involved, the originator and the recipient'.[4] The focus of the survey seems to be on the actors involved in such business.

Article 1(9) of the ECOWAS Convention has basically adopted the FCIAT definition of 'transfer'; it went on further to expressly include import, export, transit, trans-shipment and transport of SALW.

Therefore, there is no consistent definition on transfers either. So, it appears that 'transfers' and 'import-export' are synonymous. While the former is felt to be wider in scope as the latter is mainly commercial sales focused, both serve the same purpose. International transfers may not thus make sense without import-export.

Concerning the legality of transfers, while there is no definite description of the 'legal' trade in and transfer of SALW in general, some explain it as 'government to government transfers including aid: the sale of firearms, and/or transfers of surplus military equipment no longer required by the supplier's own armed forces'.[5] Others suggest 'a transfer is generally legal if it fully conforms to international law *and* the national laws of both the exporting and importing states'.[6] Elements of legality and scope are reflected in there.

In contrast to this, Article 1(2) of the OAS Convention on Firearms of 1997 defined the phrase 'illicit trafficking' as:

> The import, export, acquisition, sale, delivery, movement, or transfer of firearms, ammunition, explosives, and other related materials from or across the territory of one State Party to that of another State Party, if any one of the States Parties concerned does not authorise it.

[3] *Nobel Peace Laureates' International Code of Conduct on Arms Transfer*, 29 May 1997, New York. On 29 May 1997, 14 Nobel Laureates led by Dr Oscar Arias of Costa Rica met to launch the International Code of Conduct in New York. The Nobel Laureates encourage the United Nations as well as individual governments to restrain arms sales by endorsing the International Code; for its wide-ranging support (see 5.6).

[4] GIIS, *Small Arms Survey 2002: Counting the Human Cost* (Oxford, Oxford University Press) 111.

[5] Mouzos, 'International Traffic in Small Arms: an Australian Perspective', Australian Institute of Criminology *Trends and Issues in Crime and Criminal Justice* (Canberra, No 104, February 1999) 2.

[6] *SAS 2002*, above n 4, at 230–31, box 3, [italics added].

Furthermore, Article 3(e) of the UN Firearms Protocol has repeated the definition which appears in the OAS Convention except for the addition of one element, ie 'if the firearms are not marked in accordance with' the terms of the Protocol, at the end of the definition. In describing the phrase 'illicit trafficking', both instruments have emphasised two elements, cross-border transfers and non-authorisation by a state. Even so the UN Protocol deems the transfer of non-marked firearms as illegal. Article 4(2) of the latter instrument, albeit entirely, excludes 'state-to-state transactions', which also comprises authorised business of this kind. It is not clear whether this was meant to prove that every transaction between states is legal (see chapter five). On the contrary, the ECOWAS Convention, under Article 1(5) states: 'illicit covers all that is carried out in violation of this Convention'. The substantive and procedural obligations resolved in this Convention are robust, and cover state authorised transfers (see chapters five, six, seven and eight).

A number of problems arise out of these definitions. Are all transfers conducted between governments legal? Perhaps the answer is no, as states could for example make a deal against the SC arms embargoes. Since opinions vary on what is legal under international law, the reference made to international law, to define licit transfers may be difficult. Differing kinds of SALW transfers/trade complicate the matter further.

In theory, illegal transactions of SALW comprise both 'black' and 'grey market' transfers. According to the SAS, 'black market transfers are those where suppliers and receivers knowingly violate international and/or national laws of both the supplying and receiving states'.[7] 'Concealments, mislabeling, phoney documentation, and laundering of payment' have been featured. Falsified end-use certificate and clandestine means of transfer are thus at the heart of such transactions. Private entities or persons such as suppliers, brokers, smugglers and end users take part in such business. Often, it is primarily motivated 'by a desire for profit'. Although states usually hide arms purchases/sales for political and financial reasons,[8] however, 'black-market deals are conducted by private organizations and individuals'.[9]

Grey market transfers are 'those that are legally questionable, typically authorized by either the supplying or recipient government, but not by both'.[10] Kartha diligently elaborated this type of transaction as below[11]:

[7] *Ibid*, at 128.

[8] Naylor, 'The Structure and Operation of the Modern Arms Black Market' in Boutwell et al (eds), *Lethal Commerce: the Global Trade in Small Arms and Light Weapons* (Cambridge, Mass, American Academy of Arts and Sciences, 1995) 44–45.

[9] Kartha, 'Controlling the Black and Gray Markets in Small Arms in South Asia' in Boutwell et al (eds), *Light Weapons and Civil Conflicts: Controlling the Tools of Violence*, (Oxford, Rowman & Littlefield Publishers, 1999) 51.

[10] Above, n 7.

[11] Above, n 9.

> The grey market is taken to mean that element of the arms trade that involves the machinery of the state in some form, notably where the government (or its agents) has either assisted in or turned a blind eye to illicit arms transfers originating from within its own territory or being organized by its own nationals operating in other countries . . . Grey market transfers are rarely motivated by profit.

It seems to be essential for a grey market transfer that one of the two governments is aware of the transfer and the other is not so aware. The deal has to be conducted between a state or state authorised entity on the one hand, and arms dealers or non-state armed groups on the other, or vice-versa.[12] Even if these clusters of the illicit trade in SALW signify different things, they often overlap in practice and process. The reason why this is so is that arms deals which have started as a grey market could end-up being a black market, and the reverse.[13]

Hence, the trends show that the legal and illegal trade in weapons are mostly blurred at the moment. Tentatively thus the legal trade in SALW refers to any kind of transfer between states in accordance with both international law and the domestic regulations of states. Alternatively, illicit trade could be described as any transaction by states or NSAs in violation of either international law, or domestic laws of states, or both. However, any transfer of SALW that involves states will be regarded as an essential element of this work. Subsequent discussions will take into account the 'legal' and grey transactions only.

Defining the scope at the start, as to what is and what is not included in the arms trade appears to be necessary. Arms trade/transfer is described as including commercial trade in weapons, exchange of arms that embraces aid schemes and other non-monetary arrangements and military co-operation both between and among states, or other private citizens.[14] The International Code expounded the view that 'such transfers include those conducted in return for direct payment, credit, foreign aid, grants, and goods received as a result of off-set or barter arrangements'.[15]

In some domestic jurisdictions transfer includes donating, selling, letting, lending or parting with possession.[16] This means that whether it has monetary quid pro quo or other non-financial motives is not significant. After the end of the Cold War, the dominant motive has been commercial.[17]

[12] Above, n 8.

[13] Above, n 11.

[14] Frey, 'The Question of Trade, Carrying and Use of Small Arms and Light Weapons in the Context of Human Rights and Humanitarian Norms': working paper submitted in accordance with Sub-Commission Decision 2001/120, 30 May 2002, para 5.

[15] Above, n 3.

[16] See, eg *South African Firearms Act 2000*, ch 1, s 1 (xxxv).

[17] Lumpe, *Running Guns: The Global Black Market in Small Arms* (London, Zed Books, 2000) 3.

Similarly, due to various factors such as changes in political status quo and market fluctuations at global or regional levels, surplus weapons become subject to international transfers.[18]

While all the aforementioned motives for transfers are considered here, the term 'transfers or import-export' is limited to physical title transfers of the arms themselves, from or across a certain jurisdiction to another. Thus, transfers by way of licence, knowledge or technology and other similar exchanges are excluded due to a limit in scope. When reference is made to transfers of SALW, it is limited all the way through to transfers made between states themselves or a state and NSAs. Transactions exclusively between various NSAs in different countries are therefore excluded from consideration.

4.1.2 Facts

Factual data usually helps understand problems. The international trade in small arms among states is hard to determine in terms of value and volume. Certain facts on the former could give a clue to the magnitude of SALW import-export. The UN Secretary-General, in his report called 'Supplement Agenda for Peace', has stated 'competent authorities have estimated that billions of dollars are being spent yearly on light weapons, representing nearly one third of the world's total arms trade'.[19]

The overall value of global transactions is extremely difficult to get hold of. Official reports and customs data suggest that it worth $4 billion annually. Others speculate, however, as much as $12 billion a year.[20] In terms of regional shares, for instance, the EU SALW export of 2000 was estimated to be of the value of $869 million. In the same year, it has been recorded that the shares of export values of other regions were: North America-$692 million, non-EU Europe-$243 million, South America-$104 million, north east Asia-$65 million, central and south east Asia-$51 million, the Middle East–$35 million, sub–Saharan Africa-$16 million, south east Asia-$8 million and the Pacific-$4 million.[21]

More specifically, the US, Italy, Brazil, Germany, Belgium, the Russian Federation and China were top exporters of small arms in 2001 and 2002—each of them exported 'at least USD 100 million of small arms annually'.

[18] Kopte and Wilke, 'Researching Surplus Weapons: Guidelines, Methods and Topics' BICC, *Brief 3* (16 April 2002) 1.

[19] *Supplement Agenda for Peace*, Report, 13 January 1995, para 61.

[20] GIIS, *Small Arms Survey 2003: Development Denied* (Oxford, Oxford University Press) 100; see also *SAS 2002*, above n 4, at 109; see, eg for comparison purposes, the *SIPRI* estimated the military expenditure of 2002 of 15 states as $895.3 billion, at <http://projects.sipri.org/milex/mex_major_spenders.pdf>

[21] GIIS, *Small Arms Survey 2005: Weapons at War* (Oxford, Oxford University Press) 98; see also n 4, p 127, table 3.5.

Be that as it may, top exporter states of small arms vary from year to year. Making comparison among states is very difficult as a result of a lack of accurate factual information. For example, China did not supply values for military weapons and pistols in 1999. It seems too doubtful that these figures have incorporated aid or surplus transfers, other than the commercial ones.[22]

Statistics on imports of these weapons are also unavailable. Overall, in the year 2000, northern America, the EU, the Middle East and north east Asia regions have witnessed a high level of imports. On the other hand, sub-Saharan Africa, south Asia and south east Asia regions were the least heavy importers.[23] We must, however, consider issues such as the possibility of unreported imports, population and other social and political circumstances in the destination country.

Globally, South Korea, the US, the UK and Australia were the top importers of military type weapons in the year 1999. The US is the highest importer for hunting and sport firearms. Thailand, Israel and Germany appear to be some of the top importers too.[24] Angola, Ghana, Kenya and South Africa have been identified as some of the sub-Saharan Africa importers—the sub-region is not the widest regional market of SALW in the world. Yet there is lack of transparency on imports of SALW. Some mention transfers of SALW to the DRC-Congo and the Sudan as an example of such a problem.[25]

Finally, the volume is far more difficult to quantify than the value. The UN Secretary-General stated meticulously below[26]:

> Many of those weapons are being bought, from developed countries, by developing countries that can least afford to dissipate their precious and finite assets for such purposes, and the volume of the trade in light weapons is far more alarming than the monetary cost might lead one to suspect.

Certainly, the transfers of SALW take in billons of US dollars every year. Many developed and developing states are involved. The main flow is from industrialised to developing countries, in particular the 'non-civilian' type weapons. The 98 SALW manufacturing states and 1000 companies referred to in chapter three take part in global transfers. Yet, there has not been an accurate worldwide figure on dealers who conduct and facilitate such transfers.[27] Taking these into account, including the definition and scope shown above, we shall identify the legal issues.

[22] GIIS, *Small Arms Survey 2005: Weapons at War*, at 126.
[23] *Ibid*, para 2, table 3.3; see also n 22.
[24] *Ibid*, at 26.
[25] *Ibid*, at 117, para 2.
[26] *Agenda for Peace*, above n 20.
[27] UN Commission 1998, *United Nations International Study on Firearm Regulation*, New York, p 64. Majority of states responded that they have legal business in their territory concerning import and export of SALW.

4.1.3 Issues

Three fundamental issues are identified here. First, as the case between environmental and international trade concerns, a clash exists between freedom of transfer/trade and national interests on the one hand and other universal values on the other, on arms related transactions. In addition, it is usually assumed that states have an inherent right to transfer weapons to another state or territory, unless and only if, the recipient state or party is under the UN or regional arms embargoes. The first question is, therefore, apart from such embargoes, do states enjoy freedom of commerce in SALW, under contemporary international law?

Secondly, taking for granted that there is no global conventional international law on transfers, and no likelihood of developing one in the near future, could it mean that there is no international law that is relevant to this business? If not, what legal rules should be complied with in order to carry out this activity in a lawful manner? Again, this question targets the substantive customary norms which regulate the SALW trade by states.

All these issues lead us to general principles of international law, and particular rules relevant to the problem, if any. Finally, the 'legal' and 'grey' transfers of small arms are commonly understood as part and an ultimate source of the illicit trade. Why? Is it because of the absence of legal norms, or the lack of clarity of existing obligations, or is it merely a problem of violations? These questions demand an appropriate study of key difficulties and loopholes.

Overall, central to the book, the second part is dedicated to investigating the rules of substantive restrictions on the import-export of SALW, with emphasis on the supply side. So far, we have seen definition, facts and legal issues. Next, relevant norms of international law and some controversial legal considerations will be mirrored as a background.

4.2 GENERAL CONSIDERATIONS FOR SUBSTANTIVE LIMITATIONS

4.2.1 Relevant General International Law Norms

The norms of the maintenance of international peace and security, non-intervention, pacific resolution, self-determination, international humanitarian and human rights laws and international trade law are some of the most relevant areas, on which the discussion will be based.

Some of the core aspirations of the UN, as stated in Articles 1(1) and 2 of the Charter, are to maintain international peace and security, to bring about a peaceful means of dispute resolution on the basis of justice and international law, and to develop friendly relations among nations with due respect to notions of self-determination and equal rights.[28] These and other related norms will be discussed separately.

The maintenance of international peace and security is the general purpose and norm of the contemporary multilateral security arrangement. For the purposes of meeting this aim, 'the threat or use of force against the territorial integrity or political independence of any state or in any other manner inconsistent with the purposes of the United Nations' has been outlawed, as enshrined under Article 2(4) of the Charter. This has been reinforced as the principal obligation of all Member States in the Declaration of Friendly Relations in 1970,[29] which has systematically analysed and elaborated this norm. The GA's Resolution on the Definition of Aggression of 1974 makes such a war of aggression on a state an international crime against peace, which entails international responsibility.[30] The ICJ in the case of *Nicaragua v USA* underlined the obligation to refrain from the act of aggression and has acquired *jus cogens* character, which cannot be derogated, except through another universal norm.[31]

Nonetheless, the peace and security issue is more than just the prohibition of aggression, according to the spirit of the Charter and subsequent developments in international law. Generally, as noted by Wolfrum, 'peace is beyond the absence of war'. The necessity of curtailing the likelihood of war through every means possible is widely recognised nowadays. For example, it was often emphasised by the GA that international peace and security is closely linked to disarmament, development, human rights and humanitarian values. The Declaration on the Right of Peoples to Peace of 1984 and the Proclamation of the International Year of Peace of 1985 have shown that states and people shall take measures such as the prevention of war, the removal of various threats to peace including armaments, and agreements on disarmament. The prohibition of aggression is thus subordinate to the core objective of the UN on peace and security and not an exclusive means of attaining the general end.[32] The reference made to armaments and disarmament is rather more pertinent here, and needs further consideration.

[28] See also Wolfrum and Zockler, 'Commentary on Preamble, Articles 1, 18, 55(a) (b), 56' in Simma et al (eds), *The Charter of The United Nations: A Commentary*, 2nd edn (Oxford, Oxford University Press, vol I, 2002) 40, para 7; see also Cassese, *International Law*, 2nd edn (Oxford, Oxford University Press, 2005) 48. He said that these principles [general norms] 'constitute *overriding legal standards* that may be regarded as the *constitutional principles* of the international community' [emphasis original].

[29] GA Res 2625 (XXV), principles regarding the threat or use of force, para 1.

[30] GA Res 3314 (XXIX), Art 5(2).

[31] *Case Concerning Military Activities in and against Nicaragua, ICJ Repts* 1986 (Merits), see in particular *dispositif* 4 and 5; see also Shaw, *International Law*, 4th edn (Cambridge, Cambridge University Press, 1997) 781.

[32] GA Res 39/11/1984, para 3; GA Res 40/3/ 1985; see also Wolfrum and Zockler, above n 29, pp 41–42, paras 2 and 14 respectively; see also White, *The United Nations System: Toward International Justice* (London, Lynne Rienner, 2002) 48–55.

The UN Charter, under Articles 11(1), 26 and 47 has made some references to principles 'governing disarmament and the regulation of armaments' as part of the notion of international peace and security, to be generally considered by the GA. The SC is the organisation's body authorised to formulate a system of implementation, 'to the extent that there would be the least diversion for armaments of the world's human and economic resources'. In practice, the UN swiftly became involved in arms control measures on various types of weapons. Apart from the GA and the SC, the Disarmament Commission, as a 'subsidiary, deliberative, inter-sessional organ of the GA', makes suggestions relating to the field including conventional weapons' issues (see further chapter one).[33]

However, the League of Nations was much more devoted to arms control issues than the UN. Above all, Members of the League have acknowledged, as enshrined in Article 8 of the Covenant that: 'the maintenance of peace requires the reduction of national armaments to the lowest point'[34] (see chapter one, and 3.3.1). The prime focus shall be the UN Charter.

First, beyond preventive measures of disarmament, a collective security approach, as enshrined under Chapter VII of the UN Charter, is devised to maintain international security. The SC is entrusted with a power to determine whether a 'threat to the peace, a breach of the peace, or an act of aggression' exists, and to recommend and/or decide upon appropriate measures in accordance with Articles 24, 41, 42 and 39 of the Charter. The measures might include peace enforcement, law enforcement or both. The SC often interprets the threat or breach of the peace widely with wider discretion[35] (see further 5.1).

However, the peace and security general norm and the collective security framework exceptionally recognise the right of states to self-defence. Article 51 of the Charter grants states the right to self-defence, individual or collective, as an inherent right when any Member State has been subjected to an armed attack. This right is conditional, until 'the SC has taken measures necessary to maintain international peace and security'. There is also a reporting obligation in such cases to the SC.[36] Hence, the general notion of international peace and security along with

[33] See, eg Goldblat, *Arms Control: A Guide to Negotiations and Agreements* (London, Sage Publications, 1994) 3 and 24; see also Cassese, above n 29, at 333–34.

[34] *Ibid*, at 12; see also The NGO Committee on Disarmament, Peace and Security, 'Are Disarmament Efforts a Waste?' xxvi (2003) (3) *Disarmament Times* 3.

[35] See, eg Arend and Beck, *International Law and the Use of Force* (London and New York, Routledge, 2001) 47–50; see also, *Prosecutor v Tadic*, ICTY, Appellate Chamber (*Decision on the Defence Motion for Interlocutory Appeal on Jurisdiction*) 2 October 1995 (case No IT-94-1-AR72), para 28; see also Krisch, 'Arts 2(5), 39–43, Introduction to Chapter VII', in Simma et al, above n 28, at 717–29.

[36] See, eg Randelzhofer, 'Introduction, and Articles 2, 2(4), 51' in Simma et al, above n 28, at 790–94.

the exceptions is one of the major cornerstones for this study (see further chapter five).

Secondly, the rule of non-intervention is another cornerstone of international law. Article 2(1), (4) and (7) of the Charter and customary international law have often been considered as sources of the norm. The non-intervention norm affirmed that any intervention, including that of the UN, into the domestic affairs of a state, is outlawed,[37] save certain exceptions such as Chapter VII measures, as clearly stated in Article 2(7) of the Charter. The rule has clearly been elaborated later in both the 1965 Declaration on the Inadmissibility of Intervention in the Domestic Affairs of States and the Friendly Relations Declaration. The former emphasised that[38]:

> No State has the right to intervene, directly or indirectly, for any reason whatever, in the internal or external affairs of any other State. Consequently, armed intervention and all other forms of interference or attempted threats against the personality of the State or against its political, economic and cultural elements, are condemned.

The latter has also reaffirmed the 1965 declaration.[39] Furthermore, the Assembly has widened it through the adoption of the resolution on the Definition of Aggression. Here too, it reiterated the principle of non-intervention. It has listed various acts, which contravene the principle. Accordingly, military attack and bombardment in the territory of another state, against the territorial integrity and independence of a state, constitute the act of aggression.[40] It includes any direct or indirect armed attack as well as 'the sending by or on behalf of a State' any insurgents which could carry on military assaults upon another state.[41]

The non-intervention rule has been elaborated by the ICJ in the *Nicaragua* case. The Court clearly adopted this rule as a valid customary one and condemned the US for its acts of arming, financing and training the *contras*, as an intervention in violation of an international obligation 'not to intervene in the affairs of another state'.[42] This was not the first time the Court mirrored such a firm approach. It did so in the *Corfu Channel* case, by saying, inter alia, that 'the respect for territorial sovereignty is an essential foundation for international relations'.[43] Even so, in recent times, some interpret the term 'to intervene' narrowly so as to exclude humanitarian intervention from the prohibition, while the attitude of the

[37] See, eg *Nicaragua*, above n 32, at 14; see also Nolte, 'Art 2 (7)' in Simma et al, above n 28, at 151.

[38] GA Res 2131 (XX), 1965, operative, para 1; GA Res 2625, principle of non- intervention, paras 1 and 2.

[39] Res 2625, principle of non-intervention, paras 1, 2, 9 and 10; see also Shaw, above n 32, at 784.

[40] UN GA, Res 3314 (XXIX), definition, Art 3 (a), (b), (c), (d), (e), (f) and (g).

[41] See, eg *Nicaragua*, above n 32.

[42] *Ibid*.

[43] *Corfu Channel* case, *ICJ Repts* 1949, pp 3 and 35.

international community, as shown in UN resolutions and the judgments of the ICJ remains firm on the customary notion of the principle of non-intervention.[44] In short, as intervention is usually closely associated with arms, the impact of this rule on the problem in question is significant—chapter six will address this in detail.

Thirdly, both as a norm and as a mechanism, pacific resolution of disputes is set out as a primary means of treating disagreements at the dispute level, as embodied in Article 2(3) and Chapter VI of the UN Charter. Negotiation, mediation, conciliation, judicial settlement, and other regional and global forums have been predetermined as methods for, and mechanisms of, resolving disputes. For instance, the GA is entrusted with entertaining any dispute presented to it by any state, for the sake of assuring co-operation in maintaining international peace and order, as stated in Article 11 of the Charter—the Assembly can thus recommend solutions. Yet it could not treat a dispute when the SC exercises its functions upon it, unless the latter so desires The SC, however, can go to the extent of rendering binding decisions upon a given dispute. More importantly, those states that may be involved in an international dispute and other third parties are obliged not to take any action that could aggravate a situation and affect international peace and security.[45] For this reason, the pacific resolution general norm reinforces the peace and security objective of the system and is essential to the issue of armaments, as will be considered in appropriate sections later on.

Fourthly, the right to self-determination is referred to in Articles 1(2) and 55 of the UN Charter, the Declaration on the Granting of Independence to Colonial Countries and Peoples of 1960,[46] the International Covenant on Civil and Political Rights (hereafter 'ICCPR') of 1966[47] and the Friendly Relations declaration, as a principle of international law. More specifically, the Friendly Relations declaration, as an authoritative interpretation of the Charter set out the rule that '[S]tates have the duty to refrain from any forcible action which deprives peoples . . . right to self–determination'. Further, '[I]n their actions against any resistance to such forcible action in pursuit of the exercise of their right to self-determination, such peoples are entitled to seek and to receive support, in accordance with the principles of the Charter.[48]

[44] Lauterpacht, *The Development of International Law by the International Court* (London, 1958) 90; see also Nolte, above n 38, at 155, para 2; see also Brownlie, *Principles of Public International Law*, 6th edn (Oxford, Oxford University Press, 2003) 210–12.

[45] See also Friendly Relations, principle of pacific settlement of disputes, paras 1 and 2; see also Tomuschat, 'Articles 2(3), 19, 33' in Simma et al, above n 28, at 586, para 13; see also Shaw, above n 32, at 720 and 729.

[46] UN Res 1514 (XV), para 2.

[47] Came into force in 1976; see, eg Art 1(1) and (3).

[48] GA Res 3314 (XXIX), the principle of self-determination, paras 1, 2, and 6. It is notable that it was adopted without a vote but considered as an authoritative interpretation of the Charter; see also Doehring, 'Self-determination', in Simma et al, above n 28, at 48–63.

The nature and scope of the right is, however, controversial. On the one hand, as the ICJ in the *Western Sahara* and *East Timor* cases has affirmed, the right to self-determination exists in the context of decolonisation; thus, peoples under such circumstances shall choose whatever political, economic and social system they would like to adopt.[49] In addition, the principle *uti possidetis juris*, which means that existing boundaries and territories at the time of independence cannot be altered, unless there exists consent to change between or among interested parties, has to be taken into account in the application of the right to self-determination.[50] While the *uti possidetis* principle may contradict the right to self-determination, it has been regarded as an essential element of stability and territorial status quo of countries, in particular African states. This is a safeguard clause for territorial integrity of states under international law.[51]

Publicists have also shown various views on the scope of the application of self-determination. Shaw believes that 'self-determination fits in with the concept of territorial integrity' and 'it cannot apply once a colony or trust territory attains sovereignty and independence'.[52] In contrast, Doehring reflects the view that while self-determination as a positive international law emerged in the context of decolonisation, this fact 'no longer corresponds with presently applicable law', as the principle of self-determination has been inserted into many treaties, including into instruments 'which have nothing to do with colonial territories and peoples'. For this reason, although not generally recognised, 'the right of secession might arise if the group concerned is exposed to extremely brutal discrimination'.[53] Even though the interest here is not to get involved in the polemics, it is fair to mention the fact that state practice and court decisions appear to be in favour of territorial integrity of states rather than the claim of the right to secede within a state.[54]

Care must be taken to distinguish between the right to form an independent state as a right of self-determination, and internal self-determination as a human right, which demands respect for the rights

[49] *ICJ Repts* 1975 (Advisory Opinion), p 12, paras 55 and 36, and p 31, paras 70 and 71; see also *Portugal v Australia* case, *ICJ Repts* 1995, pp 90 and 102, in particular para 29.

[50] *Burkina Faso/Mali* case, *ICJ Repts* 1986, pp 565–67, paras 21–26; see also Yugoslav Arbitration Commission, *Opinion No 2, 92 ILR*, pp 168–69; *Opinion No 3, 92 ILR*, p 170. It was established by the EC and consented by former Yugoslav states.

[51] *Burkina Faso/Mali*, *ibid*, at paras 25 and 26; see also the Declaration on the Granting of Independence, above n 47, declarations 2 and 6; see also Shaw, above n 32.

[52] Shaw, *ibid* at 354–55; see also Crawford, 'State Practice and International Law in Relation to Unilateral Secession' *Report to the Department of Justice of Canada*, 19 February 1997, paras 22 and 23, at <http://canada.justice.gc.ca/en/news/nr/1997/factum/craw.html#toc>

[53] Doehring, above n 49 at 53, paras 18–19, and 57–58, paras 35–40.

[54] Warbrick, 'States and Recognition in International Law' in Evans, *International Law* (Oxford, Oxford University Press, 2003) 216–17.

enshrined in the UN Covenants on human rights[55] (see further chapter six).

Alternatively, as the ICJ in the *East Timor* case observed, the right to self-determination has evolved from the Charter and the practice of the organisation and 'has an *erga omnes* character'.

This affirms the universality of the right and the obligation it entails.[56] The ILC and others further suggested that, it has also formed part of *jus cogens* norms of international law.[57] Hence, the rules to be dealt with concerning SALW transfers could not override this well-established principle of international law (see further 6.2.1).

Fifthly, international humanitarian law (hereafter 'IHL') and international human rights law (hereafter 'IHRL') have laid down relevant norms of a universal nature with regard to the SALW issue. As part of public international law, the former addresses, inter alia, the protection of the civilian population in times of war, the rules of distinction between combatant and non-combatant, the prohibition of inflicting unnecessary suffering and superfluous injury and limiting the choice and means of warfare, as prime rules of the legal regime. It is also common knowledge that the Hague Regulations and the Geneva Conventions and their additional protocols are fundamental sources of IHL (see further chapter seven).[58]

As a result of IHL, we have several conventional and/or customary bans and restrictions on certain weapons. For example, the 1993 Chemical Weapons Convention and the 1997 Mines Convention have totally banned the manufacture and use of such armaments. Generally, such treaties address the ban or restriction of the use of weapons rather than their transfers. Later developments, however, include the prohibition of transfers,[59] as will be explored further.

Moreover, IHRL protects the human rights of individuals or groups, in accordance with the rules and standards that are incorporated in treaty and customary international law. The UN Charter, the Universal

[55] *Ibid*, at 215.

[56] *ICJ Repts* 1995, pp 90, 102, para 29; see also Doehring, above n 49, at 55, para 25.

[57] *The Draft Articles on Responsibility of States for Internationally Wrongful Acts*, adopted by the ILC, 26 July 2001, Art 40; see also Doehring, above n 49, at 62, para 57.

[58] See, eg *1949 Geneva Convention IV Relative to the Protection of Civilian Persons in Time of War; 1949 Geneva Convention III Relative to the Treatment of Prisoners of War; 1949 Geneva Convention I for the Amelioration of the Condition of Wounded, Sick and Shipwrecked Members of The Armed Forces in the Field; 1977 Geneva Protocol I Additional to the Geneva Convention of 12 August 1949, and Related to the Protection for Victims of International Armed Conflict; 1977 Geneva Protocol II Additional to the Geneva Convention Relating to the Protection of Victims of Non-International Armed Conflicts; Legality of the Threat or Use of Nuclear Weapons, ICJ Repts* 1996, para 75; see also Meron, 'The Humanisation of Humanitarian Law' (2000) 94 *AJIL* 240; see also Petrasek, 'Moving Forward on the Development of Minimum Humanitarian Standards' (1998) 92 *AJIL* (1998) 561.

[59] Gillard, 'What is Legal? What is Illegal?' in Lumpe, *Running Guns*, above n 17, at 31–32; see also Frey, above n 14, para 57.

Declaration of Human Rights (UDHR) of 1948, the International Covenant on Civil and Political Rights (ICCPR) and the International Covenant on Economic, Social and Cultural Rights (ICESCR), are often mentioned as principal sources, among others. Paragraph 1 of the Preamble of the UDHR underlined that 'recognition of the inherent dignity and of the equal and inalienable rights of all members of the human family is the foundation of freedom, justice and peace in the world'.[60] To that effect, IHRL imposes negative and positive duties upon states,[61] as will be discussed thoroughly in chapter eight.

Hence, as arms and conflict are highly connected to IHL and IHRL,[62] either in destructive or constructive terms or both, they form the basis for the discussion on arms transfers.

Finally, the GATT/WTO functions on the freedom of trade underpinning, albeit with a number of exceptions and problems. The rules of non-discrimination, and the elimination of quantitative restrictions on import-export of commodities, both nationally and internationally, are some of the prerequisites that the Contracting Parties must comply with.[63] Nevertheless, deviation from these rules is permitted upon legitimate and justifiable grounds.

The system itself has provided some general and specific exceptions to the principles. Article XXI of the GATT addressed security exceptions. The relevant sub-section of Article XXI reads[64]:

> Nothing in this Agreement shall be construed . . . b) to prevent any contracting party from taking any action which it considers necessary for the protection of its essential security interests . . . (ii) relating to the *traffic in arms, ammunition and implements of war* and to such traffic in other goods and materials as is carried on directly or indirectly for the purpose of supplying a military establishment; (iii) take in time of war or other emergency in international relations; or c) to prevent any contracting party from taking any action in pursuance of its *obligations under the UN Charter* for the *maintenance of international peace and security* [emphasis added].

[60] *Universal Declaration of Human Rights*, GA Res 217 A (iii), 1948; *International Covenant on Civil and Political Rights* 1966, Preamble, paras 1 and 2 and Art 6; *International Covenant on Economic, Social and Cultural Rights* 1966, Arts 1 and 2.

[61] See, eg ICCPR, Art 2; see also Provost, *International Human Rights and Humanitarian Law* (Cambridge, Cambridge University Press, 2002) 1–10; see also White, above n 33, at 58–60.

[62] See, eg Provost, *ibid*, at 4.

[63] See, eg *General Agreement on Trade and Tariff (GATT)* 1994, Arts I, Most Favoured Nation, III, National Treatment, and XI, General Elimination of Quantitative Restrictions.

[64] GATT, *'Analytical Index: Guide to GATT Law and Practice'*, 5th edn (official publication, 1994) 600–06, see in particular GATT Art XXI(b) (i), (ii), (iii), and (c) [emphasis added]. John Jackson is *rightly* of the opinion that the arms trade is not subject to the WTO law (private discussion with the author, Georgetown Law Centre, Washington DC, 24 October 2006); also Art 3(3) of the ECOWAS Convention on small arms of 2006 states: 'SALW . . . shall not be deemed to be goods for the purpose of Art 45 of ECOWAS Revised Treaty of 1993'.

This exception has made a particular reference to traffic in arms, episodes of war or other international emergencies, and the obligation of the maintenance of international peace and order, as reflected in the UN Charter. It is not therefore a general clause, rather contains a set of exceptions relating to security, which ranges from national interests to international obligations.[65]

This area of law promotes freedom of commerce therefore. However, the arms trade and associated issues seem to be excluded from the WTO system, inter alia, in the interest of UN Charter obligations. We shall concentrate on the latter, due to concerns of priority and economy.

In a nutshell, we have considered international peace and security as a substantive goal of the Charter system. The prohibitions of non-intervention and aggression, the obligation of states to resolve disputes peacefully, enforce this central objective too. Humanitarian and human rights norms also constitute core universal values that are obligatory in international relations. All of these norms are of paramount importance to the challenge of SALW transfers, if not all on an equal footing. Other controversial assertions relating to the arms trade need to be considered.

4.2.2 Some Controversial Considerations

These can be divided into three. The first controversy can be inferred from the judgment of the ICJ in the *Nicaragua* case. The Court suggested that international law has not produced rules which could restrict the level of armaments of a sovereign state, unless there is a consent or otherwise of a state to that effect.[66]

The second is, as indicated in paragraph 10 of the Preamble of the UN PoA, that 'each state' should enjoy the right to retain and import SALW for 'self-defence, security needs as well as for its capacity to participate in peacekeeping operations'.[67] Similarly, an export of SALW is generally considered as legal, if carried out in the context of the aforesaid purposes of use[68] (see further chapter five).

The last consideration concerns the absence of rules in international law on SALW transfers. The UN 1997 GGE Report, in paragraph 60, underlined that:

[65] Schloemann and Ohlhoff, 'Constitutionalization' and Dispute Settlement in the WTO: National Security as an Issue of Competence' (1999) 93 *AJIL* 431; see also Akande and Williams, 'International Adjudication on National Security Issues: What Role for the WTO?' (2003) 43 *VJIL* 284, 371.

[66] Above n 32, paras 135 and 269; see also Krisch and Frowein, 'Chapter VII Action with respect to Threats to the Peace, Breaches of the Peace, and Acts of Aggression' in Simma et al, above n 28, at 726, para 24.

[67] See Res 54/54 V/1999; see also *UN Firearms Protocol* 2001, Preamble, para 4; see also 4.2.1 and 4.2.2.2.

[68] See, eg *GGE 2001*, 12 March 2001, paras 36 and 15.

> There is also no international convention or agreement that restricts such trade, or a body of rules by which a given transfer can be declared illegal under international law other than the arms embargoes adopted by the Security Council.[69]

In this sense, thus, neither conventional nor customary international law give rise to limitations upon SALW transfers. The validity and the application of all these controversial assertions to SALW trade will be examined carefully. At this stage, we shall only consider questions out of the claims: (1) Is the right of a state to obtain and import weapons unlimited? (2) Do the above-mentioned positions demonstrate a freedom of action by a state, concerning the transactions in issue, assuming that there are no particular rules on SALW transfers? And (3) is the UN Panel's assertion correct in contemporary international law, or is there any development of particular rules thereafter?

This part, therefore, as a nucleus of the monograph, will have to provide a detailed analysis, with emphasis on the panel's findings and the challenges therein. It is intended to examine the specific rules of substantive limitations, if any. The peace and security norm on transfers, the notion that transfers shall only be between and among states, the IHL and IHRL limitations on arms transactions will respectively be examined in-depth, in the light of the aforesaid general norms of international law and particular developments in the SALW regime. To that end, the peace and security issue will be addressed first.

[69] *GGE 1997*; GA Res 50/70 B/1995 had also authorised the panel to look into the trade aspects of the SALW issue.

5

Adherence to the Peace and Security Legal Norm

5.1 ASPECTS OF INTERNATIONAL PEACE AND SECURITY

AN OVERVIEW OF what constitutes a threat to, or breach of the peace is useful at this juncture. This issue is not precisely defined in the UN Charter. The act of aggression gives rise to similar problems but is clarified later in the Definition of Aggression, on which we shall not concentrate. There are seven principal aspects, among others, which need to be discussed here:

(1) A textual and systematic interpretation of the first part of Article 39 implies that international peace was originally meant to address the prevention of inter-state wars and not intra-state conflicts. This inference corresponds with the obligation of states under Article 2(4) of the Charter. The SC has, however, widened the definition in later times.[1] A war between states is thus the first obvious aspect.

(2) Internal wars are at the forefront of the threat to peace in modern-day international law. Historically, for example, a civil war was taken as a leading factor to a threat to peace in the Indonesian case, pursuant to SC Resolution 54 of 1948. Similarly, the Council took the same line in the Congo in Resolution 161 of 1961. In both cases, the conflicts were purely civil wars. After the end of the Cold War, however, the Council adopted a broader interpretation on a significant scale. The former Yugoslavia, Somalia, Liberia, Angola, Rwanda, Albania, Sierra Leone, East Timor, the DRC, Sudan and many others have witnessed this wider interpretation.[2] As a result to-date 'any internal conflict of a

[1] Arend and Beck, *International Law and the Use of Force* (London and New York, Routledge, 2001) 48; see also Krisch and Frowein, 'Chapter VII Action with respect to Threats to the Peace, Breaches of the Peace, and Acts of Aggression' in Simma et al (eds), *The Charter of The United Nations: A Commentary*, 2nd edn (Oxford, Oxford University Press, vol I, 2002) 720, para 3.

[2] Krisch and Frowein, above n 1, at 723, para 18; see also UN Doc Supp No S/PV.392, 24 December 1948, pp 7–12; see also SC Res 724 and 713/1991 on Yugoslavia; see also SC Res 733/1992 on Somalia; SC Res 1555/2004 on the DRC; on the Sudan see, eg SC Res 1556/2004, Preamble, para 20, the Resolution was adopted with 12 in favour and 2 abstentions; see also Gray, *International Law and the Use of Force*, 2nd edn (Oxford, Oxford University Press, 2004) 205–11.

considerable scale can constitute a threat to international peace and security'[3] (see further 5.2).

(3) When a conflict has an impact on regional peace and security, it has often been determined as a threat to international peace, regardless of the status of the conflict. It is important to elaborate this aspect as it is of controversial nature in the small arms issue (see 5.6). For instance, the SC in response to the Somali crisis, in Resolution 794 of 1992, emphasised the 'consequences on the stability and peace in the region'. Resolution 788 of 1992 of the SC stated: 'the deterioration of the situation in Liberia constitutes a threat to international peace and security, particularly in West Africa as a whole'. As will be seen later, SC Resolution 1072 of 1996 on Burundi considered massive violations of IHL and IHRL as a threat to peace in the Great Lakes region as a whole. As shown in the unanimously adopted Resolution 1555 of 2004, the SC noted: 'the situation in the DRC continues to constitute a threat to international peace and security in the region'. A similar account has been given about the situation in Sudan, concerning the Darfur crisis.[4]

On other continents too, the SC has pursued a similar approach. Resolution 688 of 1991 of the SC against Iraq showed that the cross-border flows of refugees were considered as a threat to peace in the region. SC Resolution 1101 of 1997 on Albania has stressed: 'the present situation of crisis in Albania constitutes a threat to peace and security in the region'.[5] The same wording has been adopted in SC Resolution 1572/2004 on Cote d'Ivoire.[6] Apparently, this has been the case where inter-state conflict occurs, as the SC has demonstrated in Resolution 1298 of 2000 on Ethiopia/Eritrea. Paragraph 11 of the Resolution underlined that 'the hostilities constitute an increased threat to the stability, security and economic development of the sub region'.

To summarise, as the UN practice, particularly of the SC shows, regional instability constitutes a threat to international peace and security; yet the threshold requires a conflict of an extensive scale which ought to be prevented in advance. Even so, regional peace and security is greatly linked with civil and inter-state armed conflicts.

(4) Although it does not seem to be that the majority of states meant it during the drafting of the Charter, violations of IHRL and IHL have been raising concerns of peace and security, particularly after the end of the Cold War. Although this does not mean also that classifying such violations as a threat to peace was never acknowledged before.

[3] Kirgis, 'The Security Council's First Fifty Years' (1995) 89 *AJIL* 514.
[4] Res 1556, above n 2; on Liberia, Preamble, para 5; on Burundi Preamble, para 4.
[5] On Albania, Preamble, paras 6 and 9; on Iraq, Preamble, and para 1.
[6] Preamble, para 7.

The SC in the southern Rhodesia and South African cases of 1965 and 1970 respectively have determined for instance racial discrimination and the system of apartheid as threats to international peace. In the latter case, in Resolution 417, the Council systematically emphasised two matters; the phrase 'mindful of its responsibilities under the Charter of the United Nations for the maintenance of international peace and security', and the statement '*strongly condemns* the South African racist regime for its resort to massive violence and repression against the black people'.[7] These measures and their interpretation were highly promoted by developing countries.[8]

The case of southern Rhodesia provides an example of the link between international peace and security and the right to self-determination. The UN GA,[9] the SC[10] and the OAU[11] had recognised that the illegal declaration of independence by white minorities in southern Rhodesia constituted a threat to international peace and security.[12] The GA and the OAU went further to affirm 'the inalienable right of the people of Southern Rhodesia to self-determination'[13] (see further 6.2.1).

Since 1991, violations of IHRL and IHL have been consistently declared as a ground for a threat to international peace. The repression of the Kurdish and Shiite Muslims which brought a massive displacement over borders in 1991, the heavy loses of human life in Somalia in 1992, crimes against IHL in the former Yugoslavia in 1993, 'the deterioration of an already grave humanitarian situation' in Angola in 1993, 'the magnitude of the humanitarian crisis' of 1994 in Rwanda, 'killings, massacres, torture and arbitrary detention' in Burundi in 1996, 'humanitarian crisis' in Zaire (DRC) in 1996, 'the ongoing humanitarian crisis and widespread human rights violations' in the Sudan-Darfur region in 2004 and others have been a threat to international peace and security as per the resolutions of the UN SC.[14]

[7] Res 417/1977, para 1 and SC Res 418/1977; see also Krisch and Frowein, above n 1, at 724, para 19.

[8] Osterdahl, *Threat to the Peace: the Interpretation by the Security Council of Article 39 of the UN Charter* (Uppsala, Iustus Forlag, vol 13, 1998) 43–44.

[9] See, eg GA Res 1889 (XVII), Preamble, para 7.

[10] SC Res 217/1965, and SC Res 221/1966.

[11] OAU, *Resolution on Southern Rhodesia*, CM/Res 78 (VII), Preamble, para 5.

[12] See also Fenwick, 'When is There a Threat to the Peace?—Rhodesia' (1967) 61 *AJIL* 754; see also Kirgis, above n 3, at 512.

[13] OAU Res, above n 11, opertive para 5; GA Res 1889, above n 9, operative paras 1 and 2; see also *Year Book of the United Nations* (1963) pp 469*ff*.

[14] On Sudan, SC Res 1556, above n 2; on Iraq, SC Res 688; on Somalia, SC Res 733, Preamble, para 3; on Yugoslavia, SC Res 827; on Angola, SC Res 864, Preamble, para 3; on Rwanda, SC Res 929, Preamble, para 8; on Burundi, SC Res 1072, Preamble, para 4; see also Peter, 'The Kurdish Crisis and Allied Intervention in the Aftermath of the Second Gulf War' (1991) 2 *EJIL* 114; see also White, 'The Will and Authority of the Security Council after Iraq' (2004) 17 *Leiden Journal of International Law* 651; see also chs 7 and 8.

Therefore, extreme repression and violations of IHL, especially when they cause immense flows of people across borders, constitute a threat to international peace. This has been adopted for a number of years and in a number of cases; its uniform determination and interpretation is, however, at the discretion of the SC. This will be discussed as a legal problem.

(5) It has been evident in recent times that 'any act of international terrorism' constitutes a threat to international peace and security.[15] For instance, in the aftermath of the September 11 terrorist attacks against the US, the SC in its Resolution 1377 of November 2001 '*[D]eclares* that acts of international terrorism constitute one of the most serious threats to international peace and security in the twenty-first century'. In Resolution 1516 of 2003, the Council avowed the need to combat by all means 'threats to international peace and security caused by terrorist acts'.[16] As will be elaborated, inadequate action by states against terrorism, in particular in defiance of the Council's decisions, has been determined as a threat to the peace.[17] The ICJ in the *Lockerbie* case has affirmed that the measure by the SC against Libya rests within its powers under the Charter.[18]

Though it could not escape controversies, in particular the connection between peace and security and occasions of failure to deter such acts,[19] which cannot be dealt with in detail, the SC's position and various resolutions of the UN demonstrates that international terrorism constitutes a threat to international peace and security[20] (see further 5.2).

(6) Nuclear weapons proliferation, among others, also raises concerns in this discussion[21] (see 5.7).

(7) Violations of democratic principles have been claimed to be a threat to peace and security. The SC in Haiti and in Sierra Leone took direct or indirect measures to restore elected governments to power, since both were ousted by a *coup* d'état. Unless it is combined with civil strife, it does not appear to constitute a threat to peace and security by itself. It

15 See, eg SC Res 1373/2001, para 3.

16 See also for general statements SC Res 1189/1998, SC Res 1269/1999; see, eg the position of the GA, '*Measures to Eliminate International Terrorism*' GA Res 57/27/2003, para 7; see also GA Res 54/109/2000, Annex '*International Convention for the Suppression of the Financing of Terrorism*' para 10; see, eg the response of the Council to terrorist attacks in Istanbul of 15 and 20 December 2003, SC Res 1516/2003, para 2; see also Gray, above n 2, at 164–65.

17 See, eg on Afghanistan, SC Res 1267/1999; on the Sudan, SC Res 1054/1996; on Libya, SC Res 748/1992, para 7.

18 *Lockerbie* case, *ICJ Repts* 1992, pp 114 and 126; see also Kirgis, above n 3, at 514–15.

19 Kirgis, *ibid*, at 515.

20 See, eg Krisch, above n 1, at 725–26.

21 See, eg *Treaty on the Non-Proliferation of Nuclear Weapons (1968)*, UNTS No 10485, vol 729, pp 169–75, Preamble, para 2; see also below, n 234; see also ch 1; see, eg 'Iran to halt nuclear enrichment', *BBC News*, 22 November 2004.

> should be borne in mind that the Council considered the case in Haiti as an exceptional situation. This is not to deny that democratic governance provides a favourable environment for international peace.[22]

Two problems are worth reflecting on. The first is that the wider interpretation of the threat to peace and security has not escaped controversy on its validity in international law. While some writers have been in favour of wide and flexible interpretation of peace and security in the belief that it enables adequate response to problems, making the multilateral system effective, others have perceived it as a disadvantage or even as improper. The latter belief is on the basis of possible abuses by states, including some members of the SC. The principle of non-intervention is often invoked too, as a ground for opposing such intrusion into domestic jurisdiction.[23]

It would seem to be justified, however, that the SC enjoys a wider discretion under the Charter, partly because the nature of its functions, including executive decision making powers. Such discretion shall albeit be exercised within the spirit of the Charter, general international law and *jus cogens* norms. In this regard, and taking into account Article 31 of the VCLT, the inclusion of considerations such as internal conflicts, regional instability, grave violations of IHRL and IHL, international terrorism, and nuclear weapons proliferation into the peace and security realm, has constituted a settled rule of international law. Yet every internal situation or incident could not result in a threat to peace and security. The crisis needs to be on a significant scale. The interpretation is not boundless.[24]

The second problem is the lack of uniform application of such an approach into similar episodes. Inter alios, Kirgis believes 'the SC has turned from helpless inaction in the Cold War years, despite clear threats

[22] Krisch, above n 1, at 725, para 22; on Haiti see, eg SC Res 841/1993, SC Res 917/1994, and SC Res 940/1994, operative para 2; on Sierra Leone, SC Res 1132/1997, and SC Res 1270/1999; see also Doyle, 'Liberalism and World Politics' (1986) 80 *American Political Science Review* 1151–63; see also Kirgis, above n 3, at 514. He has noted that all undemocratic governments may not necessarily be a threat to peace and security; see also Gray, above n 2, at 49–52.

[23] Osterdah, above n 8, at 21–22, paras 2 and 3; see also Koskenniemi, 'The Police in the Temple. Order, Justice and the UN: a Dialectical View' (1995) 6 *EJIL* 325–48; see also Kirgis, above n 3, at 517; see also Martenczuk, 'The Security Council, the International Court and Judicial Review: what Lessons from Lockerbie?' (1999) 10 *EJIL* 519, 522, 540–46 and 539; see also White, above n 14, at 650.

[24] Krisch, above n 1, at 726, para 25; see also Osterdahl, above n 8, at 91–92 and 112–14; see also *Vienna Convention on the Law of Treaties*, 1969, 1155 *UNTS*, 331; for limits of the powers of the SC, see also Gill, 'Legal and some Political Limitations on the Powers of the UN Security Council to Exercise its Enforcement Powers under Chapter VII of the Charter' (1995) *Netherlands Yearbook of International Law* 30–138; see also Kirgis, above n 3, at 516–17; for the limits of the powers of the SC, see also White, above n 14, at 646, 652, 665–66; see also Gowlland-Debbas, 'The Functions of the United Nations Security Council in the International Legal System' in Byers, *The Role of Law in International Politics: Essays in International Relations and International Law* (Oxford, Oxford University Press, 2000) 293.

to international peace, to the reckless application of Chapter VII in recent years, when there has been no threat to international peace'.[25] Osterdahl submits that the criteria for a threat to the peace 'in the eyes of the Council seems fluid, especially if one takes into account also all the situations in which the Council did not intervene'.[26] Even so, responding to a threat to the peace 'in one case is not wrong because no decision was taken' to do so in another one. Alternatively, this might not be an excuse for the inconsistent practice that may have destructive consequences on the legitimacy and degree of respect for the decisions of the Council[27] (see further 5.2). In spite of the challenges and doubts on the practice of the SC the extensive power approach appears to be generally accepted by the international community.

In sum, a threat to peace and security incorporates, inter alia, actual/ potential conflicts, violations of humanitarian principles and the proliferation of weapons. Usually most of the aspects discussed occur simultaneously. The wider account of the matter might better suit the efforts to stem the excessive circulation of weapons. Relevant humanitarian norms have been separately treated and will not be emphasised here. Others, such as the peace and security threat of nuclear weapons proliferation, will give us some analogous ideas to the SALW challenge. The peace and security norm on transfers will, therefore, take into consideration all these aspects. The next section will address the question whether or not we have express prohibitions on SALW transfers, in view of peace and security concerns.

5.2 EXPRESS PROHIBITIONS: TREATIES AND RESOLUTIONS

In the League of Nations era, there were certain treaties aimed at restricting the international trade in arms. Maintaining international peace and security was among the key motives of the instruments (see further chapter seven).[28] In the UN epoch, the Mines Convention and the UN Firearms Protocol are currently the only global treaties that directly deal with the small arms issue. One of the objectives of the Mines Convention, as clearly stipulated in paragraph 4 of the Preamble, was the need for confidence building among states. Confidence building implies peace and stability in the context of such treaties. Taking this and other objectives into account, the Mines Convention imposed various obligations. For example, Article 1(b) states: 'each state party undertakes never under any circumstances: to . . . retain or transfer to any one' anti-personnel land-

[25] Kirgis, above n 3, at 516.

[26] Osterdahl, above n 8, at 109–10.

[27] *Ibid*, at 106–07; see also Martenczuk, above n 23, at 519; see also White, above n 14, at 652.

[28] See, eg 7.2.2.

mines.[29] This is a very important instrument because it has addressed both quantitative and qualitative aspects of any transfer of such weapons. The Convention was largely triggered by humanitarian concerns rather than peace and security. Also, the UN Firearms Protocol has recognised 'the harmful effect' of trafficking in SALW, 'on the security of each state, region and the world as a whole'[30] (for its status see 3.1). Article 4(2) of the Protocol expressly excluded state-to-state transactions of SALW,[31] which shall be considered below (see chapter six).

In brief, the Mines Convention could be a good model of substantive limitations on SALW transfer in the context of peace and security. Although the Protocol is trans-national boundary crimes oriented, and limited to illicit transactions among NSAs, it has regulatory provisions on the small arms trade in general.

Apart from treaties, the UN SC has extensively imposed arms embargoes upon states. These arms embargoes [Chapter VII] are express prohibitions that amount to positive international law, as discussed. Currently, more than 16 states, and some NSAs have been subjected to such arms prohibition. Until the late 1980s, in its nearly 'first forty-five years, the Security Council called for mandatory arms embargoes only twice, against Southern Rhodesia and South Africa'.[32] In both cases, the Council imposed arms bans declaring the situation as a threat to peace and security.[33] More interestingly, in the South African case, operative paragraph 2 of Resolution 418 asserts that, 'having regard to the policies of the South African Government, that the acquisition of by South Africa of arms . . . constitutes a threat to the maintenance of international security'. The sale or shipments of arms, ammunition of all types and related materials were totally banned against both regimes, including contracts and licences of exports, granted before the decisions came into being.[34]

Between then and the end of the 1990s, the Council has imposed mandatory arms embargoes on Iraq, Yugoslavia, Somalia, Libya, Liberia, Haiti, Angola/UNITA, Rwanda, Sierra Leone and the Federal Republic of Yugoslavia/Kosovo on the same reasoning as above, but in various circumstances. Also, the Council has called voluntary embargo compliance against Armenia and Azerbaijan, Yemen, Afghanistan and Ethiopia and Eritrea.[35] Three areas of interest can be drawn from the resolutions.

[29] *Mines Convention*, 1997.

[30] *UN Firearms Protocol*, 2001, para 1.

[31] *SAS 2002*, pp 238–40.

[32] Luck, 'Choosing Words Carefully: Arms Embargoes and the UN SC', Final Report, *First-expert seminar*, BICC, Bonn, 21–23 January 1999, p 3, at <http://www.bicc.de/events/unsanc/1999/pdf/luck.pdf>

[33] Above nn 9 and 10; see also on Rhodesia, SC Res 253/1968.

[34] Res 217, above n 10, operative para 8; Res 418, above n 7, operative para 2.

[35] See, eg on Iraq, Res 661/1990 and 687/1991; on Yugoslavia, Res 713/1991 and 724/1991; on Somalia, Res 733, above n 2, and 751/1992; on Libya, Res 748, above n 17; on Liberia, Res 788/1992 and 985/1992; on Haiti, Res 841, above n 23, and 873/1993; on Angola/UNITA,

The first regards embargoes against inter-state wars. For instance, as shown in paragraph 5 of Resolution 661 of August 1990, the Council imposed a generic trade ban against Iraq on the ground that the situation is a threat to peace. Accordingly, all states were duty-bound, in accordance with operative paragraph 3(c) of the Resolution, to cease 'the sale or supply by their nationals or from their territories or using their flag vessels of any commodities or products, including weapons or any other military equipment, whether or not originating in their territories'. This was significant because it dealt with transfers of arms from or through a third party. Yet, the Resolution was vague, as detailed description of weapons was not embodied. As a result, after the end of the Gulf War, in operative paragraph 3(a) of Resolution 687, 'arms and related materials of all types' including conventional weapons have been embargoed among other lists.[36] While not within the domain of this study, it is worth mentioning that the ban was much criticised for its humanitarian consequences upon Iraqi civilians.[37] Similarly, although non-mandatory, the Council banned weapon transfers to Ethiopia and Eritrea in 1999.[38]

The second consideration is bans of transfers as a result of civil wars and other human catastrophes in many countries. At the initial crises of Yugoslavia, the Council in its operative paragraph 6 of Resolution 713 of 1991,

> *Decides,* under Chapter VII of the Charter of the United Nations, that all States shall, for the purposes of establishing peace and stability in Yugoslavia, immediately implement a general and complete embargo on all deliveries of weapons and military equipment to Yugoslavia.

The same wording had been adopted in the mandatory arms bans against Somalia and Liberia in 1992.[39] In operative paragraph 19 of Resolution 864 of 1993, the Council imposed an arms embargo, with the purpose of 'prohibiting all sales or supply to UNITA of arm and related materials'. Subsequently, this has been the case, inter alia, in Rwanda,[40] Sierra Leone,[41] Kosovo,[42] the DRC,[43] Sudan[44] and Cote d'Ivoire.[45] The phrasing

Res 864, above n 14 and 976/1995; on Rwanda, Res 918/1994 and 1013/1995; on Sierra Leone, Res 1132, above n 23 and 1171/1998; and on the Federal Republic of Yugoslavia/Kosovo, Res 1160/1998; for non-mandatory arms embargoes see on Armenia and Azerbaijan, Res 853/1993; on Yemen, Res 924/1994; on Afghanistan, Res 1076/1996 and 1214/1998; and on Ethiopia/Eritrea, Res 1227/1999.

[36] *Ibid.*
[37] Drezner, 'How Smart are Smart Sanctions?' (2003) 5 *International Studies Review* 105–10.
[38] Res 1298/2000, operative para 6 (a) and (b).
[39] Res 733, above n 2, and 788, above n 4, respectively.
[40] Res 918, above n 33, operative para 13.
[41] Res 1132, above n 22, operative para 6.
[42] Res 1160, above n 35, operative para 8.
[43] Res 1555, above n 2.
[44] Res 1556, above n 2.
[45] Res 1572, above n 6, operative para 7.

of Resolution 661 against Iraq, which addresses indirect transfers, has also been maintained in all these domestic cases.

The final concern is international terrorism as a threat to the peace-based arms embargoes. In operative paragraph 5 of Resolution 748, the Council banned any weapon transfer to Libya. The reason was said to be the country's failure to comply with prior decisions to deter direct or indirect state sponsored terrorism, including handing over terrorist suspects.[46] Also, the Council did so against Afghan Taliban and Al-Qaeda, particularly against Usama bin Laden, on several occasions. As stated in both paragraph 11 of the Preamble and paragraph 5(a) of Resolution 1333 of December 2000, the Council banned any 'direct or indirect supply, sale and transfer to the territory of Afghanistan under Taliban control' of arms, ammunition and other related materials. The reason for this was Libya, the failure to fulfill the demands of the Council in Resolutions 1214 of 1998 and 1267 of 1999. Harbouring terrorism was at the forefront.[47] In paragraph 2(c) of Resolution 1390 of January 2002, the Council reaffirmed 'further that, acts of international terrorism constitute a threat to international peace and security'. Consequently, states have been called on to 'prevent the direct or indirect supply, sale and transfer' of weapons and other things to individuals, groups or undertakings associated with Usama, Al-Qaeda or the Taliban.

The SC arms embargoes pose a number of issues. Even if the sanctions against NSAs may pose various questions of international law, it is not discussed in the interest of scope. Yet the positive and negative features of such a practice and its pertinence to the SALW transfers issue need to be examined.

Four positive features of SC arms embargoes could be illustrated. First, SC arms embargoes have been taken as one legal remedy for the destabilising proliferation of SALW. As quoted by the UN Sanctions Secretariat, the SC itself believes that such measures 'imposed under Chapter VII of the UN Charter are today seen by the international community as an important tool in seeking to maintain or restore international peace or security'.[48] Also, the UN Secretary-General in his Report of 2002 to the SC underlined that 'eliminating the uncontrolled spread of small arms and light weapons constitutes one of the key tasks of the Security Council in discharging its primary responsibility for the maintenance of international peace and security'. He went on to state 'in particular the Council has repeatedly attempted to stem arms flows to conflict areas by establishing arms embargoes'.[49]

[46] Above, n 17.

[47] For demands upon the Taliban, see Res 1214, Preamble, para 2.

[48] 'Smart Sanctions, The Next Step: Arms Embargoes and Travel Sanctions', An Informal Background Paper Prepared by the UN Sanctions Secretariat, *First Expert Seminar*, Bonn, 21–23 November 1999, p 3, para 1.

[49] *Small Arms: Report of the Secretary General*, 20 September 2002, pp 1–3.

Writers have supplemented the above viewpoint. Luck has stated that:

> Curbs on the import of arms and military equipment, in short, have become a standard feature of United Nations efforts to resolve conflict, maintain peace, and discourage aggression. Keeping the peace, it has come to be recognized, often entails parallel measures to stem the flow of weapons into a region of tension.[50]

Gillard has supported such a view, in the context of the problem of small arms transfer. She stated that:

> in the exercise of its responsibility for the maintenance of international peace and security, the UN SC has, in recent years made increasing use of its power to impose binding sanctions that it determines amount to 'a threat to the peace, breach of the peace or act of aggression' under Article 39 of the Charter.[51]

Secondly, the SC seems to have achieved a coherent practice on arms embargoes in the cases it has positively responded to. These could be grouped into four elements: (1) Measures have mostly been justified by a threat to peace and security. Inter-state and intra-state conflicts, international terrorism and other human security concerns have been made part of such determination. (2) Arms and related materials of all types are often referred to. Small arms with their ammunition and parts and components have been included in the scope of most resolutions. (3) As a matter of scope, direct or indirect sale or supply of weapons, have been made a standard in all cases. (4) Chapter VII of the Charter was cited as a legal basis for sanctions.[52] All these elements of consistency will mean something regarding the rule in consideration (see 5.7).

Thirdly, legally, Chapter VII arms embargoes are binding upon all UN members. As shown in Articles 25 and 48 of the UN Charter, states are obliged to refrain from transfers of SALW to an embargoed state or a party, and to take all necessary measures in their respective domestic jurisdictions, including measures against entities or individuals on the other, to enforce the decisions of the Council. And so, a violation and failure to enforce mandatory sanctions by a state entails state responsibility under international law (see chapter nine). Conversely, when the impugned acts have been carried by individuals or companies criminal responsibility or civil liability would be the consequence, depending on the domestic laws of states.[53] As reiterated our interest in this book has been restricted to the obligation and responsibility of states themselves.

[50] Luck, above n 32, at 4.

[51] Gillard, 'What is Legal? What is Illegal?' in Lumpe (ed), *Running Guns: The Global Black Market in Small Arms* (London, Zed Books, 2000) 32–33.

[52] See, eg above n 46; see also above n 25; see also Martenczuk, above n 23, at 519.

[53] See 'State Responsibility' (ch 9); see also Gillard, above n 5, at 33; see also Martenczuk, above n 23, at 535.

Finally, the SC has taken a number of measures to make implementation of its embargoes effective. Along with other measures, it has repeatedly established committees or panels of inquiries of allegations of violations by states, entities, or individuals. For example, pursuant to Resolution 1013 of 1995, it has established an International Commission of Inquiry in the case of Rwanda.[54] Resolution 1237 of 1999 has established a Panel of Experts in the case of UNITA. The latter panel has disclosed violator states and individuals in March 2000. It affirmed that such 'violations were deliberate acts of states and individuals'. It has recommended among other things, sanctions including on arms sales against those who intentionally break the decisions of the Council for a renewable period of three years.[55] The SC has not done so.

Moreover, SC sanctions committees, which are entrusted with overseeing the implementation of embargoes, have been formed in a number of cases and is now a stable exercise. Pursuant to SC Resolution 1267 of 1999, the SC Committee on Afghanistan and Al-Qaeda has been established to do so, and has been reporting its findings and recommendations until recently. An Expert Panel and Monitoring Group has also assisted the Committee. The Committee of 1999 has been co-ordinating the whole effort while the rest have been dealing with specific assignments. In its report of December 2003 to the SC, for example, the Monitoring Group warned the international community that the 'increased availability of man-portable air-defence systems to non-state actors could be dangerous, and noted that 'measures be initiated by the UN to harmonise the various controls necessary to ensure that such missiles can not be acquired by Al-Qaeda or its associate'.[56]

The Council decided in 2000 to establish a monitoring mechanism for possible breaches, constituting five experts for Angola/UNITA. Some of the tasks were to investigate new violations of the arms embargo, including the findings of the previous panel. All states were called to co-operate in these efforts.[57] The Monitoring Group on Somalia, established by Resolution 1519 of November 2003, has also been closely monitoring the implementation of the Council's arms embargoes on the country. Unlike the panel on UNITA, however, it recommended in 2003 that the list of 'those who continue to violate the arms embargoes' should remain confidential. The Council appears to have accepted the proposal.[58] Later UN panel reports have disclosed the contraveners.

[54] Above, n 35; see also Res 1161/1998.

[55] For the Panel's Report, see UN Doc Supp No S/2000/203, 10 March 2000.

[56] The Report of the Monitoring Group on Al-Qeada, 2 December 2003, p 5, para 5; see also Report of 14 June 2002 of the Group; see also UN Doc Supp NoS/2002/101, 5 February 2002, Annex, IV. *Committee of Experts* pursuant to Res 1333/2000, para 32, and V. *Monitoring Group* Pursuant to Res 1363/2001, para 25.

[57] Res 1295/2000, operative, paras 3 and 4.

[58] UN Doc Supp No SC/8169, 17 August 2004, Annex, Background, para 8; see also SC Res 1558/2004.

In the face of such discrepancies, the aforesaid endeavours have been praised by many as a constructive evolution of the effective implementation of SC arms sanctions.[59]

In contrast, at least four negative features of SC arms embargoes are noteworthy. The first major problem is that states, companies and individuals, on the ground, often violate arms bans by the SC. As the final report of the Sanctions Committee of the SC on Angola indicated, arms supplies from Bulgaria and Ukraine, and other facilities including a provision of false end-use certificate, transit and storage by countries such as Togo, Zaire and Burkina Faso has been affirmed, in violation of SC's arms embargoes against UNITA.[60] As the chairman of the committee put it '[S]ecurity Council sanctions against UNITA have not worked well'.[61] This is not unique to Angola. For example, a tangible breach was recorded in 2003 against the arms ban on Liberia.[62] In the Council's debate of 2004 on small arms, Costa Rica unveiled the fact that '54 countries had been linked to the transfer and sale of weapons, in contradiction to existing arms embargoes'.[63]

The Council appears to have appreciated such a failure. In paragraph 4 of the Preamble of Resolution 1519 of 2003 on Somalia, it reiterated its serious concerns 'over the continued flow of weapons and ammunitions supplies to and through Somalia from sources outside the country, in contravention of the arms embargo'.[64] States are unwilling to take appropriate measures to investigate as well as to report violations of arms embargoes. The Sanctions Committee on Al-Qaeda has disclosed the fact that 'countries are reluctant to provide information concerning their seizures of illegal weapons and explosives believed destined to Al-Qaeda'.[65] However, there are plenty of evidences of violations, and these are assumed to be sufficient to show the problem. Jurists agree that arms embargoes have not worked in practice, owing to violations by states and others with impunity.[66]

The second shortcoming, as pointed out by Cortright et al, is the political reluctance of states, in particular the major powers, 'to create and

[59] Brzoska, 'Design and Implementation of Arms Embargoes and Travel and Aviation Related Sanctions', *Result of the Bonn Process*, 2001, p 32, at <http://www.bicc.de/events/unsanc/2000/pdf/booklet/ter_2.pdf>

[60] UN Doc Supp NoS/2000/1225, 21 December 2000, Annex, p 9, paras 20–23.

[61] UN Doc Supp No S/PV-4113, 15 March 2000, para 16.

[62] 'UN Officials Examine Banned Weapons Cargo That Arrived in Liberal', *UN News Service*, 3 November 2003, at <http://www.un.org/news>, it has been said that 'two 60-milimetre mortars, 149 boxes of mortar ammunition, 67 boxes of rocket-propelled grenades, 299 boxes of AK-47 rifles and about 699,00 rounds of AK 47 ammunition' had been caught. It was a cargo of 40-foot container of SALW.

[63] UN Doc Supp 7984, 29/01/2004, p 12.

[64] It was adopted unanimously.

[65] UN Doc Supp No S/2003/1070, Annex, p 5, para 3.

[66] Gillard, above n 51, at 34.

enforce an effective international arms monitoring and enforcement system'. This is said to have been linked with weapon exporter states' interests 'to promote, or at least not restrain, arms exports by their own producers'.[67] To Gillard, one of the failures is that enforcement of the embargoes is widely 'left to the discretion of states'.[68] Nonetheless, circumstances in target countries 'over which the SC and member states have no influence',[69] is too a cause for such breaches, either separately or in combination with other external factors. It is unquestionable, therefore, that breaches of this kind may have been beyond the control of the UN system. However, envisaging a situation where the SC or other states have no influence seems to be naivety in the context of present day international relations.

The third flaw is that the resolutions are inconsiderate of the legal, institutional and political weaknesses of target and/or supplier states.[70] For instance, 'not all member states have existing legislation or the capacity to enforce legislation' in accordance with their obligations under SC arms embargoes.[71] The discrepancy goes, inter alia, to the extent that 'violation of SC arms embargoes in the UK is a criminal offence while in Italy an administrative wrong'.[72] This loophole and other limitations 'have given rise to a significant industry of private suppliers, brokers, and transport agencies willing and able to violate the embargoes'.[73] Finally, the operations of the sanctions committees have been criticised for a range of problems, such as lack of transparency,[74] as discussed earlier in the case of Somalia—it was decided not to disclose contraveners of the embargoes.[75]

Overall, two different views have been entertained in respect of their particular relevance to the arms trade versus peace and security. The first view is that SC sanctions have little impact on the SALW transfers challenge. While UNITA was under a six-year embargo, it was able to arm its 300,000 combatants and carry on fighting against the government.[76] In spite of the weaknesses, many believe that an arms embargo is a preferred remedy to tackle the problem of SALW diffusion and associated breaches

[67] Cortright, Lopez and Gerber, 'Sanctions *Sans* Commitment: An Assessment of UN Arms Embargoes', *Fourth Freedom Forum*, April 2002, pp 11 and 6, at <http://www.fourthfreedom.org/pdf/ArmsEmbargoes.pdf>; see also Drezner, above n 37, at 109.

[68] Above, n 66.

[69] Above, n 61.

[70] Luck, above n 32, at 17.

[71] Epps, 'International Arms Embargoes' *Project Ploughshares* (No 02/4, Ontario) Working Paper, September 2002, p 15.

[72] Gillard, above n 51.

[73] Epps, above n 71, at 5.

[74] Brzoska, above n 59, at 19, 32 and 36.

[75] Above, n 58.

[76] Norris, 'Arms Embargoes: Making Sanctions Smarter' *Ploughshares Monitor* (March 2000) para 4.

of international norms. It appears to be that such prohibitions of transfers are essential in stemming diffusion of SALW, as they restrict the flow of weapons to areas of tension.[77] However, as they depend on the SC's determination of a threat to peace, 'they do nothing to head off situations of violence deemed to be below this threshold'. In reality, they have been imposed after conflict, violence or wars begin. As they require political will from states, both for their adoption and enforcement, and are frequently desecrated by states and NSAs, they are of limited use in preventing the excessive availability and unrestricted transfer of SALW.[78]

To conclude, the above treaties and the decisions of the SC are thus express limitations on the transfer of SALW by states. Such restrictions are legally binding. In particular, the measures of the SC have considered the maintenance of international peace and security, in the context of civil wars, inter-state conflicts, international terrorism, etc. As a result, since the end of the Cold War, transfers of SALW have been consistently banned in the interests of peace and security. Such consistency is of course limited to the cases where the SC has been responsive. Various attempts have been made to improve the enforcement of such actions. Lack of political commitment by states and an effective enforcement framework at international and national levels have exposed the restrictions to frequent breaches. SC arms embargoes are, therefore, crises or particular situations focused and could not be adequate remedy for the challenge in issue, although they are of important value as part of state practice on the subject (see 5.7).

5.3 EMERGING STATE PRACTICE: GLOBAL EFFORTS

In this and subsequent sub-sections, an attempt will be made to establish two fundamental facts: the link between the proliferation of small arms and international peace and security, and the restrictions/rules placed on their transfers, as a response to the problem. They are highly related to each other and will be examined jointly.

The UN is a vanguard of multilateral efforts by states on matters of international peace and security (see 4.2.1). Its resolutions, decisions, guidelines, studies, etc are of significant importance to investigate the normative values of the organisation's practice, on peace and security (see 5.7).

[77] Norris, 'Arms Embargoes: Making Sanctions Smarter' *Ploughshares Monitor*, para 5; see also Yihdego, 'The Role of Security Council Arms Embargoes in Stemming Destabilising Transfers of Small Arms and Light Weapons (SALW): Recent Developments and Challenges' (2007) 54 (1) *Netherlands International Law Review* 115–32.

[78] Gillard, above, n 51, at 35; see also Epps, above n 71, at 6; see also Cortright, Lopez and Gerber, above n 67, at 13–14; see also Hansard HC vol 413 col 74W (12 May 2003).

The position of the SC could be inferred from some measures and declarations made by it. The Council, recalling its primary responsibilities in maintaining international peace and security has time after time acknowledged the relationship between the proliferation of small arms and issues of peace and security. Consequently, it has imposed arms embargoes in several regions; the intention here is not to duplicate what we have seen above. The Council has made several calls, declarations of concern, and welcome statements to various measures of states, regions and NGOs. For instance, the Council welcomed and called upon both importing and exporting states to comply with the terms of the West African Moratorium, UN panel reports and others, in addition to its arm embargoes.[79] It is essential to have a look at certain examples.

The September 1999 Presidential Statement made on behalf of all Members noted the responsibility of the Council to maintain international peace. As a result, paragraph 7 of the statement has called[80]:

> For measures to discourage arms flows to countries or regions engaged in or emerging from armed conflicts. The Council encourages Member States to establish and abide by voluntary national or regional moratoria on arms transfers with a view to facilitating the process of reconciliation in these countries or regions. The Council recalls the precedents for such moratoria and the international support extended for their implementation.

The Council also called upon states, in September 2000, to discourage arms supply to nations and regions 'engaged in or emerging from armed conflict' and 'for effective international action to prevent the illegal flow of small arms' to such countries.[81] Moreover, as shown in paragraph 1 of the Preamble of Resolution 1467 of 2003, the SC has adopted a declaration entitled: '[P]roliferation of small arms and light weapons and mercenary activities: threat to peace and security in West Africa'. Paragraph 18 of the Resolution went on to call upon[82]:

> arms-producing and exporting countries that have not yet done so to enact stringent laws, regulations and administrative procedures in order to ensure, through their implementation, more effective control over the transfer to West Africa of small arms by manufacturers, suppliers, brokers, and shipping and transit agents.[83]

Even if voluntarism and domestic laws are emphasised, the link between peace and security and the trade in weapons to conflict zones has been

[79] *Statement by the President of the SC on Small Arms*, 24 September 1999, para 2; see also *A call to Control Trade to and in Africa*, 19 November 1998; see also SC Res 1467/2003.

[80] *Presidential Statement, ibid*; see also UN Doc S/PV. 4048, 24 September 1999, p 22.

[81] SC Res 1318/2000, Annex, pt VI.

[82] UN Doc Supp S/RES/1467/2003, 18 March 2003; for comparison purposes see *N by the President of the SC*, 31 January 1992, para 21, it has been noted that 'the proliferation of all weapons of mass destruction constitutes a threat to international peace and security'.

[83] Kirgis, above n 3, at 519.

clearly recognised by the Council. This must be read in the light of its recurrent views on the practical challenges of peace and security. It is of note that the Council's presidential statements are reflections of 'the consensus reached in closed sessions by the Council Members'.[83]

Several GA Resolutions have been adopted on the small arms transfers since the early 1990s. Almost all have mentioned the peace and security paradigm of such transactions. For example, the Assembly adopted Resolutions 46/36/ in 1991, 49/75 M in 1994 and 50/70 B in 1995. Within this, it has been expressly stated that small arms transfer shall consider the adverse effects that they bring against national, regional and global peace and security. Particularly, paragraph 2 of the Preamble of Resolution 50/70 has stressed on the need for 'a world free from the scourge of war and the burden of armament'.[84]

The above Resolutions have led to two significant guidelines adopted by the DC of the UN. First, Article 1(a) and (b) of Resolution 49/75 of 1994 invited the DC to work on SALW transfers, in response to Resolution 46/36 H, giving full account for peace and security issues.[85] Resolution 46/36, as will be discussed in later chapters, was an overall call by the GA on all Member States. States had been urged to control effectively their weapons and arms import-export activities.[86] The GA lauded the work of the Commission when the latter was working on the issue.[87]

Subsequently, considering Resolutions 46/36 and 49/75, The DC came up with 'Guidelines on International Arms Transfers' (hereafter 'GIAT') in 1996. Paragraph 14, general principle No 2, states:

> Arms transfers should be addressed in conjunction with the question of *maintaining international peace and security*, reducing regional and international tensions, preventing and resolving conflicts and disputes, building and enhancing confidence, and promoting disarmament as well as social and economic development. Restraint and greater openness, including various transparency measures, can help in this respect and contribute to the promotion of international peace and security[88] [emphasis added].

As clearly stated in No 8 of the introductory part of the GIAT that, 'limitations on arms transfers can be found', inter alia, in *'the principles and purposes of the Charter'*.[89] We shall address it further in 5.7.

[84] Res 50/70 was entitled 'Small Arms'; Res 46/36 was entitled 'International Arms Transfers', and adopted by consensus; Res 49/75 G, Preamble, para 1; see also Res 48/75 H/1993, entitled 'Measures to Curb the Illicit Transfer and Use of Conventional Weapons', Preamble, para 1.

[85] Res 49/75 M, for the consideration of peace and security, Preamble, para 1.

[86] Res 46/36 H, above n 85.

[87] Res 50/70 B, above n 85, Preamble, para 2.

[88] UN Disarmament Commission, *Guidelines for International Arms Transfers*, Substantive Session, 22 April–7 May 1996, New York, see also introduction, No 2 .

[89] *Ibid* [emphasis added]. Treaties and SC arms embargoes have also been taken as legal limitations.

The second work of the DC is 'Guidelines on Conventional Arms Control/Limitation and Disarmament, with particular emphasis on the consolidation of peace in the context of Resolution 51/45 N' (hereafter 'GCAC') of 1999. The first principle is set out in paragraph 8 and reads:

> In formulating and implementing practical disarmament measures for the consolidation of *peace in regions suffered from conflicts*, States should fully respect the purposes and *principles of the Charter of the United Nations*, including those contained in paragraph 14 of the guidelines for arms transfers.[90]

The adoption of these guidelines was indispensable for various reasons. The first was unanimously adopted by the DC. The GA has welcomed in particular the first set of guidelines.[91] Both of them have alluded to, and prepared in accordance with, the UN Charter and directions given by the GA pursuant to Resolutions 46/36 H, 49/75 M and 51/45 N; and finally, they emphatically underlined the need for considering international and regional peace in the light of arms transfers. The difference between the two guidelines is that the first talks about arms transfer in general with the objective of controlling illicit trafficking, and the second focuses on post conflict and disarmament matters.

Though they are a multilaterally agreed set of guidelines, they are not binding instruments. Paragraph 8(2) of the GCAC has stated that the application of the instrument should be on a 'voluntary basis and with the consent of the States concerned'.[92] This may not discredit the significance of such instruments. Zaleski arguably indicated that: 'efforts focused on elaboration of guidelines . . . or of politically binding obligations in this field have more chances for success than attempts to codify relevant regulations'.[93] Even so their status and impact on norm creation will need to be analysed later along with other UN practices.

The UN efforts were not limited to the guidelines and related resolutions. Extensive studies and global conferences have been conducted on the subject.

Among others, the 1997 GGE Panel attempted to clarify the link between the proliferation of SALW and their destabilising impacts. The following four valuable elements of the report are worth stating. First, it has reflected the ever-growing recognition of 'problems associated with the proliferation, and accumulation and use' of SALW vis-à-vis peace and stability. Yet, there has not been a global standard by which 'excessive

[90] UN Doc Supp No 42(A/54/52), 1999, Annex III, para 14. See also pt VII, para 38*ff*. [emphasis added].

[91] See, eg UN Doc Supp A/C.1/52/L.18, 13 October 1997, para 7 and GA Res 52/38/1998, para 4.

[92] Above, n 90.

[93] Zaleski, 'Precedents from the Export and Transport of War Materials: an Overview of the Multilateral Arms Regulation and Disarmament' in Dahinden, Dahlitz and Fischer (eds), *Small Arms and Light Weapons, Legal Aspects of National and International Regulation* (Geneva, United Nations, vol iv, 2002) 40.

and destabilizing levels of this class of weapon' could be determined. Secondly, four categories of weapons are identified as being most available. FN FAL, AK, M-16 and H & K G3 families of arms are said to be in use, manufactured and existent in millions. Thirdly, 'the terms "excessive" and "destabilizing" are relative and exist only in the context of specific regions, sub-regions and states'. The mere excessive availability of them might not be destabilising, as a small quantity of arms could be troublesome in some conditions. Finally, 'accumulations of small arms and light weapons become excessive and destabilizing', when both the importer and exporter states: (a) 'do not exercise proper restraint in transfers and acquisition of these weapons beyond states' legitimate needs', (b) 'cannot exercise effective control to prevent the illegal acquisition, transfer, transit or circulation of such weapons', and (c) 'the use of such weapons manifests itself in armed conflict' or other acts in violation of international and domestic laws.[94] The 1999 Panel on Ammunition and Explosives has also acknowledged that 'ammunition and explosives are an inseparable part of the problem of the excessive and destabilising accumulation, transfer, and misuse' of SALW.[95]

In their findings and recommendations, both the 1997 and 1999 Panels deemed the fact that the destabilising accumulation and transfers of small arms should be tackled by reduction and other protective measures. As illustrated in paragraph 80 of the report, one of the preventive methods on which the first panel stressed was to fully comply with the DC's Guidelines that has been set out in line with Resolution 46/36 H of 1991.[96] Subsequently, the Reviewing Panel of 1999 assured, as stated in paragraph 64 of its report, that many states have reported that they have been abiding by the guidelines of the DC in their small arms exports,[97] as will be seen further in domestic practice. The SC had welcomed the recommendations and assessments of this Reviewing Panel in September 1999.[98] As stated in preceding chapters, the GA had adopted these governmental expert reports, as they were initiated by its own resolutions.

Furthermore, as discussed in chapter three, the Consultative Committee of Experts established pursuant to paragraph 5 of GA Resolution 53/77E, to study the 'feasibility of . . . trade in small arms to manufacturers and dealers authorised by states' emphasised that: 'the international community has agreed to exercise restraint and caution when considering arms transfers that may contribute to excessive and destabilising accumu-

[94] UN Doc Supp No A/52/298, 27 August 1997, paras 34, 35, 36 and 37(a), (b), and (c); for the excessively disseminated weapons, see 3.2.

[95] UN Doc Supp NoA/54/155, 5 June 1999, para 104.

[96] Above, n 95, para 80 (a); see also *ibid*, para 94.

[97] *Report of the Group of Governmental Experts on Small Arms* (reviewing panel), in *Disarmament Study Series No 28*, 1999, p 69; see also ch 6, fn 27.

[98] See UN Doc S/PV-4048, above n 80, at 24, para 4.

lation of small arms'. The experts further concluded in their findings that a study for restricting the trade in small arms to persons authorised by states 'is both feasible and desirable'. They added that such a measure will help states and the international community to strengthen international and regional efforts to address the proliferation.[99] All these panel studies and recommendations have led to further progress in this area.

The PoA,[100] (the outcome of the 2001 UN Conference on Small Arms), in paragraph 2 of the Preamble, has shown a grave concern of states on the 'serious threat to peace, reconciliation, safety, security and stability', posed by the illicit trade and excessive accumulation of SALW, at all levels. The concern is also extended, as per paragraph 7 of the Preamble, to the link between the illicit trade in arms and terrorism, drug trafficking and organised crime, which led to the belief that the solution must consider the supply and demand sides of transfers of SALW.

In view of that, section II(1) of the PoA affirms that states will undertake various measures 'to prevent, combat and eradicate' the illegal trade in SALW in *'[A]ll its Aspects'* [emphasis added]. The measures sought have been divided into three levels. The first is actions that have to be taken at the national level—section II(2) shows the commitment of states: '[T]o put in place, . . . adequate laws, regulations . . . to exercise *effective control* over . . . the export, import, transit or transfer of such weapons, in order to prevent . . . illicit trafficking . . ., or their diversion to unauthorised recipients' [emphasis added]. Moreover, in section II(11) of the PoA, states have shown their devotion:

> To assess application for export authorisations according to strict national regulations and procedures that cover all small arms and light weapons and are *consistent with existing responsibilities of States under relevant international law* [emphasis added].

Regional measures have been illustrated at the second level—consistent with section II(26), participating states have agreed: '[T]o encourage the strengthening and establishing, . . . of moratoria or similar initiatives in affected regions or sub regions on the transfer . . . of small arms and light weapons, and/or regional action programmes'. Finally, at the global stratum, states have decided to take various measures, inter alia, 'to cooperate with the UN system', and the 'Department for Disarmament Affairs', as explicitly stated in section II(32) of the PoA. The Biennial Meeting of States (hereafter 'BMS') conducted in July 2003, to consider the implementation of the PoA, in which national reports had extensively been heard, has also reiterated the position of states on peace and security concerns and arms transfers.[101]

99 UN Doc Supp No A/45/160, 6 July 1999, paras 8 and 23.

100 For details of the PoA see ch 3, fn 30*ff*.

101 See Report of the BMS, UN Doc Supp No A/CONF.192/BMS/2003/1, Annex. 'Chairman's Summary', paras 5 and 30.

In sum, the UN Conference and its process on the issue exhibited that states have recognised the destabilising outcomes of the problem in all its aspects. Yet the PoA is full of difficulties. First, it's not a binding instrument, rather a political declaration of states. Even so it has a framework through which its application could be reviewed. One of these mechanisms is the BMS and review conferences.[102] For instance, a majority of states reported to the BMS of 2003 that they do have adequate import-export laws to enable them to regulate SALW transfer.[103] Unfortunately, the UN Small Arms Review Conference of June 2006, which was held at UN Headquarters in New York, did not reach a substantive conclusion at all.

The second problem regards its scope. It is aimed at the illegal trade in small arms. As discussed in the introductory part, however, illicit transfer can be interpreted widely or narrowly (see 4.1.1). According to the GGE of 1999, illicit trade includes 'all types of illicit transfers' of SALW. In that sense, the black and grey markets have presumably been included in the scope of the UN PoA. The phrase 'in all its aspects' is also meant to embrace 'the issue of legal transfers in so far as they are directly related to illicit trafficking'. It has been repeatedly stated in the Conference 'the legal and illegal trade of small arms and light weapons were two sides of the same coin'. Yet the issue is far from certain.[104]

Finally, it is worth noting that both domestic law and existing international law obligations have been mentioned to regulate the transactions of SALW. The Italian representative to the BMS of 2003, on behalf of the EU declared that 'the Union believed that export authorizations should be assessed . . . taking into account such factors as respect for international commitments'.[105] Although such a reference to international law is ambiguous, it does not seem unfounded to think that maintenance of peace and security, as a nucleus Charter obligation of states, should be considered as a relevant international law commitment, for the purposes of SALW transfer. Alternatively, effective domestic control is much more emphasised in the PoA. The interpretation of such a control has also been left to individual states.[106] It is not yet clear whether the phrase 'effective control' has some thing to do with substantive limitations on transfers. The contribution of the PoA, to the emergence or otherwise of the norm peace and security based restriction on arms transfer will be examined further (see 5.7).

It is interesting to note also that GA Resolution 61/89 of 2006 has recognised the significance of arms control 'for the maintainance of peace

[102] UN Doc Supp No A/CONF.192/15, 9–20 July 2001, s IV, para 1 (a) and (b); see also Fischer, 'Outcome of the UN Process: the Legal Character of the UN Programme of Action' in Dahinden et al (eds), above n 93, at 159.

[103] BMS, above n 102, paras 65–69.

[104] Fischer, above n 103, at 160–61; see also GGE 1999, above n 98, paras 129–32.

[105] *Press Release*, UN /2877, 11 July 2003, para 13.

[106] Fischer, above n 103, at 160.

and security', and the fact that the absence of binding global standards on conventional arms transfers has been 'a contributory factor to conflict . . . and terrorism'. It follows that the overwhelming majority's decision (153 votes in favour) as shown in operative paragraph 2 of the Resolution (UN Doc Supp A/61/394-XXXI), calls upon the UN Secretary-General to establish a panel of experts 'to examine the feasibility, scope and draft parameters for a comprehensive, legally binding instrument establishing common international standards for the import, export and transfer of conventional arms'. This will be started in 2008. It seems most likely that peace and security concerns would be incorporated in the forthcoming draft treaty parameters (for the nature and scope of this development see chapter ten).

Similarly, among non-UN efforts, the Wassenaar Arrangement (hereafter 'WA'), as a global voluntary arms export control regime which embraces 33 exporting states, 'has been established in order to contribute to regional and international security and stability'.[107] On 3 December 1998, the plenary session of the WA approved a paper entitled 'Elements for Objective Analysis and Advice Concerning Potentially Destabilising Accumulations of Conventional Weapons'.[108] As expressly mentioned in No 1(b) (c) and (d) of the paper, the motives of a weapon importing state need to be assessed, inter alia, in the light of Article 51 of the UN Charter, a risk of diversion of both end-use and end-user of weapons, 'the general direction of the state's foreign policy' vis-à-vis possible violations of Article 2(4) of the UN Charter, and whether 'the quantities involved' are 'consistent with its "requirements"'. These and other elements help determine the destabilising impact of a certain transaction in conventional weapons.[109] While these are useful tests, they do not distinguish the problem of SALW transfers from that of other conventional weapons.

However, in the year 2002, the exporting states adopted the British proposed 'Best Practice Guidelines' for export of SALW. Some of the objectives of this instrument, as shown in part I(ii) and (iii), are to prevent the destabilising accumulation of these weapons and deter terrorism. Finally, as per No 1(a) and (b) of the Guidelines, they have agreed to take into consideration the elements of peace and security in the recipient state and region whenever they deal with the trade in small arms. The words of the OSCE criteria have been reiterated in the 'Best Practice Guidelines' as will be elaborated later[110] (see 5.4). It is notable that Member States have

[107] *The WASSENAAR Arrangement on Export Controls for Conventional Arms and Dual-Use Goods and Technologies*, Initial Elements, Plenary of 11–12 July 1996. See, eg Purpose, No 1 at, <http://www.wassenaar.org/docs/IE96.html>

[108] <http://www.wassenaar.org/docs/criteria.html#paper>

[109] *Ibid.*

[110] *Best Practice Guidelines for Export of Small Arms and Light Weapons*, Plenary of 11–12 December 2002.

agreed to reflect these principles in their respective domestic legislation and policies[111] (see further chapter seven).

Interestingly enough, noting that it is a security threat, participating states of the WA only came to consensus in 2003 to restrict the transfers of portable surface-to-air missile systems only to foreign governments. Restriction No 2 of the 2003 document also stated that such transactions shall be decided at the senior policy level of exporting governments and could not be transferred through non-governmental brokers.[112]

The WA arrangement is global in nature. With the exception of China, Belarus, Israel and Brazil, the other leading exporters of SALW are all embraced therein. In this regard, therefore, it is an important forum and initiative. Yet the system works on consensus and even a single country could block any decision, as was the case in the 2002 plenary session. Russia disagreed with the proposal that seeks out the annual information exchange of exports of SALW.[113] State practice at the regional level may give us additional insight into the issue.

5.4 REGIONAL INSTRUMENTS

Such instruments may have two aspects; treaties such as the OAS Convention, the SADC and Nairobi Protocols, and political declarations like the ECOWAS Moratorium, the EU Code of Conduct and OSCE documents. Although the EU instruments fall into a grey area, discussing them in chorus under the second aspect will help to better understand their essence. The relevant aspects of these instruments to the peace and security versus SALW transfers will now be discussed, starting with treaties.

The OAS Convention on Illicit Firearms, as has been shown in paragraph 1 of the Preamble, acknowledged 'the harmful effects of these activities [illicit trafficking of firearms, etc.] on the security of each state and the region as a whole'. According to Article IX thus '[S]tates Parties shall maintain an effective system of export, import, and international transit licenses or authorisations for transfers of firearms'.[114] This obligation has considered, inter alia, the need for all exporting and importing states 'to take necessary measures to prevent, combat and eradicate the illicit . . . trafficking' in SALW, and relevant GA resolutions, as expressly stated in paragraphs 5 and 8 of the Preamble respectively.[115]

[111] See ch 7, fn 61.

[112] *Elements for Export Controls of Man-portable Air Defence Systems* (MANPADS), agreed at the 2003 Plenary, at <http://www.wassenaar.org/2003Plenary/MANPADS_2003.htm>

[113] Boese, 'Wassenaar Members Adopt Small Arms Initiatives' *Arms Control Today* (January/February 2003) paras 2, 4 and 7.

[114] *OAS Convention on Firearms* 1997, see also Preamble, paras 8 and 10 and Art X, [clarification added].

[115] *Ibid*.

Similarly, paragraph 2 of the Preamble of the SADC Protocol on the Control of Firearms of 2001 clearly accepted the contribution of 'illegal firearms' to conflict, instability and violence. Paragraph 4 of the Preamble added that 'the excessive and destabilising accumulation, trafficking . . .' need to be prevented on time. Therefore, States Parties are obliged as stated in Article 5(3)(f) of the Protocol to maintain 'legal uniformity and minimum standards' for import-export of firearms. Such measures include matters of marking, licensing, etc, as indicated in (g) and (h) of the same provision.[116]

The Nairobi Protocol for the Prevention, Control and Reduction of Small Arms and Light Weapons in the Great Lakes Region and the Horn of Africa of 2004, which has been signed by 11 states of the sub-region, has also endorsed the devastating consequences of SALW proliferation corresponding to conflict and terrorism.[117] Paragraph 3 of the Preamble has emphasised the concern of states 'about the supply of small arms and light weapons into the region and conscious of the need for effective controls of arms transfers by suppliers'. Consequently, Article 2 of the Protocol sets out some objectives, inter alia, preventing the illicit trafficking in weapons and excessive accumulation of small arms.[118] Finally, Article 10 of the instrument has reiterated the necessity of an effective system of control on SALW transfers at the national level,[119] as indicated earlier in both the OAS Convention and the SADC Protocol.

These instruments are important in that they all addressed the peace and security concerns attached to SALW. The remedies of control they have set out have included both NSAs and states. Although they emphasise the illegal trade in arms, they also talk about the need for restricting the legal SALW transit. Further, the reference made to GA Resolutions needs to be emphasised. Similar to the global treaties discussed above, they are narrowly designed and restricted to the illicit transfer of firearms. The focus is on effective import-export control at the national level. It is not clear whether not such control is meant to take account of substantive limitations on arms transfer. Regional conventional international law could thus be of limited help. It is therefore imperative to turn to regional political instruments.

The Heads of States of ECOWAS Member States have considered under paragraph 2 of the Moratorium the fact that[120]:

[116] See also ch 3, fn 7.

[117] *The Nairobi Protocol for the Prevention, Control and Reduction of Small Arms and Light Weapons in the Great Lakes Region and the Horn of Africa*, 21 April 2004, signed by Burundi, Djibouti, Eritrea, Rwanda, The Sudan, Tanzania, DRC, Ethiopia, Kenya, Seychelles and Uganda, not yet in force.

[118] *Ibid.*

[119] *Ibid.*

[120] *West African Arms Moratorium*, 1998.

> The proliferation of light weapons constitutes a destabilising factor for ECOWAS Member States and a threat to the peace and security for our people.

Accordingly, they have decided under paragraph 10 of the instrument to impose:

> a moratorium on the *importation, exportation* and manufacture of light weapons in ECOWAS member states.[121]

This framework instrument entails both quantitative and qualitative total limitation on international transfers to and from countries of the community. Even so it has made certain exceptions for legitimate uses of the states in the sub-region. Gillard thinks that the Moratorium 'quite simply prohibits' the import-export of SALW and 'any transfer would be illegal and would give rise to state responsibility of the exporting and importing states'.[122] Mubiala alternatively believes that the instrument provides only 'a basis for the adaptation of concrete measures, including mandatory decisions'[123] on arms transactions. Indeed, as we examined before, it is not a binding instrument; it does not seem, however, to be a mere declaration either (see 3.3.3.1 and chapter ten). From June 2006 onwards, however, the Moratorium has been transformed into a Convention. Chapter II of the Convention has imposed a total ban on SALW transfer into, or from, the sub-region, with some exemptions—the exemptions are very similar to those of the Moratorium as discussed in previous chapters. As per Article 6 of the Convention, making an exception/exemption 'shall' be prohibited if 'the arms are destined to be used' in internal conflicts, terrorism, aggression, to adversely affect regional security, and so forth (see further chapter ten).

The EU Joint Action ('EUJA') and the Code of Conduct on Arms Exports are of major importance for the issue at hand. The EUJA under Article 1(1) sets out some objectives, inter alia:

> to combat and contribute to ending the destabilising accumulation and spread of small arms,
> to contribute to the reduction of existing accumulation of these weapons.[124]

Article 3(a) and (b) of the EUJA has also highlighted the need for principles and restrictive export criteria on SALW transfers. The key reason for such an approach is to prevent further destabilising accumulations of small arms. The EU, as expressly mentioned in Article 3(b) of the Programme, 'shall aim at building consensus' of weapon exporting countries, to adhere

[121] *West African Arms Moratorium*, 1998 [emphasis added].

[122] Gillard, 'What is Legal? What is Illegal? Limitations on Transfers of Small Arms under International Law' (Cambridge, Lauterpacht Research Centre for International Law) p 9, para 39 at, <http://www.armslaw.org>

[123] Mubiala, 'The ECOWAS Moratorium on Small Arms in West Africa' (2000) 3 *YBIHL* 248–49.

[124] *Amended Joint Action*, 19 July 2002; see for details ch 3, p 63.

to 'appropriate international and regional restrictive arms export criteria, as provided in particular in the EU Code of Conduct' on arms export. According to Article 14(1) of the EU Treaty of Nice, the EUJA falls under Common Foreign and Security Policy of the Union and is thus legally binding[125] (see further chapter seven). For example, Article 5(3) of the UK Export Control Bill of 2002 provides[126]:

> International obligation includes an obligation relating to a joint action or common position adopted, or a decision taken, by the Council under Title V of the Treaty on European Union (provisions on a common foreign and security policy).

As per Articles 3(d) and 9(2), the EUJA's implementation is essentially left to national legal systems,[127] and the EU Code of Conduct.

It is necessary to turn to the details of the Code of Conduct at this point. The Code of Conduct's[128] criteria have attracted greater attention in this legal regime. As stated in paragraph 2 of the Preamble, the EU Council introduced the Code 'recognising the special responsibility of arms exporting states'. For instance, Criterion 1(a) and (b) propounded that:

> An export licence *should* be refused if approval would be inconsistent with, inter alia: the international obligations of member states and their commitments to enforce UN, OSCE and EU . . . arms embargoes, their commitment not to export any form of anti-personnel landmine [emphasis added].

Moreover, the first paragraph of Criterion 3 has considered the internal situations of a country of final destination of SALW export. Possibilities of tensions and armed conflict have been emphasised in the Criterion. The second paragraph of the same Criterion added that: '[M]ember States will not allow exports which would provoke or prolong armed conflicts or aggravate existing tensions or conflicts in the country of final destination'.

More details have been set out, in Criterion 4, under the title 'preservation of regional peace, security and stability'. It reads:

> Member States will not issue an export licence if there is a clear risk that the intended recipient would use the proposed export aggressively against another country or to assert by force a territorial claim. When considering these risks, EU Member States will take into account inter alia: a) the existence or likelihood of armed conflict between the recipient and another country; . . . d) the need not to affect adversely regional stability in any significant way.

Operative provision 1 of the Code states 'each EU Member State will assess export licence applications for military equipment made to it on

[125] Craig and De Burca, *EU Law: Text, Cases and Materials*, 3rd edn (Oxford, Oxford University Press, 2003) 25, 37

[126] *UK-Export Control Bill 2002*, 24 July 2002 at, <http://projects.sipri.se/expcon/natexpcon/UK/act2002.htm>; for later developments see ch 10, fn 10.

[127] See also, SIPRI at <http://web.sipri.org/contents/expcon/eujointact.html>

[128] *EU Code of Conduct on Arms Exports*, 1998.

case-by-case basis against the provisions of the Code of Conduct'. Yet, operative provision 2 indicated that states are at liberty 'to operate more restrictive national policies' than the Code's criteria. It should be borne in mind that non-military weapons are subject to the Code's criteria by virtue of operative provision 6 of the Code and EU Council Regulation No 1334/2000 of 22 June 2000 setting up a Community regime for the control of exports of dual-use items and technology.[129]

The Community regime exhibited that transfers which could have direct or indirect risk in helping aggression, conflict or other kind of instability should not be certified. However, Member States have not chosen the word 'shall' other than 'should', as shown in Criterion 1. Also, individual countries of the Union ought to interpret the phrase 'clear risk' and take measures accordingly, in the course of export authorisation. The Code has been criticised for its emphasis on, and requirement of, 'a clear risk rather than only a risk'[130] of the dangers, including conflict and instability. However, regular meetings of the Council's Working Group on the subject and annual reports of implementation of Member States 'have been used as tools to harmonise the Code's application and to narrow the scope of national interpretation of the criteria'.[131]

Germany, in its 2001 annual report declared that its political principles on the export of war and military weapons including small arms have been amended to integrate the EU Code of Conduct's criteria. It has been reported too that the Italian law 185/1990 had included the EU Criteria for the export of arms.[132] While it is not a legally binding instrument, actual discussions have been ongoing to transform 'the code into common position' of the Union. For instance, the Committee on Foreign Affairs of the European Parliament 'reiterated the call for the Code to be legally binding, and considered the possibility of it being transported [sic.] into national law'.[133] In fact, 'the code has spilled over into national law (in Austria, Belgium, Finland and the UK) and other policy areas'.[134]

Likewise, the instruments of the EU have got a wider support from the international community. Inter alia, 'the associated countries of Central and Eastern Europe, Cyprus, Malta and Turkey . . . have aligned themselves'

[129] See also for the Regulation *OJEC (OJ) L 159*, 30 June 2000, pp 1–215 (as amended by Council Reg (EC) No 149/2003 of 27 January 2003.

[130] Bauer, 'The EU Code of Conduct on Arms Exports-much accomplished much to be done' *SIPRI*, 27 April 2004, p 6.

[131] *Ibid*, at 4.

[132] Annual Report on the Implementation of the EU Joint Action, 1 August 2001, p 4, para 3; see also Second Annual Report on the Implementation of the EU Joint Action, 12 July 2002, p 4, para 27.

[133] Fifth Annual Report According to Operative Provision 8 of the European Code of Conduct on Arms Transfers, 31 December 2003, p 1.

[134] Above, n 130.

with the EUJA.[135] Six European largest arms producing countries namely France, Germany, Italy, Spain, Sweden and the UK negotiated a treaty called Framework Agreement in July 1998 to facilitate the restructuring and operation of the European defence industry. It entered into force on 18 April 2001. The EU Code's Criteria including the peace and security factor have been endorsed in this treaty.[136] UN Member States, as mentioned in the PoA,[137] have acknowledged these efforts on several occasions. The US 'has welcomed and expressed its strong support for the principles embodied in the EU Code of Conduct' as indicated in paragraph 3 of the US-EU Declaration on Responsibility in Arms Exports of 18 December 2000.[138] The EU has also repeatedly imposed arms embargoes, as will be seen against countries that are believed to have instability (see 7.2.3.2).[139]

By way of recapitulation, note as follows: EU efforts have brought crucial developments in the combat against the unrestricted international trade in SALW.[140] While the general objectives to arrest the problem constituted legal commitment, the actual measures are political in nature. Despite the instruments and the embargoes, Member States continue to transfer small arms to conflict torn regions as discussed in IHL.[141]

The OSCE is another forum for the problem of small arms. In 1993, it adopted 'Principles Governing Conventional Arms Transfers'.[142] Since then, the 1999 Decision[143] and the 2000 Vienna Document[144] on small arms came into being. In these three instruments, Member States have acknowledged their duty to restrain conventional arms transfer in compliance with the UN Charter and other relevant international obligations, including the EUJA, with particular emphasis on international, regional and national peace and security.[145] Yet section VI(6) of the Vienna Document, for example, expressly stated 'the norms, principles and measures in this

135 Third Annual Report on the Implementation of the EU Joint Action, 6 November 2003, Annex, p 3, para 2.

136 Explanatory Memorandum for an Agreement to facilitate the Restructuring and Operation of the European Defence Industry, Geoff Hoon, Secretary of State for Defence, 2 November 2001, at <http://www.mod.uk/issues/edi/>

137 PoA, above n 101, Annex, p 25.

138 < http://www.useu.be/SUMMIT/arms1200.html>

139 See ch 7, p 211.

140 *Ibid.*

141 See ch 7, fn 67; see also BASIC Research Report, 'NATO and Small Arms: From Words to Deeds' 4 October 2000, p 7, para 4 at, <http://basicint.org/pubs/Research/2000from_words.htm>

142 *Principles Governing Conventional Arms Transfers*, OSCE, 49th Plenary Meeting, Vienna, 25 November 1993.

143 OSCE, Decision No 6/99, 16 November 1999.

144 *OSCE Document on Small Arms and Light Weapons*, Vienna, 24 November 2000.

145 *Ibid*, s I(1); *1999 Decision*, above n 144, Preamble, paras 1and 4, and Decisions in paras 8 and 9; *Principles*, above n 143, No 3(a) (d), 4(a)(ii) (b)(ii) (iv) (v) and 5(a); see also Dahinden, 'Meeting the Challenges of Small Arms Proliferation: Example of the OSCE Document', in Dahinden et al, above n 94, at 14.

document are politically binding'. Remarks about this and correlated issues will be made below.

Section III(1) of the 2000 Vienna Document on small arms enumerated export criteria, with the objective of setting out 'the norms, principles and measures aimed at fostering responsible behaviour with regard to the transfer of small arms'. Pursuant to section III(A)2(a) of the Document, participating states, will have to 'take into account', in their SALW transfer decision making, inter alia,

> (ii) The internal and regional situation in and around the recipient country, in the light of existing tensions or armed conflicts; (iii) The record of compliance of the recipient country with regard to international obligations and commitments, in particular on the non-use of force, and in the field of non-proliferation, or in other areas of arms control and disarmament, and the record of respect for international law governing the conduct of armed conflict.

Section III(A)2(b) went on further to set out the grounds for denial of small arms export license. The most pertinent ones are:

> (b) Each participating State will avoid issuing licences for exports where it deems that there is a *clear risk* that the small arms in question might:
> (v) *Prolong or aggravate an existing armed conflict,* taking into account the legitimate requirement for self-defence, or threaten compliance with international law governing the conduct of armed conflict;
> (vi) *Endanger peace,* create an excessive and destabilizing accumulation of small arms, or otherwise contribute to *regional instability;*
> (ix) Support or encourage *terrorism;*
> (x) Facilitate *organized crime;* etc.[146]

As regards implementation, Member States decided in section III(A)4(i) and (ii) of the Vienna Document to reflect the principles in their domestic legislation and policies and to assist others in the efforts to achieve such effective restraint. For that reason, the OSCE's influence has been something valuable in the development of the legal regime of SALW. For example, the organisation had been invited to present its 2000 Document, in particular the export criteria, to the Third PrepCOM of the UN Conference on Small Arms in the year 2001. The statement made to the Committee was well received by states.[147]

The GA in paragraphs 6 and 7 of Resolution 58/55 of 2003 commends 'the adoption' of the Vienna Document on SALW and 'the work done so far within the framework of the Organisation'. The Assembly has also invited all Member States to develop and adopt such regional measures 'to combat the illicit trade' in SALW 'in all its aspects' and to contribute 'to international peace and security'.[148]

[146] Emphasis added.
[147] Dahinden, above n 146.
[148] UN Doc Supp A/RES/58/55, 17 December 2003, No 3.

Four remarks are of note regarding the OSCE's efforts. First, the organisation has embarked upon peace and security criteria for the trade in SALW. Participating states have agreed not to transfer small arms whenever there is a clear risk that such import-export could exacerbate existing conflicts, endangering regional peace and stability, favouring terrorists and conducive to organised crime. An assessment of a risk in the destination state and the region is therefore a prerequisite before authorising any supply of SALW. Secondly, there has been a consensus to integrate the rules into domestic legal jurisdiction. Thirdly, relevant international law principles, including the UN Charter and other appropriate obligations, have been referred to in all the documents. It may not imply political commitment only. Finally, the fact that these measures were in existence since the early 1990s, the majority of participant states are SALW producers/suppliers, and the arrangement is consensual, will have an important impact on the development of the peace and security norm on arms transfer.

Even so this is not to say the arrangement is without defects. It seems that implementation and interpretation of the key phrases like 'taking into account' and assessing 'a clear risk' is retained by individual states. This might lead to abuses by Participating States.

A multilateral global or regional effort, in the endeavour to establish the peace and security factor in SALW transfers has been seen. It is also equally important to assess the practice of states in their individual capacity. Some major exporters' laws and policies are discussed in that case.

5.5 DOMESTIC INSTRUMENTS

In June 1999, the US Congress passed a bill on the Code of Conduct for arms assistance and transfers by voice vote, which is also called the 'McKinney Rohrabacher Code of Conduct'. Under section 3(a)(3) of this law, the prohibitions on arms transfers extend to any government which is engaged in armed aggression and violation of international law. Section 4(b) states that 'the President shall promote' multilateral efforts for the sake of limiting 'arms transfers worldwide'. To that effect, for example, reference is made to the UN and WA. However, as per section 3(c)(1) of the Act, an exemption could be made in the account of the country's security interests or when emergency exists and in such situations, the President shall present the case to Congress for exemption. According to sections 2 and 5 of the legislation, it seems to be limited to military weapons and not inclusive of civilian firearms. Even so section 3(a) has embraced both aid and commercial transfers.[149] It is of note that the US law is not restricted

[149] *Code of Conduct on Arms Transfers Act of 1999*, HR 2269 IH, 106th Congress, First Session, 17 June 1999.

to export restrictions. The Export Control Act, under section 47.52 (a), has banned any importation of weapons to the US, 'if an import is not in furtherance of world peace'.[150]

Similarly, the People's Republic of China's Regulation on Export Control of Military Items, under Article 5(2) states: 'that any military exports should not jeopardise the peace and security and stability in the relevant regions and around the world'. Pursuant to Article 2 of the Regulation, the scope of such limitations is restricted to commercial exports of military purpose equipments.[151] Other known transferors of European countries such as Austria and Italy have also promulgated relevant provisions in their laws, consistent with the EU Code of Conduct on arms transfers[152] (see 5.4).

Policy statements and declarations are more widely available than primary legislations on the issue. France made a Policy declaration in 1995, which set out criteria for export licence permits. The Policy considers the impact of the export on international tensions, terrorism and the security of France and European countries.[153] Consequently, it has denied conventional arms transfers to Iraq and Iran.[154] The 2001 report presented to the French Parliament also stated that 'particular vigilance is paid to areas of latent tension (Middle East, Central Asia, north-east Asia, etc). Even in the absence of an international embargo, refusal to export is presumed if there is open conflict'.[155]

The UK Policy of export in arms of 1997 embraced the criterion and commitment not to transfer weapons if they could harm the peace and security of states and regions. The Policy refers to EU Criteria and other international obligations that shall be fulfilled in export licence permits.[156] In 2002, the UK 'has initiated unilateral export restrictions against 32 states', on the basis of its relevant international commitments and national policy.[157] The reasons for each case are hardly known. Such information is

[150] *The Arms Export Control Act of 1976*, (AECA), 22 U.S.C. 2778.

[151] *People's Republic of China, Regulations on Export Control of Military Items*, Decree No 234, 22 October 1997, effective from 1 January 1998.

[152] Above n 133; see also Austria- *Legal Gazette I*, No 57 of June 2001, para 28.

[153] *French Policy on Export Controls for Conventional Arms and Dual Use Goods and Technologies*, information provided by France to the Wassenaar Arrangement on Export Control, at <http://projects.sipri.se/expcon/natexpcon/France/frenchpolicy.htm>

[154] Anthony, 'Causation and the Arms Trade, with Reference to Small Arms', in Dhanapala, Donwaki, Rana and Lumpe (eds), *Small Arms Control Old Weapons, New Issues* (Aldershot, Ashgate, 1999) 70.

[155] *Report on Armament Exports to Parliament from France*, 2001, p. 14, para 1, at <http://www.defense.gouv.fr/english/files/d163/pdf/2.pdf>

[156] *'Criteria to be Used in Considering Conventional Arms Export Licence Applications'*, Statement by the Secretary of State for Foreign and Commonwealth Affairs of the UK, 28 July 1997, at <http://projects.sipri.se/expcon/natexpcon/UK/ukcriteria.html>; see also Hansard HC vol 413 col 855W (8 May 2003).

[157] Marsh, 'Two Sides of the Same Coin? The Legal and Illegal Trade in Small Arms' 9 *BJWA* (Spring 2002) 218.

not consistently revealed even to the parliamentary 'Quadripartite Committee', which has been set to watch over government's licensing decisions on arms export, as expressly stated in paragraph 9 of the 2004 Report of the Committee.[158] It may well be that the refusals of arms export took into account peace and security considerations.

Moreover, most participant states of the Lancaster House Conference on tightening arms exports in January 2003 affirmed that they do use national guidelines such as 'the impact of arms transfers on internal tensions and conflict' and 'regional peace and security'.[159]

Even so similar laws and policies may not be found in all jurisdictions of supplying countries. Article 6(3) of the Federal Law of 1998 of the Russian Federation speaks about restrictions on transfers. As a result, arms exports from the country are subject to international commitments concerning arms control issues.[160] However, neither Article 4 of the law, in which principles for arms exports and military assistance are outlined,[161] nor other relevant regulations of Russia have made a reference to the peace and security standard. The Russian Federation Committee for Military-Technical Cooperation with Foreign States is responsible for an approval or denial of export licences and to formulate policies for such transfers. The President also has the power to impose restrictions.[162] We do not know thus the real policies on which the Committee depends in authorising or otherwise weapons transfer.

Yet the Russian Federation representative to the SC has affirmed in 1999 that 'specific measures to rid crisis regions and the world as a whole of illegal flows of small arms and light weapons' deserves attention. He mentioned also his country's awareness on the issue of 'restricting and reducing legal supplies' of small arms.[163] Russia too is a party to the WA.

In general, the above examples demonstrate that major exporters of small arms have legislation which seeks out restrictions on weapon transfers as a result of the peace and security consequences of such supplies—the US, Austria, Italy and China's laws have affirmed this. The policies of France and the UK are also keen to restrict arms transfers on these grounds. Some address both military and other weapons; others rely

[158] Quadripartite Committee: *Strategic Export Control—Annual Report for 2002* (HC 390, 18 May 2004) p 7, para 9.

[159] *Implementing the UN PoA: Strengthening Export Controls*, Chairman's Summary, Lancaster House Conference, 14–15 January 2003, pp 2–3.

[160] *Military-Technical Cooperation of the Russian Federation with Foreign States*, Federal Law of the Russian Federation adopted by the State Duma, 3 July 1998, approved by the Federation Council, 9 July 1998.

[161] *Ibid.*

[162] *Presidential Decree No 1953*, 1 December 2000 to Form The Russian Federation Committee for Military–Technical Cooperation with Foreign States, s III, Art 7, paras 5 and 6; see also *Presidential Edict No 1953*, 1 December 2000, a Statute on Commission on Questions of the Federation's Military–Technical Cooperation with Foreign States, s I, para 1.

[163] Above, n 80.

on the former; many address aid and commercial transactions; China has only mentioned commercial exports. Some laws leave the whole power to committees and/or commissions and others involve parliaments. Though it is hardly possible to get primary legislation that prohibits imports from the importers side, the West African states have, for example, agreed to adjust their national laws and policies along the lines of the ECOWAS Moratorium and the 2006 Convention. The US prohibits imports of SALW if they jeopardise international peace, too. Several national laws and policies thus favour the restriction of arms transfer to states or regions which have difficulties of peace and security.

5.6 NGOS AND WRITERS

As essential endeavours of NGOs, the FCIAT[164] and the ICCAT[165] will be considered here (see 4.1.1).

The 2003 Draft of the FCIAT classified existing international law prohibition of SALW transfer into three categories: 'express limitations', 'limitations based on use', and prohibitions upon 'other considerations'. First, as shown, inter alia, in Article 2(a) and (b) of the aforementioned draft, any small arms transfer against the UN Charter, including decisions of the SC and treaties have been considered as express ones. Secondly, Article 3 has provided the limitations based on the use of SALW; the chapeau of Article 3 states that 'a Contracting Party shall not authorize international transfers' of SALW when 'it has knowledge or ought reasonably to have knowledge' that such supply is 'likely to be': inter alia, '(a) used in breach of the United Nations Charter or corresponding rules of customary international law, in particular those on the prohibition on the threat or use of force in international relations'.

The commentary on the 2003 draft has affirmed that use of arms against the UN Charter and customary law based prohibitions include Article 2(4) violations of the Charter and 'related principles concerning threats to the peace, breaches of the peace and acts of aggression in Article 39 of the Charter'. Furthermore, contraventions against 'standard-setting UN resolutions' are also made part of the root bases for such bans on the arms trade.[166] However, much more emphasis has been placed on aggression and Article 2(4) of the Charter.

Thirdly, Article 4 submitted that 'Contracting Parties shall take into account' whether arms transfers 'are likely to': '(a) be used for or to facilitate the commission of violent crimes; (b) adversely affect political

[164] *Draft Framework Convention* (FCIAT), 2003.

[165] *International Code of Conduct* (ICCAT), 1997.

[166] FCIAT 2003, above n 165, Commentary, p 5, para 10; see also FCIAT Draft 3 of 3 March 2001, Art 1, at <http://www.armslaw.org/fccomment.html>

stability or regional security'. As paragraph 14 of the commentary on the 2003 Draft clearly acknowledged, limitations derived from 'other considerations' do not restrict states from transfers, rather remind them to 'take into account' the effects of their transfer on regional security and violent crimes, including other economic and social impacts.[167] This will be elaborated later.

Arguably, the FCIAT is an essential initiative to codify and clarify existing rules of international law on the SALW trade by states. Number I of the commentary on the 2001 draft underlined that '[T]he Framework Convention focuses on limitations on states' freedom to transfer arms. In doing so it codifies rules that currently exist in international law. 'It does not attempt to impose new limitations or rules'.[168] The references made to the Charter, customary international law, threat to peace, the standard-setting of UN resolutions and others are significant to the subject in discussion. The draft had been presented to the 2001 UN Conference on Small Ams. However, the PoA was the only instrument, which was adopted in the 2001 negotiation. It was also circulated to Member States during the UN BMS in July 2003[169] (see chapter nine).

Three difficulties may arise regarding its scope and its clarity. The first is that regional security has not been taken as a ground for restricting arms transfer. The background work explains 'there is currently no basis in international law for prohibiting' SALW transfers that may 'adversely affect' inter alia 'regional security'; they are rather mere suggestions.[170] As was seen in express prohibitions (see 5.2) the validity of this position is disputed, and will be analysed in mind with writers later.

The second problem is that the FCIAT has restricted itself to exporting states. It has been intended to establish 'a supply-side arms control regime'.[171] Undoubtedly, 'the supply of such weapons has to be arrested if we are to make any impact on current conflicts'.[172] This could not justify the exclusion of weapon recipient states' obligations, from the efforts on going to codify and clarify the norms applicable to the arms trade. Finally, the distinction among 'express', 'based on use', and 'other considerations' kinds of restrictions, may cause confusion to some extent.

In 1997, under the leadership of 17 peace laureates, an International Code of Conduct on Arms Transfers (ICCAT) was drafted.[173] Article 8 of

[167] FCIAT 2003, *ibid*, at p 6; see also FCIAT 2001, *ibid*, Art 4(1) and (2).

[168] FCIAT 2001, *ibid*, at p 1 [emphasis added].

[169] Amnesty International, 'Arms Flows and International Law: the G8 must also obey the rules', *The Terror Trade Times Issue No 3* (June 2002) p 1.

[170] Gabelnick, 'Conventional Arms Control in the Asia-Pacific Region: The Case for a Supply-Side Regime on International Law' *Federation of American Scientists* (October 2001), paras 14 and 21, at <http://www.armslaw.org/hawaiipaper.html>

[171] *Ibid*, para 31.

[172] Scoblic, 'Illuminating Global Interests: the UN and Arms Control' *Arms Control Today* (September/October 1999).

[173] For details see above, n 168.

the Code under the title 'commitment to promote regional peace, security and stability', laid down the conditions under which arms transfer should only be conducted. The relevant conditions are as follows: as stated in sub-paragraph (a) of Article 8, transfers can be carried out if the recipient state 'is not involved in armed conflict in the region'. The exception to this are measures that fall under self-defence, which are recognised or mandated by the UN under the Charter. Secondly, as per sub-paragraph (f) of the provision in issue, weapons can only be transferred if the destination state is not engaged in armed actions, which might lead to displacement of people or refugees.

Finally, according to Article 9(a) and (c), transfers are not legal if the destination state does not have adequate commitment against international terrorism. This could be assessed by ratification of treaties on terrorism and their practical implementation. It can also be measured by ensuring that a certain state does not harbour terrorists. These and other conditions need to be fulfilled cumulatively for a valid legal transfer, as specifically indicated in the chapeau of section II of the Code. Section III of the Code provides implementation mechanisms, some of which calls the incorporation of the Code into national laws and into formulating an international monitoring framework.

The ICCAT has been endorsed and welcomed by various NGOs and eminent persons. For example, American Friends Committee, Amnesty International, Arias Foundation for Peace and Human Rights, the Council on Economic Priorities and Saferworld have endorsed it as a remedy for the proliferation.[174] Also, former US President Jimmy Carter expressed his support by stating: (1) such endeavour is a 'critically important step toward defining a moral benchmark' to which all states in the world have to comply; and (2) the Carter Centre's Council of Freely Elected Heads of States, after the conclusion of its consultations on 20 May 1997 has called the states in America to sign the ICCAT.[175]

In sum, the Draft Convention and the Code of Conduct initiated by peace activists, with full involvement of NGOs and the support of international law experts, have been major contributions to the endeavours to codify and elaborate customary norms on transfer of arms. Evidently, armed conflicts, threats or breaches of the peace, regional security and international terrorism are explicitly taken as criteria, although with varied degrees of emphasis. Such situations should result in a prohibition of transfers of small arms. These two instruments focus on the obligations of exporting states. The Draft Convention is purported to be a treaty on SALW, the Code governs all conventional munitions and seeks to be signed by states. It is not

[174] See, eg for NGOs support, at <http://www.basicint.org/WT/armsexp/codes.htm#International%20Code>

[175] The Carter Centre, *A Letter to the Peace Laureates, May 20, 1997,* Signed by Jamey Carter, at <http://www.basicint.org/WT/armsexp/carter.pdf>

clear whether the NGOs intended it to be a treaty or a political declaration. Though these drafts have marked important progress on the arms trade regime, their actual impact on restricting transfers of SALW remains to be seen. What is clear in arms control issues is that NGOs have the ability 'to improve the political climate', disseminate information, provide technical expertise, and to 'influence the position of governments'.[176] In the SALW issue in particular, NGOs 'will continue to be essential actors',[177] in strengthening the SALW transfer legal regime, as has been reiterated in the UN PoA of 2001.[178]

The views of writers should now be discussed. Analysis of the peace and security norm as a condition for the small arms trade is rare in the works of publicists. Some have made valuable endeavours. To Gillard for instance, 'it is well established that an accumulation of weapons has destabilising effects' and can 'amount to a threat of use of force in violations of the Charter'. This situation 'imposes responsibilities upon both importing and exporting states to limit the quantity of imports'.[179] If arms transfers are conducted with an aggressor state, as adopted in the FCIAT, it is deemed that both the importing and exporting states are violating international law. The latter are considered as participants in the illegal conduct of the receiving state[180] (see further chapter nine). She identified a list of core prohibitions. Use of force and terrorist activities are the only conditions she put forward[181] as far as peace and security is concerned. The focus of Gillard is on the quantitative legal limitation on SALW transfer, considering their use against certain international norms.

It is not clear whether Gillard intends to exclude those internal and regional conflicts, which might not fall under the issue of aggression. Gabelnick clearly excluded regional security as a factor to limit arms transfer. He pointed out, as has been shown above, that there is no such customary norm—rather a pure proposal, to be taken into account by states.[182]

In contrast, Anthony has identified the norms that have been developed out of multilateral, regional and national efforts on arms transfer limitations. He underlined that after the Cold War, one of the main objectives of arms transfer control regimes has aimed at conflict prevention and maintaining regional peace and stability. He has given several examples in support of his view; inter alia, 'regional stability has been a

176 Jasentuliyana, 'The Process of Achieving Effective Arms Control Law', in Dahlitz and Dicke, *The International Law of Arms Control and Disarmament: Proceedings of the Symposium, Geneva* (New York, United Nations, 1991) 197.

177 *SAS 2002*, p 218.

178 Above n 101, s I, para 16, s II, para 40, s III, para 2, and s IV, para 2(c).

179 Gillard, above n 122, at p 5, para 22 at <http://www.armslaw.org>

180 *Ibid*, para 23.

181 *Ibid*, p 14, para 55.

182 Above n 170.

central issue for the Wassenaar Arrangement since it was established in 1995'.[183]

To date, it is firm practice of the UN, especially the SC, that regional security problems constitute a threat to the peace. The DC guidelines, a number of regional and national laws and policies have duly considered this factor as a criterion for purposes of SALW transfer. Adopting a restrictive approach to international peace, in regard of arms transfer appears to be ill founded. Regional security issues and other social and political impacts of SALW transfer must be duly separated from one another. In this account, the view of Anthony seems to be satisfactory.

5.7 THE PEACE AND SECURITY NORM

Two correlated problems arise concerning the peace and security legal norm. The first is whether the obligation of states to maintain international peace and security includes SALW transfer. There seems to be no simple answer to the problem. As Gillard pointed out, 'the UN Charter neither expressly prohibits nor permits the use or transfer of any specific weapon'.[184] This leads to the question of whether or not states are at liberty to import-export SALW. Some general discussion on the freedom of action of states vis-à-vis general international law obligations could give us a better understanding.

The ICJ, in the *Nuclear Weapons Advisory Opinion* concluded that 'customary or conventional international law' has not provided 'any specific authorisation' or 'any comprehensive universal prohibition' of the threat or use of nuclear weapons. Even so, their use or threat is subject to Article 2(4) of the Charter and IHL norms and prohibitions.[185] As Falk observed, the Court favoured the 'soft *Lotus*' approach, that is to say, state's freedom of action must be limited upon 'the consent of the state or the application of legal rules and principles to the context of actual use'. Alternatively, the view that 'whatever is not explicitly forbidden to a state is permitted', which is also known as the 'hard *Lotus*' approach has not been adopted by the majority of judges.[186] Indeed, Judge Shahabuddeen, in his dissenting opinion argued that:

> There is not any convincing ground for the view that the '*Lotus*' Court moved off on a supposition that States have an absolute sovereignty that would entitle

[183] Anthony, 'Decision Making Procedure for Export Controls: relevance to small arms', in Dahinden et al, above n 93, at 78; see also Shaw, *International Law*, 5th edn (Cambridge, Cambridge University Press, 2003) 1043.

[184] Above n 51, at 35–36.

[185] *Legality of the Threat or Use of Nuclear Weapons, ICJ Repts* 1996, para 105(2)(b) and (2)(d).

[186] See also Falk, 'Nuclear Weapons, International Law and the World Court: A Historic Encounter' (1997) 91 *AJIL* 66, 91 [emphasis added]; see also *ibid, Declaration* of Judge Bedjaowi, paras 12–16.

> them to do anything however horrid or repugnant to the sense of the international community, provided that the doing of it could not be shown to be prohibited under international law.[187]

He added:

> However far-reaching may be the rights conferred by sovereignty, those rights cannot extend beyond the framework within which sovereignty itself exists; in particular, they cannot violate the framework. The framework shuts out the right of a State to embark on a course of action which would dismantle the basis of the framework.[188]

Other jurists appear to appreciate the soft *Lotus* approach also. Cassese underlined that 'the unrestricted freedom of states has been subjected to increasing qualification since the First World War'. Increased level of international obligations in various fields, the restraint on the use of force and the emergence of *jus cogens* norms have assured such qualification.[189] Shaw acknowledges the fact that the freedom of action of states only 'exists within and not outside the international legal system and it is international law which dictates the scope and content' of rights or actions 'and not the states themselves individually and unilaterally'.[190]

It could be argued in our case, that the obligation of states to refrain from destabilising international peace and security applies to every weaponry legal regime,[191] including small arms transfer. Certain analogous weaponry legal regimes will be considered later. The SC as a supreme guardian of such responsibility, and the GA as a multilateral forum for states, have frequently referred to SALW transfers, along with other weapons, in their efforts to maintain the peace and security objective.[192] Particularly, as considered earlier, the GIAT of 1996 adopted the notion that SALW transfer could be limited upon the norms and purposes of the UN Charter.[193] Generally, the peace and security norm applies to small arms transfer and thus states are not at liberty to conduct such transactions contrary to the norm.

While this reality alone might not tell the existence or otherwise of a *specific* peace and security norm on the small arms trade, it is a necessary benchmark to look at the rule of law which governs the transfer of arms.

The second problem is that treaties are scarce on the subject and so custom must be examined. Whether state practice, accompanied by *opinio*

[187] *Dissenting Opinion of Judge Shahabuddeen*, Nuclear Weapons, p 11, at <http://www.icj-cij.org/icjwww/icases/iunan/iunanframe.htm>

[188] *Ibid.*

[189] Cassese, *International Law* (Oxford, Oxford University Press, 2001) 11–12; see also Allott, *The Health of Nations: Society and Law beyond the State* (Oxford, Oxford University Press, 2002) 300–01.

[190] Shaw, above n 183, at 190.

[191] Gillard, above n 122; see, eg on the use or threat of nuclear weapons, ch 1.

[192] See, eg 4.2.1 and 5.2.

[193] Above, n 88.

juris,[194] (see 3.4) has emerged on the matter as a factor for restriction depends on appropriate analysis of the practices that we went through.

The element of constant and uniform usage[195] is considered first. It is sensible to start with practices at the global level. The SC has consistently imposed arms embargoes, including SALW, in no less than nine cases. All prohibitions embrace any transactions of small arms, including state authorised ones. Internal strife, regional instability and international terrorism were some of the overriding grounds that have constituted a threat to peace and security. The Council has been doing this, thinking that arms shall not be sent to nations and regions of conflict and gross IHRs and IHL violations / abuses. It has been repeatedly stated that transfer of weapons in breach of the embargoes by themselves constitutes a threat to peace. Apart from its decisions on case-by-case bases, it has taken the position, on many occasions, that arms transfers to problem areas cause instability and insecurity. It may be argued that such transfers are a threat to peace only if they are so determined by the Council. As the Council is constituted by states, particularly of those highly interested in SALW supplies, it appears to be logical to value its deeds as part of state practice within the UN system. It will be explained further in the generality element of state practice. Similarly, resolutions of the GA, particularly the two guidelines, concerning arms transfer have clearly established the link between peace and security and the arms trade to conflict zones. The need for restraint of transfers by states has been endorsed as a solution. Although the guidelines and resolutions are political declarations of states and not binding instruments per se, they connote state practice and norms on transfers.[196] As will be elaborated, 'resolutions may be binding if they reflect rules of customary international law'.[197]

Moreover, the GGE 1997 factors regarding the phenomena of destabilising and excessive availability of SALW, such as the unregulated availability of weapons; the use of them in conflict and in violation of international norms; the absence of adequate restraint on transfers by importing and exporting states and other circumstances in the recipient state or region of arms,[198] may constitute part of the peace and security standards for weapon transfers (see 7.2.1). As Brownlie thought, we have to bear in mind that international organisations are 'channels for expert opinion' on various legal problems. Such opinions are also 'highly influential'.[199]

[194] For details on elements of custom, see ch 3, 3.4; see also Brownlie, *Principles of Public International Law*, 5th edn (Oxford, Oxford University Press, 1998) 1–4; see also Brownlie, *Principles of Public International Law*, 6th edn (Oxford, Oxford University Press, 2003) 6.

[195] See ch 7, p 226*ff*.

[196] On SC's practice see 5.2; see also n 206; see also 5.3; for the guidelines and the role of multilateral organisations on custom creation see 6.3.

[197] Shaw, *International Law*, 4th edn (Cambridge, Cambridge University Press, 1997) 831.

[198] Above, n 94.

[199] Brownlie, above n 194, at 663.

Regional and security organisations have further widened the practice and clarified the norm in question. The EU, OSCE, the West African states and the Wassenaar Arrangement have all recognised the need to limit small arms transfers by states as a concern of peace and security. States 'shall not' therefore transfer such arms when there is 'a clear risk' that they will be deployed against peace and security. Although the instruments are dominantly political, they have shown exporting and importing states' commitment to stem the flow of weapons into countries and regions of tension. The ECOWAS Convention's robust prohibitions have to be borne in mind here. One common element of all these instruments is that countries have agreed to incorporate the criteria in discussion into their national laws and policies.[200] In particular, significant EU exporter states have done this. Some European major suppliers have not taken such clear steps, as is the case of Russia.[201] Other major exporters of SALW such as the US and China have incorporated the peace and security rule into their domestic legislation.[202]

One may question the consistency and uniformity of the norm in discussion, because of the contraventions of arms embargoes and other restrictions on SALW transfer.[203] As the ICJ in the *Nicaragua* case made clear, such breaches could not disprove the reality of the peace and security norm on the trade in small arms. Also, a norm of customary law does not require absolute conformity on the part of each state with the practice in discussion (see chapter seven).[204] It appears to be that consistent and repeated state practice has been apparent concerning the peace and security based restriction on small arms transfer.

The second factor for norms is the generality[205] of a practice. For instance, the SC 'acts on behalf of the members of the organization as a whole in performing its functions and decisions',[206] and so, its arms embargoes represent all UN Member States; the UN PoA is a consensus document of States[207]; the GIAT of 1996 is also a consensus instrument of the DC[208]; the EU, OSCE, Wassenaar and African instruments[209] reflect state practice of both supplier and recipient states on the SALW trade in respect of peace and security. The generality element is thus reasonably satisfied.

[200] See, eg 5.4.
[201] See 5.5.
[202] *Ibid*.
[203] See, eg above, nn 61, and 141.
[204] See ch 7, p 228.
[205] See ch 3, p 75.
[206] See, eg Shaw, *International Law*, 4th edn, above n 198, at 827.
[207] See ch 3, p 57.
[208] Above, n 88.
[209] See 5.4.

Thirdly, although there is no a rigid duration required for the formation of such a custom, the efforts in question have been carried out for more than a decade.[210]

Therefore, the state practice we have seen in global and regional organisations is of immense importance here. To Brownlie, international organisations are forums for state practice and their practice in such forums 'provide evidence of customary law'.[211] Although their resolutions may not be binding by themselves, 'the mere formulation of principles may elucidate and develop the customary law'.[212] Resolutions on new legal challenges also 'provide a means of corralling and defining the quickly growing practice of states'.[213]

Furthermore, Shaw has indicated that resolutions 'are significant as instances of state practice that may lead to the formation of a new customary rule'. He goes on to state that:

> [T]here is no doubt that the contribution to international law generally made by the increasing number and variety of international organisations is marked. In many fields, the practice of international organisations has had an important effect and one that is often not sufficiently appreciated. State practice within such organisations is an increasingly significant element within the general process of customary law formation.

This is the case in the law of arms control too.[216] The views of publicists on this will be assessed.

Consequently, all factors for state practice on peace and security vis-à-vis the small arms trade appear to be satisfied. State practice in various forums and levels, including domestic laws and policies has so attested.

Yet, has the *opinio juris* element of custom[217] been duly established? Again, this question will take us to the practice we have gone through. Globally, for instance, the UN panels have suggested the need for full compliance of states with the DC guidelines on transfers.[218] In particular the 1999 GGE Panel has ascertained that states had been reporting their compliance with the guidelines, as expressly shown in section II(11) of the UN PoA. Moreover, states have demonstrated their intention to assess export authorisation of SALW in accordance with their 'existing responsibilities' under international law.[219]

[210] See ch 7, p 228.
[211] Above, n 199.
[212] *Ibid.*
[213] *Ibid.*
[214] Above, n 198.
[215] *Ibid,* at 908, for the role of the EU and the OSCE in particular, see pp 895–904.
[216] See ch 7, p 296.
[217] Above, n 194.
[218] Above, n 96.
[219] Above, n 101.

The same spirit of legal obligation is found in regional and security organisations. The WA,[220] the ECOWAS Moratorium (transformed into a Convention),[221] and the EUJA[222] have specifically given assurances that the restriction in question needs to be adopted in national laws and principles. The Joint Action (EUJA) is a legally binding instrument and this should be borne in mind. Above all, the EU Code of Conduct, in Criteria 1(a) and (b) entertained the importance of limiting small arms transfers 'consistent with international law obligations of Member States'. The debates to promote the Code into a legally binding instrument might also give some clues on the official belief of several states. The OSCE's Document on small arms has been introduced, as reflected in section III(1) of the Document, with the intention of setting out 'the norms and principles' on SALW transfers.

At the national level, the EU Code Criteria, which includes the peace and security factor, has spread out into the legislation and policies of several Member States.[223] The McKinney Rohrabacher Code of Conduct on arms transfers has been considered by the US Congress as an adequate instrument to initiate negotiations for purposes of multilateral treaty on the subject. The President of the US has accordingly been ordered to do so.[224]

Even so, the existence of *opinio juris* on the norm in discussion could be questioned. For example, the EU Code, in Criteria 1 adopted the wording 'should be refused' and not 'shall be refused',[225] to indicate the commitment of Member States on the small arms trade. It may be interpreted to show non-legal commitment. Additionally, the qualifying phrase 'on case-by-case-bases'[226] for the peace and security criterion may weaken the global or regional dimension. As prominent writers on the small arms issue strongly felt, although 'many governments were previously inclined to permit exports unless their illegality is proved', there is an explicit 'reversal of the burden of proof' in the practices and policies of many eastern and central European governments that they 'are increasingly willing to deny export licenses unless their legality is established'.[227]

Taking into consideration, inter alia, peace and security and humanity objectives of international law, the Secretary-General of the Conference on Disarmament had pointed out in 1991 that 'a flexible, non-restrictive interpretation of new initiatives, arrangements, consensus documents, declarations, understandings, and agreed practices, including those

[220] Above, n 111.
[221] Above, n 123.
[222] Above, nn 124–28.
[223] Above, n 135.
[224] Above, n 149.
[225] Above, n 128.
[226] Above, n 130; see also Marsh, above n 157, at 220.
[227] *SAS 2003*, p 120.

related to disarmament, is needed'.[228] This means that contemporary international law of arms control need not necessarily adhere to 'conservative interpretation and definition of sources of international law'.[229] The aforesaid doubts and others could hence only show the problem of collective enforcement and not the absence of *opinio juris* on the norm at hand.

Also, most publicists and NGOs, who are working on the small arms problem, have acknowledged the validity of the peace and security customary norm versus SALW transfers. All the same, there seems to be lack of clarity regarding the wider reach of the norm among publicists and in some works of NGOs, as discussed in previous sections.[230]

For purposes of comparison, similar notions of restriction exist in major conventional armaments and non-proliferation of nuclear weapons. The Treaty on Conventional Arms Forces in Europe (hereafter 'the CFE Treaty') of 19 November 1990, in paragraphs 5 and 6 of the Preamble have aimed, inter alia, at preventing 'any military conflict in Europe' and achieving 'greater stability and security' in the continent.[231] In view of that, as stated in Article II(A), (B), and (C) of the CFE Treaty, States Parties have agreed that they shall not arm themselves with more than 20,000 battle tanks, 30,000 armoured combat vehicles and 20,000 pieces of artillery. To Koulik et al, this arrangement operates on the basis of 'the sufficiency rule', which is intended to allow countries to have adequate weapons for self-defence purposes, 'but to prevent any one country from having a military potential which might pose a threat to another alliance'.[232] This could be comparable to the need to arrest the excessive and destabilising availability of small arms.

Some of the objectives of the Treaty on the Non-Proliferation of Nuclear Weapons ('NPT') of 1970, as shown in paragraphs 12 and 13 of the Preamble of the NPT are 'to further the easing of international tension', and the 'maintenance of international peace and security'. For that reason, Article I obliges all states with nuclear weapons, 'not to transfer to any recipient . . . nuclear weapons or other nuclear explosive devices'. Similarly, Article II has imposed an obligation upon non-nuclear states, 'not to receive the transfer from any transferor' of such weapons. Enshrined in Article IV(2) of the Treaty, transfers of equipment or technology, 'or the peaceful use of nuclear energy' is explicitly permitted and even encouraged.[233] Nevertheless, States Parties to the Convention on

[228] Komatina, 'Address Delivered at the Formal Plenary Session' in Dahlitz and Dicke (eds), above n 176, at 33–34.

[229] *Ibid.*

[230] See 5.2; see also 5.6.

[231] *The Treaty on Conventional Arms Forces in Europe*, Paris, 19 November 1990.

[232] Koulik and Kokoski, *Conventional Arms Control: Perspectives on Verification* (Oxford, Oxford University Press, 1994) 25.

[233] See also ch 1, p 7.

the Physical Protection of Nuclear Material of 1980, being inspired, inter alia, by 'the potential dangers posed by the unlawful taking and use of nuclear material' as has been stated in paragraph 3 of the preamble, have agreed to impose restrictions on the transfers of 'nuclear material used for peaceful purposes'. Article 4(1) and (2) of the Convention prohibit any export or import of nuclear material 'unless the State Party has received assurance that such material will be protected' in the course of transfers. As illustrated in Annex 1 3.L (a), the protection includes complying with the laws and regulations of both exporting and importing states of the material in question.[234]

Although this Convention has focused on technical aspects of protection, it has specifically been intended 'to reduce the risk of diversion of nuclear material to non-peaceful purposes'.[235] In general, the nuclear weapons or material transfers issue seems to be analogous to the small arms problem in two respects. First, the former as the latter is of a dual-use nature; and secondly, the nuclear weapon or material transfer issue considers the peace and security factor and the non-proliferation remedy.[236] The major difference between the two appears to be that the nuclear weapons or material regime has achieved global verification framework for its enforcement. The International Atomic Energy Agency (IAEA) for example oversees the implementation of such treaties.[237]

5.8 CONCLUSIONS

From earlier discussions, five remarks have been identified which summarised the points made on peace and security. The first remark, the norm of the maintenance of international peace and security, as general conventional and customary norm of international law applies to the small arms transfers issue. It may not, however, render a particular norm on such activities.

Secondly, it seems that states, including major exporters, have demonstrated state practice and *opinio juris* in the SC, the GA, regional organisations, and to some extent, in their domestic systems, to restrict SALW transfers, with the aim of preventing and/or non-aggravating international peace and security problems. It ought to be emphasised here that those states that are not party to the Mines Convention may well be duty-bound to comply with this rule of customary law.

234 *Convention on the Physical Protection of Nuclear Material*, entered into force 8 February 1987. As of 12 March 2002, 74 states are parties to the Convention.

235 Zaleski, above n 93, at 33.

236 *Ibid*, at 33–34.

237 See, eg the *NPT*, above n 233, Preamble, para 5; see also n 234, Art 5.

The features of this customary rule are: (a) the actual or potential use of small arms in inter-state, intra-state conflicts and international terrorist activities, and the destabilising accumulation of such weapons have constituted the core essence of the prohibition. Regional instability has also formed part of the rule. However, factors such as international crimes and other similar impacts of the trade in small arms do not seem to constitute the norm in question. (b) Various tests have been widely adopted to apply the rule, inter alia, evident use of SALW in conflicts, the excessive and destabilising diffusion of such weapons in destination, motives of weapon importing states and their foreign policy, records of compliance of weapon recipient states with their international peace and security obligations and arms control commitments, possibilities of diversion of end-uses and end-users, the absence or otherwise of effective control over small arms transfers, and whether or not a state supports or encourages terrorism. These indicators, either cumulatively or otherwise, may constitute an apparent risk of the illegal use of SALW. It has been reiterated in state practice that restrictive arms export criteria have to be employed by states. Yet, the application of the tests fully depends on the circumstances of each case. (c) The norm gave much more emphasis to the supply side of the challenge. Arms supplier states are therefore particularly required to refrain from such transfers, whenever there is a clear risk of the use of SALW against international peace and security (see further 'IHL'). (d) With the exception of the Mines Convention, the limitations are all quantitative in nature. And (e) although some countries only regulate commercial military small arms, the developments highlighted undoubtedly show that all transfers, either aid or sales are subject to such a rule of transfer. In addition, the scope of small arms covered by the norm seems to be imprecise. Some considered military small arms alone and others all weapons, as a subject to the restriction in issue. Manifestly, there seems to be a consensus on military type SALW, as a package. Although the civilian SALW have not been included in national or regional arrangements, the dominant position at the international level shows inclusion of civilian firearms in the peace and security arena (see further chapter two).

All these *may* reflect the customary norm on SALW transfers. It is noteworthy that this peace and security norm is also found in other arms control measures, most notably in nuclear material and nuclear weapons transfers' regime.

Even so, on appropriate appreciation of the complexity of the determination of a threat to the peace, the massive flows of weapons to conflict areas by states and their reluctance to enter into binding agreements, and if one adopts a conservative approach to custom creation, it can also reasonably be argued that the aforementioned claim is just emerging, and so states' obligations are limited to regional treaties and mandatory arms embargoes (eg UN, EU, ECOWAS). Arms suppliers or recipient states may also consider the peace and security criterion if they wish to. Due to the reasons discussed earlier (see 5.7) and recent developments in the field, however, this does not appear more persuasive than the former claim.

Thirdly, neither the general norm nor the specific norm under consideration deny the right of a state to supply or receive small arms for legal purposes, inter alia, for self-defence, national security and participation in peacekeeping operations. States are permitted to supply and/or import small arms for *reasonable* uses and *legal* purposes, in accordance with domestic and international standards; their legitimate security and economic interests must also be respected as sovereign rights under international law.[238] Violations of the general or specific norm could not be justified by abuses of these rights (see chapter nine). The application of the norm and its exceptions shall thus consider the overall circumstances of each transfer and destination. Yet, the need to strengthen, refine and develop the detail tests/factors for the rule must be left to the progressive development of international law (see ICRC indicators in 'IHL'). Finally, a contravention of this norm may lead to state responsibility of both a supplier and an importer state (see chapter nine).[239]

[238] See, eg *Judge Bedjaoui*, in his dissenting opinion, in the *Case Concerning Fisheries Jurisdiction (Spain v Canada)* of 1998 entertained the view that in order to resolve the dispute arising from the legislation of Canada regarding the conservation and management measures on the high seas and the rights of third states, the 'economic logic and legal logic have to combine—and indeed do so in all international instruments—in order to avoid the *chaos both of uncontrolled over fishing and of illegal regulation.* Compatibility with international law is an integral part of the international definition of conservation and management measures', at <http://www.icj-cij.org/icjwww/idocket/iec/iecframe.htm>, para 29 [emphasis mine]; see also Cassese, above n 189, at 11. While he accepted the restriction on states' freedom of action, however, he recognised that: 'the legal order [international law] adopted a *laissez-faire* attitude, thereby leaving an enormous field of action to individual states'.

[239] See also the *Draft Articles*, p 120, Art 1.

6

Adherence to the Non-intervention Norm

AS CONSIDERED IN the general norms section above, inter alia, Article 2(1) of the UN Charter has recognised the sovereign rights of states on an equal basis. This right imposes a corresponding obligation upon all states to respect the sovereignty of any other state. In this regard, the principles of sovereignty and non-intervention are well-established norms with which all states have to comply in their international relations. This is also true in arms transfers, as any direct or indirect interference of any kind in domestic affairs of a state is forbidden under international law (see further 4.2.1).[1]

Considering the peculiar features of SALW (see chapter two), their adverse effects upon national security and stability, the political affairs of a state (see chapter five), and a state's inherent legislative and executive powers over imports, sales and use of weapons in its own territory, a wider approach has been adopted in respect of the principle of non-intervention based restriction upon arms transfers,[2] save certain exceptions to the rule (see 6.2). While it's not the main concern here, *consensual* transfers of weapons among states may not always be in compliance with the non-intervention rule (see 6.3, 6.4).

Although there may be no doubt on the application of the principle in question to the SALW transfers, the central concern of this section is whether the principle of non-intervention is embodied into the SALW legal regime, at the level of a rule of transfer. This may generate two different but related questions; first, should transfers be limited to state-to-state transactions? If yes, what could be the content of this particular rule? And second, is there any 'exception' to this rule? The next section deals with the first question.

[1] See, eg ch 4, p 92.
[2] *Ibid.*

6.1 TRANSFERS ONLY BY AND TO GOVERNMENTS OF STATE

At first, questions relating to the scope of applicable law and actors relative to the problem have to be briefly considered. As defined in 4.1.1 above, the legality of arms transfers may be seen in the light of conformity with relevant domestic and/or international law. Certainly, the vast majority of states restrict, and require authorisation for, the possession, use, domestic sales and import-export of weapons.[3] Though transfers of small arms in violation of such domestic laws and regulations are illegal and mostly serve as evidences of a breach of the norm under consideration,[4] the reach and emphasis of this work has been founded on the norm of non-intervention.

The actors involved in these controversial transactions are governments and NSAs. Governments here are agents and constituents of states, with a capacity to enter into international relations, as evolved in customary international law.[5] By contrast, for the purposes of this section and as shown in the Canadian proposal, any group, entity or an individual, who fully operates outside the machinery of a state, could generally be regarded as NSA; broadly it includes: (1) armed opposition groups that resist their governments; (2) criminal or terrorist organisations; (3) legal or natural persons engaged in arms business; (4) national liberation movements (hereafter 'NLMs'); (5) special territories of international law; and (6) inter-governmental organisations (IGOs).[6]

Bearing in mind the concern of the international community and the nature of the actors, the primary focus of this section will be on categories 1, 2 and 3, the details of which will be addressed later.[7] It has to be noted that any direct or indirect SALW transfers by governments have been deemed as acts of states (see 4.1.1). IGOs and their missions are fully

[3] See, eg *The United Nations International Study on Firearms Regulation* 1998, pp 9–11.

[4] Mathiak and Lumpe, 'Government Gun-Running to Guerrillas' in Lumpe, *Running Guns: The Global Black Market in Small Arms* (London, Zed Books, 2000) 54.

[5] Shaw, *International Law*, 5th edn (Cambridge, Cambridge University Press, 2003) 181; see also Brownlie, *Principles of Public International Law*, 6th edn (Oxford, Oxford University Press, 2003) 71; see also Shaw, *International Law*, 4th edn (Cambridge, Cambridge University Press, 1997) 140; see also *Western Sahara Advisory Opinion, ICJ Repts* 1975, paras 23–74, pp 12, and 43–44.

[6] 'A Proposed Global Convention Prohibiting the International Transfer of Military Small Arms and Light Weapons to Non-state Actors' Canadian Discussion Paper, Canadian Mission to the UN, New York, December 1998, para 14; see also 'Rebel Groups and Weapons: Limiting the Damage' *Hd Bulletin*: Small Arms and Human Security No 3 (June 2004) p 1; see also *Small Arms Survey 2002: Counting the Human Cost* (Oxford, Oxford University Press) 129; for other subjects of international law in general see Cassese, *International Law* (Oxford, Oxford University Press, 2001) 66–85; see also Arts, Noortmann, and Reinalda, *Non-State Actors in International Law* (Gateshead, Athenaeum Press, 2001) 1; see also ECOWAS Convention on Small Arms, 2006, Art 1 (10); any actor other than states is considered to be a NSA.

[7] For NSAs 4–5 see 6.2.1.

excluded from consideration, in order to concentrate on the major problems.

In this section, the relevance of the norm in discussion to the SALW trade and such rule-based responses of states to the problem will be established, with emphasis on the latter. As two of them are intimately related, they will be discussed jointly.

6.1.1 Global Efforts

Valuable treaties and draft conventions have been negotiated to regulate the transfers of weapons, including SALW, during the League period (see 3.3.1 and 7.2.2). It is of note that 'The Draft Convention for the Control of the International Trade in Arms, Ammunitions and Implements of War' of 1925, under Article 2(1) of Chapter II, underlined that the export of armaments, inter alia, machine guns, automatic rifles, mortars, grenades and machine pistols of all kinds 'shall be for direct supply to Government of the importing State or, with the consent of such government, to a public authority subordinate to it'. Exceptionally, however, Article 3(1) of the same Chapter permits the export of these weapons to arms industries, provided that 'their import has been duly authorised by the Government of the importing country'.[8]

In a different way, Article 5 of the instrument has set out the rule that weapons such as 'pistols and revolvers', 'firearms designed, intended or adopted for non-military purposes, such as sport or personal defence', 'swords and lances', 'shall only be exported' upon a licence to be issued 'by the competent authorities of exporting country'. Nonetheless, if the 'legislation of the importing country requires the endorsement of a duly authorised representative of its Government' for arms imports, the exporting state has to obtain an authorisation from the destination state, if it is so aware of the legislation. If 'the size, destination or other circumstances of a consignment', shows that such weapons 'are intended for war purposes', the restrictions of Articles 2 and 3 would apply to Article 5 transactions.[9]

The main purpose of such limitations, as shown in paragraph 2 of the Preamble of the Draft, does seem to promote transparency in arms transfers.[10] This Draft Convention was adopted by the League's Conference on the subject and signed by 22 states, which include a range of countries such as Abyssinia and the United States.[11] It did not come into force (see

[8] League of Nations, *Proceedings of the Conference for the Supervision of the International Trade in Arms and Ammunition and in Implements of War*, 4 May–17 June 1925, pp 32–40.

[9] *Ibid*.

[10] *Ibid*, at 8.

[11] *Ibid*, at 13.

7.2.2). As stated also in chapter five, the endeavours did not continue to address the question of arms transfers to NSAs.

In the UN era, there has been no global treaty which expressly incorporated the non-intervention rule. Sadly, the Firearms Protocol, under Article 4(2) says 'this protocol shall not apply to state-to-state transactions or to state transfers in cases where the application of the Protocol would prejudice the right of a State to take action in the interest of national security consistent with the UN Charter'. The negotiating history witnessed that some countries had rejected and others had expressed reservations on the national security exception.[12] India for instance registered a reservation saying that 'the exclusions as expressed in the drafting of Article 4 were so broadly defined'. It has suggested therefore that the 'exclusions in that paragraph must be viewed in narrow terms'.[13] Prima facie, the view to exclude state-to-state transfers, from the ambit of the Protocol has prevailed. The reference to the UN Charter was suggested by the US as a compromise in the context of sharp differences among states.[14]

Although the reference to the Charter is something positive, as reiterated in various sections, the Protocol's interest is restricted to NSAs and transnational boundary crimes. As there is not a single phrase in the entire Protocol which considers the non-intervention norm in the course of arms transfers, it does not appear to be clear whether the exclusion of state transfers is an exception. Therefore, the instrument could not solve the question we are trying to address.

Other global efforts, such as resolutions of the GA and the SC, the DC guidelines, the UN panels, the UN Conference and the PoA, and the Canadian proposed Convention have specifically dealt with the issue. The factual circumstances have been grouped into six categories.

The first regards GA and SC Resolutions on the relevance of the duty of non-intervention to arms transfers. Section I(4) of GA Resolution 55/2 of 2000 has declared the determination of Member States, on 'the sovereign equality of all states, respect for their territorial integrity and political independence'. In view of that, as stated in paragraph 10 of section II(9), they agreed, inter alia, 'to take concrete action to end illicit traffic' in SALW. This includes the measures to be defined by the UN Conference on Small Arms.[15] We shall come to the details of the Conference later. Furthermore, the SC has reiterated the pertinence of the non-intervention obligation to arms flows against the sovereignty and integrity of a state. Among others, the Council reaffirmed the sovereignty and territorial

[12] *SAS 2002*, above n 6, at 240.
[13] See, eg *Press Release*, GA/9866, 31 May 2001; see also *ibid*.
[14] *SAS 2002*, above n 6 at 238–39.
[15] The Resolution was entitled '*UN Millennium Declaration*'.

integrity of Iraq,[16] Somalia,[17] Bosnia Herzegovina,[18] the states in the Great Lakes Region[19] and Albania,[20] despite the imposition of arms embargoes against these states. Most notably, the Council highlighted in Resolution 1519/2003, under paragraph 3 that states, 'should not intervene in the internal affairs of Somalia', through the supply of SALW. On the contrary, although they may not show the prevalent practice of the Council, some arms embargoes, such as the case of Haiti[21] and Rwanda,[22] have not referred to the principle of non-intervention. Notably, in the context of civil war, while the Council imposed arms embargoes upon NSAs, it has never authorised or encouraged arms transfers to such actors (see 5.1).

Secondly, this category refers to the UN DC's two guidelines on conventional arms transfers. The GIAT, under paragraph 14 affirmed that: 'states should respect the principles and purposes of the Charter of the United Nations . . .; the sovereign equality of all its Members; non-interference in the internal affairs of States'. It went on to state, in paragraph 22 that 'international arms transfers should not be used as a means to interfere in the internal affairs of other States'. Even so, it is unclear whether the 1996 Guidelines advocate the notion that transfers shall only be conducted between states. As indicated in paragraph 33 of the Guidelines, it has emphasized reducing 'the possibility of diversion of arms to unauthorized destinations and persons',[23] and has not resolutely declared the prohibition of arms transfers to NSAs.

The GCAC has expressly touched the government-to-government transfers issue. Annex III paragraph 37, under the title 'national measures', propounded that:

> States considering measures to ensure that arms are exported only to Government of sovereign States, either directly or through duly licensed or authorised agencies acting on their behalf, are encouraged to draw upon already existing provisions in this field.[24]

Both guidelines have thus adopted the principles of sovereignty and non-intervention, concerning arms transfers. The second has given a clear indication that such transactions should be carried out between governments or their legally authorised entities only. The GA has adopted these efforts as considered previously[25] (see 5.3).

16 SC Res 688/1991, Preamble, para 7.
17 SC Res 794/1992; see also SC Res 1519/2003.
18 SC Res 836/1993, Preamble, paras 3 and 4, operative para 3.
19 SC Res 1080/1996, Preamble, para 4.
20 SC Res 1101/1997, Preamble, para 8.
21 SC Res 940/1994.
22 Res 929/1994.
23 UN Doc Supp No 42(A/51/42), 1996, Annex. 1.
24 UN Doc Supp No 42(A/54/52), 1999, Annex III.
25 GA Res 50/72 D/1996; see also Res 53/79 A/1998; see, eg part I, 1 (7).

As a third, the indications given by the UN panels on small arms in respect of the question of transfers to NSAs are worth examining. The 1997 Panel revealed in paragraph 51 of its report the fact that states engage themselves in covert transfer of arms to NSAs. It has also added that such transfer may not necessarily be illicit. When the transfer is made without the authorisation of the destination state, however, such transfers could be declared to be illegal by the latter state. As shown in paragraph 80(a) of its report, it has recommended the application of the principles of the 1996 DC Guidelines.[26] Here, the problem seems to be that it unclear on what grounds a transfer to NSAs may not be illegal.

The Report of the second Panel (Reviewing Panel) of 1999, as shown in paragraphs 74 and 75, expounded that several states have replied to the Secretary-General, in accordance with Resolutions 52/38 J and 53/77 E, the fact that they implement the guidelines. To the Panel, the elements of the guidelines are also reflected in the OSCE principles, the EU Code of Conduct, the OAS Convention, the ECOWAS Moratorium, the SADC Protocol and in the East Africa Co-operation initiative. The Panel praised the support to, and implementation of, the guidelines by states. It has stressed that full implementation of the guidelines by all Member States is still required.[27] Similarly, the 2001 GGE Panel on 'the feasibility of restricting the legal trade in small arms' accentuates the paramount importance of these guidelines to weapon transfers, as so pointed out under paragraph 61 of its report.[28]

The fourth category of facts is related to the UN Conference on SALW. The restriction in question was one of the contentious issues in the 2001 UN Conference on small arms. At the outset, the PrepCom of the UN Conference on Small Arms, in its Third Session (19–30 March 2001) had adopted a draft PoA (hereinafter 'DPoA'), which was circulated to states for comments. The draft under part II(13) advocates the view that states shall:

> '[S]upply small arms and light weapons only to governments, either directly or through entities authorised to procure arms on behalf of Governments.'[29]

Even so, sharp differences of view had been revealed in the meeting and negotiations, which led to the adoption of the final PoA. A majority of states from Europe, Africa and Canada have thought to expressly include the prohibition of transfers to NSAs. A joint EU-Canada position letter submitted to the PrepCom of the Conference said '[T]he EU and Canada

[26] GGE 1997, 27 August 1997.

[27] *Report of the Group of Governmental Experts on Small Arms*, 3 August 1999.

[28] *Feasibility of Restricting the Legal Trade*, 12 March 2001.

[29] *Draft Programme of Action to Prevent, Combat and Eradicate the Illicit Trade in Small Arms and Light Weapons in All Its Aspects (DPoA)*, Working Paper by the Chairman of the Preparatory Committee, 12 February 2001.

will promote international and regional efforts to ensure that small arms and light weapons are only transferred to states or state authorised entities'.[30] It has cross-referred to the purpose of transfers, which should only be for the self-defence needs of states[31] among other things. Additionally, Switzerland suggested that the PoA must express a commitment 'to supply arms and light weapons only to governments or entities duly authorised by Governments'.[32] The US, took a different view on the matter. In the words of John Bolton to the Conference:

> We do not support measures limiting trade in SA/LW solely to governments. This proposal, we believe, is both conceptually and practically flawed. It is so broad that in the absence of a clear definition of small arms and light weapons, it could be construed as outlawing legitimate international trade in all firearms. Violent non-state groups at whom this proposal is presumably aimed are unlikely to obtain arms through authorized channels. Many of them continue to receive arms despite being subject to legally binding UNSC embargoes. Perhaps most important, this proposal would preclude assistance to an oppressed non-state group defending itself from a genocidal government. Distinctions between governments and non-governments are irrelevant in determining responsible and irresponsible end-users of arms.[33]

Despite the above, the endorsed version of the PoA, in paragraph 8 of the Preamble shows that states have reaffirmed their 'respect for and commitment to . . . the *sovereign equality of States, . . ., non-intervention and non-interference in the internal affairs of States*'[34] [emphasis added]. For this and other reasons, participating states have recognised their primary responsibility 'for solving the problems associated with the illicit trade in small arms in all its aspects', as stated in part III(1) of the PoA. Due to the strong objection of the US, the proposal shown in part II(13) of the DPoA had been omitted both from the operative and preambular sections of the final PoA. It is of note that no state did advocate the US's position.[35]

The concluding statement of the President of the Conference could give a clearer picture in this regard; he stated:

> While congratulating all participants for their diligence in reaching this new consensus, I must, as President, also express my disappointment over the Conference's inability to agree, *due to a concern of one state*, on language

[30] *N Verbal dated 29 June 2000 from the Permanent Mission of Portugal to the UN addressed to the secretariat of the Preparatory Committee*, Annex, para 6.

[31] *Ibid*, para 7.

[32] *N Verbal dated 30 March 2001 from the Permanent Observer Mission of Switzerland to the UN addressed to the secretariat of the Preparatory Committee, transmitting working paper on the revised draft Programme of Action*, Annex II, s ii, para 13.

[33] *Statement by Bolton, United States Under Secretary of State for Arms Control and International Security Affairs*, UN Conference on SALW in All Its Aspects, Plenary, July 9, 2001, para 12, at <http://usinfo.state.gov/topical/pol/arms/stories/01070902.htm>.

[34] UN Doc Supp No A/CONF.192/15, 9–20 July 2001 [emphasis added].

[35] *SAS 2002*, above n 6, at 224–25.

> recognising . . . the need for preventing sales of such arms to non-state groups[36] [emphasis added].

In addition, the President made an historic remark on the disagreement that 'states of the region most affected by this global crisis, Africa', had come to consensus to the deletion of this and other issues with an extreme reluctance. African states 'did so strictly' in order to reach a compromise agreement; this will not, however, prevent them from pursuing their efforts to address the issues in the future.[37] As he has accurately pointed out, several states have continued their efforts to expressly forbid small arms transfers to NSAs, as had been observed in the UN BMS of 2003.[38]

Certain observations are worth noting in respect of the UN Conference's position on the problem. The first is that a majority of states were in support of the inclusion of the prohibition of transfers to NSAs; the second point is that the only objector was the US. The last is that the reasoning of the US considered, inter alia, the fact that violent non-state groups do not obtain arms through 'legal' transfers; the habitual violations of legally binding norms; the irrelevance of distinction between government and non-government for legitimate end uses of small arms and the concern of assisting armed resistance against oppression and genocide. The US distinction between violent and non-violent/responsible NSAs is difficult to understand. The US does not seem to have a problem regarding the first category; it is difficult however to envision a non-violent actor, which might need to arm itself without the authorisation of a state. Whether these arguments are widely accepted and well founded in international law, is something which will be explored further (see 6.1.3 and 6.3).

As a fifth fact in point, Canada's proposed global Convention of 1998 rejects some of the contentions of the US, with respect to the transit of arms to NSAs. Only a state, its agencies or other entities that are duly authorised to do so by a state shall be permitted to carry out such transactions, as specifically stated in paragraphs 13 and 14 of the Proposal. Thus, it has been intended to ban any transfers of military small arms to NSAs. An international transfer is widely defined in this proposal to also include sales, gifts or aid to NSAs.[39]

As stated in paragraph 15, the proposed Convention had envisaged certain criticisms of the kind made by the US. One of these was the notion that prohibitions of SALW to NSAs affect those who fight against their own repressive regimes, while the latter are at liberty to acquire such

[36] Above n 34, Annex. *Statement by the President of the Conference after the Adoption of the PoA*, p 23, para 2 [emphasis added].

[37] *Ibid*, para 3.

[38] See, eg Statement, *U Kyaw Tint Swe*, Permanent Representative of the Union of Myanmar to the UN, 18 July 2003, p 1, para 3.

[39] A Proposed Global Convention. above n 6.

weapons.[40] The commentary of this instrument has clarified Canada's views as below:

> Whatever the international law is with respect to this point, Canada, as a matter of policy, does not advocate the transferring of arms to opposition groups in order to overthrow unpopular regimes. It is doubtful, in our view, that the deliberate arming of non-state actors in order to effect political change is a viable option. If such a policy is applied, the inevitable result is that people will be killed, no matter what the politics of the situation may be. Prohibiting transfers of military small arms and light weapons to non-state actors must not, in our view, be interpreted as providing any right for States to acquire and use these weapons in any way they wish.[41]

The Proposal was delivered to a meeting of 21 states on small arms in 1998. It is important to emphasise that the British, German and Norwegian Governments had extended their express support to the proposal. The Russian Government has also shown some degree of support to the proposal. The US nonetheless strongly rejected the idea on the aforementioned grounds. EU Member States, in their Joint Action (EUJA) of 1998, have 'picked up' the principle embodied in the Canadian proposal, as will be elaborated. The draft had been criticised for excluding handguns, hunting rifles and shotguns from its ambit.[42]

As a sixth fact, section I(5) of the Wassenaar Best Practice Guide clearly stipulates that: '[P]articipating States will take *special care* when considering exports of SALW other than to governments or their authorised agents' [emphasis added].[43] It appears that transfers to NSAs are permitted to some extent. Whether this reflects the real position of all participating states or it is so for the interest of compromise and diplomacy, as it was the case in the UN Conference of 2001, will have to be seen along with regional practice, as the majority of OSCE and EU members have been taking part in the Wassenaar process. It has to be noted also that the Wassenaar states have banned any shoulder-fired missile transfers to NSAs.[44]

It is fair to draw the conclusion that the UN and other global practice have proved the fact that a majority of states, with the exception of the US, appear to be determined to apply the non-intervention principle to the SALW transfers issue in general, and to the prohibition of transfers to NSAs in particular. Conversely, the exclusion of specific prohibition from the actual measures section of the PoA signifies one major failure of this political instrument, as has been emphatically stated by the Chairman of

[40] *Ibid.*

[41] *Ibid,* paras 16 and 17; see also Gray, *International Law and the Use of Force,* 2nd edn (Oxford, Oxford University Press, 2004) 58

[42] Mathiak and Lumpe, above n 4, at 74.

[43] *Best Practice Guidelines for Export of Small Arms and Light Weapons,* Plenary of 11–12 December 2002 [emphasis added].

[44] See ch 5, pp 119–120.

the Conference. The 1999 UN Panel had also taken a lenient position on the issue. The Wassenaar arrangement's lax approach does not seem to be in favour of the ban in discussion. The implications of all these global practices to the formation of a rule of law will be dealt with below in 6.3. The responses of the international community to the problem may be stronger and clearer in forums other than the global forums.

6.1.2 Regional and National Efforts

Regional instruments and domestic systems have handled the issue with diverse emphasis and approach. First, as regional treaties, the OAS Convention,[45] the SADC[46] and Nairobi[47] protocols on firearms, and the ECOWAS Convention on small arms have reaffirmed the principles of sovereignty, non-intervention and of the territorial integrity of a state, in the context of the international trade in small arms. Article III of the OAS Convention asserts that:

> States Parties shall carry out the obligations under this Convention in a manner consistent with the principles of . . . and that of non-intervention in the domestic affairs of other states.

As a result, by virtue of Article IX(2) of the Convention:

> States Parties shall not permit the transit of firearms, ammunition, explosives, and other related materials until the receiving State Party issues the corresponding license or authorisation.

Further, sub-section (3) of the aforementioned provision affirms that 'States Parties, before releasing shipments of firearms. . .for export, shall ensure that the importing and in-transit countries have issued necessary licenses or authorisation'. For the Convention, 'illicit trafficking' of SALW includes non-authorised transfer of such weapons, by 'any one of the States Parties Concerned', as discussed in chapter four. In addition, Article 10(b) of the Nairobi Protocol of 2004 propounded that:

> Before issuing export license or authorisations for shipments of small arms and light weapons, each State party shall verify; (i) that the importing Sates have issued import licences or authorisation; and (ii) that, . . ., the States have, at a minimum, given notice in writing, prior to shipment, that they have no objection to the transit.

The Protocol has been signed by ten states of the sub-region and has not yet entered into force, as discussed in relation to the peace and security norm earlier.

[45] *OAS Convention on Firearms*, 1997, Preamble, para 13.
[46] *SADC Protocol on the Control of Firearms*, 2001, Art 2.
[47] *The Nairobi Protocol on SALW*, 2004, Preamble, para 9.

Conversely, the SADC Protocol is silent in adopting the specific rule under discussion, apart from reiterating the principle of non-intervention in its preamble. So far, it has been signed by 14 states of the sub-region.

Albeit Article 3(2) of the 2006 ECOWAS Convention asserts: 'Member States shall ban, without exception, transfers of small arms and light weapons to non-state actors that are not explicitly authorised by the importing state'. Despite that Art. 4 (1) states:

> A Member State can request exemption from the provisions of Article 3(b) in order to meet legitimate national defence and security needs, or to participate in peace support or other operations in accordance with the decisions of the United Nations, African Union, ECOWAS, or other regional or sub-regional body of which it is a member.

The exception regarding peace keeping or related operations is clear and explicable. While the 'national defence and security' parameter seems to be subject to decisions of global or regional organisations (as the exemption request is to be made to ECOWAS Secretariat), the practical side of it would not appear to be uncomplicated, as we shall later see.

Therefore, some regional treaties have adopted the rule that small arms import-export shall only be conducted on the will and full knowledge of destination, supplier and even transit states. The OAS Convention is significant, as it has been ratified by 16 states of the region.[48] The ECOWAS Convention came up with a robust and comprehensive ban on arms supplies to NSAs, but with one controversial exception, as discussed earlier.

Secondly, other regional instruments are of paramount value in clarifying the rule that prohibits the provision of arms to NSAs. To begin, the EUJA (as amended in 2002), under Article 3(b), has acknowledged the need for international and regional consensus on:

> A commitment by exporting countries to supply small arms only to governments (either directly or through duly licensed entities authorised to procure weapons on their behalf) in accordance with appropriate intentional and regional restrictive arms export criteria, as provided in particular in the EU Code of Conduct, including officially authorised end-use certificates.[49]

According to Criterion 7 of the EU Code, transfers should be denied if there is 'a risk that the equipment will be diverted within the buyer country' or 'export goods might be diverted to an undesirable end user'. Possibility of diversion of exports to terrorist groups has been particularly emphasised as a reason for refusal of export authorisation. Although the Code has not directly addressed the issue at hand, it could be assumed that the Code and the EUJA have to be mutually enforced, as indicated earlier. Criterion 1(a) of the Code has cross-referred to the OSCE commitments of Member States too.

[48] See ch 3, fn 5.

[49] *OJEC, No 2002/589/CFSP*, 19 July 2002; see also ch 3, fn 61.

The OSCE document, under section III(C)(1), took the position that no transfers of SALW were to be made, 'without an authenticated end-user certificate, or some other form of official authorisation . . . issued by the receiving State'.[50] As expressly stated in section VI(6), moreover, 'the norms, principles and measures in this document are politically binding' (see further 5.4). Although there were concerns of freedom of commerce of states,[51] the Criterion in issue has been adopted by the Participating States as a whole.

From the importers' viewpoint, African states have overtly tackled the difficulty. In 2000, African ministers came up with a common African position to the UN Conference on Small Arms, and strongly appealed to the international community—particularly to SALW supplying states—'to accept that trade in small arms should be limited to governments and authorised registered licensed traders'.[52] The ECOWAS Moratorium has also adopted fundamental principles of international law, including those incorporated in the OAU Charter.[53] The recent Convention is, however, very straightforward in its stance on the problem.

This position mirrors the perception of other developing counties. For example, the Latin American and Caribbean states, in their Brasilia Declaration on Small Arms of November 2000, expressed their 'unshakeable commitment to the basic norms of international law'; the 'non-intervention in the internal affairs of States', has been explicitly referred to.[54]

In sum, the rule of non-intervention has been incorporated into the OAS and ECOWAS Conventions, and other regional protocols. The EUJA, as a binding instrument,[55] has also given an indication that governments of states shall only be parties to transactions of SALW. Although not legally binding, the OSCE, EU, African and Latin American states' declarations have considered the relevance of the non-intervention principle to the small arms trade.

Finally, it is essential to explore the position of the laws and policies of some representative states such as France, China, India, and the US, regarding arms transfers and NSAs. According to Article 13(3) of the

[50] *OSCE Document on Small Arms and Light Weapons*, 24 November 2000.

[51] Dahinden, 'Meeting the Challenges of Small Arms Proliferation: example of the OSCE Document' in Dahinden et al, *Small Arms and Light Weapons: Legal Aspects of National and International Regulation*, (Geneva, United Nations, 2002) 9–10.

[52] *Bamako Declaration an African Common Position on the Illicit Proliferation, Circulation and Trafficking of SALW*, Bamako, Mali, 1 October 2000, paras 4(i) and 6.

[53] *West African Arms Moratorium*, Abuja, 31 October 1998, the Moratorium has referred to the *OAU Charter*. The latter emphatically incorporated the principles of sovereign equality, non-intervention and territorial integrity of a state in Arts II(1)(c), III(1), (2), and (3); see also ECOWAS Convention, Preamble, para 7, Arts 3 and 4.

[54] *Brasilia Declaration on the Illicit Trade in Small Arms and Light Weapons*, The Latin American and Caribbean States, Brasilia, 24 November 2000, No 4.

[55] See ch 5, p 123.

Legislative Decree of 18 April 1939, France's arms exports are only legitimate if authorised by a recipient state.[56] Likewise, the Chinese Regulation on Export Control of 1997, under Articles 2 and 5(3) has restricted all commercial exports of arms including SALW, if they would amount to intervention into the internal affairs of small arms recipient states.[57] This has been reiterated as one of the country's arms export principles in the UN BMS of 2003. It has been declared that the 1997 Regulation on export of arms has been amended in October 2002 to manifestly include this and other principles.[58]

India has confirmed in the BMS of 2003 that it has a stringent regime of export which permits transfers only between governments.[59] This restriction is also integrated with the domestic laws of Canada and Switzerland.[60] It ought to be remembered that several EU Member States have incorporated the principles of the EUJA and the EU Code into their domestic laws and national policies.[61]

With regard to policies, in January 2002, Edward Peartree, a US foreign affairs officer, explained the country's policy as below:

> What is gained by a global ban on transfers to non-state groups? Some argue that it establishes the norm that it is improper to supply arms to groups other than governments. *In many cases, this would be a good thing*. Of those non-state groups that are currently active today and under embargo-Al-Qaida, the RUF, UNITA, Somali warlords, and others not currently under international embargo such as the FARC in Colombia — *all of us would like to see that their supply of arms cut off immediately* [62]

Even so, he tried to devise an exception by saying:

> We would be irresponsible not to consider some other cases too: a resistance group fighting against a tyrannical government; an oppressed ethnic or religious minority confronted by a genocidal regime . . . It is these *exceptional circumstances* that we must consider. Because we are not talking about whether we will 'usually' prohibit transfers to non-state groups, or most of the time with perhaps a few exceptions.[63]

[56] *Legislative Decree of 18 April 1939*, see also No 3 (a), at <http://projects.sipri.se/expcon/natexpcon/France/frenchpolicy.htm>

[57] Decree No 234, 22 October 1997.

[58] *National Report of The People's Republic of China on the Implementation of the UN SALW Programme of Action*, Ministry of Foreign Affairs, 7 July 2003, p 6, para 2.

[59] TP Seetharam, Minister, Statement, First Biennial Meeting of States on the Implementation of the PoA of 2001, 7–11 July 2003, New York, p 1, para 5.

[60] Mathiak and Lumpe, above n 4, at 74.

[61] See ch 5, p 124; see also Hansard HC vol 413 cols 29–30WS (18 November 2003).

[62] Edward Peartree, Foreign Affairs Officer, *US Views: Ban on Transfers of Small Arms to Non-state Groups*, Remarks at Follow-up Meeting on the UN Conference on the Illicit Trade in Small Arms', Tokyo, 24 January 2002, para 4 [emphasis added], at <http://www.state.gov/t/pm/rls/rm/2002/8766.htm>

[63] *Ibid* [emphasis added].

This reinforces and clarifies Bolton's position as seen earlier. What is interesting in Peartee's approach is that while the US accepts in principle the view that transfers shall only be between states, it is of the view that there should be exceptions. It is of note too that the McKinney Code of Conduct on Arms Export,[64] a novel law on many areas of transfers, is silent on the matter.

The domestic laws and policies of several states, including some major exporters of arms, advocate the notion that SALW transactions shall preclude unauthorised NSAs, including brokers. It is true that domestic regulations such as the Russian Federation are silent on this issue. Nonetheless, Russia backed the OSCE arrangement and expressed its commitment to international obligations corresponding to weapon transfers.[65] It has also supported the Canadian proposed Convention of 1998. The US is the only country that has been claiming the legitimacy of arms provision to NSAs on the ground of fighting repression and genocide. Whether or not the US practice constitutes a valid exception, to the rule in question, will be seen later, along the newly devised 'national defence and security' exception of ECOWAS.

Despite the prevailing position of the international community, several instances of transfers of SALW to NSAs exist. Above all, this was apparent during the Cold War era. Arms supplies of the US to Nicaragua's *contras* (1981–84), Libya to the Irish Republican Army (IRA) (1970s–1980s), India to Sir Lanka's Liberation Tigers of Tamil Elam (LTTE) (1983–87), China to Cambodia's Khmer Rouge until 1991, and Thailand's support to Burmese operating along the Thai-Myanmar border (1980–1990s) are worth mentioning. Some of the supplies were conducted by two or more states in unison. The Mujahideen in Afghanistan was supplied $2 billion worth of weapons aid by the CIA between 1979-89 through the Pakistani intelligence agency known as ISI. This aid included shoulder fired anti-aircraft missiles.[66]

Since the end of the Cold War, the US and the Soviet Union (Russia) have discontinued such programmes substantially. In spite of the rhetoric that weapons supplies to NSAs by governments has ceased, the practice is continuing, at a reduced degree, either for political or commercial reasons,

[64] See ch 5, p 127.

[65] Amnesty International, *A Catalogue of Failures: G8 Arms Exports and Human Rights Violations*, 19 May 2003, p 23, paras 3 and 4.

[66] *SAS 2002*, above n 6, at 129; see also Mathiak and Lumpe, above n 4, at 58–66; Khan, 'Linkages between Arms Trafficking and the Drug Trade in South Asia' in Dhanapala et al, *Small Arms Control: Old Weapons, New Issues* (Aldershot, Ashgate Publishing, 1999) 243; Pirseyedi, *The Small Arms Problem in Central Asia*: *Features and Implications* (Geneva, United Nations Publications, 2000) 14–18; see also Boutwell and Klare, 'Small Arms and Light Weapons: Controlling the Real Instruments of War' *Arms Control Today* (August/September 1998) 4; see also *Case Concerning Military Activities in and against Nicaragua, ICJ Repts* 1986, para 206; the Court has noted that 'there have been in recent years a number of instances of foreign intervention for the benefit of forces opposed to the government of another State'.

or both.[67] For instance, Russia had supplied arms to the insurgents in Georgia and Moldova, as a means of political coercion over these new states.[68] The US and Uganda in southern Sudan, Sudan in southern Uganda, Uganda in Angola, Turkey in Chechnya, Greece, Syria, Armenia and Russia for Kurdish guerrillas in Turkey, official Pakistani aid to Kashmiri militants, French military aid for ex-armed forces of Rwanda and for the Interhamwe militia, multiple regional states sponsoring warring militias in central Africa, and Chinese transfers to African rebels are some of the allegations of transfers to NSAs in the 1990s.[69]

The 2002 study of the SAS on the Middle East, which considered state practice during the last ten years, claims that six governments have been involved in supporting 19 NSAs in the region. Countries such as Iran, Sudan, Syria, Algeria, Iraq, Lebanon and Libya are involved in assisting Islamic movements in and outside the region. These countries have aided about 27 NSAs in general. Notably, the governments usually deny most of the allegations and the transfers are often made for non-economic reasons.[70]

Although controversial in the context of terrorism, the Russian Federation, Uzbekistan, Tajikistan, Iran, India, and US involvement in Afghanistan, through arming the Northern Alliance, was also another reality of this kind.[71] In 2001 the US jointly with the Northern Alliance overthrew the de facto Taliban Government. Arms transfers to NSAs go to the extent of violations of arms embargoes of the SC,[72] which amounts to a breach of an international obligation of a state.

In summary, for political, economic and other motives, states have been continuing transfers of SALW to such actors. The measures are covert and in many cases denied by states. The question is whether this practice implies the absence of the rule in consideration. Or, does it show the emergence of a new norm, replacing the customary law that restricts arms transfers to NSAs? Or, can we think of any exception out of the practices examined above? The views of the ICJ and publicists may have some answers to the problems (see further 6.3).

6.1.3 The ICJ and Publicists on the Question

The US, through the CIA, as indicated in paragraphs 82, 94 and 95 of the judgment of the ICJ in the *Nicaragua* case,[73] had been arming the *contras* in

[67] See, eg Mathiak and Lumpe, above n 4, at 66; see also Boutwell and Klare, *ibid*, at 4.

[68] Anthony, 'Illicit Arms Transfers' in Anthony (ed), *Russia and the Arms Trade* (Oxford, Oxford University Press, 1998) 217–32.

[69] Mathiak, above n 42, at 66–67.

[70] *SAS* 2002, above n 6, at 130, table 3.6.

[71] *Ibid*, at 130–31.

[72] See ch 5, p. 110; see also 'The International Dealers in Death: Ian Traynor in Odessa' *Guardian Unlimited* (9 July 2001).

[73] *Case Concerning Military Activities in and against Nicaragua, ICJ Repts* 1986.

Nicaragua since the early 1980s with the purpose of toppling the Marxist government in the country. On 9 April 1984, Nicaragua took legal action before the ICJ against the US. In its memorial Nicaragua requested the Court to declare that the US, inter alia, breached its customary law obligation not to intervene in the domestic affairs of Nicaragua, and its 'particular duty to cease and desist immediately . . . all intervention, direct or indirect in the internal affairs of Nicaragua'; this includes 'the provision of training, arms, ammunition . . . to any organisation, movement, or individual' in the country. The US in its part, as stated in paragraph 208 of the judgment 'justified its intervention expressly and solely by reference to the right to collective self-defence'. Three areas of interest can be deduced from the case.

First, consulting relevant instruments and its own cases (see 4.2.1), the ICJ, as stated in paragraph 209 of the judgment, ruled in favour of Nicaragua and underlined that:

> [N]o such general right of intervention, in support of an opposition within another State, exists in contemporary international law. The Court concludes that acts constituting a breach of the customary principle of non-intervention will also, if they directly or indirectly involve the use of force, constitute a breach of the principle of non-use of force in international relations.

D'Amato rejected the notion of customary rule of non-intervention and claimed that:

> the Court thus completely misunderstands customary law. First, a customary rule arises out of state practice; it is not necessary to be found in UN resolutions and other major political documents. Second, *opinio juris* has nothing to do with 'acceptance of rules in such documents'.[74]

Morrison, one of the counsels for the US in the jurisdictional phase of the dispute, thinks that the Court has relied on two GA resolutions, the Friendly Resolution and the Definition of Aggression, and its decision 'goes much further than its predecessors in transforming them from exhortations or "soft law" principles into "hard law" prescriptions'.[75]

In contrast, several legal scholars welcomed the conclusion of the Court. In the opinion of Farer, the verdict 'is the one that most effectively reconciles the international system's pre-eminent interests: conflict containment and national sovereignty'.[76] European scholars, inter alios, De Arechaga considered both the *Corfu Channel* and *Nicaragua* cases as significant contributions of the ICJ in the development and elucidation of the 'duty of non-intervention', in the context of assisting 'opposition

[74] D'Amato, 'Trashing Customary International Law (1987) 81 *AJIL* 102.

[75] Morrison, 'Legal Issues in the Nicaragua Opinion' (1987) 81 *AJIL* 161.

[76] See Farer, 'Drawing the Right Line' (1987) 81 *AJIL* 113; see also Briggs, 'The International Court of Justice Lives up to its Name' (1987) 81 *AJIL* (1987) 78–86.

groups in another state'.[77] Besides, as Sloan acknowledged with reference to the *Nicaragua* case, it is now well established that resolutions of international organisations, such as GA resolutions 'may satisfy the subjective element (*opinio juris*) of customary international law'. This is correct in particular when the resolutions are declaratory of principles and rules of international law.[78] The details are discussed below (see 6.3).

The second divisive issue is the question of whether the principle of non-intervention has been abolished by a subsequent new norm, or whether certain exceptions have emerged out of it. Indeed, under paragraph 202, the Court said 'examples of trespass against the principle are not infrequent'. In paragraph 206, the Court acknowledged the fact that 'There have been in recent years a number of instances of foreign intervention for the benefit of forces opposed to the government of another state'. The Court in paragraph 207 of its decision, made a reference to the *North Continental Shelf* cases and asked itself whether such instances constitute state practice accompanied by *opinio juris*, to the effect of establishing a new rule or an exception to the existing principle. In response to the question, as discussed in the aforementioned paragraph:

> [T]he Court find that States have not justified their conduct by reference to a new right of intervention or a new exception to the principle of its prohibition. The US authorities have on some occasions clearly stated their grounds for intervening in the affairs of a foreign state for reasons connected with, for example, the domestic policies of that country, its ideology, the level of its armaments, or the direction of its policy. But these were statements of intentional policy not an assertion of rules of existing international law.

In paragraph 208, the Court added that:

> In particular, as regards the conduct towards Nicaragua which is the subject of the present case, the US has not claimed that its intervention, which is justified in this way on the political level, was also justified on the legal level, alleging the exercise of a new right of intervention regarded by the US as existing in such circumstances . . . 'Nicaragua too has not argued that this was a legal base for an intervention, let alone an intervention involving the use of force.

Furthermore, in paragraph 186, the Court underlined that 'it is not to be expected that in the practice of States the application of the rules in question should have been perfect'. For instance, for the existence of the customary rule in issue, 'complete consistency' of states to refrain 'from intervention in each other's internal affairs', is not required. First, 'instances of state conduct inconsistent with a given rule should generally have been *treated as breaches of that rule, not as indications of the recognition of a new rule*'. And secondly, if a state attempts to justify its 'incompatible'

[77] See, eg De Arechage, 'The Work and the Jurisprudence of The International Court of Justice 1947–1986' [1987] *BYIL* 14.
[78] Sloan, 'General Assembly Resolutions Revisited (Forty Years Later)' [1987] *BYIL* 74–75.

conduct vis-à-vis an established rule, '*by appealing to exceptions or justifications contained within the rule itself*, whether or not the State's conduct is in fact justifiable on that basis, the significance of that attitude is to *confirm rather than to weaken the rule*'.[79] Yet, D' Amato disagreed with the Court's position saying:

> [T]his procedure similarly robs state practice of independent content. All we need is the original alleged rule and the empty theory that any practice inconsistent with it does not count. The poverty of the Court's theory is matched by the absence of supporting research into state practice.[80]

More clearly, Franck claims that customary rule only exists if the practice 'is demonstrably adhered to by the actual conduct of the large preponderance of international actors capable of violating it'. Yet, the non-intervention norm is 'adhered to, at best, only by some states' and has been 'ignored, alas, with impunity in at least two hundred instances of military conflict since the end of World War II'.[81] The Court, as shown in paragraph 207, had declined to examine state practice, other than that of the US and Nicaragua relying on lack of jurisdiction on other states that were not parties or connected to the dispute.

Among many others, Cassese's view rejects the above assertions in that after the Second World War, the non-intervention norm 'acquired new vigour' due to several reasons, inter alia, 'far-reaching legal restrains on the use of force' has been introduced, and 'the drive towards international-cooperation, which entailed the expansion of international organisations' have become helpful in harmonising conflicting sovereign interests[82]:

> [T]he principle of non-intervention thus acquired the fundamental value of a solid and indispensable 'bridge' between the traditional, sovereignty oriented structure of the international community and the 'new' attitude of States, based on more intense social intercourse an closer co-operation.[83]

The last but the most relevant issue concerns the legality of supply of arms to NSAs, for purposes of preserving human rights in destination. As shown in paragraph 268 of the judgment, the Court underlined that:

> With regard to the steps actually taken, the protection of human rights, a strictly humanitarian nature, can not be compatible with . . . the training, arming and equipping of the *contras*. The Court concluded that the argument derived from

[79] [Emphasis added]; see also n 132, para 178, Judge Schewebel, in his dissenting opinion noted that 'the Court rightly observed that for such a general right to come into existence would involve a fundamental modification of the customary law principle on non-intervention'.

[80] Above, n 74.

[81] Franck, 'Some Observations on the ICJ's Procedural and Substantive Innovations' (1987) 81 *AJIL* 119.

[82] Above n 6, at 99.

[83] *Ibid*; see also 4.2.1.

> the preservation of human rights in Nicaragua cannot afford a legal justification for the conduct of the United States.[84]

The observations of contemporary writers, on the legality of transfers of arms to those who resist their own repressive regimes, may further clarify the response of international law to the problem. The controversies among publicists range from the impact of such transfers to that of their legality under international law. Concerning the first, Mathiak and Lumpe believe that arms transfers to NSAs 'fuel armed conflict and instability, as they are generally intended to destabilise and topple governments. Because of the unaccountable nature of covert arms supply, such operations also feed directly into the global black arms market'.[85] In contrast, Smith thinks that:

> Not all these customers (NSAs) are by definition destabilizing or inherently any more wrong than transfers and exports to governments . . . potentially disturbing trend is to see all arms transfers to non-governmental forces as counter productive from a security perspective.[86]

His argument resembles the US position reflected in the 2001 UN Conference. He did not deny the fact that such transfers could intensify problems, including conflicts.[87] Undoubtedly, transfers to such actors before or after the Cold War, and their unbearable impacts on peace and security and human rights and humanitarian norms do not seem difficult to comprehend.[88]

The controversy on the state of law deserves more attention. Mathiak et al identified two most relevant UN Charter principles to the issue; the first is the principle of respect for human rights and the self-determination of peoples, and the second is the prohibition of non-intervention and the act of aggression[89] (see further 4.2). Dean, relative to the aforesaid principles expounded that:

> Whether support of insurgency is either permissible or desirable in any particular situation ultimately will depend upon the relative weights one accords these principles. In light of the Charter's stated purpose, these two principles were designed to be mutually reinforcing. In the context of insurgencies and national movements, striking the balance between these has become a continuing source of controversy within the international legal community.[90]

84 Above, n 73.

85 Mathiak and Lumpe, above n 4, at 75.

86 Smith, 'Light Weapons—the Forgotten Dimension of the International Arms Trade' in (1998) *Brassey's Defence Year Book* 277 [clarification added].

87 *Ibid.*

88 See ch 1; see also 6.1.3.

89 Mathiak and Lumpe, above n 4, at 70.

90 Dean, 'Self-Determination and the US Support of Insurgents: A Policy Analysis Model' *Military Law Review*, vol 122 (Fall, 1988).

In addition, Mathiak et al reflected the view that the Friendly Resolution, as an authoritative interpretation of the Charter, imposes a duty upon states, to respect the right to self-determination and human rights. When peoples have been subjected to forcible deprivation of their right to self-determination, they 'are entitled to seek and receive support in accordance with the purposes and principles of the Charter'. They went on to write[91]:

> [A]t the same time, the resolution requires that states respect the territorial integrity and political independence of states. This statement, along with a subsequent decision by the International Court of Justice, implies that respect for territorial and political integrity is grounded in the presumption that fundamental human rights and other protections are being provided by a state to its populace in compliance with its duty under the UN Charter.

Could this mean that arms transfer to resistance groups, those who fight against tyrant regimes, is legal?[92] Three facts could be inferred from what has been written to answer the question. First, 'given the spread of this norm through regional and national laws', they thought that the Canadian Proposal should 'deserve support'[93]; secondly, they referred to the *Nicaragua* case and highlighted that there is no general right to support opposition groups in a state's territory; in fact, they emphasised that the ICJ considered the support of the US to the contra rebels as an armed attack against Nicaragua.[94] Last, it is of note with respect to this issue that 'cutting off the state supply of arms to guerrilla forces must be balanced with responsible state-to-state arms transfer policies. Such policies would bar arms and military support to repressive governments'[95] (see chapter eight).

In effect, although states have to comply with both human rights and the non-intervention principles, arming NSAs has not been suggested as a legal response to repressive regimes. Rather, the action needs to be directed against the regimes themselves.

In particular, Gillard consulted, inter alia, 'customary law prohibitions on the use of force and interference in domestic affairs', and took the position that SALW transfers into the territory of another state, in violation of the latter's domestic laws and without its consent 'can be characterised as unlawful intervention in the internal affairs of another state, and, as such, prohibited'.[96] McDonald and Cattaneo indicated that the 'prohibitions on interference in the internal affairs of another state' limits small arms transfers.[97] The SAS also affirmed that an overwhelming majority of

[91] Above n 89; see for relevant resolutions ch 4, p 93.
[92] For the essence and definition of repression see ch 8.
[93] Above n 4, at 74.
[94] *Ibid*, at 71.
[95] *Ibid*, at 76.
[96] Gillard, 'What is Legal? What is Illegal?' in Lumpe (ed), '*Running Guns: The Global Black Market in Small Arms* (London, Zed Books, 2000) 36–37; see also for the resolution 4.2.1.
[97] GIIS, *Small Arms Survey 2003: Development Denied* (Oxford, Oxford University Press) 224–25.

states support the rule of 'supplying arms to governments only, although some of them engage themselves in clandestine transfers'.[98]

As has been stated by Shaw, 'aid to rebels is contrary to international law',[99] and states are not permitted to arm any opposition groups of another state, in response to repression or violations of fundamental human rights. Despite that, Karp claims that it should be possible to define,

> the circumstances when the international community wants to encourage arms transfers, especially to ethic nationals whose situation is dire and whose demands are legitimate . . . A) Credible policy to stifle the flow of small arms and light arms may have to be balanced with consultative mechanisms *to permit such transfers in desperate cases*. At a minimum, the international community can establish standards determining when such arms transfers are permissible and when they must be stopped at all costs.[100]

The problem is how to determine 'desperate and legitimate cases'? Mathiak et al noted that states have tried to justify their aiding or transfers of arms to such actors on different grounds. During the Cold War, the Soviet Bloc attempted to justify intervention by the need to oust colonial powers and racist regimes. The Regan Doctrine as a counterpart was trying to validate its deeds on the ground of democratic values. All of these, including humanitarian intervention, as justifications for arming NSAs, are open to 'subjective and politicised' interpretation and could be manipulated by states.[101] They also pointed out that 'it is not always clear-cut whether opposition groups are true representatives of a people, as defined under international human rights'.[102]

Interventions through weapon provision could be triggered by national interests and may not be the right remedy for breaches of IHRL. In fact, there is a strong argument that weapon provisions to such actors escalates abuses of human rights[103] (see 6.1.4). Therefore, it is difficult to set out some hypothetical exceptions. Whether the international community will be formulating Karp's 'desperate case' exceptions remains to be seen.

6.1.4 Position of NGOs

The prohibition of arms transfers to those who fight their own oppressors does not imply that the international community has to ignore such

[98] *SAS 2002*, above n 6, at 224–25.

[99] Shaw, above n 5, at 1043; see also Gray, above n 41, at 58.

[100] Karp, 'Arming Ethic Conflict' *Arms Control Today* (September 1999) 13 [emphasis added]; see also Gray, above n 41, at 58.

[101] Mathiak and Lumpe, above n 4 at 71–72.

[102] *Ibid*.

[103] For views of OXFAM, Amnesty international, etc, see below, n 110.

situations. 'International mechanisms and responses must be developed or strengthened to protect people from repressive regimes'.[104] This should include the problem of small arms transfers to such regimes, as shall be seen (see chapter eight). The 'national defence and security' exception of ECOWAS is a fairly new claim which needs to be debated and explored in the future. The endeavours of NGOs may explain the non-intervention rule of arms transfers further.

Article 2(4) of the 2001 draft of the FCIAT[105] set out express customary international law prohibitions on the arms trade. The commentary on the Article reads:

> It is well established that transfers of weapons by one state into the territory of another without the latter's consent may amount to unlawful interference in the affairs of the recipient state. *This is particularly the case if the weapons are destined to supply opposition forces in the recipient state.* This provision also covers any principles of customary law that may emerge in the future in relation to transfers of arms.[106]

Also, Article 2 of the FCIAT of 2003[107] reiterated this express prohibition. It says: '[A] Contracting Party shall not authorise international transfers of arms which would violate its obligations under international law'. These include, according to sub-section (d), obligations arising under 'customary international law'. Paragraph eight of the commentary explained two relevant circumstances of breaches of such customary rules; the first is that 'transfers to persons other than those exercising governmental authority may also amount to a breach of the principle of non-intervention in the internal affairs of the State'; and the second circumstance is that a transfer of small arms, which disregards the consent of a state may also be a breach of the obligation relative to 'the threat or use of force in international relations'.[108]

This has been widely supported by NGOs and pacifists.[109] During the UN Conference on small arms, NGOs such as OXFAM and Amnesty International have expressed their support for the prohibition of arms transfers to NSAs.[110]

[104] Above, n 95.

[105] *Framework Convention*, Draft 3 of 3 March 2001.

[106] *Ibid* [emphasis added].

[107] Working Draft of 21 November 2003.

[108] *Ibid*, at 5.

[109] See, eg *Meeting of Eminent Persons Group with NGOs in Support of a successful UN Conference on the Illicit Trade in Small Arms and Light Weapons*, Naval & Military Club, London, 18 June 18 2001, chair's report, para 19(d), at <http://www.geocities.com/eminentpersons group/un2.html>; see also Ezell, 'UN Confab OKs Global curb on Small Arms' *National Defence* (October 2001) para 6, at <http://www.nationaldefensemagazine.org/article.cfm?Id=618>

[110] Ch 8; they were particularly concerned about human rights abuses, if transfers are permitted to NSAs.

The ICCAT[111] has entertained a different approach. The chapeau of Section II, states 'arms transfers may be conducted only if the proposed recipient state, *or recipient party* in the country of final destination',[112] complies, inter alia, with humanitarian norms. It appears that transfers to non-governments are also acknowledged or tolerated in the Code. It is not clear whether this is so—in order to accommodate all states and/or to regulate the behaviour of NSAs. Yet, the Code was a 'call on all governments to abide by' certain rules and norms, as shown in paragraph 13 of the Preamble.

In practice, the lobby of NGOs focused on the FCIAT rather than the Code, and it seems that the former will have a significant impact on the development of the law of SALW control.[113]

So far in the assessment, the dominant idea appears to be that international transactions on small arms shall only be between and among governments of states. In particular, transfers to cluster one kind of NSAs (see p 146), including rebels, have been rejected widely (see further 6.3). There are some exceptions.

6.2 EXCEPTIONAL GOVERNMENT-TO-NSA TRANSFERS

Three categories of possible exceptions, namely, national liberation movements (hereafter 'NLMs'), special entities/*sui generis*, treaty and/or domestic law based situations (other cases), may be deduced from the principle of government-to-government transfers. The first two will be given particular attention. Even if arms transfers to such cases pose legal problems, they do no seem to be at forefront of contemporary challenges in respect of the SALW issue. Due to this and concerns of economy, the scope of discussion in this section will fairly be limited.

6.2.1 Transfers to NLMs

The first issue is the legality of arms transfers to NLMs. As a background, the features of these movements must be identified.

NLMs are those 'organised groups' who fight on behalf of a whole 'people' 'against colonial domination, a racist regime, or alien occupation'.[114] One of their features is that their international recognition and

[111] See ch 5, p 130.

[112] *Ibid* [emphasis added].

[113] See 5.6.

[114] Cassese, above n 6, at 75–76; see also Shaw, 'The International Status of National Liberation Movements' (1983) 5 *Liverpool Law Review* 19; see also Shaw, *International Law*, 5th edn, above n 5, at 220–23; see also Brownlie, *Principles of Public International Law*, 6th edn (Oxford, Oxford University Press, 2003) 61–62.

legitimacy emanates from the principle of self-determination,[115] the details of which have been considered in 4.2.1 above. The second is that the GA, the SC and other regional organisations such as the OAU and the Arab League accorded recognition to NLMs in several cases. The Angolan, Mozambican, Palestinian and Rhodesian movements were recognised by the UN GA as legitimate NLMs in 1974.[116] Some, such as the PLO[117] were also granted observer status in the proceedings of the UN GA. The third is that such movements 'are accorded the capacity to conclude binding international agreements with other international legal persons'[118] and also have rights and obligations under general humanitarian law.[119] They are subject to a limited legal personality.[120]

The last characteristic, probably not solid, is that NLMs take control over some part of the territory in which they conduct their struggle; FLN in Algeria, the two movements in Zimbabwe, and POLISARIO in Western Sahara have had control over some parts of the territories. Others such as the PLO, SWAPO and the NAC were basically conducting their struggle and military operations from friendly or neighbouring countries.[121] Though such a description has not escaped controversy, it seems to be that a movement that satisfies at least the first two features may qualify for a NLM.

It is generally uncontested, as clearly stated in the Friendly Declaration, that 'such peoples are entitled to seek and receive support', in line with UN Charter principles and purposes.[122] The question may be whether or not this includes SALW transfers by states. State practice during the colonial era, the views of the ICJ and the debate it generated, and present-day state practice may provide us with some answers and indications. Colonial era state practice will be considered.

After the illegal declaration of independence of 1965 by the white minority in Southern Rhodesia, a civil war broke out between the racist regime and two black African movements called the Zimbabwe African People's Union (ZAPU) and the Zimbabwe African National Union (ZANU). The international community condemned the declaration and supported the struggle of the people to their self-determination and freedom.[123] The UN SC imposed economic and arms embargoes against the white Rhodesian regime.[124]

[115] See 4.2.1.

[116] Brownlie, above n 114, at 62.

[117] GA Res 3237/1974; see also Shaw, *International Law*, 5th edn, above n 5, at 221.

[118] Brownlie, above n 114, at 62.

[119] *GP I*, Arts 1(4) and 96(3); see also *ibid*; see also Cassese, above n 6, at 77.

[120] Cassese, *ibid*, at 76.

[121] *Ibid*.

[122] See 4.2.1, fn 48; see also Gray, *International Law and the Use of Force*, 2nd edn, above n 41, at 52–58.

[123] See eg GA Res 1889 (XVII).

[124] McDougal and Reisman, 'Rhodesia and the United Nations: The Lawfulness of International Concern' (1962) 62 *AJIL* 3; see also ch 4.

More importantly, in Resolution 227 of 1970, under paragraph 14, the UN SC urged 'Member States to increase moral and *material assistance* to the people of Southern Rhodesia in their legitimate struggle to achieve freedom and independence'. Under paragraphs 15 and 16 of the same Resolution, the SC had requested the specialised agencies of the UN and other international organisations, 'to give aid and assist to refugees' from Southern Rhodesia; economic aid constituted part of the request.[125]

Similarly, the SC in paragraph 5 of Resolution 417 reaffirmed 'its *recognition of the legitimacy of the struggle of the South African People* for the elimination of apartheid and racial discrimination'. Under operative paragraph 2 of the same Resolution, the Council expressed '*its support for, and solidarity with, all those struggling*' against apartheid.[126] Unlike Rhodesia, the Council did mention neither material nor moral support to the movements. The OAU had been persistently calling upon all African states to provide political, material and moral support to both people who were involved in struggles and others.[127]

Although it is not clear whether material support includes weapon provision, it seems to be that the SC distinguished political and material support from humanitarian and economic aid. Moreover, the OAU went on to the extent of establishing the 'Coordinating Committee for the Liberation of Africa', which was working closely with the movements and 'a special fund' for such purposes.[128] It does not seem difficult to imagine hence that African states purported to assist NLMs in all aspects, including with weapons.

This could further be strengthened by the fact that several countries provided small arms to NLMs during the Cold War period. The Soviet Union for instance supplied small and light weapons, inter alia, to the MPLA in Angola, SWAPO in Namibia, FRELIMO in Mozambique, the ANC in South Africa and the POLISARIO in Western Sahara. It did so to the PLO too.[129] Before the outbreak of the civil war in 1975, the US, China, Romania, North Korea, South Africa and Zaire had supplied small arms to Angolan independent movements.[130] All cases involved the right to self-determination of peoples, although some may question the validity of arms provision to NLMs.

[125] [Emphasis added]; see also Fenwick, 'When is there a Threat to the Peace?—Rhodesia' (1967) 61 *AJIL* (1967) 753–55.

[126] See also, 4.2.1, p 127 [emphasis added].

[127] See, eg 4.2.1, p 129; *Resolution on Apartheid and Racial Discrimination* (CM/Res 142 (x) No 11; *Resolution on Territories under Protégées Domination* (CM/Res 137 (X) No 8.

[128] CM/Res 136 (X) Nos 1 and 3.

[129] Academician General Yuriy Kirshin, 'Conventional Arms Transfers During the Soviet Period' in Anthony (ed), above n 68, at 66–70.

[130] Mathiak, 'Light Weapons and Internal Conflict in Angola' in Boutwell et al (eds), *Lethal Commerce: the Global Trade in Small Arms and Light Weapons* (Cambridge, Mass, American Academy of Arts and Sciences, 1995) 83–84.

The ICJ's views on the subject may help clarify the legality of such transfers, taking for granted the firm support of the Court to the principle of the right to self-determination as it has been demonstrated in many cases (see 4.2.1). The Court in the *South West Africa Advisory Opinion* of 1971 expounds that:

> All States should bear in mind that the entity injured by the illegal presence of South Africa in Namibia is a people which must look to the international community for assistance in its progress towards the goals for which the sacred trust was instituted.[131]

Also, the *Nicaragua* case and the debate it has generated are of significant importance. Paragraph 206 of the judgment states that: '[T]he Court is not here concerned with the process of decolonisation', while it was talking about instances of foreign intervention and their implications for the principle of non-intervention. Judge Schwebel, in his dissenting opinion, seems to correctly observe that:

> the Court is of the view that there is or may be not a general but a particular right of intervention provided that it is in furtherance of the process of decolonisation . . . the Court may be understood as . . . endorsing an exception to the prohibition of so called 'war of liberation', or at any rate, some of such wars, while condemning intervention of another political character.[132]

He added however, that while it is lawful to provide political, humanitarian, or moral support to movements of self-determination against colonial domination, 'it is not lawful for a foreign state or movement to intervene in that struggle with force or provide arms. . .in the prosecution of armed rebellion'.[133] Even so, Farer, in support of the Court's judgment, affirms that:

> In the colonial context and in the name of national self-determination, the UN has gone behind the political institutions established by metropolitan governments to locate sovereignty in the people of the territory. There is, therefore, some precedent at the global level for regarding people not governments, as the ultimate locus of sovereignty.[134]

Furthermore, Cassese considers that due to the legitimate goals of NLMs, 'no ban is imposed on states to refrain from providing national liberation movements with humanitarian, economic, and *military assistance* short of sending troops'.[135]

[131] *Legal Consequences for States of the Continued Presence of South Africa in Namibia*, Advisory Opinion, *ICJ Repts* 1971, paras 117–27 and 133; see also Gray, *International Law and the Use of Force*, 2nd edn, above n 41, at 55.

[132] *Dissenting Opinion of Judge Schwebel*, *ICJ Repts* 1986, p 351, para 179; in contrast, see Gray, *ibid*, at 56; she noted that the Court 'deliberately and expressly left this question out of its consideration'.

[133] *Ibid*, para 180.

[134] Above n 76, at 115.

[135] Above n 6, at 76 [emphasis added]; see also Crawford, 'The Criteria for Statehood in International Law' [1976] *BYIL* 169–73.

Although it seems to be that the ICJ's exclusion of liberation movements from the non-intervention based prohibition is justified, whether it has been integrated into the SALW legal regime still needs examining.

Contemporary instruments on SALW have reflected such a notion of support to NLMs. The UN Protocol on firearms, under paragraph 4 reaffirms:

> the right to self-determination of all peoples, in particular peoples under colonial or other forms of alien domination or foreign occupation, and the importance of the effective realisation of that right.

The same wording is found in paragraph 14 of the 1996 DC guidelines for arms transfers and paragraph 11 of the UN PoA.[136]

It has been made clear, as indicated in the aforesaid paragraph of the PoA that, such affirmation to the principle, in relation to the SALW transfers issue,

> shall not be construed as authorising or encouraging any action that would dismember or impair, totally or in part, the territorial integrity or political unity of sovereign and independent states.

Additionally, despite the fact that many guerrilla movements in countries such as Sudan and Somalia considered themselves as liberation movements and some of them relied on the right to self-determination, the UN practice, relative to small arms and arms embargoes, has not supported their claims. For instance, SC Resolutions 1519 of 2003 on Somalia and 1556 of 2004 on Sudan did not make any mention of the right to self-determination, while they have affirmed the sovereignty and unity of both states.[137] This is also true with respect to regional instruments on small arms, such as the OAS Convention, SADC and Nairobi protocols and the EU Code of Conduct on arms exports. While all have underlined the principles and certain exceptions, inter alia, of sovereignty and the right to self-defence, they have not addressed the right to self-determination in the sense of assistance to NLMs.[138]

This appears to be the case due to the diminishing existence of NLMs and does not show the defiance of states from the principle of self-determination. This conclusion is evident in the UN PoA and the UN Firearms Protocol. As mentioned earlier, these two instruments are dedicated to fight the illicit SALW international trafficking. However, they

[136] See also GA Res 50/70 B/1995, para 4 of the Preamble has repeated the words of the Protocol and the GIAT; see also ch 5, p 117.

[137] See also GA Res 46/36 L/1991; SC Res 1318/2000; SC Res 1265/1999, while all are about the contemporary problems of SALW, including their transfers, no reference is made to self-determination; rather they have emphasised on the sovereignty and territorial integrity of African states in particular.

[138] See, eg *EU Code of Conduct on Arms Exports*, para 8; *OAS Convention on Firearms*, above n 45, para 13; *SADC Protocol*, above n 46, Art 2; *Nairobi Protocol*, above n 47, para 9.

clearly exclude peoples' struggle against colonial, alien and foreign occupation from the ambit of the restrictions, in a similar way to the ICJ.

In brief, state practice in the Cold War era, the ICJ and various global instruments on SALW have shown that arms transfers to NLMs may not be subject to arms transfer restrictions where the requirements discussed so far are met. Regardless of its topicality in today's international law, the international community supports such notions of assistance. The movements in question are also entitled to such backing. The claim of Judge Schwebel appears therefore to be unproven.

Although Crawford wrote in 1979 that 'assistance by States to local insurgents in a self-determination unit, may possibly and *exceptionally*, be permitted',[139] it does not seem to be so, as the principle in issue could not be an exception, inter alia, to the non-intervention rule. Rather, the rights of states and NLMs emanate from an independent obligation of *erga omnes* character, ie the principle of the right to self-determination.[140] It appears that both principles co-exist depending on the circumstances of particular cases.[141] As Cassese diligently pointed out, such movements 'seem to be on the wane'[142] and thus arms assistance to NLMs does not come into sight as a prime issue of the SALW legal regime.

Further, care must be taken on the right of states and NLMs in respect of arms transfers. The right to assist rebels in the aforesaid situations may not be an absolute one, as cases of national self-determination could be resolved through peaceful means if the parties involved and/or the international community so wishes.[143] For example, the ICJ in the *Western Sahara Advisory Opinion* concluded that:

> the decolonization process envisaged by the General Assembly is one which will respect the right of the population of Western Sahara to determine their future political status by their own freely expressed will. . . . This right to self-determination . . . leaves the General Assembly a measure of direction with respect to the forms and procedures by which the right is to be realised.[144]

Of course, the UN has to exercise such powers and good offices in accordance with UN Charter principles.[145] It has to be recalled that states

[139] Crawford, above n 135, at 173[emphasis added].

[140] See, eg *East Timor* case, *ICJ Repts* 1995, para 29.

[141] Cassese, above n 6, at 13.

[142] *Ibid*, at 76.

[143] For the principle of pacific resolution of disputes see ch 4, p 93; see also De Arechage, above n 77, at 4–6; see also Crawford, above n 135, at 155.

[144] *Western Sahara Advisory Opinion, ICJ Repts* 1975, 12, paras 23–74.

[145] See, eg *Voting Procedure on Questions Relating to Reports and Petitions Concerning the Territory of South- West Africa*, Advisory Opinion of 7 June 1955, para 18, the ICJ noted that 'the degree of supervision to be exercised by the General Assembly should not therefore exceed that which applied under the Mandates System'.

are under obligation to refrain from aggravating disputes.[146] Weapons transit contrary to the UN process may thus amount to a breach of international law, subject to considerations relating to the overall circumstances of particular cases (see 6.2.1).

6.2.2 Transfers to Special Entities

The second crucial issue is about the 'legality' of SALW transfers to territorial entities.[147] Such entities include Taiwan, Palestine, northern Cyprus, Western Sahara, and the Holy See.[148] The central interest here is not to deal with controversies over statehood, recognition and/or self-determination of exceptional territories of international law; although we will need to touch on such issues as a background. The following four elements lay down the basis for dealing with the problem.

First, as a matter of fact, there are exceptional territories which are not states as illustrated above.[149] Secondly, these entities have limited international legal personality. Crawford pointed out that these,

> special cases' must have some legal status, even if, for what ever reason, they do not qualify as states. They are clearly not *terrae nullius*, and there is no reason of principle or practice why they should not be subject to relevant international legal rules.[150]

Thirdly, 'it can't be assumed that all territorial entities will necessary have the same rights and obligations, or the same particular status'[151] and so determination of their relations with other states depends on the particular circumstances of each territory and the nature of the international transaction which is to be involved. The legitimacy of the conduct of such entities vis-à-vis sovereign states can only be determined on case-by-case bases.

Finally, as a rule, SALW transfers shall only be between governments. Apart from NLMs, therefore, NSAs are not entitled to take part in arms transactions (see 6.1). The question is thus whether these entities can be

[146] *Friendly Relations*, GA Res 2625 (XXV), Principle II, para 4; see also Cassese, above n 6, at 103; see also J Collier, *The Settlement of Disputes in International Law: Institutions and Procedures* (Oxford, Oxford University Press, 2000) 19–20.

[147] See in general Crawford, *The Creation of States in International Law* (Oxford, Oxford University Press, 1979) 142–66; Shaw, *International Law*, 5th edn, above n 5, at 207–13; Brownlie, *Principles of Public International Law*, 5th edn (Oxford, Oxford University Press, 1998). Brownlie, *Principles of Public International Law*, 6th edn (Oxford, Oxford University Press, 2003) 169; Warbrick, 'States and Recognition in International Law' in Evans, *International Law* (Oxford, Oxford University Press, 2003) 230–31.

[148] Shaw, *International Law*, 4th edn, above n 5, at 165–67; see also Crawford, 'The Criteria for Statehood', above n 135, at 143; see also Brownlie, above n 114, at 63–65.

[149] See, eg Brownlie, *ibid*, at 76.

[150] Crawford, 'The Criteria for Statehood', above n 135, at 142.

[151] *Ibid*.

seen as another exception to the rule. Palestine and Taiwan are chosen as examples, in the belief that they illustrate the complexity of the issue. In a short historical and political assessment of these territories, the endeavour is to examine the rights and obligations of such entities and states, if any, regarding arms transfers.

6.2.2.1 The Palestine Authority[152] and the SALW trade

In the aftermath of the Second World War, after the end of the British mandate over the Palestine territory, the international community intended to solve the Israel-Palestine problem through establishing two independent states—Palestinian Arabs and Jewish people have to exist side by side.[153] Nevertheless, the State of Israel declared its independence in 1948. By 1967, the latter was in control of the whole of the Palestine territory, including the West Bank and Gaza Strip. The SC in its Resolution 242/1967 called on Israel to withdraw from territories it occupied in the 1967 conflict.[154] Subsequent developments, as shown in the 1974 GA Resolution, affirm the fact that the international community was/is in support of the inalienable right to self-determination of the people of Palestine. The GA set up a committee to implement this right, and at the same time granted the PLO with a permanent observer status in the UN GA.[155] While this was occurring, as shown for example in SC Resolution 298 of 1971, the UN was condemning Israel for its measures, inter alia, its attempts to change the status of Jerusalem.[156]

Following ruinous armed conflicts, which also involved other states within the Middle East, a peace process had been initiated to cease the war in the region. Authoritative resolutions of the UN SC played a significant role in doing this.[157] As a result, the 'land for peace formula' had been negotiated between the State of Israel and the PLO, as the representative of the people of Palestine. This led to the signing of the 'Declaration of Principles on Interim Self-Government Arrangements' in Washington DC, on 13 September 1993.[158] This agreement, as indicated in Article IV of the Declaration, establishes an Interim Palestine Council with jurisdiction over the West Bank and Gaza Strip territories. In accordance with this

[152] For general understanding on the problem see Shaw, *International Law*, 4th edn, above n 5 at 174–75 and 220–23; see also, *Legal Consequences of the Construction of a Wall in the Occupied Palestine Territory Advisory Opinion*, ICJ, 9 July 2004, paras 117–33; see also UN documents on the Palestine issue at <http://www.un.org/Depts/dpa/ngo/history.html>

[153] See, eg GA Res 181(II)(A+B)/1947.

[154] See also *Legal Consequences*, above n 152, paras 73–74.

[155] See GA Res 3236 (XXIX)/1974; Res 3237 (XXIX)/1974.

[156] See also *Legal Consequences*, above n 152, para 75.

[157] SC Res 242/1967; see also SC Res 338/1973.

[158] Annex. *Declaration of Principles on Interim Self-Government Arrangements*, Report of the Secretary General, 11 October 1993; see also Brownlie, above n 114, at 77–78.

arrangement, elections to the Palestinian Council and Presidency of the Authority had taken place later.[159]

As the ICJ, in paragraph 77 of the Legal Consequences Advisory Opinion observed, the obligations of Israel to transfer certain powers and responsibilities to the Palestine Authority 'remained partial and limited' due to 'subsequent events' and disagreements. Four remarks could be drawn from the brief historical assessment that we have gone through.

First, the UN, as reiterated in SC Resolution 1397 of 2002, has, as things stand now, only a vision of two states[160] and thus we have both the State of Israel and the Palestine Authority in the region. However, it is also suggested that Palestine is a nascent state, that is to say an entity recognised by the world community and the parties concerned, 'as having an entitlement to statehood'.[161]

Secondly, despite the persistence of the problem, the 1993 provisional arrangement and subsequent developments have been achieved on the basis of the will of both parties and under the auspices of the UN. Thirdly, although questions of statehood and self-determination of the people of Palestine are at the heart of the conflict, violations of humanitarian law, violence and terrorism are also real concerns in the area.[162]

Finally, there seems to be a general consensus, among some elements of the parties and the international community, to resolve the matter peacefully, and not through armed struggle. The UN Secretary-General, following the death of the Palestinian President Yasser Arafat, called on the parties to the conflict and the international community to make greater efforts 'to bring about the peaceful realization of the Palestinian right of self-determination'.[163]

These conclusions could lead us to identify threefold relevant elements to the issue of small arms transfer to the territory of Palestine. The first is that the PLO/Palestine people have an inherent right to seek and receive assistance from the international community for purposes of ensuring their right to self-determination (see 6.2.1). This may not include military assistance, as armed struggle has been abandoned as a means of attaining the objective in question—measures which defeat the peace process could therefore be in violation of the principle of pacific resolution of disputes (see 4.2.1).

159 See also Shaw, *International Law*, 4th edn, above n 5, at 174–75.

160 It was adopted, 14 in favour, none against, and 1 abstention (UN Doc Supp No S/2002/1397) para 2.

161 Brownlie, above n 114, at 77–78; for self-determination as *jus cogens* norm see 4.2.1.

162 See, eg SC Res 1515/2003, para 3, and operative, para 2; the SC has called unanimously the cessation of violence; see also SC Res 1397/2002, para 5, and opertive para 5, the Council expressed its concern about the protection of civilians; see also *Nuclear Weapons*, para 78.

163 *Press Release*, 'Secretary General Deeply Moved at Death of President Arafat' SG/SM/9585, PAL/2016, 11 November 2004 [emphasis added]; see also Gray, *International Law and the Use of Force*, 2nd edn, above n 41, at 57–58.

As a second element, the transitional administrative arrangement in the territory has brought some special circumstances. Articles VIII and IX of the Declaration of Principles have empowered the Palestine Council to make and enforce laws within its authority, including establishing law enforcement bodies. Article VIII in particular states that 'in order to guarantee public order and internal security for the Palestinians of the West Bank and the Gaza Strip, the Council will establish a strong police force'. The administration adopted a basic law in 1997, which was signed by the President in 2002. Article 75(1) of this law stipulated that the police and security forces formed regular armed forces to protect the homeland, the people and preserve peace and order; although this is not without contention on the part of Israel—claiming that the Authority can only have police forces under the Oslo Agreement of 1996. The police force is estimated to be up to 30,000 (18,000 in Gaza and 12,000 in the West Bank), including the Public Security Force, Civil Police, Emergency and Rescue, Preventive Security Force, the General Intelligence Service (Mukhabarat) and the Presidential Security Force known as Force 17.[164] Data published on 10 October 2004 claims that the total number of regular personnel of security forces of the Authority in the year 2003 had reached 45,000.[165]

Finally, while countries such as the US give economic aid, some countries render military assistance to the Palestine Authority. Russia donated armoured personnel carriers and training to the Palestinian police in 2001 [166]; it has been said that it supplied SA-7 shoulder-launched SAMs via Croatia in the year 2000[167]; Iran is also said to have transferred Sagger ATGMs, MRLs, and 120mm mortars to the Authority in 2001. Other countries such as Algeria, Egypt, Jordan, Libya, Pakistan, Yemen, UAE, etc provide military training to the Palestinian security forces, both in Palestine and abroad.[168]

These legal, political and factual circumstances/elements may support or otherwise the legality of arms supplies to the Palestine Authority. Arguably, such a practice in combination with the special arrangement agreed by the parties and the future of the territory could imply that the entity in question may have certain rights and duties regarding securing arms transfers, although it is difficult to justify the legitimacy of every case of weapon transfer to the Authority, as will be seen.

Alternatively, due to peace and security, terror, humanitarian and arms diffusion concerns in the region, it may well be argued that any weapon provision to the territory is illegal under international law. Such

164 Palestinian Legislative Council, *Basic Law Draft Resolution*, Third Reading, Passed 2 October 1997, signed by Arafat on 30 May 2002; see also <http://www.pna.gov.ps/>

165 *Russia to give Palestinian Police 45 APCS*, September 16 1994, p 5, at <http://csf.colorado.edu/dfax/matn/matn9409.htm#T-0047>

166 *Ibid.*

167 <http://www.tau.ac.il/jcss/balance/Pa.pdf>

168 *Ibid.*

subsequent change of circumstances[169] may also raise the question of the validity of the agreements, which led to the special arrangement discussed above.

With all its challenges, the peace process is still on track—taking into account the will of the parties to the conflict, the safety of the Palestine people, the legitimacy of the administration with law enforcement capacity, its recognition by the international community and its future, it appears that the Palestine Authority is entitled to import small arms for public order end-uses in the territory. To that extent, states may have the right to supply arms to this entity in the form of aid or sale, provided that the quantity and quality of SALW to be transferred do not: (1) exceed the threshold of purposes of end-use (eg maintenance of public order); and (2) contradict other norms of arms transfers, in particular the rules on peace and security and IHL (see chapters five and seven).

In reality the Palestinian territory is flooded with SALW and militant groups who are not part of the administration but are alleged to have connections with it. According to the SAS, *Tanzin* groups alone possess about 70,000 guns, mainly AK-47s and M16s. Some Middle Eastern countries are alleged to be shipping enormous weapons to such actors in the territory.[170] Such covert transfers by a state shall thus be excluded from the exception made above (see 6.1). This assessment was made before the Hamas-led Authority came into being.

6.2.2.2 Taiwan[171] and the SALW Trade

Taiwan was ceded by China to Japan in 1895 in perpetuity through the Treaty of Shimonoseki. The aggressor, Japan, 'coerced the losing party, the Qing government' of China, to sign such a treaty in 1895. While the Allies, Britain, the US and China in 1943 and Japan in 1945 affirmed their acceptance of the return of Taiwan to the Republic of China, Japan withdrew its control, without denoting any beneficiary of all the rights over the territory and declared that it had no sovereignty over the island. After the end of the Chinese Civil War, the nationalist regime established itself on Taiwan, while the communist regime took control over the mainland. Both had been claiming to be governments of the whole of China.[172]

[169] eg, Art 62 of the VCLT provides *robus sic stantibus* grounds for termination of a treaty; yet breaches of obligations, among others, are not valid reasons for claiming so.

[170] *SAS 2002*, above n 6, at 131, box. 3.6; see also, 'Iran-Palestine Weapons Link likely', *BBC News*, 5 February 2002.

[171] See generally Crawford, *The Creation of States in International Law*, above n 147, at 141–52; Shen, 'Sovereignty, Statehood, Self-determination, and the Issue of Taiwan' (2000) 15 *Am.U.InT'LL.Rev* 1102–60; Brownlie, *Principles of Public International Law*, 6th edn, above n 114 at 64–65; and Shaw, *International Law*, 5th edn, above n 5, at 211–12.

[172] Shaw, *International Law*, 4th edn, above n 5, at 166; see also Shen, *ibid*, at 1108; see also Lovelace, 'Is there a Question of Taiwan in International Law?' 4 *Harvard Asian Quarterly* (Summer 2000) 1; see also Crawford, *The Creation of States in International Law*, above n 147, at 143–44.

However, in 1971 the UN General Assembly adopted Resolution 2758 (XXVI), 'which expelled the representatives of the Taiwan authorities and restored the seat and all the lawful rights of the government of the PRC in the United Nations'.[173] Further, the Guidelines for National Unification of One China of 1991, which was endorsed by the parties shows that 'both the mainland and Taiwan are parts of Chinese territory'. It has also been said as a principle that ensuring the unification is a 'common responsibility of all Chinese people'.[174] This and other situations led some writers to raise the question whether there is a Taiwan issue in international law.[175]

Taiwan is seen claiming 'a special state-to-state' relation with China, and in some cases, an independent sovereign status.[176] For example, in response to the February 2000 'White Paper on The One China Principle and Taiwan Question', issued by the PRC,[177] Taiwan emphasised that[178]:

> The government of the Republic of China will definitely not agree to the PRC's unilateral definition of 'one China'. The Republic of China has always been a sovereign state. The release of a 'white paper' cannot change this fact. If China were unified, then why is there a unification issue?

On 18 March 2000, the territory undertook a presidential election, in which the Democratic Progressive Party candidates Chen Shui-bian and Annette Lu won over their rivals of the Independent and Kuomintang parties. President Chen insisted, inter alia, sovereign independence of the island and the promotion of human rights in his triumph speech. The immediate response of Beijing was that Taiwan is part of sovereign China, and thus the claim for independence is unacceptable.[179]

For the PRC, as clearly shown in part IV paragraph 4, and part I paragraph 7 of the White Paper of 2000, Taiwan's status as part of China is unequivocal. Numerous reasons are given for this: (1) As yet, 161 countries have diplomatic relations with it. All these countries, including the US have accepted the one China principle and recognised the regime in Beijing. (2) Sovereignty over Taiwan belongs to all the Chinese people. Since Taiwan had never been a state, the question of self-determination

[173] The Resolution was adopted by 76 votes in favour, 35 against, and 17 abstentions, on a draft introduced by Albania and 20 other states.

[174] *Guidelines for National Unification of One China*, adopted by the National Unification Council, Third Meeting, 23 February 1991, and by the Executive Yuan Council (Cabinet), 2223rd Meeting on 14 March 1991, III. Art 1, at <http://www.president.gov.tw/2_special/unification/te.html>.

[175] See, eg Lovelace, above n 172, at para 6.

[176] See, eg President Lee's (ROC), *Deutsce Welle Interview*, 9 July 1999, para 9, at <http://www.taiwanheadlines.gov.tw/state/1.htm>

[177] *Ibid.*

[178] *Taipei Update*, 29 February 2000, para 3 ,at <http://www.roc- taiwan.org/dc/press/20000315/2000031502.html>

[179] See, eg Lovelace, above n 172, paras 2 and 3.

could not arise, and therefore the conflict between the two should be characterised as an internal dispute. (3) This position is notwithstanding the high degree of autonomy of Taiwan, which includes the capacity to make cultural, economic and social relations with other states. And (4) a claim for military presence in Taiwan is intolerable, and any foreign involvement beyond the aforesaid matters amounts to an intervention to sovereignty against the UN Charter.[180] Recently, Beijing 'enacted a law authorizing the use of force against Taiwan if it moves toward formal independence'.[181]

Taiwan maintains first, since 1949 it has had a separate government ruling the island, and thus the PRC and ROC are different jurisdictions. Secondly, it has its own constitution; for instance, the Constitution of 1947 had declared the existence of armed forces under the command of the president, as a sovereign state. Thirdly, it has promoted a democratic political system, which is non-existent in the mainland and fourthly, the island has established foreign relations with many countries, including military agreements. As it had been an independent state since 1912, and was not colonised in history, there has been no need to declare independence.[182]

At least four legal issues and the prevalent position of jurists on them must be discussed, without which it is hardly possible to tackle the main issue. The first issue is the fulfilment of the criteria of statehood by Taiwan. Nunathan, Charney and Prescott think that the territory existed since 1947, with 23 million people and its own de facto government. It has upheld international relations with various countries, including military agreements. For example, it is a member of the WTO as a customs territory. Hence, it satisfies the four criteria for statehood.[183] In contrast with this, Shen thinks that Taiwan does not fulfil statehood as 'it lacks sovereignty over a territory of its own, and does not have a government capable of independently entering into relations with other nations'.[184]

Probably the third and more sensible argument about the statehood of Taiwan, as reflected, inter alios, by Crawford is that 'Taiwan is not a state, because *it does not claim to be*, and it is not recognized as such: its status is that of a consolidated local de facto government in a civil war situation'.[185]

[180] PRC White Paper, *The One China Principle and the Taiwan Issue*, the Taiwan Affairs Office and the Information Office of the State Council, 21 February 2000, at <http://www.taiwandocuments.org/white.htm>; see also Lovelace, *ibid*, para 5.

[181] 'China Puts Threat to Taiwan into Law' *Washington Post*, 14 March 2005, p A01.

[182] President Lee's (ROC), *Interview*, above n 176); see, eg Lovelace, above n 172, para 14; see, eg *The Constitution of the Republic of China*, adopted by the National Assembly, 25 December 1946, promulgated by the National Government on 1 January 1947, effective from 25 December 1947, Art 36, at <http://www.gio.gov.tw/info/news/constitution.htm>

[183] Charney and Prescott, 'Resolving Cross-Strait Relations between China and Taiwan' (2000) 94 *AJIL* 464–65.

[184] Shen, above n 171, at 1160.

[185] Above, n 147, at 151[emphasis added].

Lovelace supports this saying 'whereas it [*Taiwan*] would appear to meet the conditions of statehood, it is not a separate state because it *formally claims to be part of China*'.[186]

The second issue is whether territorial title could be reversed under international law. It is not generally denied that 'China held indisputable sovereignty' over Taiwan, until the conclusion of the treaty of Shimonoseki, as the island was found and acquired by China before any other state. Yet, the territory was under Japan until 1945 and then under the authority of the ROC. Since then, the PRC has never exercised governmental authority over the island.[187] The Permanent Court of Arbitration, in the *Eritrea v Yemen* case has claimed 'reversion of territorial title is unproven in international law'.[188] Conversely, some argue that if a state is unable to have authority over a territory for a significant period of time, it may lose title to it.[189] It should not be forgotten that the mainland has been persistently claiming Taiwan as its territory. China has been making diplomatic efforts and some minor military activities to realise its claims over Taiwan. Accordingly, it has managed to oust the ROC from the UN forum.[190] As Shaw noted corresponding to such situations thus 'protests by the dispossessed sovereign may completely block any prescriptive claim'.[191]

As a third issue, some ask whether the ROC is a government of China as a whole, as it does not claim an independent sovereignty from mainland China. In history, the PRC took control of mainland China in 1949 and has been considered as the successor of the government of China. The community of states and international organisations, with the exception of some, has recognised both the government and the State of the PRC.[192] In particular, the collective non-recognition of the ROC by the UN GA may reinforce 'the legal position' of the PRC over Taiwan.[193]

The final issue is the controversy over the applicability of the principle of self-determination to the Taiwan question. Nunatham et al argues that:

> Today, a non-state entity may hold territory in opposition to the state with sovereignty over that territory, and the population of a territory may have rights of self-determination that deny the sovereign state the unqualified

[186] Lovelace, above n 172, para 8 [clarification and emphasis added].

[187] Charney and Prescott, above n 183, at 458–59.

[188] *Eritrea/Yemen* Arbitration Award, *Permanent Court of Arbitration* (phase I), 9 October 1998, para 125; see also Brownlie, *Principles of Public International Law*, 6th edn, above n 114, at 141–42 and 640.

[189] *Temple of Prech Vihear* (*Cambodia v Thaiand*) *ICJ Repts* 1962, 6, 45 (June 15) (sep.op. Judge Alfaro); see also Charney and Prescott, above n 183, at 462.

[190] Charney and Prescott, *ibid*, at 463; see also Shen, above n 171, at 1124–25.

[191] Shaw, *International Law*, 5th edn, above n 5, at 427.

[192] See, eg Charney and Prescott, above n 183, at 460–1; see also Shen, above n 171.

[193] Crawford, 'Statehood' in *The Creation of States in International Law*, above n 147, at 122; see also 1 *Oppenheim's International Law* 1999 (Sir Robert Jennings and Sir Arthur Watts, 9th edn, 1992, at 120; see also, Lauterpacht, *Recognition in International Law* (Cambridge, Cambridge University Press, 1947) 142.

> authority to control that territory and its population. Clearly, Taiwan is independent of China, having achieved economic and governmental autonomy despite Beijing's efforts to the contrary. Traditionally, only states could have sovereignty over territory or rights under international law. This state-centred approach, however, has eroded.[194]

Yet they suggested that, as the Taiwanese do not want to be under Beijing rule, their right to a higher degree of autonomy should be respected. They added that this might not imply an automatic right to independence from China. The UN could play a key role in resolving the problem for purposes of maintaining international peace and security.[195]

In contrast, Shen viewed such a wider interpretation of the right to self-determination to the case of Taiwan as an abuse of a legal concept. He underlined that 'the territory of Taiwan is not a colony of China, a trust territory, nor is it any other type of non-self-governing territory within the meaning of the UN Charter'. It is rather an 'administrative unit' or 'an integral part' of China, in which the notion of self-determination is inapplicable.[196] He did not contest that 'the people of Taiwan have a broad range of rights to choose their political system and participate in or influence the political life in the locality'[197] (see further 4.2.1). The common element of both arguments is that they end with a solution of autonomous administration for the entity.

In conclusion, having considered the historical and legal circumstances of the case and the limited application of the right to self-determination to cases of statehood (see 4.2.1). Taiwan is a non-state territory; but, with its own authority, population and some degree of international relations.[198] With this legal and political backdrop, the main question can be explored.

At present, Taiwan manufactures SALW and their ammunitions,[199] imports military small arms from various countries,[200] and several states such as the US, France, Ireland, and Canada have been exporting billions of US dollars worth of major conventional weapons to the island. Such deals include light weapons such as FIM-92A portable stinger, AGM-114K Javelin anti-tank missiles. It has to be noted also that Taipei's defence budget in 2001 was about $7.4 billion a year.[201]

[194] Above n 183, at 465.

[195] *Ibid*, at 466; see also Crawford, *The Creation of States in International Law*, above n 147, at 151, he noted that the issue of self-determination in respect of Taiwan 'must be resolved without endangering peace and security under Art 33 of the UN Charter'.

[196] Shen, above n 171, at 1158–60.

[197] *Ibid*.

[198] Shaw, *International Law*, 5th edn, above n 5, at 298 and 166; see also 4.2.1.

[199] *SAS 2002*, above n 6, at 45, table 1.11; *SAS 2003*, above n 97, at 50–51, App 1.1.

[200] *SAS 2004*, p 111, table 4.3; see also '*EU 4th Annual Report*' 8.3.2, n 139, p 25; see, eg Austria 6, Belgium 8, and Germany 17 of export licences authorisation to Taiwan.

[201] See *Transfers and License Production of Major Conventional Weapons: Exports to Taiwan, Sorted by Suppliers. Deals with Deliveries or Orders made 1993–2003, at* <http://projects.sipri.se/armstrade/tai_imports93-2002.pdf>; see also country profile at <http://www.fas.org/asmp/profiles/taiwan.htm>

Prima facie, China has been persistently objecting to such transfers of arms to Taiwan as an intrusion of its sovereignty. In the year 2000, Beijing emphasised that[202]:

> No country maintaining diplomatic relations with China should provide arms to Taiwan or enter into military alliance of any form with Taiwan. All countries maintaining diplomatic relations with China should abide by the principles of mutual respect for sovereignty and territorial integrity and non-interference in each other's internal affairs, and refrain from providing arms to Taiwan or helping Taiwan produce arms in any form or under any pretext.

In addition, in August 1997, the Permanent Representative of China to the UN had strictly protested the US inclusion of transactions of weapons with Taiwan in its report of arms transfers to the UN Register. China noted 'the arms transfers from the United States to Taiwan are neither legitimate nor transfers between sovereign states'.[203] The UN responded to the Chinese claim saying that any report received from countries does not imply any position of the organisation, as to the legal status of any territory or a country. They are reproduced as delivered[204] (for the UN Register see chapter two). These conditions demonstrate that China has been determinedly objecting to the practice of arms dealings with Taiwan, as interference in domestic affairs.

The question before us is thus whether this could mean Taiwan and other states have no certain rights and obligations, in respect of SALW transfers, given that Taiwan is not a sovereign state.

Overall, Taiwan has some rights and obligations under international law. The mainland and the international community accept that Taiwan is a territorial entity, with its own de facto administration and some capacity to make international relations. The latter includes cultural, commercial and some economic relations with sovereign states.[205] Although the situation differs, the ICJ in the *Western Sahara Advisory Opinion* accepted in principle that a non-state legal entity could exist 'enjoying some form of sovereignty'.[206] Yet matters related to the arms trade involving such entities in general and Taiwan in particular are controversial indeed. Let us address the question of rights first, if any.

Three possible views could be construed with respect to rights on small arms transfer. The first argument is that, as Taiwan has 'some degree of

[202] See the White Paper 2000, above n 180, pt v, para 5.

[203] *China and UN Register of Conventional Weapons*, para 2, at <http://www.nti.org/db/china/rocaorg.htm>

[204] *Ibid*, paras 4, 5 and 7.

[205] See, eg Crawford, *The Creation of States in International Law* above n 147, at 152; see, eg Taiwan's diplomatic relations with 29 countries, membership in 16 inter-governmental organisations (IGOs), observer status in 10 IGOs, and membership in 986 NGOs at, <http://www.canada-taiwan.org/english/issues/>

[206] Above n 144, para 148, see also Brownlie, *Principles of Public International Law*, 6th edn, above n 114, at 169.

juridically cognizable existence', under international law, which includes conducting international relations with sovereign states,[207] international law does not appear to deny it to have certain rights with respect to arms transfers, for purposes of maintaining its internal security, including the safety of its people, administration, infrastructures, institutions, etc within the territory. Issues of external security may also arise regarding the right to prevent itself and its inhabitants from internal or trans-boundary crimes, inter alia, piracy and global terrorism.[208] For these end-uses, therefore, its arms imports could *exceptionally* be justified. In effect, other states may not also be prohibited to transfer SALW to the territory.

At least five justifications could be given in support of the claim in question. First, the reference made to the interests of the inhabitants of Taiwan and the exceptional circumstances of this entity is not without legal basis, under international law. The Court in the *Western Sahara Advisory Opinion*[209] emphasised that,

> in examining the propositions of Mauritania regarding the legal nature of ... the Mauritanian entity, the Court give full weight ... to the *special characteristics of the Saharan region and peoples* with which the present proceedings are concerned [emphasis added].

Secondly, Taiwan has been maintaining its own law and order for many decades and this seems to be a relatively settled practice now.[210] Also, the notion of greater autonomy for Taiwan may include internal security powers. Wider autonomy for Taiwan, including having international relations with states, appears to be acceptable to Beijing, as long as it claims to be part of China.[211] Thirdly, other states have been trading small arms with this entity for many years; the US, South Korea, Italy, Spain and Germany are among main known suppliers of SALW to the territory.[212]

Fourthly, although the position of the WTO on the arms trade lacks clarity, nevertheless, Taiwan, as a member of the WTO, may have a legal competence to trade in arms, unless and otherwise exporting states deny it such a right, due to their national and international security concerns and interests, as clearly stated in Article XXI of the GATT.[213] And finally,

[207] See, eg Pegg, 'Defacto States in the International System' Institute of International Relations, University of British Colombia, *Working Paper* No 21, February 1998, pp 16 and 13; see also Charney and Prescott, above n 183, at 466; see also, the White Paper, above n 180; even the PRC recognises the right of Taiwan to have certain international relations.

[208] At a ministerial meeting in June 2003 of the Asia-Pacific Economic Cooperation Forum, Taiwan's Economic Minister voiced Taiwan's strong support for counter-terrorism efforts in the Asia-Pacific region, which focused on plans to enhance security measures in airplanes, airports, ships, and harbors, at <http://hongkong.usconsulate.gov/uscn/state/2004/042901.htm>

[209] Above n 144 [emphasis added].

[210] Above n 182, Art 137.

[211] White Paper, above n 180.

[212] Above, n 200.

[213] See 4.2.1, p 96.

exercising security powers, by an entity having no sovereignty over a territory, is not unknown in international relations. After the end of the Second World War, for instance, the GDR had its own strong police and army while it was under the sovereignty of the USSR.[214]

The opposing argument may have four interrelated dimensions. Firstly, such assertion of a right for Taiwan could be against the sovereignty of China and the non-intervention principle. Secondly, the general consensus on the notion of greater autonomy for Taiwan may not include military affairs either; in this respect, the continuing objection of China may imply that the territory did not have such rights. Thirdly, the practice of importation of arms by Taiwan goes to the extent of 'national' defence of the territory; and fourthly, supply of weapons to Taiwan may well be in violation of the duty not to aggravate disputes; in this sense, therefore, the state practice we have relied on, to assert the right of Taiwan may only be evidence of breaches of international law (see 4.2.1 and 6.1).

While both views could have their own legal basis, the first one appears to be more persuasive, and reflective of the exceptional features of the Taiwan issue. It seems to be plausible that Taiwan may need, as a matter of necessity, to import SALW for its own public order and security, as the safety of the people and their wellbeing need to be sheltered. Its borders, as a territory shall also be protected from any internal or external crimes. This position could be reinforced by the fact that the mainland has not been exercising such sovereign functions in Taiwan. However, the imports of arms, beyond the abovementioned purposes should be illegal under international law.

Yet, Taiwan is now one of the newly emerged manufacturers of small arms. Will it have a right to export arms to other jurisdictions? Generally, a 'legal supply' of arms by a NSA to a state appears to be illegal in international relations (see 6.1). Also, it is difficult to envisage any exception of this kind at this stage, and the wise solution could be to wait and see further legal developments in the area.

At any rate, Taiwan has to be bound, at least, by norms of *jus cogens*.[215] The obligation to adhere to fundamental rules of arms transfers, which are highly related to peremptory norms, applies to Taiwan. For instance, it can't be at liberty to destabilise countries or regions by providing weapons, either through the diversion of its imports, or from its own manufacture (see 4.2.1, chapters five and seven). This is so because the international community does not accept any behaviour of territorial entities which could defeat the core values of the multilateral legal framework.[216]

[214] See eg Shaw, *International Law*, 5th edn, above n 5, at 204–05, GDR under the USSR.

[215] Crawford, 'The Criteria for Statehood', above n 135, at 145.

[216] *Ibid*; see also, n 150; see, eg PGIIS, 2005, *SAS*, p 20, 'in January 2005, a news report suggested that the US intended to purchase 300 million 5.56mm cartridges, for around $62.5 million, from Taiwan', for the use of the US military, including in Iraq.

Some analogies regarding transfers of nuclear materials and hazardous wastes could clarify these restrictions. Among others, Canada and the US, in their exchange of letters of 24 February 1993, concerning 'non-proliferation assurance to Canadian uranium retransferred from the US to Taiwan', have agreed that:

> 3. [T]he United States of America shall ensure that Canadian uranium and special nuclear material produced therefrom are, while in Taiwan, subject to all provisions of the Agreement for Cooperation Concerning Civil Uses of Atomic Energy, signed April 4, 1972 . . . 4. The United States of America shall ensure that Canadian uranium and special nuclear material produced therefrom are, while in Taiwan, subject to the Safeguards Transfer Agreement.[217]

Therefore, apart from the peaceful use of nuclear energy, Taiwan has been prohibited from developing nuclear weapons and from transferring such materials to third parties.[218] Such measures underpin the norms on nuclear weapons non-proliferation. Likewise, in respect of environmental issues, Pegg notes[219]:

> individual states will, for example, want to ensure that proper controls are placed on the transfers of dangerous substances such as agricultural pests or toxic wastes regardless of their foreign origin or destination.

Similarly, Taiwan has the obligation to comply with the rules of international law of arms transfer and their end-uses. Whether it has or otherwise the right to export arms, moreover, Taiwan cannot be held to be free from relevant international law obligations. This is notwithstanding the legal duty of any state that wishes to have small arms transactions with Taiwan, to ensure that relevant international rules have been met.

Four remarks sum up the discussion on territorial entities relating to arms transfers. First, it appears that international law has not developed apparent and universal rules relevant to such conditions. In principle, governments of states are only entitled to acquire and use weapons for their legitimate needs. Such exceptional situations should therefore be assessed on entity-by-entity bases.[220] The views of the parties directly concerned, international organisations, the practice of states and the overall interests of the inhabitants of such entities, have to be carefully assessed. This shall therefore be the first golden rule for purposes of such transactions.

Secondly, it has to be emphasised that territorial entities must comply with general international law principles, including with basic rules of

[217] <http://www.lexum.umontreal.ca/ca_us/en/cts.1993.05.en.html>; see also the same treaty between Australia and the US, 31 July 2001, at <http://www.aph.gov.au/house/committee/jsct/nst/treaties/taiw_nia.pdf>

[218] *Ibid*, Annex, para 1; see for nuclear material transfers, below n 235.

[219] Above n 207, at 12–16.

[220] See, eg Lovelace, above n 172, para 17; Warbrick private discussion, 4 October 2003, Department of Law, Durham University.

small arms transfers and use. This does not diminish the obligations and responsibilities of states that might arise from their involvement in such transfers (see chapter nine).

Thirdly, international law may not deny transfers of small arms, as an exception to the non-intervention rule, to the extent that the threshold is not exceeded. The quantity and quality of weapons to be transferred shall be commensurate to the public order and peace end-uses of an entity and its populace. Arms sales or aid for such entities, beyond this line, may not be justified under international law. They could also lead to serious security, humanitarian and other concerns. The Palestine and Taiwan cases, among others, express both sides of the problem, on the one hand, the *exceptional rights* of the entities and on the other, *possible abuses* of such situations. Nonetheless, every exceptional entity might not enjoy such an exceptional right. Small arms transfer has nothing to do, for example, with the Holy See as a spiritual entity, although it has an undisputed international legal personality, comparable to states.[221]

6.2.3 Other Cases

Two further exceptions deserve a mention. The first regards the absence of licence requirements by a state, for imports of certain types of small arms to its own territory. For instance, the US Code of Federal Regulations of 1974 does not require any permit for the importation of firearms from Canada of less than .50 calibre[222]; also, customs officers 'may permit the export without a license' of such arms to Canada, inter alia, for 'end-use' in Canada.[223] Correspondingly, section 35(1) of the Canadian Firearms Act[224] permits an individual(s) to import a firearm such as a rifle or a shotgun to Canada, without an import licence, on the condition that it has to be declared to customs officers there. Exports of these sporting or hunting firearms can also be authorised, similar to the US practice.[225]

However, first, in both the US[226] and Canada,[227] the exception applies to non-business transfers and individuals only; secondly, it is basically limited to firearms intended for hunting and sport; and thirdly, such a practice is virtually non-existent in the vast majority of states, as transfers

[221] See, eg Shaw, *International Law*, 5th edn, above n 5, at 218–19; see also Brownlie, *Principles of Public International Law* 6th edn, above n 114, at 63–64.
[222] 22 U.S. ss 47.41(c) and 47.21.
[223] *Ibid*, s 126.5.
[224] *Firearms Act* 1995, ch 39.
[225] *Ibid*, ss 37 and 38.
[226] Above n 222, s 47.61.
[227] Ch 39, ss 43–53.

of 'civilian firearms' to, and from, their territories have to be authorised in advance.[228]

Regardless of those cases where the domestic legislation of a state does not entail a permit or licence for importation of certain firearms, a state's exports of arms to a territory may not amount to a violation of the non-intervention rule to the extent that the laws of the recipient state accommodates such situations.

Treaty-based arms transfers to NSAs may possibly be the second exception. Hypothesis could be of help here; if states A, B and C, who have a legal interest upon entity D, agree to intervene to restore law and order, in case of internal disturbance in the latter, a supply of weapons to D by the parties to the agreement could be justified, subject to compliance with the terms and purposes of the treaty and other relevant rules of international law.

In summary, both exceptions in this sub-heading are founded either upon the explicit consent of a state or a general understanding of consent and therefore may not contradict the rule relating to government-to-government transfer.

6.3 THE NON-INTERVENTION RULE

Does the discussion so far suggest that there is a rule of law which restricts SALW transfers to be between states alone? If yes, what could be the sources, contents, exceptions and problems of the rule? In order to address these and related questions, it may be necessary to discuss the general application of the non-intervention norm to the small arms problem, relevant contemporary developments and their legal implications, and other analogous legal regimes which may help clarify the rule in question.

As discussed above (see 4.2.1 and 6.1.3), it is generally uncontested that the customary rule of non-intervention exists and applies to the arms trade.[229] Moreover, breaches of the rule could amount to a violation of the prohibition of the threat or use of force against another state, if they constitute a direct or indirect armed attack against that state. Hence, compared with other norms of transfers considered in this work, the principles of non-intervention and sovereignty appear to imply a clear-cut position on arms transfers in that—weapons supply to the territory of a state, particularly to violent NSAs, without the consent and knowledge of that

[228] See, eg '*UN Study*', above n 3, at 10; *EC Directive* (91/477/EEC), 18 June 1991; and *Chinese Law on Control of Firearms*, 1996, Art 13.

[229] For general restrictions on the freedom of action of states see, eg ch 5, p 134; see also Charney, 'Universal International Law' (1993) 87 *AJIL* 543–45.

state, is illegal intervention upon the sovereignty of the latter, save for certain exceptions. Furthermore, it has to be noted here that the non-intervention based prohibition of arms transfer applies to anyone (including governments) in a conflict area (eg civil war), with certain lawful and legitimate exceptions, such as SC authorised measures and the co-operation between states to fight terrorism (see 6.4, and chapters four and five).

The next question should be whether the non-intervention rule has been specifically adopted in the small arms legal regime of transfers. The answer considers the entities involved and the circumstances of transfers; the supply of arms by a state, to rebel, terrorist, criminal, etc groups of another state, in a situation of security or political crisis or otherwise, will be of principal concern here. Three possible responses could be given to the question in such a context. The first is that the instruments/practices we have seen at all levels may amount to acceptance of the duty of non-intervention by states and international organisations, to the small arms trade.[230] This may not show albeit a full picture of the rule in discussion. The second response relies on treaty obligations. As seen earlier, the OAS Convention,[231] the ECOWAS Convention and the EUJA[232] on small arms transfer, as legally binding instruments, have clearly adopted it. Their scope of application as treaty obligations is however limited to the parties concerned.

Most importantly, we need to address the question whether a customary rule on SALW affirms or rejects the non-intervention general norm. In other words, does state practice and *opinio juris*[233] on SALW transfers, reinforce, or deviate from, the universal rule of non-intervention? We shall examine it in the light of the elements of custom.

Regarding the usage requirement, the global, regional and domestic instruments we have discussed have clearly demonstrated two realities: first, that SALW transfers must comply with the non-intervention rule; and secondly, that such transactions shall be between, or on the authorisation of, states only. In particular, the OAS and ECOWAS Conventions, the Canadian Proposal, the DPoA and the PoA have witnessed the support of an overwhelming majority of states to such claims.[234] Many states have made the rule part of their primary legislation—for instance, China, Germany, France, Austria, Canada and India did so.[235] Importer states

[230] See, eg above n 25; see also Brownlie, *Principles of Public International Law*, 6th edn, above n 114, at 663.
[231] Above, n 45.
[232] Above, n 49.
[233] See, eg on custom in general 3.4; see also Akehurst, 'Custom as a Source of International Law' (1974–75) 47 *BYIL* 1; see also Shaw, *International Law*, 5th edn, above n 5, at 59–60.
[234] See 6.1.1.
[235] See 6.1.2.

such as African countries have also taken a similar position on many occasions.[236] Scott has convincingly reached the conclusion[237]:

> Given the elements required to create binding customary international law, it is conceivable that the Conference [UN, 2001], or at least the policies espoused, may well become binding. As states are numerous, uniform, and consistent in applying curbs on illicit transfers, and such application is of sufficient length, the material element would be met.

Hence, taking into account the detailed analysis made on the nature of these global, regional and domestic efforts (see 5.7), it could fairly be argued that we have a consistent, uniform,[238] and general[239] practice, which has been evident since the early 1990s.[240]

Despite this, the US has repeatedly rejected restrictions, as clearly demonstrated in the UN Conference, on the ground that such a limitation might hamper the need to assist a just cause.[241] The 1997 UN Panel,[242] the Wassenaar Guidelines,[243] the ICCAT[244] and some writers[245] have shown a lenient view on, or some degree of support to, the legality of arms provision to NSAs. The practice of covert transfers of arms by states to such actors[246] may show the inadequacy of the practice in question too.

Nonetheless, the ICJ in the *Fisheries* case, in respect of the usage element of custom, underlined that 'the evidence should be sought in the behaviour of a great number of States, possibly the majority of States, in any case the great majority of interested states'.[247] In this case, unlike the controversy over the ban of the use of nuclear weapons, greater majority of exporting and importing states of SALW, with the exception of the US, support the prohibition of weapon supplies to NSAs.

As revealed later, however, the US seems to claim an exception to the prohibition, and not denying the rule in its entirety.[248] The ICJ in the *Nicaragua* case made it clear, moreover, that although states *frequently* breach the rule of non-intervention, there is no customary rule which supports the emergence of an exception to it. The Court emphasised that

[236] Above, n 52.

[237] Scott, 'The UN Conference on the Illicit Trade of Small Arms and Light Weapons: An Exercise in Futility', 31 *GAJINT'L and COPM.L.* 694 [clarification added].

[238] For consistency and uniformity of the practice see, eg 5.7, fns 195 and 196).

[239] For generality of the practice see 5.7, fns 205–10.

[240] *Ibid*, fn 210.

[241] Above, n 33.

[242] Above, n 26.

[243] Above, n 43.

[244] Above, n 111.

[245] Above, n 100; see in general for the non-binding nature of the instruments Zaleski, ch 5, fn 93, pp 36–37; see also Marsh, 'Two Sides of the Same Coin? The Legal and Illegal Trade in Small Arms' 9 *BJWA* (Spring 2002) 220.

[246] Above, nn 65 and 66.

[247] *Fisheries* case, *ICJ Repts* 1951, p 128.

[248] Above, n 63.

the non-intervention customary rule could only be modified if the exception in question [*the right to intervene*] is 'shared in principle by other states'. It added also that instances of claims of legitimate interference by the US were only statements of international policy and not assertions of legal rules.[249] Certainly, the developments on the small arms regime, following the Court's verdict, reinforce the proposition found in the judgment, and not the current claims of the US. A single state is not seen claiming the right of arms transfers, in response to genocide, repression or tyrannical rule in another state. Rather, as discussed in the Canadian Proposal, states challenge, or at least have not supported, such a claim.

It is true, as the UN High-Level Panel of 2004 underlined, that the international community has to collectively respond and prevent atrocities including genocide, large-scale violations of IHL and ethnic cleansing. However, there has been no '"right to intervene" of a State, but the "responsibility to protect" of *every* State'.[250] It has added in paragraph 203 of the report that there shall be 'collective international responsibility to protect, exercisable by the Security Council'. In particular, the Panel suggested the ban of small arms supply to conflict areas, as one method of preventing, or responding to human catastrophe.[251] So, current practices do not back the US view; they appear in fact to oppose it.

Briefly, the material element of the rule in question seems to be sufficiently satisfied.

Yet, is such practice accompanied by *opinio juris*? The fact that the rule has been clearly included in certain treaties and domestic legislation, and the Canadian and the UN DPoA proposals—and the attention they have attracted on the part of an overwhelming majority of states, undoubtedly shows the intention of states to be bound by the rule of non-intervention in their SALW transactions.[252] It has to be emphasised that, inter alia, Article IX(2) and (3) of the OAS Convention,[253] Article 10(b) of the Nairobi Protocol,[254] Article 3(b) of the EUJA,[255] section III(c)(1) of the OSCE Document,[256] the ECOWAS Moratorium[257] and the ECOWAS Convention have all included the non-intervention rule in general and the restriction of arms transit to NSAs in particular. In addition, Fischer suggests:

> from a legal point of view, we may assume that the *opinio juris* is established since a clear majority—173 of the 174 states participating in the Conference—

[249] See 6.1.3; see also *Fisheries* case, above n 247, at 138, para 2.

[250] *A More Secure World, Our Shared Responsibility: Report of the Secretary General's High-Level Panel on Threat, Challenges and Change,* November 2004, para 201.

[251] *Ibid*, para 96, see also para 178.

[252] See also detailed discussion, pp 138–40.

[253] Above, n 45.

[254] Above, n 47.

[255] Above, n 49.

[256] Above, n 50.

[257] Above, n 53.

> supported the consensus to have this measure (*the ban of arms transfers to NSAs*) introduced into the Programme of Action. The feeling was expressed within the international community that States should be bound by this norm.[258]

However, Fischer questioned her own view saying that out of the 191 states of the world only '174 States were present. Because of the absence of these States, we cannot confirm in absolute terms whether the psychological element is fulfilled'; that, as a particularly interested state, the US does not 'feel bound by it; consequently, the proofs for customary norm are not present'.[259]

At least three main reasons could challenge Fischer's assertion. First, as Judge Lachs, in his Dissenting Opinion, in the *Continental Shelf* cases underlined, 'for the rule to become binding, a rule or principle of international law need not pass the test of universal acceptance'.[260] As discussed earlier too, a single state that has a particular interest cannot block the formation of customary rule. The reference should be to the 'great majority of interested states'.

Secondly, the notion of the rule is embodied in the Preamble of the PoA, although states failed to agree on an explicit prohibition of arms supply to NSAs. And thirdly, the UN Conference and the debate over the PoA is only one process; so Fischer's conclusion has not considered other crucial efforts. Therefore, the aforesaid failure of the PoA should not imply the absence of the rule at hand.

Moreover, as discussed in a greater detail above, the ICJ's opinion in the *Nicaragua* case and the views of a majority of jurists' strengthens the view that there was/is adequate *opinio juris* regarding the prohibition of arms supply to armed groups of another state.[261] Such notion of restriction is also found in environmental law. For instance, Cook wrote that:

> Many agreements such as the Basel Convention, the Rotterdam Convention and the Cartagena Protocol provide for some form of advance notification of export to the State of import, a system referred to as 'prior informed consent' or 'advanced informed agreement'. This type of control is particularly appropriate where the goods to be exported may be potentially hazardous or harmful . . . In this respect, the regimes concerned with potentially hazardous products may provide a closer substantive analogy with the type of regime envisaged for small arms and light weapons.[262]

258 Fischer, 'Outcome of the UN Process: the Legal Character of the UN Programme of Action' in Dahinden et al (eds), *Small Arms and Light Weapons, Legal Aspects of National and International Regulation* (Geneva, United Nations, vol iv, 2002) 165 [clarification added].

259 *Ibid*, at 166.

260 *North Sea Continental Shelf* case, *ICJ Repts* 1969, p 229, paras 2 and 3.

261 See 6.1.3.

262 Cook, 'Precedents from the Export and Transport of Endangered Species: CITES and other Trade-related Multilateral Environmental Arrangements: Models for Control of Trade in Small Arms and Light Weapons?' in Dahinden et al (eds), above n 258, at 61–62.

There can be no doubt that SALW are lethal and dangerous, especially when they are not under the strict control of a state. Indeed, the notion of prior informed consent in environmental law is analogous with authorised transfers of small arms by states. However, in the latter case, the risk assessment factor seems to be irrelevant to the rule in discussion. The non-intervention rule, as opposed to other rules of transfers (peace and security, IHL, IHRL), does not seem to depend on the actual or future use of arms in a destination state.

6.4 CONCLUSION

Therefore, the non-intervention rule of small arms transfer seems to have been appropriately established. This particular rule strengthens the general rule of non-intervention. The contents of this particular rule include: (1) small arms transfers shall only be, as a rule, between states or their governments; (2) a direct or indirect supply of arms by a state, to opposition groups in another state, is illegal and prohibited; (3) any SALW transfers to a territory of a state has to be authorised by that state, and thus the consent and knowledge of a concerned state of the transactions in question is an intrinsic element of the rule. As mentioned above, however, care must be taken that every consent of a recipient state/government may not justify the legal supply of weapons to the territory of a sovereign state;[263] and (4) this applies to all kinds of small arms, with emphasis on military type weapons, as shown, inter alia, in the League's and contemporary practice.

However, three accepted exceptions exist: first, this rule is not withstanding the right of peoples or NLMs, to get assistance, including SALW, to resist colonial, alien or racial rule/domination; this may only be the case in the absence of a pacific framework, established by the parties concerned and/or the international community. Secondly, state-to-individual transfer of civilian firearms could be lawful when it's permitted under the domestic law of the destination state, or when common understanding relating to this exists between the countries concerned; businesses of arms and military type SALW have clearly been excluded from such an exception. Lastly, states may have the right to supply arms to a NSA, pursuant to a valid treaty between them. The last two exceptions rely on

[263] See, eg Cassese, *International Law*, 2nd edn (Oxford, Oxford University Press, 2005) 368. He states that: 'Clearly state practice makes extensive use of the consent exception [to the duty of non-intervention], even though this practice hardly conforms to present-day international law'; consent is valid if it is given freely, by the lawful government, on an ad hoc basis, does not legitimise illegal use of force against the integrity or political independence of the consenting state and does not conflict with *jus cogens* norms. However, he also indicated (at 472) that a state 'may not oppose its sovereign rights to any foreign State that intends lawfully to use force against those (*terrorist*) organisations' [clarification added].

the will of a state, and so a question of intervention may not arise in such circumstances. Although not the main focus of the chapter, it is worth noting here that SC measures and exceptions to arms embargoes in areas of UN or authorised forces is legal too.

In addition, there is one controversial exception; arms transfers by a state may be possible to territorial entities (eg nascent states), for purposes of public order and law enforcement uses, in such exceptional territories. Such cases have to be determined: (1) on a case-by-case basis; (2) taking into account the practice and the attitude of the parties and the international community; and (3) in full compliance with other norms of general international law, including the rules on small arms transfers (eg peace and security). Similarly, the entities in question owe the international community the obligation to comply with its basic norms of arms transfers. Thus, any breaches or abuses of such exceptional circumstances, either by states or by entities, shall not be acceptable.

Prima facie, arms provision by a state, to NSAs, to oust tyranny, etc is illegal intervention on the sovereignty of a state and should not therefore be regarded as an exception to this rule.

This rule and its exceptions are not without problems. The first difficulty is that states frequently violate this rule of transfer, acting on national and political interests. Covert transfers are thus the major challenge of the rule. The second is that states are reluctant to codify the rule, as was the case in the UN Conference. This clearly hinders the process of elaborating the details of the rule and its application. The last problem is that exceptions can lead to abuse if their application is entirely left to unilateral decision-making. However, contraventions of the rule, especially the prohibition of arms supply to NSAs engaged in armed conflict, may bring about state responsibility (see chapter nine).

In the end, it has to be borne in mind that every consignment of arms undertaken in conformity with the rule of non-intervention is not necessarily legal under international law, as will be observed in subsequent chapters.

7

Humanitarian law [IHL] Limitations on SALW Transfers

7.1 IHL IN GENERAL

HUMANITARIAN LAW IS a deep-rooted body of international law (see 4.2.1). Examining the essential features and particular relevance of IHL to the problem at hand is imperative. Issues of sources, relevant principles, scope of application, and the questions that have to be raised for our purposes are considered next.

IHL, also called *jus in bello,* deals with the rules and customs of war and constitutes a part of international customary law.[1] Its sources are primarily custom and treaties. The Hague Regulations and Geneva Conventions have established the far-reaching treaty regime of IHL.[2] As the ICJ in the *Nicaragua* case has affirmed, however, IHL is 'customary law and the treaties as reflections of it'. In particular, the Court has so deemed common Articles 1 and 3 of the Conventions.[3] The former Article deals with the universal character of the instruments, and the latter extends the application of IHL to non-international conflicts (see. 7.2). Also, the ICRC observes that IHL 'is older than' the Geneva Conventions and 'independent of them'.[4]

However judges Jennings and Ago in the *Nicaragua* case expressed their doubts on the customary law character of the provisions of the Conventions, including common Article 1. Inter alios, Meron thinks that there is no evidence which shows that the negotiating states had concluded the treaties of 1949 in the belief that they were codifying customary

[1] Green, *The Contemporary Law of Armed Conflict*, 2nd edn (Manchester, Manchester University Press, 2000) 52–53; see also Shaw, *International Law*, 4th edn (Cambridge, Cambridge University Press, 1997) 806.

[2] See for the treaties, ch 4, p 95; see also Green *ibid*, ch 2 and p 122; see also Shaw, *ibid*, at 807.

[3] See *Case Concerning Military Activities in and against Nicaragua, ICJ Repts* 1986, para 42.

[4] Pictet, *The Geneva Conventions of 12 August 1949, Commentary* (*Geneva Convention I*, ICRC, 1952) 39, para 2; see also for the customary status of IHL Greenwood, 'The Development of International Humanitarian Law by the International Criminal Tribunal for the Former Yugoslavia' in Frowein and Wolfrum (eds), *Max Planck Year Book of United Nations Law* (London, Kluwer Law International, vol ii, 1998) 128.

law, and thus some provisions of the Conventions are customary and others are not. Yet, he regards Article 1 of the Geneva treaties as customary law.[5]

By and large, it appears to be well recognised that the treaties reflect customary rules of armed conflict. Alternatively, as the treaties are widely accepted by states, and such universal obligations could originate either from treaties or a custom, the debate on this line might not make any difference for our purposes. The core interest shall therefore be on relevant IHL principles.

At least five principles could be described at this juncture. First, IHL protects civilians who are not or no longer taking part in hostilities, along with their civilian premises, at the time of armed conflict; this is also called a rule of distinction in combat.[6] Sandoz et al have diligently spelt out the nature and extent of protection for civilians as including:

> The dangers arising from military operations. This means that the obligation does not consist only in abstaining from attacks, but also in avoiding, or in any case reducing to a minimum, incidental losses, and in taking safety measures.[7]

Beyond that, women and children, especially those who have been affected in one way or another by the effects of conflict have received particular attention in IHL. For instance, children should be treated with special care; those under 15 years of age shall not be recruited into the armed forces, and both sides are obliged to prevent them from taking part in a conflict.[8]

Secondly, it lays down the principle that the purpose of armed conflict is to defeat an enemy, with the least human and resource losses, rather than total destruction or extermination; thus providing protection for combatants. In this way it embodies the rules of necessity and proportionality in its ambit.[9]

Thirdly, it sets out the rule that the means and methods of warfare in war are not unlimited. The first dimension of this principle is that weapons that have the effect of causing unnecessary suffering or super-

[5] For dissenting opinion of Judge Jennings and for views of Judge Ago see *Nicaragua* case, above n 3, p 527, para 3, and p 184, para 8 respectively; for the Conventions as a whole as customary law see Meron, *Human Rights and Humanitarian Norms as Customary Law* (Oxford, Oxford University Press, 1989) 154; see also Meron on Art 1: 'The Geneva Conventions as Customary Law' (1987) 81 *AJIL* 370 and below, n 32.

[6] See, eg *GC IV*, Arts 2, 3, 24–26, 27–78; *GP I*, Arts 1, 48–60 and 35(2); *GP II*, Art 13; see also Green, above n 1, at 229–30.

[7] Sandoz, Swinarski and Zimmermann (eds), *Commentary on the Protocol Additional to the Geneva Conventions of 12 August 1949* (Geneva, ICRC, Martinus Nijhoff, 1987) 1448–49, paras 4761 and 4770; see also Provost, p 38.

[8] See, eg *GP I*, Arts 76, 77(1), (2), (3); *Convention on the Rights of the Child*, 1989, 28 I.L.M.1448, Art 38(2); see also Green, above n 1, at 118–19; see also SC Resolutions 1261/1999, 1314/2000, 1379/2001, and 1460/2003.

[9] The Hague rules focus on combatants' protection; see eg, *HC IV*, Annex, Art 4; see also Green *ibid*, at 122, 350.

fluous injury are prohibited from use as a means of warfare. In other words, a principle of humanity has to be adhered to.[10] The bans and/or restrictions upon incendiary weapons, anti-personnel mines, and some WMD can be included here (see chapter one).[11] As a second aspect of the principle, certain prohibited methods of armed conflict, such as perfidious attacks upon an adversary have also been proscribed.[12]

Finally, in the absence of clear rules in relation to armed conflict, the principles of humanity and the dictates of public conscience apply; this is commonly known as the Martens Clause. These rules of IHL are widely incorporated in treaties.[13]

Furthermore, IHL's scope of application includes both international and internal armed conflicts. The first scenario is that when armed conflict arises between states 'through the medium of their armed forces', *jus in bello* treats such situations as international armed conflicts. The central feature is that the conflict is inter-state.[14] In the course of hostilities, therefore, states have to comply with several obligations of IHL. Acts such as wilful killing, torture or inhuman treatment, causing great suffering or serious injury to body or health and unjustified extensive destruction of civilian property all amount to grave breaches of IHL. Parties to a conflict have to refrain from, and prevent the commission of, these breaches. Such breaches constitute war crimes, on which states have assumed a legal obligation either to punish perpetrators in their respective jurisdictions or to extradite them to any country party to the Convention whenever that country makes a prima facie case. This is an introduction of the concept of universal jurisdiction to IHL, with regard to grave breaches of IHL. This has been clearly stated in all four Conventions and also applies to all states, whether or not party to the Convention. Two points are worth mentioning here; first, the notion of grave breaches and their legal consequences only apply to international conflicts, as far as the classic position of IHL is concerned. Secondly, the prosecution of individuals may not exonerate a state from its responsibility, depending on the circumstances of the breach (see. 7.8).[15]

[10] See Green *ibid*, at 125–26; see also Gillard, 'What is Legal? What is Illegal? Limitations on Transfers of Small Arms under International Law' (Cambridge, *LRCIL*) 2 and below, n 96.

[11] See 4.2.1, p 121; see, eg *1925 Geneva Gas Protocol, 1972 Biological and Toxin Weapons Convention, 1980 CCW [Mines, booby traps and incendiaries]*; see *Res XXVIII of the XXth International Red Cross Conference*, Vienna 1965, the fourth principle is 'that the general principles of the law of war apply to nuclear and similar weapons'; see also Green on nuclear weapons *ibid*, at 128–32.

[12] See, eg *Hague Regs*, Art 24; *P I*, Art 37 (2); see also Green *ibid*, at 144–50.

[13] Ticehurst, 'The Martens Clause and the Laws of Armed Conflict' *International Review of the Red Cross* (No 317, 30 April 1997) 125–34.

[14] See, eg Green, above n 1, at 54–55.

[15] *GC I*, Arts 49–50; *GC II*, Arts 50–51; *GC. III*, Arts 129–30; *GC IV*, Arts 146–47; see also, ICRC *Commentary* on Art 146 of the IVth GC, at <http://www.icrc.org/IHL.nsf/Web COMART? OpenView>; see also Pictet (1952), above n 4, at 362–73; see also, Green *ibid*, at

The second scenario applies to armed conflicts of non-international character. According to Article 1 of GP II, all armed conflicts that occur in the territory of a state, 'between its armed forces and dissident armed forces or other organised armed groups', have been deemed to be non-international armed conflicts.[16] Minimum humanitarian protection for civilians, including those *hors de combat*, is set out for such cases. Common Article 3 of the Conventions prohibited:

> (a) violence to life and person, in particular murder of all kinds, mutilation, cruel treatment and torture; (b) taking of hostages; (c) outrages upon personal dignity, in particular humiliating and degrading treatment.

The minimum guarantee under this common Provision is therefore the obligation to provide 'humane treatment', to civilians and those captives who fall into the hands of the adversary. Although neither definition nor explanation of such a treatment had been given, three absolute prohibitions, inter alia, torture, murder and hostage taking have been listed, and should be met without any excuse and in all circumstances. The list of such prohibitions is not exhaustive, but rather flexible. Even so protections and obligations applicable to international conflicts have been extended as customary rules to the non-international conflicts. For example, Article 8(2)(c), (d) and (e) of the ICC Statute stipulates that serious violations of common Article 3 of the Geneva Conventions would amount to war crimes of the same severity as grave breaches of IHL. More precisely, the ICTY in the *Prosecutor v Delalic et al* case has considered Common Article 3 violations as grave breaches of war.[17] In 2002, the ICJ in the *Yerodia* case has used, obiter dicta, the term 'serious crimes' to indicate universal jurisdiction on violations of IHL.[18] Moreover, the Appeals Panel of the Special Court for Sierra Leone has ruled that 'recruiting child soldiers was established as a war crime at the time of the civil war in that country'.[19]

45–46, 297–300; see also, *Rome Statute of the International Criminal Court (ICC Statute), 37 ILM* (1998) 999–1019, Art 8(2) (a) talks about grave breaches of Geneva Conventions as a war crime, but in (c) crimes committed in non-international conflicts have been termed as serious violations and not grave breaches; see also, *Prosecutor v Tadic* (4.2.1, n 35) para 71, the Tribunal has stated that Art 2 of its Statute which deals with grave breaches only applies to international conflicts.

[16] See also Green, *ibid*, at 65–67.

[17] Pictet (1952), above n 4, at 52–53, and 59–61; see also, *ICC Statute*, above n 15; see also, *Prosecutor v Delalic et al* (*Celebici* case), ICTY, Trial Chamber II (Judgment), 16 November 1998, IT-96-21-T, paras 202, 235, while finding the conflict in Bosnia and Herzegovina to have been international throughout 1992, suggested, obiter dicta, that violations of common article 3 of the Geneva Conventions should now be considered as 'grave breaches' of the Conventions.

[18] *The Arrest Warrants* case, *ICJ Repts* 2002 (Merits), 121, p 22, para 59; *Separate Opinion of President Guillauma*, p 7, para 12, in his view, the 'only true case of universal jurisdiction' under international law is piracy, in contrast to, see *Separate Opinion of Judge Wyngaert*, p 30, para 59, she believes that war crimes against civilians are subject to universal jurisdiction.

[19] 'Child Recruitment was War Crime', *BBC News*, 01 June 2004, at <http://news.bbc.co.uk/1/hi/world/africa/3767041.stm>

One thing which is clear is that grave breaches and serious violations of IHL, particularly those committed against civilians, are war crimes which entail individual criminal responsibility, whatever the status of conflicts. The interest in this work is, however, limited to an individual state's duties and responsibilities.

Due to the fact that SALW use and transfer may conflict with the aforesaid principles of IHL, as will be explored further, the application of IHL to the transactions of arms has to be studied appropriately. General IHL obligations of states, specific standards for restriction and some forgotten dimensions of humanitarian law to the arms trade will give us some insights on the matter. Addressing these issues will provide some answers as to how IHL responds to the global arms trade.

7.2 THE OBLIGATION TO RESPECT AND ENSURE RESPECT FOR IHL VIS-À-VIS SALW TRANSFERS

Does IHL apply to small arms transfers? If yes, on what basis, and to what extent? To answer these and other related questions, the general application of a state's obligations 'to respect and ensure respect' for IHL to the SALW transfers regime will need to be seen in the light of particular developments. The nature and extent of these obligations will be dealt with first. Common Article 1 of the Geneva Conventions of 1949 reads:

> The High Contracting Parties undertake *to respect and ensure respect* for the present Convention *in all circumstances* [emphasis added].

This Article is embodied in all Geneva Conventions of 1949. This means that: first, it applies to all states, to the extent of customary international law, as the Geneva and The Hague treaties are declaratory of such customary law, as assured by the ICJ in the *Nicaragua* case (see 7.1).[20] Secondly, by virtue of Article 26 of the Law of Treaties, ie the principle of *pacta sunt servanda,* the rules of IHL apply to all states who have signed and ratified the treaties at issue.[21] With this in mind we need to discuss the nature and scope of this obligation to some degree.

Three phrases often cause controversy, namely, 'to respect', 'to ensure respect' and 'in all circumstances'; yet, we will focus on the second one. Undoubtedly, states are under an obligation 'to respect' the rules of IHL in their respective territories and authority. They are also obliged to abide by them 'in all circumstances'. This means that 'application of the Conventions does not depend on the character of conflicts. Whether a war is "just" or "unjust", whether it is a war of aggression or of resistance to

[20] Above n 3, p 114, para 218; see also ICRC, above n 4.
[21] *VCLT,* ch 5, p 103.

aggression', states shall comply with the rules of IHL, as soon as armed conflict arises.[22] This might not answer however whether IHL rules are *erga omnes* (general and non-reciprocal) obligations.

As to the ICRC, common Article 1 was intended 'to give a more formal character to the mutual undertaking by insisting on its character as a general obligation'. Thus, 'it is not an engagement concluded on a basis of reciprocity, binding each party to the contract only insofar as the other party observes its obligations'.[23] It went on to state further that:

> It is rather a series of unilateral engagements solemnly contracted before the world as represented by the other Contracting Parties. Each State contracts obligations vis-à-vis itself and at the same time vis-à-vis the others. The motive of the Conventions is such a lofty one, so universally recognized as an imperative call of civilization.[24]

Moreover, the phrase 'to ensure respect' could give us some more guidance towards understanding the problem, as it contains twofold obligations. The first is limited to domestic enforcement. A state's engagement 'extends to all those over whom it has authority'. Giving necessary orders to military authorities or civilians, and supervising the execution of the Directives are among the obligations, which a state has to uphold in the course of ensuring respect for the Conventions. Further, states are under obligation to make peace time preparations on 'the legal, material or other means of loyal enforcement of the Conventions as and when the occasion arises'. The second dimension of the obligation is universal in nature. When a power fails to respect its legal obligations, 'the Contracting Parties (neutral, allied or enemy) may, and should endeavour to bring it back to an attitude of respect for the Convention'[25] (see chapter nine).

Later developments have supported a wider interpretation of such duties in general. The first one was the Teheran Conference on Human Rights of 1968, which was held under the auspices of the UN. A Resolution was adopted with the support of a vast majority. The Preamble of the Resolution states:

> States Parties to the Red Cross Geneva Conventions sometimes fail to appreciate their responsibility to take steps to ensure the respect of these humanitarian rules in all circumstances by other state, even if they are not themselves directly involved in armed conflict.[26]

[22] Pictet (1952), above n 4, at 26–27; see also Pictet (1960), *The Geneva Conventions of 12 August 1949, Commentary, Geneva Convention II'* 26; see also Sandoz et al (eds), above n 7, at 37.

[23] See, eg Pictet (1952), *ibid*, p 25, para 3.

[24] *Ibid*.

[25] *Ibid*; see also Pictet (1960), above n 22, at 25–26; see also Sandoz et al (eds), above n , at 35–36, the interpretation of the protocols is consistent with the interpretation of the Conventions.

[26] Res XXIII, 12 May 1968, '*Human Rights in Armed Conflicts*' (A/CONF.32/41), final Act, p 18, the Resolution has been adopted by 67 in favour, none against and 2 abstentions; see also, GA Res2444 (XXIII), 19 December 1968.

The second key development was attached to the *Nicaragua* case. In particular, the ICJ took the position that the US had an obligation to '"respect" the Conventions and even "to ensure respect" for them "in all circumstances"', in accordance with common Article 1 of the Conventions. In the end, it concluded that the US had 'an obligation not to encourage persons or groups engaged in the conflict in Nicaragua to act in violation of the provisions of Article 3 common to the four 1949 Geneva Conventions'.[27] The Court, in the *Nuclear Weapons Advisory Opinion*, has also emphasised that the basic rules of IHL are 'intransgressible' in character.[28] It should also be noted that the ICJ in the *Barcelona Traction* case has mentioned the prohibition of genocide as one example of *erga omnes* obligation. It has been said that such rights might be derived in general from the 'principles and rules concerning the basic rights of the human person'[29] (see chapter eight). In the *Legal Consequences of the Construction of a Wall in the Occupied Palestine Territory Advisory Opinion* too, the ICJ has maintained the position that IHL 'rules incorporate obligations which are essentially of an *erga omnes* character'. An expressed mention has also been made of common Article 1 of the Conventions.[30]

Opinions of jurists vary on the issue. Kalshoven believes that states are legally responsible for ensuring respect for IHL by their armed forces and other armed groups under their control, and by the population. 'The primary legal obligation arising from common Article 1 is for States Parties to impose respect for the applicable rules' of IHL along with their treaty obligations. For that reason, 'it cannot be said to impose upon states a legal obligation to act against other states that fail in their respect of the Conventions'. This is because Article 1 of the instruments was not intended by the Contracting Parties to be so interpreted. Rather, it was intended to get rid of the *si omnes* clause, which frees states from legal obligation in case of conflict with non-Contracting Parties to the Conventions; it was meant to embrace populations as a whole in a state; and also to reveal that the duties are non-reciprocal. The 1952 and 1960 commentaries of the ICRC were therefore inventions of the writers. With respect to the Tehran Conference's Resolution, he is of the opinion that the text was adopted without debate and the participants 'may not all have been aware of the various possible interpretations of Article 1'. In the same vein, the ICJ was 'wanting to see customary law and therefore finding it'. Even so states have a moral obligation to ensure respect for IHL outside their jurisdiction.[31] In

[27] See above n 3, p 114, paras 218, 220.

[28] *Legality of the Threat or Use of Nuclear Weapons, ICJ Repts* 1996, p 257, para 79.

[29] *Barcelona Traction* case, *ICJ Repts* 1970, p 32, para 34.

[30] 9 July 2004, paras 157, 158.

[31] Kalshoven, 'The Undertaking to Respect and Ensure Respect in all Circumstances: from Tiny Seeds to Ripening Fruit' (1999) (2) *YBIHL* 10, 14, 22, 27, 28, 30, 32, 44, 47, 56, 57, and 59–61.

contrast, Meron regards the treaties in total as *erga omnes* obligations and expounds that[32]:

> The *erga omnes* character of many of the norms in these conventions implies that third states have not only the right to make appropriate representation urging respect for these norms to states allegedly involved in violating them, but also a duty not to encourage others to violate them. Insofar as the norms whose observance is urged are obligations *erga omnes*, the words 'to ensure respect' (common Article 1) may indeed reflect a principle of customary law.

In addition, Suter has highlighted the fact that those states which actively support belligerents have to be reminded of their duty to comply with common Article 1 of the Conventions, which deals with their duty to ensure respect for IHL. Luigi Condorelli and Laurence Boisson de Chazournes jointly entertain the idea that 'since each state owes respect of humanitarian law to all other states, every state had a legal interest to require that its colleagues meet their humanitarian obligations'.[33]

Despite that, whether states enjoy only *erga omnes* rights and not *erga omnes* duties, corresponding to IHL breaches by third states has not escaped debate. Cassese, while acknowledging IHL as *erga omnes* obligations, clearly noted that 'it is more appropriate to speak of a *right* of other States to appeal to the parties involved to respect the law'. He has described this as a first stage. He goes on to state that 'another stage is reached' in cases such as 'aggression and serious breaches of the right to self-determination', where 'there is also a possibility of adopting much more effective and much more binding measures than a mere appeal of invitation'.[34]

Conversely, Meron thought that 'the Geneva Conventions address rights and duties, the importance and gravity of which is well recognised by the international community'. States are obliged to bring a violator 'back to an attitude of respect for the Conventions'. The types of measures might consider, inter alia, the UN Charter.[35] Crawford has also indicated that the fundamental rules of IHL are justified as peremptory in character, along with the prohibition of torture and the right of self-determination.

[32] For scope and nature of Article 1 see Meron, 'The Geneva Conventions as Customary Law', above n 5, at 370, 355; see also Gillard, 'International Humanitarian Law and Extraterritorial State Conduct', in Coomans and Kamminga (eds), *Extraterritorial Application of Human Rights Treaties* (Oxford, Oxford University Press, 2004) 27. She stated that 'unlike human rights treaties, the protections of the four Geneva Conventions and the Additional Protocols are not expressly limited on the basis of 'jurisdiction' or territory'.

[33] As translated and quoted by Kalshoven, above n 31, at 58; see also Suter, *International Law of Guerrilla Warfare* (New York, St Martin's Press, 1984) 25–26.

[34] Cassese, 'Critical Remarks on the Application of the Concept of Crimes of States to Humanitarian Law' in Weiler, Cassese and Spinedi (eds), *International Crimes of State* (Berlin, Walter de Gruyter, 1988) 233.

[35] Meron, 'Is there already a Differentiated Regime of State Responsibility in the Geneva Conventions?' in Weiler et al (eds), *ibid*, at 228, 230 and see below, n 147.

Such universal obligations and rights were clearly envisaged by the law of treaties.[36]

It should be remembered, as will be seen in IHRL limitations, that *erga omnes* obligations in the human rights realm, are generally wider than IHL. As stated previously, the ICJ has, for example, referred to principles and rules of basic rights of the person to explain obligations of such a nature. Even so, it is not clear as to which rights are included in *erga omnes* obligations. Some say the basic ones, and others say human rights related to the natural dignity of human beings. As approaches vary to determine such rights, many believe that 'each should be assessed on its own merits, with a view to ascertaining whether or not it is an obligation *erga omnes*'.[37]

Overall, in spite of certain controversies, the dominant views can be summarised as follows: (1) States have to respect IHL by themselves. (2) They have to ensure respect for IHL in their domestic jurisdiction and outside their territories; the universal obligations include positive and negative duties. States shall, thus, refrain from any encouragement of such violations in other countries. Furthermore, they are obliged to respond to violations of IHL by other states, so that the latter would comply with *erga omnes* obligations of *jus in bello*. The provisions in the Conventions, the ICRC, the ICJ and a number of writers have affirmed this.[38] (3) They have to do so in all circumstances; and (4) in contemporary IHL, whether a war is inter-state or intra-state is irrelevant, as far as the obligation of states to respect the basic rules of IHL is concerned. In a nutshell, as a matter of customary, treaty and *erga omnes* obligations of IHL, states assume wide-ranging duties, which are generally applicable to all weaponry legal regimes.

The next question should, therefore, be how these universal obligations have been reflected in the SALW transfers regime in general, and relevant instruments at all levels will now be discussed. Global treaties have not fundamentally covered the area. In the recent past, however, the Mines Convention, stressing 'the role of public conscience in furthering the principles of humanity', as shown in its Preamble paragraph 8, has outlawed any transfers of anti-personnel landmines under any circumstances, as clearly assured in Article 1(1)(b) and (c) of the Treaty. Inducing, encouraging or assisting, in any way, any one to engage in such prohibited activity is also forbidden. While there has been no other global treaty of similar nature on small arms in modern international law, history has recorded some treaties and drafts (see 7.2.1).

[36] Crawford, *The International Law Commission's Articles on State Responsibility: Introduction, Text and Commentaries* (Cambridge, Cambridge University Press, 2002) 246–47; see also *VCLT* (p 103) Arts 53, 64; for the obligations of third states, see further ch 9.

[37] Ragazzi, *The Concept of International Obligations Erga Omnes* (Oxford / New York, Oxford University Press, 1997) 135–45.

[38] See, eg Pictet (1960), above n 22, at 25–26; see also, *Tehran Conference*, above n 26; see also, *Nicaragua*, above n 3; see also, Meron, 'The Geneva Conventions as Customary Law', above n 32.

Some important global instruments and studies on small arms have made either implicit or explicit allusions to IHL. The UN PoA, under paragraph 5 of its Preamble has recognised 'that the illicit trade in small arms and light weapons in all its aspects . . . undermines respect for international humanitarian law and impedes the provision of humanitarian assistance to victims of armed conflict'. Consequently, states have agreed, as has been stated in part II paragraph 11 of the PoA, to address the problems associated with arms transfers. In addition, UN agencies such as the Commission on Human Rights have studied the subject and concluded that the small arms trade should adhere to humanitarian norms and criteria.[39]

As was reflected in previous topics and will be seen further, the UN has expressed its concerns on the proliferation of small arms and their impact on humanitarian norms. For instance, the UN Secretary-General, in the Supplement to an Agenda for Peace, emphasised that first, small arms are 'responsible for most of the deaths in current conflicts'; secondly, 'the world is awash with them and traffic in them is very difficult to monitor, let alone intercept'; thirdly, 'the causes are many: the earlier supply of weapons to client States by the parties to the Cold War, internal conflicts, competition for commercial markets'; and finally, he suggested that the search for a solution 'should begin now'.[40] The GIAT of 1996 has also recognised the 'humanitarian' dimension of 'illicit trafficking in arms'.[41]

Furthermore, the SC has reiterated its humanitarian concern with respect to SALW proliferation, in particular their indiscriminate use against civilians, especially against children and women. Taking into account 'the considerable volume of this trade', the SC has highlighted the crucial importance of 'effective national regulations and controls on small arms transfers'. It has noted too that it 'encourages the Governments of arms-exporting countries to exercise the highest degree of responsibility in these transactions'.[42] SC arms embargoes have also been considering protection of IHL (see 5.2).

At the regional level, the EUJA, under Articles 4(b) and 6(1) and (2) affirmed the commitment of EU Member States to aim at achieving consensus on the reduction of the existing accumulation of small arms and their ammunition 'for the realisation of the following principles', inter alia, 'respect of human rights and humanitarian law'. As a result, the EU has

[39] Frey, The Question of Trade, Carrying and Use of Small Arms and Light Weapons in the Context of Human Rights and Humanitarian Norms' 30 May 2002, pp 1–26.

[40] *Supplement to an Agenda for Peace*, 3 January 1995, para 63; for further concerns of the GA see also, GA Res50/70/1995; Res 52/38/1998, Preamble, para 6; Res 56/24/2002, p 17, Preamble, para 1, pp 24, 33.

[41] UN Doc Supp No 42(A/51/42), 1996, Annex. 1, Introduction, No 3; for recent developments see also, GA Res 61/89/2006 (UN Doc Supp A/61/394–XXXI) Preamble, para 7.

[42] *Statement by the President*, 24 September 1999, paras 3, 4, 5, 6; SC Res 1265/1999, para 17; for arms embargoes and IHL considerations, see 7.2.1.

expressed its readiness for international co-operation, including financial and technical assistance, taking into account the 'compliance with international humanitarian law' of the countries to whom assistance could be granted.[43]

Moreover, the European Parliament Resolution on Small Arms of 2001, under Preamble D and operative paragraph 6, has voiced its satisfaction with the commitment of Member States to assess export applications and the authorisation of small arms in accordance with 'states' existing responsibilities under relevant international law'. This has been adopted as 'having regard to the Joint Action', in effect IHL. Further, it has called on Member States to bring all national and regional export control systems in line with such responsibilities, and to negotiate a binding legal instrument on norms and procedures.[44] The EU Code's relevant criteria will be considered in the subsequent section.

From the importers' perspective, the OAU, in its Bamako Declaration in December 2000 recognised that the illicit proliferation of SALW threatens international humanitarian law; and so 'it is vital to address the problem of the illicit . . . circulation and trafficking of small arms and light weapons . . . through . . . the respect for international humanitarian law'. Although illicit transfer has been emphasised, such a focus must be read in the light of the whole context of the declaration in general, and the call made on exporting countries to consider international law principles in their export of weapons to Africa in particular.[45] More precisely, the impact of the arms trade in general on humanitarian law and the need to totally ban such transactions within and outside the West African States in particular, with express intention of safeguarding such norms, have also been recognised in the Preamble and Article 6(2)(b) of the ECOWAS Convention on Small Arms.

In addition, the Latin American and Caribbean States, in November 2000 have acknowledged in their Brasilia Declaration that they 'share unshakable commitment to the basic norms of international law' in the field of small arms transfers.[46] It has been agreed in the same declaration that the illicit SALW problem has to be addressed 'in a manner which would alleviate the plight of populations besieged by . . . armed conflicts'. They have also called on the international community to support 'national measures taken by affected states in post conflict situations', relative to SALW circulation.[47] It is thus reasonable to assume that the Brasilia Declaration's commitment was meant to embrace IHL.

43 *OJEC, No 2002/589/CFSP*, 19 July 2002.

44 *EU Parliament Resolution on Small Arms* (B5-0723, 0729 and 0730/2001), November 2001.

45 *Bamako Declaration on African Common Position on SALW*, Mali, 1 October 2000, vol 1(i), and vol 2(ix).

46 *Brasilia Declaration on the Illicit Trade in SALW*, Brasilia, 24 November 2000, No 4.

47 *Ibid*, No 8, and 14(c).

Along with regional efforts, individual states, including considerable suppliers, have incorporated the notion of IHL in their domestic legislation and national policies. In the interest of avoiding duplication, we shall not discuss them here (see 7.2.3.3, 7.2.4).

There seems to be a common understanding among NGOs and peace activists, that exports of SALW are a major concern for IHL. They also think that IHL should be a key factor as a standard for legitimate transfers of small arms, as the application of the rules of IHL mitigates the consequences of war and related catastrophes. For example, the ICRC 'has in a variety of national, regional and international fora urged States to integrate consideration of respect for international humanitarian law into arms-export decision-making', as their legal obligation.[48]

In conclusion, except in the recent ECOWAS Convention, IHL rules are not expressly integrated in small arms treaties, as the international community has paid little attention to the problem of SALW transfers.[49] Even so the latter is linked with IHL, not only in terms of its devastating humanitarian consequences, but for purposes of compliance with its standards, as an existing legal duty of states. The state practice we went through has not denied this reality as will be analysed further. Regional organisations and important NGOs such as the EU, OSCE, OAU, ECOWAS and the ICRC have affirmed the pertinence of this body of rules to the small arms trade; writers have also complemented this general conclusion. As this legal duty is not limited to their respective jurisdictions, any arms deals by themselves and/or their business firms, with foreign elements, either states or NSAs, shall not defeat their IHL obligations. In short, the *erga omnes* obligation of states concerning respect and ensuring respect for IHL extends to the trade in arms. Yet this could only serve as a general yardstick on the problem. The specifics of the obligation and the responsibilities therein will now be appropriately identified.

7.2.1 IHL Standards for SALW Transfers

Small arms could serve both legal and illegal end-uses (see chapter two). The focus here is on the illegal and illegitimate use of SALW by reference to principles of IHL. There are two major standards: the use and excessive availability of weapons. Although these areas are closely related and even overlap, we will discuss them separately in this section. It is useful to look first at the legal background of both standards.

[48] ICRC, *Report to the First BMS*, New York, 7–11 July 2003, p 2, para 5; see also, p 71; see also, ICRC, below n 87, at p 2, para 2; see also, *SAS 2002* below n 70 at p 180; see also, Eminent Persons Group (p 72) pp 1–2.

[49] ICRC, '*Arms Availability*', below n 87, p 20, para 4; see also Herby, 'Transfers, Humanitarian Assistance, and Humanitarian Law' in Boutwell and Klare (eds), *Light Weapons and Civil Conflicts: Controlling the Tools of Violence* (Boston, Rowman & Littlefield) 200.

7.2.2 The Legal Background to the Standards

Three pre-UN bodies are worthy of consideration. First, the 1890 Brussels Act prohibited the introduction of firearms and ammunition to some parts of Africa, in particular to the Congo basin countries and territories, as clearly stated in Article VIII of the Treaty. The obligation to refrain from transfers, and prevent the entry of these weapons, was triggered by the belief that these tools were, and would be, used in slave trade operations, and wars between tribes. The Treaty was adopted by 15 countries; almost all of whom were, and still are, the chief producers and exporters of SALW.[50]

Secondly, in the 1919 St Germain-en-Laye Convention for the Control of the Trade in Arms and Ammunition, the Contracting Parties agreed under Articles 1 and 2 of the instrument, 'to prohibit the export of firearms and ammunition' to specified parts of Africa, save for exceptions to be granted by governments. It was originally intended to enhance the Brussels Act and cope with later developments. Introductory paragraphs 1, 2, and 3 of the Treaty show that: '[T]he task of preventing bloodshed in great parts of Africa and in the countries which border the Red Sea' would extremely be difficult to achieve, 'if the inhabitants have access to unlimited quantities of arms and munitions'—therefore it was intended to deny tools of carnage and prevent the 'uninhibited spread' and accumulation of such arms, which proliferated during the First World War.[51]

Although there was not the slightest doubt of 'the grave and sordid scandals connected with the trade in arms', by members of the League, the Treaty was only ratified by eleven countries. Another four expressed their willingness to adhere to the principles of the Convention. Germany and Austria were among great producers of arms who bound themselves by the Convention which was also signed by 22 principal states, including countries such as China and Cuba. Even so, due to the US refusal to ratify it, the Convention never entered into force. Most importantly, the principal parties of the instrument agreed to a Supplementary Protocol 'to the effect that they would bring its provisions into immediate effect without waiting for formal ratification'. The Protocol was, however, 'acted upon by few principals'. It is noteworthy that such efforts fell under the mandate of

[50] *General Act of the Brussels Conference, and Declaration*, Brussels, 2 July 1890, Arts IX, X, XIII, and XIV, *ATS* 1920 No 117 [emphasis added], the instrument was legally binding, specially its provisions on the arms trade. The participating states were Great Britain, Austria-Hungary, Belgium, Denmark, France, Germany, Italy, the Netherlands, Portugal, Russia, Spain, Sweden and Norway, Turkey and the US.

[51] LN, *Conference for the Control of the International Trade in Arms, Munitions and Implements of War (CCITAMIW)*, Geneva 1925, for the prohibition see the signed Convention p 29, for the historical survey see p i, and ii, for parties to the Treaty see Preamble, para 1; see also Goldblat, *Arms Control: A Guide to Negotiations and Agreements* (London, Sage Publications, 1994) 13–14 and below, n 53; see also, *The Covenant of the League of Nations*, Arts 23(d) and 8.

the League of Nations, as it was entrusted with the power to oversee the international trade in arms in the light of common interest of states, in accordance with Articles 23(d) and 8 of the Covenant.[52]

Finally, the failed Geneva Convention on the Supervision of International Trade in Arms of 1925 also addressed SALW transfers, including those suitable for both military and civilian uses, as shown in Article 1 categories I and II of the Treaty. As stated in Article 2(1), it was not intended to reduce the international trade in weapons, but rather to prevent the illicit trade through export licensing and other similar regulatory measures. It was not welcomed by those non-producing and importing countries of the time for the reason that such states were fearful of the potential for abuse by exporter states. For this reason this also failed to enter into force. In fact, 'of the documents signed simultaneously with the 1925 Geneva Convention, only the Protocol' banning asphyxiating, poisonous gases and bacteriological weapons, became a reality.[53]

This Second World War state practice enlightens us about five things. First, states attested nearly a century ago that arms including SALW should not be transferred to regions of 'bloodshed'. Secondly, this view was widely accepted by both suppliers and importer states. The involvement of countries such as China in the 1919 process seems to be worth underlining. Thirdly, states were then reluctant to codify their obligations when the question of a treaty arose. Fourthly, the scope of the restrictions was limited to the African continent. Finally, since 1925, the attitude changed as far as treaties were concerned, into the regulatory dimensions of the arms trade and, of course, into specific weapons control, for example, WMD and other certain inhumane weapons (see chapter one).

While the issue was generally neglected for some time, a renewed focus has been exerted by states in the aftermath of the Cold War.[54] In the light of this, we now turn to the details of contemporary IHL standards for SALW transfer.

7.2.3 Actual or Potential Use Standard

The use-oriented standard, also called the use-based rule (UBR), embraces twofold matters of concern: the behaviour of recipient states and the risk of the use of such weapons on arrival at the destination, as factors for such prohibition. Relevant practice at different levels and the contributions of NGOs and writers will be assessed.

[52] *CCITAMIW*, above n 51; see also, Goldblat, *ibid*.

[53] LN, *Proceedings of the Conference for the Supervision of the International Trade in Arms and Ammunition and in Implements of War*, Geneva, 4 May–17 June 1925, pp 29–67; see also, Goldblat, *ibid*, at 14.

[54] Lombard, 'Small Arms and Light Weapons: a Neglected Issue, a Renewed Focus' *Disarmament Diplomacy* (No 49, August 2000) 1.

7.2.3.1 *Global Efforts*

As discussed earlier, the UN expressed its concerns on the impact of the illicit arms transfers on IHL (see 7.2). We shall concentrate on specific measures of its organs, in particular the SC.

The SC, considering the peace and security norm, has been imposing arms embargoes on humanitarian law grounds. To state some examples, the Council expressed its grave concerns at 'the heavy loss of human life and widespread material damage' both in Yugoslavia and Somalia, as a ground for its decision to impose arms embargoes. In the latter case, the deteriorating humanitarian situation was specifically emphasised. It has been focused on the 'systematic, widespread and flagrant violations of international humanitarian law in Rwanda', particularly the massive killings of civilians. In its persistent embargoes against Angola since 1992, the Council noted 'with consternation the further deterioration of an already grave humanitarian situation' in the country. In 2000, the Council took the step, in the war between Ethiopia and Eritrea, of imposing an arms ban on both sides, '[N]oting with concern that the fighting has serious humanitarian implications for the civilian population of the two States'. The wide-ranging arms supply bans against Sierra Leone, and Kosovo were/are motivated, inter alia, by the belief that they would be used as tools of IHL violations.[55]

Concerning the Darfur case, the Council, through its Resolution 1556 of 30 July 2004, 'reiterated its grave concern at the ongoing humanitarian crisis' and 'violations of . . . humanitarian law by all parties to the crisis, in particular by the Janjaweed'. The latter are known as government-backed Arab militia, who are alleged to be committing atrocities in the region. It has accordingly decided, under Chapter VII of the Charter, that 'all states shall take necessary measures to prevent the sale or supply . . . of arms and related materials', to all NSAs, entities and individuals, operating in that region.[56]

Although some of the aforementioned conflicts were mainly matters of *jus ad bello,* such as the case of Ethiopia and Eritrea, the Council has also looked at their *jus in bello* aspects, which is why they have been considered as relevant cases here (see further 5.1).

Alongside its embargoes, the September 2000 call by the Council to discourage arms supply to troubled areas has some relevance too (see pp

[55] See on *Yugoslavia,* Res 713/1991, Preamble, para 3; on *Somalia,* Res 733/1992, Preamble, para 5; on *Angola,* Res 733/1992 and 788/1992, Preamble, para 3, operative, paras 7 and 19; on *Rwanda,* Res 918/1994, Preamble, paras 9, 10 and operative, para 13; on *Ethiopia-Eritrea,* Res 1298/2000, Preamble, para 9; on *Sierra Leone,* Res 1132/1997 and Res 1343/2001, Preamble, para 5, the Council recalled to the ECOWAS Moratorium; on *Kosovo,* Res 1160/1998; see also, pp 104–05.

[56] See, eg Preamble, paras 6, 7, and operative, paras 7, 8; see also, *Report of the Secretary-General on the Sudan,* 3 June 2004.

112–14). Article VI of the Resolution has not only dealt with arms transfers to conflict zones, but has stressed its concern about violations of IHL[57]; it seems to be clear that the Resolution was passed in the context of IHL.

Therefore the UN SC consistently considered actual and/or subsequent possibilities of violations of IHL as a ground for the prohibition of arms transfers to various countries and territories. It should be emphasised, as shown in the cases of Yugoslavia and Somalia,[58] that serious breaches of IHL, mass killings and flows of refugees were taken as factors for these decisions.[59]

Three global efforts are particularly noteworthy in this regard. First, the Oslo meeting of July 1998, in which 21 states took part, was a major breakthrough on the small arms problem. A number of chief exporters of small arms agreed to take action to 'respect and ensure respect for international humanitarian law with regard to the use of small arms and light weapons', and expressed their commitment to develop sufficient mechanisms both at regional and national levels. This includes reduction, and restraint on transfers, of SALW. The meeting was important as it evidenced the common understanding of participating States on IHL vis-à-vis the trade in small arms.[60]

Secondly, the Wassenaar Best Practice Guidelines for Exports on SALW of 2002 confirmed that Member States shall avoid transfers if they will have a negative impact on IHL norms in the destination country. It is a word-by-word duplication from the EU and OSCE agreements (see 7.2.3.2). It ought to be noted that these 33 states have agreed to reflect this and related principles in their respective legal jurisdictions.[61]

Last but not least, in a more realistic manner, the 28th International Conference of the Red Cross and Red Crescent of December 2003, in which 191 States Parties to the Geneva Conventions took part adopted a comprehensive approach to the topic. The use and misuse of weapons, among other things are considered all together as threats to human dignity and therefore are urgent contemporary humanitarian challenges. In their Declaration entitled 'Protecting Human Dignity', participants, 'in recognition of States' obligation to respect and ensure respect for 'IHL', have agreed to take the following actions: (1) '[S]tates should make international humanitarian law as one fundamental criteria', for arms transfer decision making; they are also encouraged to integrate IHL into national

[57] SC Res 1318/2000, Annex, pt VI.

[58] See on *Yugoslavia*, Res 1318/1991; on *Somalia*, Res 794/1992, Preamble, para 8, operative, paras 2 and 4.

[59] See also Osterdahl, *Threat to the Peace: the Interpretation by the Security Council of Article 39 of the UN Charter* (Uppsala, Iustus Forlag, vol 13, 1998) 81.

[60] The Oslo Meeting on Small Arms, Final Communiqué, *An International Agenda on Small Arms and Light Weapons: Elements of a Common Understanding*, 13–14 July 1998, paras 5–6.

[61] Wassenaar, *Best Practice Guide for Exports on Arms*, 2002, 1(c), 2(e), 3(a).

and regional laws and policies; and (2) to take 'concrete steps' for the prevention of misuse of SALW, as an urgent matter, in accordance with the UN PoA and other existing regional frameworks. States shall ensure, therefore, that SALW 'do not end up in the hands of those who may be expected to use them to violate' IHL.[62] It has to be noted that states affirm their commitment to the Declaration, as members of the Conference.

Briefly, significant practice has been demonstrated at the global stratum, in respect of the use based standard for SALW transfers. Most of all, the Red Cross conference and the declarations therein are remarkable. Yet regional efforts could be vital for further clarification of such a benchmark.

7.2.3.2 *Regional and Security Organisations' Efforts*

Among others, the EU, OSCE and NATO have positively spelt out their obligations on the question. The EU Code of Conduct on Arms Exports, for example in Criteria 6(b), advocates that:

> Member States take into account *inter alia* the *record of the buyer country* with regard to . . . its compliance with international commitments, . . ., including under *international humanitarian law applicable to international and non-international armed conflicts* [emphasis added].

The Code underscores four important elements. First, it presupposes either prior compliance or violation of IHL norms for export decisions. This proves that such transactions have to consider the behaviour of a buyer country on its compliance with IHL. Secondly, it has acknowledged IHL as an existing legal responsibility of states on small arms transfers. Thirdly, the call on Member States, which was made to bring all domestic and regional systems of arms transfers control in compliance with such principles, is highly significant. Finally, the call includes the commitment to take necessary steps towards codifying such legal norms into a treaty. Yet the wording of the papers has to be reflected in the deeds of Member States.

In fact, the EU imposes two types of arms embargo, full scope and less than full scope. The former deals with arms, munitions and military equipment and the latter with arms and munitions alone, subject to a case-by-case basis determination. The common list of items embargoed includes, inter alia, SALW. The EU Council decides the embargoes, known as the common position of Member States. As enshrined in Articles 15 and 2 of the EU Treaty, such common positions are legally binding for Member

[62] 28th International Conference of the Red Cross and Red Crescent (Conference 2003), Declaration, '*Protecting Human Dignity*', Geneva, 2–6 December 2003, p 3, para 2, for the agreed measures see '*Agenda for Humanitarian Action*', 6 December 2003, p 7; in particular see, *Final Goal* No 2, it should be noted that 181 national societies, their international federations, and the ICRC have taken part in the Conference, at <http://www.icrc.org/eng/conf28>

States. This is because Article 15 based measures fall under Title V, ie 'Common Foreign and Security Policy' of the Treaty.[63]

Accordingly, the EU Council has imposed a number of arms embargoes which are relevant to the arms trade and humanitarian law. For example, the EU Council in March 1998 maintained its full scope arms embargoes on the Federal Republic of Yugoslavia ('FRY'). Some of the main humanitarian concerns which led to the arms embargoes were: (1) the use of force against the Albanian community in Kosovo; and (2) the withdrawal of humanitarian organisations and its impact on the civilian population and the peacekeepers.[64]

In a slightly different approach, the EU decided a full scope arms embargo on Sierra Leone in June 1998, in accordance with SC Resolution 1171 of 1998. This was a sequel to the 'urgency for all rebels to put an end to the atrocities' in the country. However, this measure did not ban arms transfers to the Government of Sierra Leone, as stipulated by the UN SC.[65] In the Ethiopia and Eritrea full scope arms embargo, however, the EU didn't mention humanitarian concerns other than citing the UN SC Resolution.[66]

The EU initiatives demonstrated, therefore that a combination of both export criteria and arms embargoes have been considered to prevent transfers of arms which might be used in breach of IHL.

There are certainly some indications of positive achievements. EU members have, for example, been issuing reports of the implementation of the Code. The first year report of this instrument has proved that 'a large number of denial notifications have been circulated and Member States have engaged in active consultations on specific export licensing issues'. Some of the denials of the licensing of exports of weapons, including small arms, included 5 issued by Belgium, 27 by Germany, 16 by the Netherlands, 43 by the UK and 50 by France. There are countries, moreover, which neither report the details of their exports nor declare any denial.[67] The refusals and the reporting practice cited above are indeed encouraging.

[63] Craig and De Burca, *EU Law: Text, Cases and Materials*, 3rd edn (Oxford, Oxford University Press, 2003) 25; see also, *Consolidated version of the Treaty of the European Union*, 24 December 2002; see also for the kinds of embargoes in General, at <http: / / projects.sipri.se / expcon / euframe / eu_commonlist.htm>

[64] *Common Position of 19 March 1998 defined by the Council on the Basis of Art J. 2 of the EU Treaty on Restrictive Measures against the Federal Republic of Yugoslavia*, 27 March 1998, pp 1–3, Preamble, para 1, and operative, para 6, the embargo on export of weapons was lifted in October 2001 by Common Position (2001 / 719 / CFSP). Note: the EU maintained its arms embargoes while the UN SC's arms embargoes on Bosnia and Herzegovina, Croatia and the FRY were lifted by Res 1021 / 1998.

[65] *Common Position of 29 June 1998 Concerning Sierra Leon*, 1 July 1998, pp 0001–0002, Preamble, para 2, and para 1.

[66] *Common Position 15 March 1999 Concerning Ethiopia and Eritrea*, 18 March 1999, p 1, para 1.

[67] *Annual Report in conformity with operative provision 8 of the European Union Code of Conduct on Arms Exports*, para 7, No 6, at <http: / / projects.sipri.se / expcon / eucodear1999.htm>

Even so, the existence of a genuine and robust regime of implementation of the embargoes and the Code raises doubts, even in the recent past. For instance, the Third Annual Report of 2002 of the EU on small arms shows that only Spain and Germany have reported their compliance with arms embargoes obligations. Spain 'has implemented all embargoes in force', which includes UN, the EU and OSCE measures. Germany disclosed that it enforces arms embargoes strictly, and provides serious penalties against violators. Others such as Italy have said nothing about embargoes in their reports[68]; silence on reporting might not, however, necessarily denote infringements.

Concerning the Code, it is open to criticism from NGOs on the ground that it does not regulate the companies and individuals which facilitate transfers from Europe. The arms transfer from Bulgaria to Sierra Leone in contravention of the arms embargoes, organised from London by a company called 'Sandline', was referred to as an example.[69] Another difficulty of the EU Code is that detailed reasons for refusals of exports by Member States were/are not revealed. This is due to the confidential nature of consultations on denials between Member States, as stipulated under operative provision 4 of the Code,[70] a subject which is not the main focus of this book.

To sum up, while some of the criticisms deal with brokerage, they generally focus on the shortcomings of the EU Code and the embargoes. Problems of scope and enforcement have also been raised. Be this as it may, the system has, however, been understood as a promising model, in the endeavours to prevent the transit of arms to areas where actual or potential abuses of IHL exist.

In addition, the OSCE, in its 2000 Document on SALW, reiterates Criterion 6(b) of the EU Code on Arms Transfer. States have expressed their commitment to reflect the principles of IHL in their national legislation and policies.[71] For example, section III (A)2(b)(v) underlines:

> Each participating State will avoid issuing licences for exports where it deems that there is a clear risk that the small arms in question might . . . threaten compliance with international law governing the conduct of armed conflict.

The OSCE appears to be one step ahead of the EU Code, in that regardless of a record of prior compliance or infringement, any clear risk of the use of

[68] *Third Annual Report on the Implementation of the EU Joint Action*, 22 December 2003, for Spain, para 36, for Germany, para 24, for Italy, para 8.

[69] *Memorandum submitted by the UK Working Group on Arms*: the EU Code of Conduct on Arms Exports, Minutes of Evidence, UK House of Commons, 2 December 1998, para 4.4, at <http://www.parliament.the-stationery-office.co.uk/pa/cm199899/cmselect/cmtrdind/65/65a01.htm>

[70] See also, *SAS 2002: Continuing the Human Cost*, p 117.

[71] See also, *OSCE Document*, 24 November 2000, s (III) (A)2(a) (iii), (A)4(i).

arms at destination in contravention of the law of armed conflict is a ground for export licence's denial.

Aside from the EU and the OSCE, the November 2000 NATO Parliamentary Assembly Resolution on Small Arms Control urges member governments and parliaments to enhance 'evaluation of recipient States' records of adherence to international humanitarian law'.[72] Unlike the aforementioned organisations, however, NATO has never imposed arms embargoes.

In contrast, the ECOWAS Convention of 2006, under Article 6(2)(b) underlines:

> A transfer *shall not* be authorised if its authorisation violates obligations of the requesting States as well as those of Member States, under international law including: . . . (b) universally accepted principles of international humanitarian law [emphasis added].

This Convention is the first of its kind in contemporary international law to expressly put in place IHL—based ban on arms transactions, set aside anti-personnel landmines (see further 7.2, and chapter ten).

By and large, three elements have been manifested in practice. First, regional organisations and some global arrangements which embrace the majority of key producers and suppliers of small arms, including the US, Russia and other European countries, have declared the propriety of considering compliance of a recipient state with IHL and possible risks of contraventions of IHL, as a matter of existing IHL obligation. To some degree, this belief has been accompanied by certain arms embargoes against some states and NSAs. Secondly, the approach adopted, and emphasis placed, has, in effect, been on the use rather than the nature of weapons. Finally, almost all have recognised, as stated earlier, that these principles should be an integral part of domestic legislation and polices.

7.2.3.3 Domestic Efforts

Certain major exporters have incorporated the rules of IHL into their domestic legal regimes of arms transfer. Principle 2 of the US International Arms Sales Code of Conduct of 1999 for instance, requires a recipient country to be free from persistent gross violations of human rights including 'grave breaches of international laws of war or equivalent violations of the laws of war in internal armed conflicts'. Moreover, the US has to make sure that the recipient country 'provides access on a regular basis to humanitarian organizations in situations of conflict or famine'. This law has been adopted by Congress and reflects the fact that Congress wanted the Act to be a model for a global treaty on arms transfers.[73]

[72] *NATO Parliamentary Assembly Resolution on Small Arms Control*, November 2000, 8(d).
[73] *US International Arms Sales Code of Conduct*, 1999, No 2 (A) vi, (F).

Belgium has also integrated the EU criteria for arms transfers, which has considered both retrospective and prospective IHL impacts of transfers, in its legislation covering arms exports in June 2003.[74] Still, few states mention respect for IHL by a recipient state as a criterion for arms dealings in their legislation.[75]

Despite this states have also adopted pertinent national policies. The French national policy on arms exports has directly taken the IHL criteria set out in the OSCE and the EU Code. This has been affirmed by France in its document submitted to the Wassenaar Arrangement.[76] Germany also revealed in 2000 the fact that the EU Code and other commitments constitute part of its national policy in arms dealings.[77] The October 2000 House of Commons criteria for arms transfers clearly states: 'The Government will not issue an export licence if approval would be inconsistent with, inter alia . . . the OSCE Principles Governing Conventional Arms Transfers and the EU Code of Conduct on Arms Exports'. The interesting aspect of this political instrument is that it gives equal importance to the relevant OSCE and EU instruments with regard to the Mines and Inhumane Weapons Conventions.[78] More specifically, the UK Export Control Bill of 2002 is intended to empower the Secretary of State 'to impose export controls when there is a clear risk that the exportation of the goods or technology in question might be used to carry out, or facilitate the carrying out, of acts contravening the international law of armed conflict'.[79]

All these domestic efforts indicate the ever-growing concern expressed by states on the question of the trade in arms and their use against IHL.

In contrast, as previously stated, Chinese and Russian legislation do not expressly refer to IHL in relation to the behaviour of a buyer country. It is equally difficult to say definitively that they have totally omitted these elements from their legislation since they have generally recognised the necessity of compliance with general international law obligations, and there has been no record of objection on the matter.[80]

Indeed, a number of states refer to their general international law duties, as a ground for restricting small arms transfer. For instance, in section 1 sub-section (5) of No 185 of 1990, Italian law prohibits the export of

[74] ICRC '*Report to the BMS*', above n 48, p 7, para 4.

[75] Herby, 'Humanitarian Implications of Small Arms Proliferation and Proposed Codes of Conduct: Arms Availability—A Matter of Urgent Humanitarian Concern' in Dahinden Dahlitz and Fischer (eds), *Small Arms and Light Weapons: Legal Aspects of National and International Regulation* (Geneva, United Nations, vol iv, 2002) 100–01.

[76] *French Policy on Arms Exports*, No 2, para 2.

[77] Germany, *Policy Principles for the Export of War Weapons and Other Military Equipment*, January 2000, p III, 7.

[78] *The Consolidated EU and National Arms Export Licensing Criteria*, Hansard HC cols 199–203W (26 October 2000).

[79] The *UK Export Control Bill* 2002, sch 4, (5), D, (b).

[80] See p 265.

weapons contrary to the country's 'international commitments' and where sufficient guarantee is not obtained as to the 'final destination' of the arms.[81] Section 15(f) of the South African Act of 2002 has also clearly stipulated that conventional weapons transfers from the country shall 'adhere and to international law, norms practices and the international obligations and commitments of the Republic'.[82] These are of paramount importance to the topic at issue, as IHL obligations regarding arms transfer have been an inherent ABC of international law (see 7.2).

In reality, state practice has been characterised by two features, the constructive and the detrimental, concerning the use-based standard for arms transactions. The following two cases might show the constructive practices of states. The US claims that it 'has one of the strongest systems in the world for regulating the export of arms'. One US official has, for example, told the UN SC in October 2002 that 'In the past six years, we have interdicted thousands of illicit arms and cut-off exports to countries that failed to comply with U.S. law'.[83] Similar to the EU confidentiality barrier, however, details of denials of small arms are not normally disclosed in the country.

Furthermore, in 2002, India wanted to 're-equip its special forces operating in Kashmir'. Although ' "its first choice" was to import SALW from Europe, "Berlin refused an export licence", . . . for fear that the weapons could be used in armed conflict'. The arms company called Keckler & Koch was thus 'forced to withdraw its bid'.[84] This has to be read in the light of the application of IHL to the Kashmir conflict and the breaches of it in the area. It is widely acknowledged that the Kashmir conflict has evidenced enormous violations of IHL, including massive killings of civilians, carried out by both government forces and the militants.[85]

On the other hand, in reality detrimental practice in regard to the use-based standard of arms transfer has been witnessed. The deal of automatic weapons transfer between Nepal and Belgium of 2002 is a good case in point. There was/is a civil war going on in Nepal since 1996, in which 7000 civilians have been killed. A cease-fire was signed between the government and the guerrillas in 2003, but the cease-fire had been signed after the start of delivery of the guns. In such a situation, the Belgian Government has concluded a contract of sale of 50,000–60,000 M16 rifles and other small arms with Nepal. The delivery of these weapons had been started in

[81] *Italian Law* No 185, July 9 1990, *Decree of Ministry of Foreign Affairs*, 14 July 1990.

[82] *National Conventional Arms Control Act* 2002 (Act No 41, 2002), *Government Gazette*, vol 452, Cape Town, 20 February 2003, No 24575.

[83] Richard Williams, US Alternate Representative to the UN for Special Political Affairs, '*Small Arms and Light Weapons*', statement in the SC, New York, 11 October 2002, para 4.

[84] GIIS, *Small Arms Survey 2003: Development Denied* (Oxford, Oxford University Press) 112.

[85] 'Behind the Kashmir Conflict: Abuses by Security Forces and Militant Groups Continue' *Human Rights Watch*, Report 1999, at <http://www.hrw.org/reports/1999/kashmir/>

January 2003. As 'the best publicised small arms deal', and a good test for the applicability of the EU Code of Conduct for Arms Transfers, it has attracted divided opinions. Opponents of the deal 'spoke of the fears that the weapons would be used in the civil war'. They also thought that the 'guns might contribute' to 'extra-judicial killings of civilians'. Even so, governments, including the Bush administration in the US, supported the deal. The most worrying aspect of this deal was that Germany rejected the same deal on the grounds of its EU Code commitments.[86] This case therefore proves a lack of the uniform application of standards of transfers.

In addition, there are still actual transfers by states to recipients who are best known for their violations of IHL, and to situations where the use of small arms in violation of the norms is apparent (see chapter six). It is thus the perception of prominent humanitarian organisations that few practical measures have been taken to restrict international transfers of SALW to such situations. The reason is that national security issues have usually taken dominance over considerations of IHL, in respect of the arms trade.[87] Regardless of non-compliance, however, the use-based standard with regards to norms of humanitarian law appears to be established in domestic state practice.

To sum up, despite the positive contribution of domestic legal systems on the development of the use-based standard, there appears to be a gap in state practice with the result that detailed indicators for such a standard have not yet been set out. For instance, while EU countries generally refer to IHL obligations, the US emphasises grave breaches of such norms. It is thus important to consider cases, NGOs and publicists' views on the use-based humanitarian law standard.

7.2.3.4 *Cases, NGOs and Publicists*

With respect to case law, although the ICJ has considered the provision of weapons to the *contras* in Nicaragua as a failure to meet the obligation not to encourage violations of IHL,[88] the European Commission of Human Rights, in the case of *Tugar v Italy*, seems to have differed on the problem. The facts of the case could briefly be described as follows: (1) a delivery of 5,750,000 anti-personnel landmines was made to Iraq between 1982-83, as per the contract between the Iraqi Foreign Minister and an Italian company called V.M. which was concluded in 1982; (2) in February 1991, the latter along with other companies was found guilty of illegal arms trafficking to Iraq by the Brescia Court in Italy; (3) the defendant had no law to regulate the arms trade at the time, and such transactions were

[86] *SAS 2003*, above n 84, p 113, box. 3.3.

[87] *Arms Availability and the Situation of Civilians in Armed Conflict*: a study presented by the ICRC, 1 June 1999, ICRC publication, p 19, para 4, and p 20, para 3; see also, ch 1.

[88] See *Nicaragua*, above n 3, para 220.

generally treated as the same as any commodity export; (4) the case was brought on the basis of Article 2 of the European Convention on Human Rights; and (5) Tugar, who was a mine cleaner by profession had brought a case against Italy in 1993; he complained that 'he suffered life-threatening injury', as a result of: first, the provision of the indiscriminate anti-personnel landmines by Italy to a country 'which has been condemned for extraordinary violations of human rights and humanitarian obligation'; and secondly, Italy has failed to protect him from the harm he suffered 'by means of an effective arms transfers licensing system'. The Commission freed the defendant on the ground that 'the applicant's injury cannot be seen as a direct consequence of the failure of the Italian authorities to legislate on arms transfers'. Accordingly, the case was unanimously declared inadmissible.[89]

Sadly, the Commission did not discuss the IHL obligations of supplier and importer states in such situations, although the applicant had indicated not only human rights, but IHL obligations. It was also apparent that Italy had been treating the arms trade in the same way as any other goods. However, the transferor was later declared guilty of illegal arms trafficking to Iraq.

Generally, the decision seems to imply that only users of light weapons are under obligation and not third states. Yet, as it is limited to human rights obligations, it might not be said in conclusive terms that it contradicts the ICJ's decision. State responsibility and other aspects of the case will be discussed later.

NGOs have expressed their views on this issue too. For instance, the 1999 ICRC's Study on Arms Availability states:

> As a step towards limiting the availability of arms and ammunition among users likely to commit violations of international humanitarian law, codes of conduct for arms transfers, containing clear references to and indicators of respect for international humanitarian law, should be developed. Such references and indicators should also be added to existing standards which do not include them. These measures would be a means of reinforcing Article 1 common to the Geneva Conventions and of improving implementation of the whole fabric of international humanitarian law. They would be complementary to criteria taken from other fields.[90]

Further, admitting that there have been no clear criteria for the restriction in mind, the 1999 study has suggested certain *indicators,* which might help elaborate the details of the use-based IHL standard for arms transfers. Part 5(B) expounds[91]:

[89] *Haje Tugar v Italy*, European Commission of Human Rights, First Chamber, Admissibility of Application, 18 October 1995, pp 1–5.

[90] ICRC, above n 87, pp 7, 21, and 14; see also, ICRC, *BMS*, above n 48, p 8, para 4.

[91] *ICRC*, above n 87, pp 21–22, pt 5, (B), 1–5 [emphasis added]; see also, ICRC, *BMS*, above n 48, p 2, para 5.

> [T]he points below illustrate the types of *indicators* of likely respect for humanitarian law which could be incorporated in future national and international codes of conduct governing the transfer of arms and ammunition: **1**. whether the recipient has made a formal engagement to apply the rules of international humanitarian law; **2**. whether the recipient has trained its armed forces in the application of international humanitarian law; **3**. whether the recipient has taken the measures necessary for the repression of serious violations of international humanitarian law; **4**. whether a recipient which is, or has been, engaged in an armed conflict has failed to punish those responsible for serious violations of international humanitarian law and to cause such breaches to cease; **5**. whether stable authority structures capable of ensuring respect for international humanitarian law exist in the area under control of the recipient.

Therefore, actual respect for IHL, preventative measures, peace and stability at the destination, etc, have been considered as pointers to determine the application of the standard under discussion. These indicators supplement and elaborate the UN regional and national endeavours to apply the standard. The rest of the indicators associated with the availability of arms will be considered below in 7.2.8.

The ICCAT and FCIAT have duly considered the behaviour of a recipient state and risks of violations as pre-conditions for transactions. Article 4 of the former set out a rule as below:

> Arms transfers may be conducted only if the proposed recipient state, or recipient party in the country of final destination: (A) Does not engage in, or sponsor, grave breaches of the laws and customs of war as set forth in the Geneva Conventions of 1949, and additional Protocols of 1977, and other rules and principles of international humanitarian law applicable during inter-state or intra-state armed conflict which, for example, prohibit arbitrary and summary execution, indiscriminate killing, mutilation, torture and cruel treatment, and hostage taking; (B) Provides access on a regular basis to humanitarian non-governmental organizations in time of conflict or humanitarian emergency, including access of the International Committee of the Red Cross to detainees. (C) Co-operates with international tribunals, either ad-hoc or general, with the power to adjudicate violations of the rules listed under (A).[92]

In a slightly different manner, the FCIAT has focused on situations other than the conduct of 'the recipient state or party'. Article 3 (3) states:

> Contracting Parties shall not license international transfers of arms in circumstances in which there exists a reasonable risk that the arms would: (3) be used to commit serious violations of international humanitarian law applicable in international or non-international armed conflict.[93]

[92] *Nobel Peace Laureates' International Code of Conduct on Arms Transfer*, 29 May 1997; see also p 84.

[93] Working Draft, 21 November 2003.

The Code contains detailed indicators which are of significant importance for the use-based standard. For instance, the attitude towards humanitarian activities as a benchmark reinforces and clarifies some of the ICRC's indicators and the US domestic law on transfers. The prohibition has also included NSAs in its ambit. Yet, in the draft Convention, the reasonable risk factor seems to be wider in scope, which could embrace the attitude of a recipient state and other circumstances. International and non-international armed conflicts have also been referred to. In addition to this, the draft emphasises the probable use of the guns against humanitarian norms. Although the phrase 'reasonable risk' has not been defined in the draft Convention, the situations enumerated in the Code of Conduct and the ICRC's indicators could give a good understanding of such a risk, among others.

It is of use here to look at one analogous situation. The UN Secretary-General, in his report of 1999 to the SC, regarding protection of civilians in armed conflict, has suggested an enforcement action by the Council, taking into account, inter alia,

> (a) The scope of the breaches of human rights and international humanitarian law, including the numbers of people affected and the nature of the violations; (b) The inability of local authorities to uphold legal order, or identification of a pattern of complicity by local authorities; (c) The exhaustion of peaceful or consent-based efforts to address the situation[94];

The conduct, ability, and willingness of states to abide by, and ensure respect for, IHL have been properly taken into account as reflected in the ICRC's indicators. Much emphasis is also placed on the extent of breaches and their impacts. The report has also direct relevance to the arms trade as will be seen later.

Moreover, writers have entertained different views on this specific norm of transfers. Quigley, for example, has underscored that '[S]tates have recognized a duty not to facilitate violation by other States of the humanitarian law of warfare'. He added that the 'provision of material used by another state to violate rules of warfare has engendered protest by States'. As a result, 'donor states have cut off supply of such materials upon learning of the wrongful use'.[95] Further, Gillard, emphasising the fact that small arms which are not unlawful by their nature could be subject to limitation for transfers due to the manner of their use in contravention of against IHL, asserts that: 'a state which transfers weapons in circumstances where it is likely they will be used to commit serious

[94] *'Report of the SG to the SC on the Protection of Civilians in Armed Conflict'*, 8 September 1999, para 72, recom. 9.

[95] Quigley, 'Complicity in International Law: a New Direction in the Law of State Responsibility', (1986) 57 *BYIL* 77, 90–91.

violations of IHL would clearly be failing its duty to ensure respect for IHL'.[96]

In contrast to this, Frey, in her proposed work submitted to the UN Sub-Commission on the Promotion and Protection of Human Rights, believes that excepting expressed prohibitions of the UN SC, 'there are no binding international standards that prohibit state-authorized transfers of small arms'. The reason given is that such transfers are largely free of international control even though they are an urgent matter of humanitarian concern. Nevertheless, she appears to acknowledge that common Article 1 of the Geneva Conventions 'could be interpreted' to impose an obligation upon a state to refrain from 'transferring small arms knowing that they will be used to violate human rights'.[97] We shall address the final analysis of this crucial question later.

It should be stressed at this level that while Gillard and others clearly supported the IHL standard of transfers under discussion, Frey relied only on SC arms embargoes. Of course, she referred to common Article 1 as a matter of probable interpretation. Considering the practice of the international community, however, such an argument does not seem persuasive. The dominant view of publicists is, therefore, in favour of the use-based standard of the arms trade. Even so they also appreciate the problem of lack of comprehensive indicators through which the respect of IHL in destination and other risks should be determined.[98]

Up to this point, we have examined the practice of states at different levels, including cases, NGOs and the views of publicists on the use-based standard of transfers. In general, the trend has been in support of this standard, as will be analysed further (see 7.2.5). We shall now turn to the next one.

7.2.4 Excessive Availability Standard

The second IHL standard of small arms transfer pertains to the excessive availability of SALW. Although it is not entirely detached from the previously discussed standard of transfer, it could be useful to look at it separately in some depth.

At the global level UN practice could be a wise place to start. The GGE of 1997 examined the availability factor of SALW with respect to armed conflict. As stated in paragraph 7 of the report, the mandate of the Panel was to examine the role of SALW in 'armed conflicts being dealt with by the United Nations'. In paragraphs 14 and 15, the Panel made certain

[96] Gillard, 'What is Legal what is Illegal? Limitations on Transfers of Small Arms under International Law' (*LRCIL*, Cambridge) p 8, para 32.

[97] Frey, above n 39, paras 70 and 74.

[98] Herby, 'Humanitarian Implications', above n 75, at 102.

remarks, inter alia, 'many of these conflicts have inflicted heavy causalities on the people involved. The vast majority of the causalities have been civil mostly women and children'; and 'countries throughout the world were at risk of facing civil strife either owing to ongoing humanitarian crises or as a result of a slow recovery from past ones'.[99] The report has thus embraced the rudiments of IHL.

The Panel has, however, found it difficult to determine the excessive accumulation of SALW. Failure to restrict and prevent transfers and circulation of weapons by importer and export states, in accordance with states' legal needs of SALW, and the use of small arms in conflicts and in violation of international law have been mentioned as some of the tests to determine the existence or else of excessive availability of small arms in a country.[100]

Even so, the Panel, under paragraph 60 of its report categorically denies the existence of any body of rules, by which transfers of SALW could be considered illegal. Its analysis on, and reference to, international and domestic law violations and its absolute denial of binding rules, do not, however, seem to be justified.

In any case, either as a matter of direct relevance to IHL or as analogous to it, the analysis of the Panel has to be considered to be a valuable contribution to the development of the excessive availability standard of IHL—the report was adopted by the GA and also praised by the SC, regional organisations and states. For example, the GA welcomed the report saying that it 'contains measures to reduce the excessive and destabilizing accumulation and transfers of small arms and light weapons in specific regions or the world and to prevent such accumulations and transfers from occurring in future'.[101]

In addition, in February 1999, the SC for instance recognised the consequences of the proliferation of small arms on the security of civilians; in particular the Council was concerned about the targeting of civilians 'in flagrant violation of international humanitarian and human rights law'. It also affirmed the close link between armed conflicts and IHL violations. It has accordingly called on arms producing and exporting states to restrict 'arms transfers which could provoke or prolong armed conflicts or aggravate existing tensions or armed conflicts in Africa'.[102] Most recently, the Council unequivocally recognised that the proliferation of SALW in West Africa has been contributing to serious violations of IHL and human rights.[103]

[99] UN Doc Supp No A/52/298, 27 August 1997.

[100] See 5.3, p 116*ff*.

[101] GA Res 52/38G/1998, Preamble, para 6; see also, Draft UN First Committee Res 52/38 J/1998, Preamble, para 7; see also ch 5; for the wide-ranging acceptance of the Report, see ch 2.

[102] UN Doc S/PRST/1999/6.

[103] SC Res 1467/2003 entitled *Proliferation of SALW and Mercenary Activities to Peace and Security in West Africa*, Annex, para 1.

The 1999 UN Secretary-General's Report to the SC also pointed out that the 'widespread availability' of small arms 'has had a significant impact on the scope and level of violence that affects the civilian populations in armed conflict'. The 'absence of control on transfers' and the features of such weapons 'have made it much easier to turn children into soldiers'. Further, 'their easy availability . . . has also greatly increased the risks of delivering humanitarian assistance in affected areas'. In the end, 'controlling the availability of arms' has been suggested as one solution.[104]

States have also raised the problem in the UN 2001 Conference on Small Arms. For instance, the Minister for Defence of Rwanda, as the Chairman of the National Focal Point on Small Arms and Light Weapons, told the conference that the 'genocide of 1994 in Rwanda was made possible by the easy availability of small arms'.[105]

Paragraph 2 of the Preamble of the UN PoA on small arms has demonstrated two pertinent elements: first, Member States of the UN have expressed their grave concern about the 'transfer and circulation of small arms and light weapons'; and secondly, they have recognised the fact that the 'excessive accumulation and uncontrolled spread in many regions of the world' of SALW 'have a wide range of humanitarian . . . consequences'.

Such an effort does not seem to be confined to the UN. The 28th International Conference of the Red Cross and Red Crescent has acknowledged the need to strengthen controls on the availability of weapons, in particular SALW, as a threat to human security and as an urgent humanitarian challenge of contemporary international law. Common Article 1 of the Geneva Conventions has been referred to. In the document called 'Agenda for Humanitarian Action', the participating states have consented, as a matter of urgency and final goal, to take 'concrete steps' for the 'prevention of the uncontrolled availability' of SALW, along the lines of various global and regional arrangements.[106]

Thus, global practices have reasonably affirmed the link between the excessive availability of SALW and IHL violations; it has also affirmed that transfers must consider such a problem. Yet the indicators need to be further clarified. Resort to regional and national instruments is therefore essential here.

At the regional level, for instance, Article 4(b) of the EUJA has aimed at the reduction of 'existing accumulation of small arms', taking into account, inter alia, the principle of 'respect for humanitarian law'.[107] The OSCE Document on Small Arms of 2000, under section III(A)(b)(vi) of the criterion for arms exports, prohibits arms transfers, 'where it deems that

[104] Above, n 94, paras 23 and 55.

[105] *UN Conference on the Illicit Trade in Small Arms*, 5th meeting (AM), 11 July 2001, para 3; see also p 244*ff*.

[106] Above n 62, Final Goal, 2.3.2.

[107] Above n 43; see also, pp 63 and 107.

there is a clear risk that the small arms in question might', inter alia, 'create an excessive . . . accumulation of small arms'. This needs to be seen in the light of the general consensus that excessive accumulation of small arms is of concern for IHL.[108]

African states have declared their 'grave concern' about the illicit proliferation and circulation of small arms. Part V(1)(i) of the Bamako Common Position of 2000, contains the statement that the problem of proliferation of SALW 'sustains conflicts . . ., contributes to the displacement of innocent populations and threatens international humanitarian law'. Accordingly, they called on exporters of arms to consider the IHL impacts of their transfers to Africa,[109] as elaborated above with respect to the *erga omnes* character of IHL obligations on transfers.[110] The Nairobi Protocol on small arms also acknowledged the problems associated with the proliferation of small arms, as shown in the Bamako Declaration. One of the objectives of the instrument, as stated in Article 2(b) of the Protocol is: 'to prevent the excessive and destabilizing accumulation of small arm and light weapons in the sub-region'.[111]

The 2003 UN BMS has revealed some of the responses by individual states to the excessive availability standard of IHL. Israel believes that the 'illicit proliferation' of SALW 'has affected many societies worldwide, causing suffering primarily to civilian populations'. And so, 'it generates humanitarian problems'.[112] Ambassador Gunter Pleuger of Germany to the UN has demonstrated his concern on the proliferation subject, stating that 'zones of conflict are still awash with weapons, child soldiers and small arms are all too prevalent'.[113] For Ambassador David Broucher of the UK to the UN, it' is widely acknowledged by states that 'the easy availability of small arms and light weapons is a major source of human misery'.[114] The Netherlands has taken the UN PoA as 'a useful first base for better international cooperation on the control of the proliferation of SALW to conflict areas'.[115] As reiterated in previous sections and explicitly stated in paragraph 64 of the Chairman's Summary of the BMS, states have reaffirmed their commitment 'to adopt laws . . . to exercise effective controls over the export, import, transit and transfer of small arms'.[116] It appears to be that the humanitarian impacts of the proliferation of small

[108] Capie, 'Armed Groups, Weapons Availability and Misuse: an overview of the issues and options for action' *Briefing paper*, CHD, Geneva 25 May 2004, p 7.

[109] *Bamako Declaration*, above n 45.

[110] See pp 203–06.

[111] *Nairobi Protocol for the Prevention, Control and Reduction of SALW*, 21 April 2004, Preamble, para 2; it has been signed by 11 states of the sub-region.

[112] *Statement of the State of Israel*, UN BMS, New York, 8 July 2003, p 1.

[113] *Statement of Germany*, UN BMS, 7 July 2003, p 1.

[114] *UK Policy and Strategic Priorities on SALW*, UN BMS, July 2003, p 1.

[115] Sanders, Ambassador to the Conference of Disarmament of the Netherlands in Geneva, *National Statement*, UN BMS, New York, 7 July 2003, p 1.

[116] *Chairman's Summary*, UN BMS, 14 July 2003, p 18.

arms and the need for restraint in the arms trade have been a concern of states.

Turkey, however, is more concerned about peace and security effects than IHL of small arms proliferation. For that country, 'SALW proliferation in Iraq and its possible repercussions on the regional security is a serious cause for concern'.[117] Many tend to believe, however, that 'the widespread availability of small arms' in Iraq, combined with other factors, results in 'daily incidents of injuries and deaths from small arms attacks on civilians and military personnel'.[118] While the Turkish assertion has some elements of truth, it's also equally correct that the excessively diffused SALW in Iraq have been a serious threat to IHL in the country.

The ICRC considers the availability of weapons as an element of restraint for transfers. In its study of 1999 on the SALW problem, it has affirmed the link between a decline of the situation of civilians in conflicts and arms availability. This means that violations of IHL are more likely to occur during or after armed conflict, a time when arms are available in a society. Similar to the position of the UN Panel, however, it is believed that the unregulated availability of arms increases 'tensions, facilitate their indiscriminate use and lead to a rise in civilian casualty levels'.[119]

Along with the indicators suggested in the first standard, and for purposes of the 'limiting the availability of weapons' to violators of IHL, Part 5(B)(6) and (7) of the study submits the following conditions / tests for arms transfers:

> the recipient [state] maintains *strict and effective control* over the internal distribution of arms and ammunition and their further transfer across international borders; the recipient is the *actual 'end user'* of arms and ammunition, will *accept verification* of this and will undertake *not to transfer these to third parties* without the authorization of the supplier State.[120]

In addition, publicists seem to realise the need for export restriction whenever there is excessive availability of small arms[121] (see 7.2.7).

This situation can be summarised as follows: first, various instruments and efforts at *all* levels have recognised the fact that the excessive availability of small arms is a threat to IHL. This has been reiterated by both the ICRC and publicists. Some of the impacts mentioned are: increased risks for humanitarian assistance; facilitating the turning of children into soldiers; and a decline of the safety and security of civilians

[117] Pamir (Ambassador), *Turkish Statement*, UN BMS, 8 July 2003, p 3.

[118] Jackman, 'Small Arms and Security in Iraq' *Ploughshares Monitor* (2003), Ontario, paras 10 and 12.

[119] *ICRC*, above n 87, pp 7, 21, and 14; see also, *Report to the BMS*, above n 48, p 8, para 4.

[120] *ICRC*, above n 87, pp 21–22; see also, ICRC *Report*, *ibid*, p 2, para 5 [emphasis added].

[121] Herby, 'Arms Transfers, Humanitarian Assistance, and Humanitarian Law', above n 49, at 102.

in conflict zones. Even so it is the uncontrolled and unregulated accumulation which most clearly endangers IHL.

Secondly, although there has not been a common definition of phrases such as 'excessive availability' and 'proliferation' of small arms, at the global echelon, the 1997 Panel's report and the ICRC have given some tips on the nature of availability that we have to consider. There exists excessive availability whenever there is: (a) a failure to control strictly weapons either in importing or exporting states; (b) a lack of competence to prevent illegal acquisition; (c) a lack of commitment to avoid diversion; and / or (d) when they are used in actual conflict and violation of humanitarian norms.[122] Some of the indicators clearly show the overlap between the first and the second standards of transfer. Generally these and other indicators may be applied on a case-by-case basis. SALW transfers must to take into account the availability standard of IHL.

Lastly, a careful review of the practice gone through in this chapter fairly demonstrates a general consensus that restrictions upon arms transfer must give paramount consideration to the proliferation of small arms in destination countries. There has been serious commitment by states to prevent the problem and even to use it as a criterion for transfers. Despite this the UN Panel boldly declared the absence of rules of legal restriction.

Centrally therefore, the questions we seek to answer are—do states' humanitarian law obligations cover the use and availability of SALW based specific rules for SALW transfer? Does the practice discussed above constitute a rule of international law? The two standards have more or less the same sources and greatly overlap each other. They will be treated together in the following section, with emphasis on the second question.

7.2.5 Have Use and Availability Based Legal Rules Emerged?

As IHL has been developed as both customary and codified law, we will look at the question from both perspectives, with emphasis on the former. The elements of custom[123] with regard to the standards at issue will now be examined. First, is the *uniformity and consistency* requirement of usage satisfied on this issue? It is worth mentioning here that, even though state practice was stronger in the League era than in the UN on the arms trade, it could not be said that there was consistent practice up until the last two decades.[124]

The first response to the question can still be in the affirmative. At a global level, resolutions and statements by the SC have been affirming that

[122] See *ICRC*, above n 91.

[123] For general discussion, see 3.4, 5.7, 6.3; see also, *Fisheries* case, *ICJ Repts* 1950, p 266, 17 ILR, pp 276–77.

[124] For the interruption of state practice see, eg Lombard, above n 54, at 1.

weapons should not be transferred to areas where IHL values are violated or where any risk of this kind exists. The GA, the GGE 1997 and the UN PoA have complemented this position in general terms. Remarkably, almost all exporters of arms have entered into various arrangements and consider these conditions as criteria for transfers. The standards have been continuously adopted by the OSCE and the EU. As shown in the general obligations section, the Wassenaar and NATO arrangements have supported such considerations. The OSCE and the EU instruments have evolved consistently; in particular the development of the latter was both in words and deeds. The 191 states, who attended the 28th International Conference of the Red Cross and Red Crescent, reiterated their IHL obligation to refrain from transfers of weapons to areas where actual and/or potential violations are apparent, including the availability of arms at the ultimate destination. IHL was firmly incorporated in the ECOWAS Convention of 2006. All these phenomena indicate that not only international organisations, but individual states have continually adopted the practice. Besides this, a number of major exporters have incorporated this practice in their national laws and policies. Global efforts in this direction and the call of African states to stem transfers that take place without due account of IHL, could also represent the view of destination and victim countries on these particular rules of transfers.[125]

The second possible response is that state practice is not adequate for a number of reasons. Firstly, as stated by the ICJ in the *Asylum* case, uncertain and contradictory practices do not amount to 'constant and uniform usage',[126] and the practice at hand is full of contradictions and so unsettled. The violations of arms embargoes by states, and transfers of weapons to countries and regions where breaches of IHL are evident[127] may be invoked to challenge the claim in question. Secondly, a practice ought to be 'both extensive and virtually uniform' in order to constitute custom[128]; and it is clear that certain major exporters of SALW seem to be reluctant to accept the norm. For instance, China is neither a member of the regional organisations nor has it officially adopted such criteria as a policy or law. The same is true with Russia in respect of domestic legislation. Both are among the leading producers and suppliers of small arms.[129] Similarly, importing states do not clearly demonstrate any prohibition in their domestic laws and policies. Finally, the factors that should be adhered to in determining risks of violation are not authoritatively identified or well developed, as recognised by the ICRC. The worst

[125] For state practice in the SC, UN, OSCE, EU, OAU, Wassenaar, NATO and domestic level, see 7.2.1; for the role of international organisations in custom formation, see 5.7, 6.3.

[126] *Asylum* case, *ICJ Repts* 1950, p 277.

[127] For violations and transfers, see p 217, nn 86 and 87.

[128] *North See Continental Shelf* case, *ICJ Repts* 1969, p 3.

[129] Above, n 80.

scenario is expressed in the fact that the UN Panel of 1997 entertained the view that we have no rules on transfers.[130]

Even so such a view can be challenged upon several grounds: (1) a practice need not necessarily be 'in absolute rigorous conformity' with the intended customary norm, as clearly underlined in the *Nicaragua* case. The Court stated that 'in order to deduce the existence of customary rules, the Court deems it sufficient that the conduct of states should, in general, be consistent with such rules'. (2) Incompatible practices against a rule cannot thus justify the absence of a certain practice[131] (see p 162). (3) China and Russia are both members of the UN SC. Russia is also a party to the OSCE and Wassenaar arrangements. Above all, their domestic laws on arms transfer clearly refer to their international obligations.[132] (4) Almost all importing states have backed the UN PoA, and all African countries have called upon the rest of the world to consider IHL impacts of arms transfers; and (5) although the absence of universally agreed indicators of risk is deemed to be a challenge, there has never been a doubt about, or a protest against, the use and/or availability based restrictions upon the arms trade,[133] as opposed to the rule on state-to-state transfers.[134] The second response, therefore, does not seem to be sound.

As a second requirement, the *duration* element now needs to be touched on. International law does not require a rigid time factor for a custom to develop and thus depends on the circumstances of the usage.[135] As discussed in the *erga omnes* character of IHL, this body of international law and the obligations therein are older than the 1949 Geneva Conventions. The question is, therefore, since when states have demonstrated the practice at issue? It is hard to give a precise date and year. It is essential, if not decisive, to point out that states were taking multilateral measures, including codified ones, to restrict transfers to regions where actual or potential atrocities were apparent since the second half of 19th century. These practices did not consistently continue after the failed conventions of the League in the 1920s. What is clear is that during and after the end of the Cold War, it became obvious that SALW are the tools most responsible for extensive violations of IHL and that the practices at global, regional and national levels on these particular standards have developed since the early 1990s, and remain a major concern of states up to the present. It is

130 For lack of indicators, see GGE 1997 and the ICRC (pp 218, 222).

131 See *Nicaragua*, above n 3, at 98; see also Dahlitz, 'The Role of Customary Law in Arms Limitations' in Dahlitz and Dicke (eds), *The International Law of Arms Control and Disarmament* (New York, United Nations, 1991) 176–77.

132 For China and Russia, see p 213.

133 For the position of states, including importing states, and the absence of any objection, see 7.2.

134 See ch 6.

135 Brownlie, *Principles of Public International Law*, 5th edn (Oxford, Clarendon Press, 1998) 5; see also Shaw, above n 1, at 60; see also, *North Sea Continental Shelf*, above n 128, at 43.

important to note that the OSCE has deemed both standards to be operative since 1991, and has subsequently elaborated up on this. The boom of UN initiatives, including arms embargoes commenced in the aftermath of the Cold War. These specific measures have existed therefore for a decade or more.[136]

Yet 'in a society constantly faced with new situations because of the dynamics of progress, there is a clear need for a reasonably speedy method of responding to such changes by a system of prompt rule formation'.[137] Considering the gravity and urgency of the challenge, therefore, progress could have reasonably been faster than it is now.

The third one is the *generality*[138] requirement. This could be deemed to have a threefold dimension in our case. First, major exporters of arms have shown their dedication in various instruments, though the level of commitment varies. Those who have not integrated the criteria into their domestic law made it clear, to state the least, that they respect their international law obligations in the course of arms transfers. Secondly, the victim states, as shown above, are generally sympathetic to tighter measures on the matter. Finally, on some occasions, both the suppliers and recipient states have agreed to consider the use, misuse and availability of SALW in the endorsing or otherwise of transfers, as evidenced by the declaration of the 28th Conference of the Red Cross and Red Crescent in 2003 and 191 states, as parties to the Geneva Conventions have clearly said so (see 7.2.1). The generality aspect of the practice appears to be fulfilled.

For these reasons, the elements of state practice/usage, regarding the use and/or availability standards seem to be appropriately established. The next question is whether this practice is considered *as a law* by states.[139] Four sources will be looked at: state practice, judicial decisions, and the works of jurists and the views of NGOs, particularly of the ICRC.

First, interested states, both exporters and importers have expressed their commitment in various fora to halt transfers of weapons which may represent violation of IHL. In doing so, almost in all global and regional instruments and measures, it has been clearly acknowledged as an existing international law obligation with reference to IHL. The ECOWAS position has to be borne in mind here. This has also been adopted in some major supplier countries' domestic legislation and policies. Those who have not done so have repeatedly been committing themselves to make the use and availability based restrictions part of their domestic legal and political systems. Such beliefs and measures of states existed during early days of the League of Nations, which also led to the establishment of some

136 For the development, see 3.3.3.2 and 6.3; see also, Lombard, above n 54, at 1.

137 See, eg Shaw, above n 1, at 62.

138 *North Sea Continental Shelf*, above n 128, at 42–43; see also *ibid*, at 62–63; see also, ch 3, 3.4.

139 For *opinio juris*, see ch 3, pp 74, 76.

treaties. Commitment has, however, been renewed during and after the Cold War era, and is still continuing.[140] Although some might argue that most of the instruments referred to are merely political declarations, it seems that states engaged in this are aware of the legal nature of this practice as they have been saying it plainly[141]; so, while the majority of interested states are committed to codifying their existing obligations, it would be illogical to consider such practice as 'purely a political or moral gesture'.[142]

Secondly, the ICJ in the *Nicaragua* case, as a subsidiary source of international law and of 'immense importance', has affirmed the customary law obligation of states, concerning provision of weapons for contraveners of IHL, as real.[143] Yet the *Tugar* case[144] declined to adopt or clearly reject the ICJ position. As the former is an ICJ case and dealt with the subject in-depth, its view might be more valued than that of the European Commission of Human Rights. Thirdly, the view a of majority of writers is in favour of the existence of the legal standards at hand, merely on the basis of common Article 1 of the Geneva Conventions.[145] This could therefore be a further proof for the existence of *opinion juris* on both standards.

Fourthly, the role of NGOs, above all of the ICRC is considerable on the subject. Both as an initiator and a partner of states, in humanitarian norms development, the ICRC firmly believes that states are under an obligation to ensure respect for IHL, which includes the duty to cease small arms provision to violators, unsafe areas and countries that suffer from the unregulated availability of such arms. As a matter of custom, therefore, the ICRC may be deemed as an authoritative source of interpretation or an indicator of likely legal development on the subject, although not included in Article 38 of the ICJ Statute.[146] To Meron, for example, this is 'authoritative commentary'.[147] Others, however, think that some NGOs such as the ICRC 'exercise considerable influence',[148] on promoting humanitarian norms.

140 For state practice, see 7.2.1.

141 See, eg *Lotus* case *PCIJ*, Series A, 10, 1927, p 28, the Court emphasised the need for consciousness of states of their legal duty; see also Dahlitz, above n 131, at 177 and 174.

142 Shaw, above n 1, at 70.

143 *Nicaragua*, above n 3, at 114 and 135; see also *ibid*, at 86.

144 Above, n 89.

145 See pp 288–89; see also p 287, some academics are involved in the drafting of the FCIAT; for the role of publicists see Shaw, above n 2, at 88.

146 Sandoz et al (eds), above n 7, at xxix–xxxv; for the role of NGOs see also, McCorquodale, 'The Individual and the International Legal System' in Evans, *International Law* (Oxford, Oxford University Press, 2003) 317–20.

147 Meron, 'Is there already a Differentiated Regime of State Responsibility in the Geneva Conventions?' above n 36, at 228.

148 Burnett, 'International Organisations', at <http://www.asil.org/resource/intorg1.htm>

In any event, no one has disputed that the views of the ICRC deserve special consideration. The ICJ in the *Legal Consequences Advisory Opinion* for instance refers to the interpretations given by the ICRC of the Fourth Geneva Convention, in order to determine questions of the 'Convention's *travaux préparatoires*'.[149] The position of other NGOs has also proven public conscience on the problem; in addition to their role of influencing states' laws and policies at all levels, they strongly express the view that transfers should not be allowed in the stated circumstances—with the result that the use of them against humanitarian norms might be averted.[150]

Finally, as an analogy, such an approach has been adopted in the Amended Protocol II, to the CCW of 1980. Article 3(7) and (8) of the instrument prohibits, for example, the indiscriminate use of mines and booby traps against civilians. Pursuant to Article 8(a) (c) and (d), a State Party is obliged, inter alia, first, 'to exercise restraint in the transfers of any mine', if non-compliance of a party with the rule of distinction is evident; secondly, to ensure that any transfer is in compliance with the obligations therein and rules of IHL; and finally, not to transfer mines to non-parties to the Protocol unless a recipient state is ready to abide by the rules of the Treaty.[151]

Therefore, it appears to be plausible to conclude that state practice accompanied by *opinio juris* have emerged on both the use and proliferation based restrictions of SALW transfers. Actual and/or possible uses of SALW against IHL, including their unregulated availability, have constituted the basic features of the rules.

The second perspective focuses on treaty obligation. Do the Geneva Conventions and other related agreements cover the use and availability based restrictions? As there is no direct reference to these situations and the Contracting Parties have not specifically intended SALW transfers, it might reasonably be argued that the texts of the treaties of IHL do not cover them.[152] Consistent with Article 31 of the law of treaties, however, the object and the purpose of such instruments and subsequent practice of the parties ought to be considered too.[153]

First, consistent with the *travaux preparatoires*, one of the objects and purposes of the Geneva Conventions is to safeguard 'the personality and

[149] Above n 30, paras 95 and 97.

[150] See ch 5, 5.6; see also 8.3.4; for the role of NGOs see *SAS 2002*, above n 70, at 242, box. 6.3.

[151] 1980 UN Convention: *Amended Protocol on the Prohibitions or Restrictions on the Use of Mines, Booby-Traps and Other Devices*, (Amended Protocol II, 1996); see also Aust, *Handbook of International Law* (Cambridge, Cambridge University Press, 2005) 255–56.

[152] See 7.1.

[153] *VCLT* (p 103); see also, *Libya v Chad* case, *ICJ Repts* 1994, p 6, paras 21–22, the Court noted that Art 31 reflects customary international law; for the significance of subsequent practice in general, see White, *The United Nations System: Toward International Justice* (London, Lynne Rienner, 2002) 38–43; see also, McGoldrick (ch 8, fn 202) p 49.

dignity of human beings' as a universal principle, which is binding without a need for any reciprocal legal relationship.[154] By virtue of Article 31(1) of the law of treaties[155] the use of small arms against this objective could thus suffice to the application of the treaties to the small arms transfers. Such a restriction on SALW might also make the treaties effective in application terms.[156]

Secondly, the Geneva Conventions should be interpreted 'in the light of present-day conditions'.[157] This approach of treaty interpretation has been adopted by human rights regimes and implementation mechanisms in later times.[158] Evidently, the contemporary proliferation of small arms and armed conflicts jeopardizes respect for IHL, which should be taken into account in applying the treaties. The fact that such a condition did not exist during the conclusion of the treaties is not a valid excuse for failing to engage with current problems.

Finally, the frequent practice of the SC, regional organisations and individual states has clearly referred to their obligation to respect and ensure respect for IHL in relation to SALW transfer. Then again, it could strongly be argued, in accordance with Article 31(3)(b) of the VCLT that such a situation constitutes subsequent practice,[159] in the application and interpretation of the Geneva Conventions of 1949.

In conclusion, the attitude of recipient states towards respect for IHL and / or any possible risk including arms availability, as general standards, have formed a rule of restraint on SALW transfers, which could briefly be described as 'use or risk based limitation'. This has been further clarified by the indicators set out in the ICRC Study, the UN Panel Report, and the practice of the SC and ECOWAS Treaty on small arms of 2006. In this sense, therefore, the detail indicators are in a progressive development. Such a restriction on arms transfers is, therefore, an obligation of states, as a component of IHL—they are built-in customary and / or treaty laws.

To express an extreme position, it may also be argued, without disputing the threat IHL is facing from the proliferation of small arms, that the rules have not yet clearly emerged and they lack widely agreed parameters. The Martens Clause may offer some responses to this problem.

[154] Pictet (1952), above n 4, p 21, para 3.

[155] See also Shaw, above n 1, at 656.

[156] *Ibid*, at 660; see also Ronzitti, 'Problems of Arms Control Treaty Interpretation' in Dahlitz and Dicke (eds), above n 132 at 119; see also, ICJ '*The Legal Consequences*', above n 30, at 94; see also *Soering v UK*, ECHR Series A, No 161, p 34 (1989); see also White, above n 154, at 39.

[157] Shaw, above n 1, at 659; White, *ibid*, at 41.

[158] See, eg the *Tyrer* case, ECHR Series A, No 26, p 15 (1978).

[159] Shaw, above n 1, 659; see also, White, above n 154, at 39.

7.2.6 The Martens Clause and SALW Transfers

> Until a more complete code of the laws or war is issued, the high contracting Parties think it right to declare that in cases not included in the Regulations adopted by them, populations and belligerents remain under the protection and empire of the principles of international law, as they result from the usages established between civilized nations, from the laws of humanity, and the requirements of the public conscience.[160]

The Martens Clause has formed part of humanitarian law, and has continuously been embodied in a number of conventions, regulations and protocols of IHL. The modern version of the clause is found for instance in Additional Protocol II of 1977 to the Geneva Conventions, which dealt with non-international armed conflict. Paragraph 4 of the Preamble states: '[I]n case not covered by the law in force, the human person remains under the protection of the principles of humanity and the dictates of the public conscience'.[161]

Certain questions arise, among others: first, can the Martens Clause be a source for rule of transfer by itself? And secondly, do the dictates of public conscience address other sources, particularly of NGOs, beyond the traditional sources of law? It is essential to look at the fundamentals of the clause before dealing with the first question.

Three features are of note of the clause; first, the reason for its importance is: (a) 'all the circumstances which occur in practice' may not be covered in conventions; and (b) whenever parties to a conflict, as well as in civil wars, feel that they are not bound by certain rules, including by common Article 3 of the conventions and protocols, it restricts their behaviour, regardless of their beliefs. Secondly, the very essence of the clause is that, in the absence of treaty-based rules of IHL, the principles of humanity and the dictates of public conscience apply. According to the *Oxford English Dictionary*, the former ordinarily refers to the 'compassion' or 'fellow-feeling' of 'human species', among others. Legally, it is a rule restricting the doctrine of military necessity and prohibits unnecessary death and injury. The latter constitutes two essential words: the word 'public' normally implies 'universal', or 'common' or 'widespread', and the word conscience means 'sense of right and wrong', or 'moral sense', or 'principles', or 'ethics'. In an IHL context and as a phrase, it refers to draft rules, resolutions, communications, declarations, etc, which represent the conscience of the public or is evidence of public opinion. Whether the sources should be states, IGO's or NGOs, or all three, seems to be

[160] Scott, *The Hague Conventions and Declarations of 1899 and 1907*, 3rd edn (Oxford, Oxford University Press, 1918) 101–02; see also Roberts and Guelff (eds), *Documents on the Laws of War*, 3rd edn (Oxford, Oxford University Press, 2000) 70.

[161] See also, *GC I*, Art 63, *GC II*, Art 62, *GC III*, Art 142, *GC IV*, Art 158 and *GP I*, Art 1(2); see also, *1980 CCW*, Preamble; see also, Ticehust, above n 13, at 125–34.

unsettled. Nevertheless, the will of interested states, including the most affected ones, and independent societies have been referred to, as possible sources of public conscience. Finally, it has generally been maintained that it exists 'independently of the conventions', as universal customary law although its vagueness has been acknowledged as a drawback.[162] The perception of states and publicists is thus critically divided regarding the legal status and value of the clause.

Contemporary positions of states on the relevance and interpretations of this vary greatly. As was revealed in the Advisory Opinion of the ICJ on *The Threat and Use of Nuclear Weapons*, the views of states can probably be classified into three parts. Some states consider the clause as outdated; the Russian Federation, for example, thought that the clause is obsolete 'as a complete code of the laws of war was formulated in 1949 and 1977'. Others, however, consider it as an independent source of law. Nauru for example argued that the clause authorises the ICJ to determine the scope of IHL by looking at the dictates of public conscience.[164] The final category is neither acceptance nor denial of the importance of it. The UK and the US are typical examples of this. The former think that the clause 'does not itself establish' the illegality of a weapon; however, it also implies that the use of every weapon which is not outlawed by treaty does not mean that the weapon is legal. In the end, the UK has referred to the need for express prohibition.[165] The US seems to have preferred to remain silent on this matter.[166]

Despite the question of how appropriate the opinion of the ICJ on nuclear weapons, it has affirmed that the Martens Clause 'has proved to be an effective means of addressing the rapid evolution of military technology', and the views of the Russian federation and the UK was accordingly rejected. The Court underlined that the legal existence of the clause should not be doubted. The ICJ affirmed also that the clause is a customary rule with a normative value.[167]

In addition to this, publicists take diverse opinions on the issue. One trend entertains the idea that the clause 'operates only at the level of inter-

[162] Sandoz et al (eds), above n 7, at 1341, paras 4433–35; see also Ticehust, *ibid*; see also Green, above n 1, at 34, paras 1 and 2; see also, *Nuclear Weapons*, above n 28, *Dissenting Opinion of Judge Shahabuddeen*, p 21; see also, Pictet (1952), above n 4, at 413, and (1960), above n 22, at 282.

[163] *Russian Federation-Written Submission on the Opinion Requested by the GA on the Legality of the Threat and Use of Nuclear Weapons*, p 13, para 3.

[164] *Nauru-Written Submission on the Advisory Opinion Requested by the World Health Organisation*, September 1994, p 68.

[165] *United Kingdom-Written Submission on the Opinion Requested by the GA on the Legality of the Threat and Use of Nuclear Weapons*, p 21.

[166] *USA-Written Submission on the Opinion Requested by the GA*, 21 June 1995, pp 21–33.

[167] *Advisory Opinion*,, above n 28, paras 78(2), 79, 84 and 87; see also Ticehurst, above n 13, at 12; see also Sandoz et al (eds), ICRC, above n 7, at 1341; see also, p 305, the 1890 declaration refers to a 'usage established between civilised nations', Protocol II has also mentioned 'established custom'.

pretation of international principles and rules'. The second inclination of scholars and judges is that the phrase has an impact on 'sources of international law', at least in the area of IHL. According to this line of argument, the laws of humanity and public conscience have become principles of international law. Finally, the clause is an expression of ideas 'that have motivated and inspired' the progression of IHL.[168] The views are highly related to each other; it seems, however, that the second gives more value to the clause as a source of law.

For our purposes three points can be made at this stage: (1) as reflected by Nauru and the ICJ, and firmly endorsed by the ICRC, it seems to be a convincing argument that the clause generally stands by its own as a principle of customary rule of IHL in prohibiting the use of weapons, particularly of the newly innovated technologies, although legitimate doubts might arise as to its complete separation from customary rules of IHL; (2) the clause is relevant for weapons regulation be it as a source of law, a tool of interpretation or as a motive for the evolution of IHL; and (3) the elements it has embraced are really ambiguous,[169] in particular the basis for the phrase called 'dictates of public conscience'.

Where is the phrase to be found? Some argue that the dictates of public conscience, as enshrined in the Martens Clause confers authority to consider the views of independent societies, such as the ICRC and writers who are 'highly qualified to identify the rules of *jus in bello*, as a source of customary law, and as an expression of *opinio juris*', in addition to the sources illustrated in the ICJ Statute. A restriction on weapons may, therefore, emanate from the legal views of international societies or others who are believed to reflect the views of the public on concerns of IHL.[170] In this account the views of the ICRC and others are worth consideration, either as an expression or evidence of public conscience.

The ICRC submits that 'as international arms transfers, particularly of small arms, have become easier the promotion of respect for IHL has become vastly more difficult'. Therefore, all national laws and policies, including regional and international norms shall consider the IHL impact of exports. This comprises the production, transfer and availability of arms. The availability aspect is much more focused by the ICRC. States are therefore, according to the ICRC, under an obligation to 'respect and ensure respect' for IHL in the light of these obligations (for details see 7.2.1).[171]

[168] Cassese, 'The Martens Clause: Half a Loaf or Simply Pie in the Sky?' (2000) 11 *EJIL* 189–90; in comparison, see Meron, 'The Martens Clause, Principles of Humanity, and Dictates of Public Conscience' (2000) 94 *AJIL* 78–89.

[169] ICRC, 'Weapons and International Humanitarian Law', 4 March 2003, p 1, para 3, at <www.icrc.org>

[170] Nauru's Submission, above n 164, para 2; see also, Cassese, above n 168, at 214–15.

[171] *ICRC's Report to the BMS*, above n 48, p 2, para 3; see also, ICRC, above n 87, at 25, 2; ICRC, 'The ICRC and Various Issues Related to the Use of Weapons' *Statement made at the UN GA*, 55 Session, 2000, para 5.

Moreover, the FCIAT and the ICCAT are the best examples of efforts of civil societies and prominent activists, who took a firm position on restricting the trade in, and transfers of weapons which are likely to be used in violations of IHL. Eminent NGOs and peace laureates are playing a leading role on this issue. For instance, Amnesty International, OXFAM and IANSA had jointly launched a campaign in October 2003, which was conducted in 60 countries. This was generally against the unregulated international arms trade. These NGOs claim that 'the easy availability of arms increases the incidence of armed violence, acts as a trigger for conflicts, and prolongs wars'; the movement is not intended 'to ban the trade, but to adopt far stricter controls', taking into account actual or potential IHL violations and other international law norms. The interesting aspect here is that they have identified certain weapons, as the most diffused SALW in the world: the Russian AK-47, the US M16, the German G3 and the Belgian FAL. They have called on all states, particularly of the major exporters of arms, to sign the arms treaty in 2006.[172]

Others have, however, relied on sources such as the resolutions of the GA as an authoritative declaration of the state of public conscience. Judge Shahabuddeen, in his dissenting opinion on the 'Nuclear Weapons Advisory Opinion' stated that the Court 'must confine its attention to sources which speak with authority'. He went on to state that although GA resolutions are not binding and may not pass with unanimity, they 'do provide evidence of the public conscience' and not the *opinio juris* of states.[173]

As indicated in previous parts of the book, the GA has passed various resolutions since 1988 on the problem of arms transfer. For example, the UN GA, in Resolution 52/38 J of 1998, welcomed the GGE Report of 1997, with emphasis on the need for 'measures to reduce the excessive and destabilizing accumulation and transfer of small arms and light weapons'; it also acknowledged 'the guidelines for international arms transfers in the context of General Assembly resolution 46/36 H of 6 December 1991, which were adopted by consensus by the "Disarmament Commission"', which set out the obligation of states to exercise restraint over transfers of arms to ease international tensions and conflicts in general. The Assembly also welcomed the BMS held in 2003, in which the indiscriminate and pervasive use of SALW was referred to as a concern of states, among other things.[174]

[172] See for gun-control activists' position, *The FCIAT* and *the ICCAT* (5.6, 6.1.4, 7.2.3.4); see, eg 'Charities Campaign against Arms Trade' *BBC News*, 9 October 2003, at <http://news.bbc.co.uk/1/hi/uk/3176416.stm>; see also for the role of NGOs in general, p 231.

[173] Above n 162, pt III, No 3, para 22; see also Ticehurst, above n 13, at 2–3.

[174] UN Doc A/52/38 J, Res 52/38, Preamble, paras 7 and 8; see also the first *DC Guidelines*, above n 41, para 19; Chairman's Report of the BMS, above n 116, p 6, para 4; see also, GA Res 61/89/2006 adopted by a vote of 153 states in favour.

In brief, four concluding observations will have to be made. First, the clause is one of the valued principles of IHL. It might be of help to fill gaps in the obligation 'to respect and ensure respect' for IHL, relating to SALW transfers. It should generally be emphasised that the attitude of the world public is against irresponsible transfers of arms that endanger humanitarian norms, irrespective of being represented by NGOs or the UN GA[175] and has to be considered as an indicator for transfers. Secondly, it helps enhance the participation of non-state parties in the small arms control regime. Apart from the main actors of international law, non-governmental societies or activists might represent the public conscience on such problems. As demonstrated earlier, the circulation of certain types of weapons has been causing immense humanitarian challenges and deserve paramount consideration. These voices must be heard as a potential source of IHL rules in order to mitigate the consequences of these challenges. Thirdly, and most unfortunately, the elements, legal status and actual implementation of the clause have not escaped vagueness. As reflected by Cassese, for example, the criticism valid to the extent that the clause is in conflict with the state sovereignty based reality of the international order.[176] Finally, the clause does not seem to form part of the ongoing efforts to regulate the SALW flow from suppliers to violators of IHL; it is one of the forgotten dimensions of IHL in relation to the SALW control regime. In order to control the trade in light weapons their devastating humanitarian consequences, attention is needed to make the most compelling use of these IHL norms.[177]

7.3 CONCLUSIONS AND PROBLEMS

Four key points are believed to summarise the chapter. First, from a weapons specific prohibition perspective, the use of most SALW currently in circulation might not be declared illegal under IHL. Moreover, those who have taken or may take part in armed conflict (states or NSAs) have a primary obligation to respect and ensure respect for IHL norms. The manner of use of these arms in violation of such norms has, however, brought legal restrictions, in accordance with states' duties under common Article 1 of the Geneva Conventions and customary IHL, as established by ICJ's interpretation of the Article pertaining to arms supplies. As a rule, a state owes the international community the

[175] See, eg Shahabuddeen, above n 162, para 29, sub-para 4, he noted in relation to the use or treat of nuclear weapons that '[A] civilized society is not one that knowingly destroys itself, or knowingly allows itself to be destroyed'.

[176] Cassese, above n 168, at 216, paras 1 and 2; see also n 13, at p 4, para 3.

[177] For further recommendations, see Yihdego, 'Irresponsible Arms Transfers and Humanitarian Norms: Principles of Humanity and Public Conscience Perspective' (2006) 3 *Australasia Journal of Human Security* 29–42.

obligation not to engage itself in, and in addition to prevent transfers of SALW, which may be used in contravention of IHL. The supplier, importer, transit and facilitator states of such undertakings are all subject to these *erga omnes* obligations. These are existing customary and conventional legal duties of states.

Two basic standards of restriction have thus been set out; a transfer is illegal if: (a) recipients have a record of non-obedience or if a risk of violations is evident; and (b) whenever a destination is flooded with unregulated SALW. These cases have jointly constituted the use and/or availability based restrictions of transfers. The best example of such a violation is the use (actual or potential) of weapons against non-combatants. These and other standards have widely been adopted in state practice, on the understanding that they reflect existing legal obligations. The development of detailed indicators by which situations of this nature can be determined is still in progress. The inclusion of these restrictions in the 2006 ECOWAS Convention asserts the dynamic nature of such a progress.

Secondly, regardless of the confusion over the application of IHL to SALW transfer, there is a consensus on the harmful humanitarian consequences of the use and proliferation of small arms, particularly with regard to civilians. The international community has to be reminded of one essential tool in this regard. In such a state of confusion, humanitarian law is equipped with a golden principle called the Martens Clause. The principles of humanity and the dictates of public conscience have to apply in such situations. This principle, with all its haziness and controversies, might help improve the perception of the world community on the challenge of small arms. For instance, NGOs have persistently called for a legal restraint on the most dispersed weapons such as AK 47/77, M16, G3 and NFL. They went to the extent of drafting laws and regulations of arms transfer in view of the behaviour of importers and other situations of risk and availability of arms. All these concerns have been reflected in the resolutions of international organisations. The Martens Clause may thus help fill the gaps of IHL-based rules of arms transfer.

Thirdly, efforts have to be made to clarify and remind states of their IHL obligations on arms transfer, and also that violations by states and the absence of a framework of application are serious challenges to the rules of arms transfer considered in this chapter.

Finally, questions of state responsibility may arise out of the violations of these rules (see chapter nine). Yet the human being is protected not only by IHL, but by IHRL regarding SALW transfers.

8

International Human Rights Law [IHRL] Limitations on SALW Transfers

DOES IHRL OR its related norms restrict small arms transfer? We shall address first the salient features of human rights obligations of states in general and their duties regarding the use of firearms in particular.

8.1 IHRL IN GENERAL

Identifying the core features of international human rights (henceforth 'human rights') and their link with SALW diffusion will enable us to appreciate some key problems.

The word 'right' relating to human rights can be described as 'immunity against encroachments of certain fundamental interests' of the human person.[1] As opposed to other rights or legal regimes such as IHL, 'human rights attach to individuals as against any state bound by the international norm' and, therefore, 'apply always and everywhere'.[2] Human rights have generally two mainstream sources, treaty and custom.[3] The UN Charter,[4] the ICCPR, the ICESCR and other regional conventions can be mentioned among the core treaties on IHRL.[5] Also, GA resolutions such as the UDHR and the Friendly Relations have constituted the customary law of human rights.[6]

[1] Provost, *International Human Rights and Humanitarian Law* (Cambridge, Cambridge University Press, 2002)17; see also Joseph, Schultz and Castan (eds), *The International Covenant on Civil and Political Rights: Cases, Materials, and Commentaries*, 2nd edn (Oxford, Oxford University Press, 2004) 4–6.

[2] Provost, *ibid*, at 18–19.

[3] Rehman, *International Human Rights Law: A Practical Approach* (England, Pearson Education, 2003) 16–21; see also Shaw, *International Law*, 4th edn (Cambridge, Cambridge University Press, 1997) 204.

[4] See, eg Art 1(3).

[5] See ch 4, p 95; *ECHRs,*, below n 34; *The African Charter on Human and Peoples' Rights* (ACHPRs) 5, 21 I.L.M. 58 (1982); *American Convention on Human Rights* (ACHRs) (1978) O.A.S.T.S. No 36.

[6] See further (p 96).

International human rights are generally divided into three categories: civil and political rights, social, economic and cultural rights, and group or people's rights. Although very close to and even overlapping each other, the first cluster of rights is regarded as more precise and authoritative than the rest.[7] The focus of this chapter will therefore be on these rights.

Civil and political rights include the right to life and recognition as a person before the law and equality; freedoms of thought, conscience and religion and the prohibition on torture, slavery, and retroactivity of criminal law and imprisonment solely on the ground of failure to comply with contractual obligations. These are non-derogable legal rules, which shall be respected and ensured by states.[8] Even so, all of them are not absolute rights and obligations. The right to life is not for instance unlimited, as a lawful deprivation of life is not forbidden in human rights law.[9]

By contrast, the conventions on the prohibition of torture and genocide have set out absolute freedoms and obligations. The former, as indicated in Article 1(1) outlaws 'any act by which severe pain or suffering, whether physical or mental, is intentionally inflicted on a person', to obtain confession or information, by a state official or another person in such a capacity. It grants an absolute right to a person not to be subjected to torture or other cruel and inhuman treatment.[10] By virtue of Articles 1, 2 and 3 of the Genocide Convention, moreover, any act of conspiracy, complicity or incitement to kill, cause serious bodily or mental harm, etc, 'with intent to destroy, in whole or in part, a national, ethnical, racial or religious groups as such', is made a crime of genocide.[11] These protections and obligations must also be complied with both in times of peace and war.[12]

In addition, the prohibition of genocide, torture, slavery, the slave trade, and racial discrimination and apartheid have acquired a peremptory status under international law. Some also call them special value rights. Others extend such norms to the right to life, equality, liberty and security and a fair trial. However, there has been no exhaustive list of such norms in international law,[13] and every right, therefore, has to be assessed on its merits.

[7] Rehman, above n 3, at 20 and 55; see also Joseph, Shultz and Castan (eds), *The International Covenant on Civil and Political Rights: Cases, Materials, and Commentaries* (Oxford, Oxford University Press, 2000) 28, para 1.76.

[8] See, eg *ICCPR*, Arts 4 (2), 6, 7, 8, 11, 15, 16 and 18; ECHRs, Art 15; ACHRs, Art 27; ECHRs, Art 15(2); see also, Rehman, above n 3, at 56; see also Higgins, 'Derogations Under Human Rights Treaties' 48 *BYBIL* (1976–77) 281; see also Shaw, above n 3, at 196.

[9] Joseph et al (eds), *The International Covenant* (2000), above n 7, at 20, para 1.52; see also Shaw, *ibid*, at 204; see, eg ECHRs, Art 15(1).

[10] *Convention against Torture and Other Cruel, Inhuman or Degrading Treatment or Punishment* (1984).

[11] *Convention on the Prevention and Punishment of the Crime Genocide* (1948).

[12] Joseph et al (eds), *The International Covenant* (2000), above n 7 at 20, para 1.50; see also Shaw, *International Law*, 4th edn, above n 3, at 209–12.

[13] Crawford, *The International Law Commission's Articles on state Responsibility: Introduction, Text and Commentaries* (Cambridge, Cambridge University Press, 2002) 246; see also Provost,

Further, the protection of fundamental human rights on the whole is an obligation *erga omnes*, and 'not reciprocal between states'.[14] States are hence obliged 'to respect and ensure respect' for human rights. This implies both refraining from violations, and positive actions to prevent violations and/or abuses. The duty of states to respect and ensure respect applies albeit 'within their sovereign territory, and within territory over which they have effective control', as clearly stated under Article 2(1) of the ICCPR. Yet, it appears that a state is not permitted to commit violations of human rights, through its agents on foreign soil[15]—it is submitted that the application of IHRL to extra-territorial situations is complex. However, controversies relating to the actions of the armed and security forces of a state outside its territory *may* be distinguished from the question of extraterritorial conduct (which may include authorising arms exports) of a state carried out within its territory (see further 8.3, 8.3.5).

Two observations should be made here. First, the obligations of human rights are of a general nature in the sense that they embrace both negative and positive duties. This is so without discrimination of any kind as to ethnicity, origin, sex, etc.[16] Secondly, the *erga omnes* obligations of human rights may give rise to rights and some duties of third states in response to non-compliance of a state with such norms, as will be seen later. With this background, therefore, we shall assess the impacts of small arms proliferation on international human rights.

As the UN Secretary-General has noted, '[S]mall arms proliferation is not merely a security issue; it is also an issue of human rights and development'.[17] The link between IHRs and SALW is multifaceted. The first one is that SALW are the dominant tools of arbitrary killings, detention, forced disappearance, genocide, torture, rape, kidnappings, injuries, and displacements. They are either in actual use or they facilitate such violations.[18]

The second is that they aggravate violations and cause them to become more serious. In the words of the UN Special Rapporteur on small arms,

above n 1, at 18–19; see also Rehman, above n 3, at 23 and 61; see also ILC, 'Best and Settled Rules of *jus cogens*' *YBILC* 1966, vol ii, pp 247–48; see also 7.2.

[14] *Barcelona Traction* case, *ICJ Repts* 1970, p 32; Rehman, above n 3, at 2; Crawford, *ibid*, at 278, paras 8 and 9; see also Shaw, *International Law*, 4th edn, above n 3, at 208, 204 and 545–46; see also IHL.

[15] Joseph et al (eds), *The International Covenant* (2000), above n 7, at 59–60 and 21–24; see also Shaw, *International Law*, 4th edn, above n 3, at 213 and 259; see, eg *Lopez Burgos v Uruguay*, HRC (52/79), 29/7/81, para 12.3; see also Joseph et al (eds), *The International Covenant*, 2nd edn, above n 1, at 91, para 4.15; see also Lawson, 'Life After Bankovic: on the Extraterritorial Application of the European Convention on Human Rights' in Coomans and Kamminga (eds), *Extraterritorial Application of Human Rights Treaties* (Oxford, Oxford University Press, 2004) 120.

[16] See, eg Rehman, above n 3 at 66–67.

[17] *Millennium Summit*, 2000, para 239.

[18] Frey, The Question of Trade, Carrying and Use of Small Arms and Light Weapons in the Context of Human Rights and Humanitarian Norms' 30 May 2002, para 33; see also *Shattered Lives*, below n 21, at 19 and 27.

'small arms have the power to transform a basic violation of human rights into a profound one. With powerful firearms, a dispute can turn into a killing, an act of revenge can turn into a massacre'.[19] The Rwandan genocide of 1994, the gross murders of civilians in Israel/Palestine, Spain, the UK and Iraq are realities of today[20] (see 2.1).

Finally, the availability and misuse of small weapons by states, NSAs and individuals has led to a widespread deprivation and abuse of human rights.[21] It has been reiterated by UN bodies and panels that strong links exist between the availability of weapons and serious crimes, violence, and hindrance of social and economic development[22] (see 7.2.4). This is so, notwithstanding the legitimate use of small arms, including for the protection of human rights[23] (see 2.1). The interest here is however on the violations and failures to safeguard human rights norms.

Briefly, states are duty-bound to respect and ensure respect for human rights in their respective jurisdictions and in all circumstances. Of course, restrictions could be placed on non-absolute rights in accordance with the rule of law. It has been established that the use and availability of SALW is closely linked to IHRL, especially with that of civil and political rights, in terms of violations and abuses of the latter. In the light of these general remarks, thus, it is necessary to take a look at the challenges to SALW transfer from an IHRL perspective. The discussion on negative and positive international human rights obligations on the use of small arms, may lay a foundation for any potential human rights law-based rule of arms transfer.

8.2 THE DUTY OF STATES REGARDING THE USE OF FIREARMS

Two different but related obligations arise out of the use of SALW, the use of force and firearms by state forces and others. The first obligation, as enshrined in Articles 6(1) and 9(1) of the ICCPR, requires states and their agents to respect and protect the right to life and the dignity and security

[19] Frey, *ibid*, para 34; see also the *Secretary-General's Report*, below n 17.

[20] See *Shattered Lives*, below n 21; see also 'Spain mourns train attack victims' *BBC News*, 12 March 2004; see also <http://www.guardian.co.uk/terrorism/story/0,12780,1523867,00.html> for London bombings.

[21] Oxfam, Amnesty International, *Shattered Lives: the Case for Tough International Arms Control*, 30 January 2003, p 26; see also, Frey, above n 18, para 38; see also the UN HRC, below n 62.

[22] *GGE 1997*, para 77(a) (c); see also *GGE 2001*, *Feasibility of Restricting the Legal Trade*, 12 March 2001, p 3, para 13; see also, *Press Release*, 'Security Council Seeks Limitation on Illicit Trade in Small Arms, Noting Harmful Impact, Especially on Vulnerable Groups' 31 October 2002, para 1; see also p 291.

[23] See, eg *Basic Principles on the Use of Force and Firearms by Law Enforcement Officials*, UN Congress on the Prevention of Crime and the Treatment of Offenders, Havana, 27 August–7 September 1990, Preamble, para 3.

of a person. For instance, as stated in Article 6(2) of the ICCPR and Article 2(2) of the ECHR, a person's life can only be deprived to enforce a competent court's judgment, in accordance with the rule of law and under some exceptional circumstances which will be discussed later. States, therefore, have to respect such rights and to prevent arbitrary killing by their agents, the police, security forces and the army.[24] Criminal acts perpetrated by individuals or groups, 'with the express or implicit permission of authorities', are also understood to be deeds of state agents.[25]

Three important UN instruments have outlined the details of the use of force and firearms and the obligations therein. The first is the 1979 Code of Conduct for Law Enforcement Officials. It is emphatically stated under Article 2 that officials of states shall 'respect and protect human dignity and maintain and uphold the human rights of all persons'. The principle, as per Article 3, is that 'law enforcement officials may use force only when strictly necessary and to the extent required for performance of their duty'. The Article underlines three elements: (1) any use of force by state agents should be an exception, in all circumstances; (2) it has to be in line with the 'principle of proportionality'; and (3) 'the use of firearms is considered an extreme measure. Every effort should be made to exclude the use of firearms, especially against children'.[26] It shall be noted that the GA has adopted the Code, as shown in introductory paragraph (e) of Resolution 34/169, 'as a body of principles for observance by law enforcement officials'.[27]

The second is the 'Basic Principles on the Use of Force and Firearms by Law Enforcement Officials', which was adopted in 1990 by the Eighth UN Congress on the Prevention of Crime and the Treatment of Offenders; Article 9 provides[28]:

> Law enforcement officials *shall not use firearms* against persons except in self-defense of others against the imminent threat of death or serious injury, to prevent the preparation of a particular serious crime involving grave threat to life, to arrest a person presenting such a danger and extreme means are insufficient to achieve these objectives. In any event, intentional lethal use of firearms may only be made when strictly unavoidable in order to protect life.

Finally, the 'UN Bluebook for Law Enforcement Officials', as guidance for UN peacekeepers, has dealt with international standards and norms on

[24] Frey, above n 18, para 40; see also Joseph et al (eds), *The International Covenant* (2000), above n 7, at 108–09; see also the *Code of Conduct*, below n 26, Art 1.

[25] Frey, *ibid*, para 46.

[26] *Code of Conduct for Law Enforcement Officials*, 1979, GA Res 34/169, Annex 34 [emphasis added].

[27] *Ibid*; see also UN Economic and Social Council Res1986/10, s IX, 21, the Council had called on UN Member States to implement the Code.

[28] *Basic Principles on the Use of Force and Firearms by Law Enforcement Officials*, UN Congress on the Prevention of Crime and the Treatment of Offenders, Havana, 27 August–7 September 1990 [emphasis added].

the subject, including on the use of firearms. Principle 1 has reinforced the aforesaid rules and stressed the obligation of law enforcement officers to respect the right to life, security and dignity of a person. Under principle 2 of the Bluebook, the duty to refrain from using weapons except in some unavoidable circumstances has also been reiterated.[29]

These instruments have to be read in the light of states' obligations under human rights treaties.[30] The HRC, in the case *Guerrero v Colombia* emphasised that the right not to be killed by the state 'is a matter of the utmost gravity'.[31] It added that, the shooting and killing of seven suspects of kidnapping by the police, 'without warning to the victims and without giving them any opportunity to surrender', was not justified as 'necessary in their own defense or others'.[32] The action which caused the death of the applicant 'was disproportionate to the requirements of law enforcement in the circumstances of the case and she was arbitrarily deprived of her life contrary to Article 6(1)'[33] of the ICCPR.

Regional instruments and courts seem to have adopted similar approach. Article 2 of the ECHRs only permits 'the use of force which is no more than absolutely necessary'. By virtue of sub-paragraph (2) a, b and c of the same provision, such exceptional actions could lawfully be taken, inter alia, in defence of a person from illegal attack, to effect a legitimate arrest and to prevent escape from lawful detention or prison.[34]

The ECHR, in the *McCann v United Kingdom* case[35] indicated that, 'a stricter and more compelling test of necessity must be employed',[36] in interpreting the threshold between the proportionality of an action and the right at stake. In particular, the Court duly considered the rules of engagement of the UK Ministry of Defence[37] and the Gibraltar Police.[38] The latter's 'Firearms-Rules of Engagement' has incorporated the following rules:

> 1. Do not use more force than necessary to achieve your objective. 2. If you use firearms you should do so with care for the safety of persons in the vicinity . . . 3. A warning should, if practicable, be given before opening fire.[39]

Police officers may, however, fire without warning if doing so or any delay to do so 'could lead to death or serious injury' either to protected persons

[29] *UN BlueBook for Law Enforcement Officials*, UN Humanitarian Affairs Division, Principle 2.5, at <http://www.uncjin.org/Documents/BlueBook/BlueBook/index.html>

[30] See, eg *Code of Conduct*, above n 26, Preamble, paras 1–3.

[31] HRC, (45/79) 31/3/82, para 13.1.

[32] *Ibid*, para 13.2.

[33] *Ibid*, para 13.3.

[34] *European Convention on Human Rights* (ECHRs), 4 November 1950.

[35] ECHR, Judgment, 5 September 1995.

[36] *Ibid*, para 149.

[37] *Ibid*, para 16.

[38] *Ibid*, para 136.

[39] *Ibid*, paras 136(1), (2), (3)(a) and 137; as shown in para 16(5), (6) and (7) of the Judgment, the UK's rules are essentially the same as those of Gibraltar.

or to themselves,[40] or if a hostage taker 'is using a firearm or any other weapon or explosive . . . or if he is about to use a firearm',[41] or if a suspect 'is in the course of placing an explosive charge in or near any vehicle, ship, building or installation'.[42]

Finally, taking into consideration the 'failure by the authorities' to take 'appropriate care in the control and organisation of the arrest operation', and the 'automatic recourse to lethal force' in such circumstances, therefore, the Court is not persuaded that the killing of the three terrorists constituted the use of force which was no more than absolutely necessary in defence of persons from unlawful violence',[43] the UK was thus found in breach of Article 2 of the Convention.[44]

The Court, in the cases of *Andronicou and Contantinou v Cyprus*,[45] and *Nachova and others v Bulgaria*,[46] has also adopted the necessity and proportionality standards concerning the use of force and firearms by state agents. In the *Nachova* case in particular, 'the use of potentially lethal firearms', in circumstances where so doing is 'not absolutely necessary', has been described as a violation of Article 2 of the ECHRs.[47]

Moreover, Article 2(e) of the Nairobi Protocol on Firearms, recognising the observance of human rights as one of its objectives, has underlined the need for accountable, legal and efficient 'control and management' of SALW 'held by States parties and civilians'.[48] It has indicated the significance of a responsible and legal use of weapons by states.

The scope of the obligation regarding the use of force and firearms has also extended to all fundamental rights and protections enshrined in the UDHR, ICCPR, the Declaration against Torture, the Genocide Convention, Standard Minimum Rules for the Treatment of Prisoners, the UN Declaration on the Elimination of All Forms of Racial Discrimination, etc.[49]

Three points are worth underlining here. First, the UN Code and the Basic Principles have been taken as sources of rules on the use of force and firearms, as they have 'received widespread acceptance by the international community', including by the UN GA and ECOSCO.[50] Also,

40 *Ibid*, para 136(3)(b).
41 *Ibid*, para 136(4)(a), (b).
42 *Ibid*, para 136(5).
43 *Ibid*, paras 212, 213.
44 *Ibid*, para 214.
45 ECHR, Judgment, 9 October 1997, para 171.
46 ECHR, Chamber Judgment, 26 February 2004, para 93.
47 *Ibid*, paras 105 and 106.
48 *The Nairobi Protocol for the Prevention, Control and Reduction of SALW*, 21 April 2004; more precisely see *The ECOWAS Convention on small arms*, 2006, Arts 10, 11, and 14.
49 *Code of Conduct*, above n 26, Art 5(a); see also, *UN BlueBook*, above n 29, principle 1, ns.
50 *BlueBook*, *ibid*, forward, para 4; see also *International Human Rights Standards for Law Enforcement Officials*, the UN Centre for Human Rights, p 9, at <http://www.unhchr.ch/html/menu6/2/pocketbook.pdf>

the ECHR, in the *Nachova* case,[51] has considered them as 'relevant international law' principles. These instruments do, however, need to be integrated into domestic laws for their implementation.[52] It is generally believed that 'the principles have not been well incorporated into the domestic laws and practices of states'.[53] Secondly, they need to be seen, however, in the context of treaty and customary law obligations on human rights[54] and the principles of necessity and proportionality.[55]

Finally, it may be concluded that the aforesaid instruments, cases and relevant human rights obligations have demonstrated that states do not enjoy a wider freedom of action regarding the use of firearms against a human being. In particular, small arms can only be used when they are absolutely necessary or strictly unavoidable to protect life and/or to prevent other similarly dangerous events. Their use must comply also with the test of proportionality.

The second category of obligations deals with the use of firearms by non-state parties and/or individuals. The general principle, the duty to regulate the use and diffusion of firearms and associated problems are seen next. As a rule, states are under an obligation to extend due diligence to secure and ensure respect for human rights in their respective territories despite the fact that the act is committed, or will be committed, by non-state parties or individuals. Examples of such duties include enacting proper laws, establishing and organising appropriate state apparatus, preventing violent crimes, condemning, prosecuting and punishing perpetrators, etc.[56]

For instance, the ECHR, in the *Akkok v Turkey*[57] case underlined that Turkey did not take reasonable measures to prevent and avert the death of Mr Akkok; the latter was shot dead despite the fact that he had reported to the state authorities the death threat he received from unknown assailants. The Court acknowledged that the European Convention on Human Rights imposes a positive duty on states, to protect a person, whose life is at risk from criminals.

[51] Above n 46, paras 67–68.

[52] See, eg *Basic Principles*, above n 23, Art 8.

[53] Frey, above n 18, para 42.

[54] Above n 30; see also, *BlueBook*, above n 29, para 3.

[55] *Case Concerning Military Activities in and against Nicaragua, ICJ Repts* 1986, para 176; see also Dixon and McCorquodale, *Cases and Materials on International Law*, 3rd edn (London, Blackstones Press, 2000) 222, para 49.

[56] See, eg *ICCPR*, Arts 2 (1) and 6(1), *ACHRs* Art 1, *ECHRs* (n 34) Art 1, *ACHPR* (n 5) Art 1; see also Provost, above n 1, at 60–61; Joseph et al (eds), *The International Covenant* (2000), above n 7, at 23–24; see also *Kindler v Canada*, HRC (470/91), 30 July 1993, see dissenting opinion of Mr Wennergren, Appendix, B, para 8.

[57] ECHR, App No 22947/93 and 22948/93, 10 October 2000, para 97; see also *Velasquez Rodriguez* case, Judgment of 29 July 29 1988, Inter-Am.Ct.H.R. (Ser. C) No 4 (1988), para 180; see also below, n 117, at 22–23, although not a direct issue of human rights, the ICJ in the *Corfu Channel Case* seems to have adopted a similar test, failure to give a notice of warning to Britain was enough to establish the responsibility of the defendant.

Publicists, inter alios, Kabaaliogu[58] and Joseph[59] have recognised the existence of the positive right to life and its corresponding obligation also known as due diligence standard. This requires states to prevent human rights abuses by non-state parties.

In the light of the aforesaid positive duty of states we shall now attempt to address states' obligations, in respect of the problem of excessive availability of small arms and their use by non-government forces in their own territories. It should be recalled that 59 per cent of the world stockpile of SALW is in the hands of civilians and 2 per cent is possessed by non-state groups (see 2.1.5). The trend of such stockpiling is also growing alarmingly.[60] Possession ranges from leisure rifles to that of automatic/military weapons.[61] There is, therefore, a good reason to focus on the regulation of firearms in use by civilians.

Undoubtedly states have the obligation to prevent human rights abuses through controlling the small arms available in their respective jurisdictions. The UN HRC for example criticised the US for failing to discharge positive duties stating:

> It . . . regrets *the easy availability of firearms* to the public and the fact that federal and State legislation is not stringent enough in that connection to secure the protection and enjoyment of the right to life and security of the individual guaranteed under the Covenant.[62]

In addition, the UN Special Rapporteur on small arms underlined that states could be 'accountable for patterns of abuses, such as the state's failure to establish reasonable regulation regarding the private ownership of small arms that is likely to be used in homicides, suicides and accidents'[63]; such responsibility includes a failure by a state to protect individuals from criminals and violence.[64]

The Special Rapporteur on violence against women has, furthermore, noted that 'private persons committing acts of violence against women frequently use firearm to carry out their abuses'; hence '[S]tates are held responsible for acts or omissions of private persons', among other things, where they fail 'to exercise due diligence in the control of private actors'.[65]

The Nairobi Protocol has also hinted at the commitment of the Parties to ensure a responsible use of civilian firearms, bearing in mind the

[58] Kabaaliogu, 'The Obligations to "Respect" and "Ensure" the Right to Life' in Ramcharan (ed), *The Right to Life in International Law* (Dordecht, Martinus Nijhoff, 1985) 179.

[59] Joseph et al (eds), *The International Covenant* (2000), above n 7, at 129–30.

[60] *SAS 2002*, p 79; see also Cukier, Lochhead, Susla and Kooistra, 'Emerging Global Norms in the Regulation of Civilian Possession on Small Arms': draft for review, SAFER-Net, July 2003, pp 20–21.

[61] *GGE 1997*, para 44.

[62] UN Doc CCPR/C.79/Add. 50, (1995) para 17 [emphasis added].

[63] Frey, above n 18, para 46.

[64] *Ibid*.

[65] UN Doc Sup No E/CN.4/1995/42, para 102.

protection of human rights (see p 245). Paragraph 17 of the Preamble of the ECOWAS Convention acknowledges the negative effects of the excessive availability of weapons on human rights and the need to 'prevent combat, and irradiate' such a problem. Accordingly, it has adopted, under Article. 14 of the instrument, stringent bans and controls on civilian possession of SALW—only small arms (it does not include light weapons) are permitted for civilian use, subject to rigorous controls and requirements including a national and sub-regional register of such weapons and users.

Even so, the positive duty under consideration is not without problems. The first problem is that 'in some states and regions there is a culture of weapons whereby the possession of military-style weapons is a status symbol, a source of personal security'.[66] This raises both legal and sociological concerns. The second and most important challenge is the claim of a human right to bear and use arms, for purposes of self and property protection. Some reflections on such a claim may clarify the positive obligations of states further. On the one hand, the school of opponents of gun-control, as Utter wrote, think that 'the right (to bear and use arms by civilians) can be defended as a basic natural, or human, right independent of any positive law'.[67]

Relative to the subject, Scott criticised the UN Conference on small arms, saying; 'it does nothing for, or rather destroys, rights to preserve one's safety from tyrants and despots'.[68] Furthermore, Keith Tidswell, a representative of the Sporting Shooters Association of Australia has warned states in the First BMS of 2003 that 'we should adopt no policy, no mode of action' to disarm a population; 'we need to be aware of the real human rights implications of what we are doing'.[69]

On the other hand, in support of the school of proponents of gun-control, Miller and Cukier thought that 'there is no evidence of a general right to unrestricted civilian access to arms under any international human rights instrument'.[70] Human rights conventions merely talk about the burden of duty on states and state authorities to respect and ensure respect for the rights in question. These include addressing 'the problem associated with misuse of firearms by civilians', against women and children in particular.[71]

[66] *GGE 1997*, para 44.

[67] Utter, 2000, *Encyclopedia of Gun Control and Gun Rights*, (Arizona, Oryx Press, 2000) x, paras 3 and 4, and xi, para 1 [emphasis/clarification added].

[68] Scott, 'The UN Conference on the Illicit Trade of Small Arms and Light Weapons: An Exercise in Futility?' (2003) 31 *GAJINT'L and COPM.L.* 687.

[69] Tidswell, 'Definitions, Reliable Facts and Human Rights Concerns' BMS, 7–11 July 2003, New York, p 2.

[70] Miller and Cukier, 'Regulation of Civilian Possession of Small and Light Weapons' *Biting the Bullet*, Briefing 16, p 6 at < http://www.international-alert.org/pdf/pubsec/BB_Briefing161.pdf> [abbreviation added].

[71] Cukier, Sarkar and Quigley, 'Firearms Regulation: International Jurisprudence' (2000) 6 *Canadian Criminal Law Review* 111.

Also, the US Supreme Court in the *United States v Cruikshank* case of 1876 has stressed that: 'only the states have the authority to protect citizens against such violations of their rights (life and property) by private persons.'[72] In New Zealand and Canada, there is no a general right to bear arms by civilians. In particular, there is no a constitutional right to bear arms in Canada. The Australian laws considers the bearing and keeping of arms to be an administrative entitlement rather than a right. States such as South Africa and the Philippines have rejected the notion of such a right on the basis that the right to life, liberty and security requires a reduction in access to arms.[73]

Similarly, as shown in the Lord Cullen's Inquiry, in the aftermath of the Dublane massacre in 1996, 'the right to bear arms is not a live issue in the United Kingdom' and thus 'a safety-first philosophy should be adopted' rather than 'any supposed inherent-right to hold guns'.[74]

State practice has not, therefore, supported the claim of the right to bear and use arms. On the contrary, it appears that the individual has no human right to bear and use firearms for the purposes of self-defence. The law enforcers of a state are rather authorised and obliged to ensure such protection. Yet the civilian possession and use of arms might be a legal right or entitlement, depending on the domestic laws and regulations of countries. As shown in Article 4(2) of the UN Firearms Protocol, small arms may also be useful for private protection and other legal activities, so long as they are properly controlled, managed and fall in the right hands.[75]

While not in the context of human rights, similar notions of positive obligation are also found in other weaponry regimes. For instance, the Chemical Weapons Convention permits states to transfer and use toxic chemicals and their precursors for lawful purposes. At the same time, it requires states to take necessary measures to ensure that such materials 'are used for purposes not prohibited under the Convention'. It also obliges states to prohibit natural or legal persons from doing so.[76]

The following points may recap the discussion in this section: first, firearms must be used by officials and agents of a state only when they are absolutely necessary; the standard of proportionality must be met in such extreme situations; this signifies the negative human rights law duties of

[72] *United States v Cruikshank,* 92 U.S. 542,553 (1876) [clarification added]; see also Utter, above n 67, at 356; see also *United States v Miller*, 307 U.S. 174 No 696 [15 May1939] 26 F.DOC.1002, Reversed, No 2, para 12.

[73] Cukier et al, above n 71, paras 5 and 6; see also Miller and Cukier, above n 70, at 12.

[74] Lord Cullen, *The Public Inquiry into the Shooting at Dublane Primary School*, 13 March 1996, Ch 7.0, para 7.14, at <http://www.archive.official-documents.co.uk/document/scottish/dunblane/dunblane.htm>; see also Cukier et al, above n 71.

[75] See p 49, fn 5.

[76] Zaleski, 'Precedents from the Export and Transport of War Materials' in Dahinden, Dahlitz and Fischer (eds), *Small Arms and Light Weapons, Legal Aspects of National and International Regulation* (Geneva, United Nations, vol iv, 2002) 35.

states. Secondly, states are obliged to take essential measures to protect basic human rights from abuses by non-government armed groups, criminals or individuals—this includes the prevention of excessive availability of weapons; these constitute the positive duties of states; thirdly, such obligations are enshrined in the international, regional and case law sources of the law of human rights; fourthly, it has to be emphasised that the obligations linked to small arms focus on the right to life, the prohibition of torture, cruel and inhuman treatment, genocide etc. Finally, the impact of actual or potential non-compliance of a state with these and other obligations of human rights law on restricting the trade in SALW will have to be examined next.

8.3 ACTUAL OR POTENTIAL USE OF SALW AGAINST IHRL: A STANDARD FOR RESTRICTING TRANSFERS

This section will explore whether there is a norm which restricts small arms transfer to regimes who have failed, or may fail, to meet their negative and/or positive IHRL obligations. It will be argued that a rule of limitation has evolved in view of human rights. Ultimately—the contents of the rule and the problems therein will need to be identified. Examining the practice at all levels is a crucial gateway to tackle the challenge.

8.3.1 Global Efforts

Although the League of Nations was concerned with transfers of arms as tools of the slave trade and bloodshed,[77] we shall concentrate on post-UN efforts.

The UN efforts could be divided into three: treaties, non-treaty instruments and Chapter VII measures of the UN SC. First, the UN Protocol on Firearms, as it has indicated in paragraph 1 of the Preamble, signifies that states are aware of the harmful consequences of arms transfer to the wellbeing of people and their right to live in peace.[78] The phrase 'human right' is not, albeit, found in the entire instrument. Currently, no global treaty deals with this issue.

Secondly, non-treaty instruments have dealt with human rights issues regarding SALW transfers. As discussed earlier, it is generally appreciated in the UN that the proliferation and unrestricted transfers of small arms have been endangering basic human rights.[79] As a result, the GA has, in various instances, called on Member States to decline from supplying

[77] See, eg 7.2.2; see also Shaw, *International Law*, 4th edn, above n 3, at 200.
[78] Above n 69, Preamble, para 1.
[79] See, eg above n 22; see also 7.2.3.1.

SALW and other assistance to states that are engaged in serious violations of human rights.[80] In the famous Resolution 46/36 L of 1991, the Assembly, being disturbed, by the 'effects of the illicit arms trade, particularly for the internal situation of affected states and the violation of human rights',[81] has called on states, as indicated in operative paragraph 1, 'to exercise due restraint in exports and imports of conventional arms'.[82]

This and other resolutions of the GA led to the adoption of the GIAT. In the unanimously adopted Guidelines of 1996, the Disarmament Commission has stated under paragraph 14 of the general principles that, 'in their efforts to control their international arms transfers', states shall bear in mind the principle of 'respect for human rights'[83] (see further 5.3). Besides, the Secretary-General's Report to the SC of 1999 highlighted that:

> In an era in which the world will no longer stand by in silence when gross and systematic violations of human rights are being committed, the United Nations is dedicated to addressing both the *supply and the demand* aspects of the trade in small arms. From the Balkans to Africa to East Asia, small arms have become the instruments of choice for the killers of our time. *We must do our part to deny them the means* of murder.[84]

The scale of violations, the scope of the trade and the duty of the international community emphasised by the Secretary-General are important indeed.

The UN PoA did recognise under paragraph 1 of the Preamble that the excessive accumulation and uncontrolled spread of SALW all over the world 'pose a serious threat' to the safety and security of individuals. As per section II paragraph 11 of the PoA, Member States have agreed to properly assess export authorisation of SALW, in accordance with 'existing responsibilities of States under relevant international law'.[85] Even so the instrument does not impose substantive limitation upon arms transfer. It's also correctly criticised for not explicitly addressing the question of human rights.[86]

The GA, in Resolution 61/89 of 2006 has albeit explicitly reaffirmed its 'respect for . . . international human rights law and international humanitarian law', as one of the grounds for its decision to study the feasibility of an arms trade treaty (see chapter ten).

[80] See, eg *Report of the Economic and Social Council, the Third Committee of the GA*, Draft Res XVII/1982, p 50; see also GA Res 43/75 I/1988, 'International Arms Transfers'; see also GA Res 48/75 F/1993.

[81] See para 7.

[82] *Ibid*; see also p 113.

[83] For the significance of the *GIAT* see p 114; subsequent UN efforts have adopted or recommended the GIAT; see, eg *DC Guidelines* of 1999 [GCAC], principles, para 8; see also *GGE 1997*, para 80(a); see also *GGE 1999* [Reviewing Panel] para 75; see also *GGE 2001*, para 61.

[84] 24 September 1999, p 2, para 8 [emphasis added]; see also p 220.

[85] See for the details of the instrument, see 3.3.1.

[86] See, eg Scott, above n 68, at 692.

The UN Special Rapporteur on small arms, in her 2002 Report[87] to the Sub-Commission on the Promotion and Protection of Human Rights has also acknowledged the negative impact of 'the availability and misuse' of SALW on human rights. And so, Part V of the Report illustrates 'existing human rights norms'. Paragraph 35 asserts:

> Some international obligations, such as the non-derogable requirement to protect the right to life under Article 6 of the International Covenant on Civil and Political Rights, place absolute limitations on States actions involving weapons.

As shown in sub (ii) of paragraph 35, states are required, among others, to:

> take effective measures to prevent the transfer of small arms into situations where they are likely to be used to commit serious human rights abuses.

This has been included in the recommendations for further action as indicated in paragraph 77 of the Report. The Sub-Commission, in its Resolution 2002/25, had endorsed the conclusions and recommendations of the Report.[88]

Finally, actual or future violations of human rights have been taken into account as grounds for SC arms embargoes in a number of cases. The Council, in its Resolutions 181/1963 and 418/1977, has decided to cease any sales or transfers of arms to South Africa. One of the motives was the massive killings, repression and violence against 'students and others opposing racial discrimination'.[89] IHRL violations-based arms embargoes have been continuously taken in the aftermath of the Cold War. In its call of compliance on states, with its arms embargo of 1992 against Somalia, the Council, in Resolution 4425/2002 emphasised that provision of weapons to the country brings 'climate of fear and impacts adversely on human rights'.[90]

In its Resolution 918 of 1994 on Rwanda, numerous killings of civilians and the 'systematic and flagrant violations of . . . the right to life' have been referred to as a ground for the measure.[91] In 1998, the Council reinforced its arms embargo on Rwanda, thinking that the arms flow to the country 'could lead to further acts of genocide'.[92] The civilian deaths, discrimination against women and other abuses of human rights have led to restrict the transfer of arms to Afghanistan.[93] In respect of the Darfur crises, moreover, Resolution 1556 prohibited the arms trade to the region and to

[87] Above, n 18.

[88] *Progress Report of Frey*, Sub-Commission on the Promotion and Protection of Human Rights, 21 June 2004, p 4, para 2.

[89] Res 181, operative, paras 2 and 3, and Res 418, Preamble, para 1 and operative, para 2; see also pp 127, 134.

[90] Preamble, para 3.

[91] Preamble, para 10.

[92] Res 1161/1998, Preamble, para 5.

[93] Res 1076/1996, Preamble, para 5; Res 1333/2000, Preamble, para 5; Res 1390/2002.

NSAs within Darfur, because of 'its grave concern at the ongoing . . . widespread human rights violations' including the attacks on civilians, forced displacements, rapes and acts of violence which put hundreds of thousands of lives at risk.[94]

Furthermore, the express prohibitions of arms transfer imposed by the SC against Angola, Burundi, Liberia, Sierra Leone, Albania, Yugoslavia and the DRC have, in one way or another, been instigated by human rights concerns.[95] Such an approach has also been reiterated by the Council in its common positions. For example, affirming the Council's 'commitment to the need for respect for human rights and the rule of law', the 1999 presidential statement[96] emphasised the 'vital importance' of preventing and curbing the 'illicit trafficking' and 'excessive accumulation' in SALW.[97]

Three remarks are notable at this point. The first is that the SC has repeatedly relied on actual and future violations of IHRL, which led to mandatory arms embargoes. The second is that, similar to the Secretary-General's approach to the problem, the Council's emphasis is on serious, systematic and massive violations. The last is that violations by state agents and abuses by NSAs are both embraced in the actions.

Briefly, UN practice highlighted the fact that arms shall not be sent to countries where SALW are used or may be used for gross violations and abuses of human rights. The main problem with efforts in this direction appears to be that there have been no clear and detailed criteria for doing so. Relevant arms export regimes and regional and security organisations might be of assistance to clarify the human rights law-based standard of transfer. It has to be mentioned here that the Wassenaar arrangement, as a global export control regime, has set out IHRL guidelines for arms transfer.[98] As these guidelines are a replica of the OSCE and EU criteria on the issue we shall not consider them separately.

8.3.2 Regional Efforts

Relevant OSCE and the EU standards for exports of SALW are seen first. Part II, 4(a)(1) of the 1993 OSCE 'Principles Governing Conventional Arms Transfers' has considered 'the respect for human rights and fundamental freedoms in the recipient country',[99] as a condition for export of SALW. This has been reiterated in section III(A)(2)(a)(i) of the OSCE 2000 Document.[100] Moreover, the same section of the latter under 2(b)(i) and

[94] Preamble, paras 6 and 7; see also p 101.
[95] See, eg 5.1.
[96] 30 November 1999, p 1, para 2.
[97] *Ibid*, p 2, para 5.
[98] Wassenaar, *Best Practice Guidelines*, Arts 1(i) and 2(h) and (i); see also p 119.
[99] See p 125.
[100] *Ibid*.

(viii) obliges each participating state to avoid export licence authorisation of SALW 'where it deems that there is a clear risk' that the weapons may be 'used for the violation or suppression of human rights and fundamental freedoms', or 'for the purpose of repression'.

It is noteworthy that the OSCE joint measures include arms embargoes.[101] In 1992, the Committee of Senior Officials of the Organisation requested participating states and others in the region to 'impose an immediate embargoes on all deliveries of weapons and munitions', to the parties engaged in combat in Nagorno-Karabakh; one of the underlining motive was to enable the population 'enjoy all their rights'.[102]

The UN[103] and commentators[104] often commend the OSCE's initiative, as a model for multilateral measures. We shall examine the details of the phrase 'clear risk' and the scope of the human rights involved, alongside the EU efforts below.

The EUJA on small arms,[105] under Article 4(b) of the 'principles on preventive and reactive aspects' of the instrument, has considered, inter alia, 'respect of human rights' and 'the protection of the rule of law', as the basis and approach to tackling the problem of small arms proliferation at all levels. The EU Code, which is meant to implement the EUJA, has illustrated important criteria for arms transfer. Criterion Two of the Code has considered 'the respect of human rights in the country of final destination'.

As stated in the chapeau of this Criterion, EU states are required to assess 'the recipient county's attitude towards relevant principles established by international human rights instruments'. Consequently, Member States will:

> (a) *not* issue an export license if there is a *clear risk* that the proposed export might be used for internal repression.
> (b) *exercise* special caution and vigilance in issuing licenses, on a case by case basis . . ., to countries where *serious violations of human rights* have been established by the competent bodies of the UN, the Council of Europe or by the EU.

In addition, paragraph 2 of sub-section (b) has given fourfold indicators which need to be considered to determine the use of SALW for internal repression; the first indicator is 'where there is evidence of the use of this

[101] See OSCE, *Best Practice Guide on Export Control of Small Arms and Light Weapons,* 19 September 2003, p 3; for the legal nature see Dahinden, 'Meeting the Challenges of Small Arms Proliferation: example of the OSCE Document' in Dahinden, Dahlitz and Fischer (eds), above n 76, at 11; see also p 125; see also OSCE, *Charter for European Security,* Istanbul, November 1999, para 14.

[102] *Decision Based on the Interim Report on Nagorno-Karabakh,* Committee of Senior Officials, Prague, 27–28 February 1992, paras 2 and 4; see also *UKMIL* (2002) 73 *BYIL* 824.

[103] See 126.

[104] See, eg Dahinden, 'Meeting the Challenges of Small Arms Proliferation: example of the OSCE Document' in Dahinden, Dahlitz and Fischer (eds), above n 76 at 4.

[105] [Emphasis added]; see also p 63; for the legal status of the Joint Action see p 123.

or similar equipment for internal repression by the proposed end-user'; the second is 'where there is reason to believe that the equipment will be diverted from its stated end-use or end-user and used for internal repression'; the third is that the Code requires Member States to pay particular attention, if the equipment 'is intended for internal security purposes'; and the last is that such assessment has to be made on case-by-case bases.

Certain crucial phrases will have to be clarified. According to paragraph 3 of sub (b) of the aforesaid Criterion, internal repression comprises:

> inter alia, torture and other cruel, inhuman and degrading treatment or punishment, summary or arbitrary executions, disappearances, arbitrary detentions and other *major violations* of human rights and fundamental freedoms [emphasis added].

Although the list is indicative, it appears to show the emphasis of EU states on the kinds and the level of violations or abuses.

The difficulty is that the phrase 'clear risk' is not defined or explained. In fact some questioned and criticised the reference to 'clear risk' rather than only 'a risk'.[106] When violations are ongoing, it may be less problematic to evaluate such a risk. For example, as shown in Criterion Two, paragraph 2 of sub (b), if past or existing use of weapons against human rights is evident, in any prospective destination of arms exports, it seems to be that such a situation may constitute the 'clear risk' element. Nevertheless, it is much more difficult to determine future risks and the use of weapons to that effect. The Code has considered the possibility of diversion of end-uses and end-users of supplies for so determining. Sadly, the *Tugar* case of the European Commission on Human Rights, when directly faced with such questions, did not address the details of the problem, as the case was simply declared inadmissible (see 8.3.5). Relevant considerations of the HRC may explain the problem better, although not in relation to SALW.

The HRC has repeatedly underlined that complaints on future violations of human rights 'must be reasonably foreseeable'.[107] In *EW et al v The Netherlands*,[108] the authors complained that the preparation for the use of cruise missiles and the presence of nuclear weapons in the country violates their ICCPR rights, particularly of Article 6. The Committee rejected the claim stating that an 'existing or imminent violation of their right to life' is not apparent. Likewise, in *Borders and Temeharo v France*,[109] the authors complained on nuclear test plans by France, as an infringement of their right to life. The Committee has considered the claim as a

[106] Bauer, Bauer, 'The EU Code of Conduct on Arms Exports-much accomplished much to be done' *SIPRI*, 27 April 2004, p 6.

[107] Joseph, *The International Covenant* (2000), above n 7, at 49–57.

[108] HRC, (429/90), 8 April 1993, paras 6.2 and 6.4.

[109] HRC, (645/95), 22 July 1996, paras 3.6 and 5.4.

'purely theoretical and hypothetical' violation. France had also managed to prove that it has safety measures in place for the nuclear tests.

By contrast, the Committee, in *Kindler v Canada*,[110] and *Cox v Canada*,[111] sympathised with the authors. In the first case for instance, the author objected to his extradition to the US on the grounds of the possibility of the death penalty and degrading and cruel treatment. Canada challenged the admissibility of the author's complaint saying, inter alia, that his claim is 'derived from assumptions about possible future events which may not materialize and which are dependent on the law and actions of the authorities of the United States'. However, the Committee rejected such a contention on the basis that[112]:

> if a state party takes *a decision* relating to a person *within* its jurisdiction, and the necessary and foreseeable consequences is that that person's rights under the covenant will be violated *in another jurisdiction*, the state party itself may be in violation of the Covenant. That follows from the fact that a State party's duty under article 2 of the Covenant would be negated by the handing over of a person to another State (whether a State party to the Covenant or not) where treatment contrary to the Covenant is certain or is the very *purpose* of the handing over . . . The foreseeable of the consequence would mean that there was a present violation by the State party, even though the consequences would *not* occur until later on.

The rule which could be deduced from this and similar cases of extradition is that states are duty-bound to avert, or not to facilitate, possible violations of a person's human rights by a third state, whenever there is an evident risk of such violations.

The clear risk element, either in the EU Code or others, therefore might refer to realistically predictable violations. Hypothesis seems to be unacceptable. The HRC has nonetheless dealt with the particular cases of individuals, and we are concerned with situations which might lead to violations and abuses.

Moreover, the indicators of the ICRC,[113] as shown in IHL earlier, might be of help in determining the existence or otherwise of a 'clear risk' of contraventions of human rights. To mention just a few: (a) stable authority and structure capable of ensuring international human rights; (b) appropriate responses to violations and violators of such norms; (c) preventive measures;[114] and (d) the unregulated excessive availability of small arms,[115] in arms recipient states, may well be useful tests to assess potential risks of arms supply to human rights values.

110 Above, n 56.
111 HRC, (539/93), 31 October 1994.
112 Above, n 56, at paras 4.2 and 6.2.
113 See 7.2.1.
114 For the details, see p 218.
115 For the details, see pp 221–28.

Indeed, Member States have been refusing licences for SALW export on the basis of the Code's principles, as reported to the EU.[116] According to operative provisions 3 and 4 of the Code, however, the details of such denials and 'elements on which the assessment is based' shall only be circulated confidentially to Member States.[117] The UK Minister of Trade revealed in 2002 that detailed information for refusals could only be shared with the Quadripartite Committee on Strategic Export Controls in the country and EU Partners 'on a confidential basis'.[118]

Thanks to the media and domestic politics, however, we have one relevant publicised case available. As examined in IHL in depth,[119] the military firearms deal between some EU countries and Nepal showed both hope and difficulty with regard to the application of the EU Code. This gave grounds for hope because the German Government disapproved of the contract of supply of arms, between Heckler & Koch and Nepal in 2001, due to the concern about 'supplying weapons to a country both at war and charged with violations of human rights'.[120] This gave rise to a problem because Belgium had transferred arms to Nepal in 2003, regardless of the possibility of the use of the guns for abuses of human rights, 'such as extra-judicial killings of innocent civilians suspected of being Maoist sympathisers', and the existence of prior German refusal of such a deal.[121] It has to be recalled that Belgium has adopted the EU Code principles in its domestic legislation.[122]

In summary, it appears that the EU human rights criterion aims at tangible and potential major violations of human rights and not at every episode of infringement. It also emphasises certain aspects of human rights such as the right to life, protection from torture, extra-judicial executions and forced disappearances. The indications given regarding sources of facts, and qualitative considerations in decision-making, are of paramount importance too, as discussed in 8.3.2. In the face of this, phrases such as 'clear risk' could prove to be ambiguous in some cases.[123] The HRC's practice demonstrates albeit that the claim of future violations must be realistic enough. The terms of the EU Code are generally important-eastern European countries, South Africa, Canada and the US have expressed their support for the Code's standards.[124] The principles

[116] For list of states see eg, p 212; see also <http://www.fas.org/asmp/campaigns/code/eucode.html>

[117] See, eg *Fourth Annual Report of the EU Code of Conduct, Council of the European Union*, Brussels, 11 November 2002, pp 10–12, at <http://www.fas.org/asmp/campaigns/code/EU codereport4.pdf>; see also IHL, p 212.

[118] *UKMIL* (2002) 73 *BYIL* 831.

[119] See p 216.

[120] *SAS 2003*, p 113, box 3.3 [emphasis added].

[121] *Ibid.*

[122] See p 124.

[123] Gillard, p 12, para 47, at <http://www.armslaw.org >

[124] <http://www.fas.org/asmp/campaigns/code/eucode.html>

of the Code are also expanding into domestic laws and policies (see p 211*ff*). As reiterated in various sections, however, the organisation has not limited itself to setting out criteria on transfers.

The EU arms embargoes against Myanmar, the Federal Republic of Yugoslavia, Afghanistan, China and Zimbabwe, among others, have been imposed as a response to human rights violations. For example, following the use of military force by the Chinese Government in 1989 to suppress student demonstrations in Beijing, the European Council strongly condemned such a 'brutal repression' and responded by adopting various measures, including 'interruption by the Member States of the community of military cooperation and an embargo on trade in arms with China'.[125] The features of this and its fate will be examined below.

Also, in 2002 the European Council 'has assessed that the Government of Zimbabwe continues to engage in serious violations of human rights'.[126] And thus Article 1(1) of the common position asserts:

> The supply or sale of arms and related material of all types including weapons and ammunition, . . . and spare parts for the aforementioned to Zimbabwe by nationals of Member States or from the territories of Member States shall be prohibited whether originating or not in their territories.

At least five key issues are worth considering with regard to the EU arms embargoes in general. The first concerns the range of human rights often considered in these measures. The phrase 'brutal repression'[127] has been used in the embargo against China. Continued, serious and systematic violations of human rights by authorities, violence and intimidation of political opponents and harassment of the independent press were among the grounds that led to the ban against Zimbabwe.[128] In the case of Myanmar, inter alia, the practice of torture, summary and arbitrary executions, forced labour, political arrests and abuses against women have been mentioned.[129] 'Violent repression of the non-violent expression of political views' was mentioned as a motive for the ban against the Federal Republic of Yugoslavia.[130] So, terms like serious, continuous brutal and violent may suggest that the violations and abuses in mind are extreme cases.

The second issue is whether or not SALW are included in the bans. supply of arms, ammunition and spare parts to Zimbabwe have been

[125] *EU Declaration on China*, Council of Ministers, 26–27 June 1989, Madrid [emphasis added], at <http://projects.sipri.se/expcon/euframe/euchidec.htm>

[126] *Council Common Position (CCP) of 18 February 2002 on Zimbabwe*, para 4 [emphasis added].

[127] *CCP on China* (n 125), para 1.

[128] *CCP on Zimbabwe*, above n 126, paras 1 and 4; see also *CCP of 16 September 1999 Concerning Restrictive Measures against the Republic of Indonesia*, para 1.

[129] *CCP on Burma/Myanmar, 28 October 1996*, No 2; see also *Council Regulation on Burma/Myanmar*, 22 May 2000, para 1.

[130] *CCP of 19 March 1998 against the Federal Republic of Yugoslavia (FRY)*, pp 1–3, Preamble, para 1.

banned.[131] 'Weapons designed to kill and their ammunition' and spare parts were among the restrictions to Burma.[132] Any 'equipment which might be used for internal repression' has been prohibited to the FRY.[133] Although the phrase 'which might be used' appears to be weak, the restriction includes both weapons designed to kill and their components.[134] Whenever the Council adopts a common position on the items to be banned, as shown in the aforesaid cases, it does not usually cause controversy.

However, the embargo against China refers to 'trade in arms with China' in general.[135] As a common position was not taken on items of the embargo, unlike the aforesaid cases, Member States are at liberty to interpret the declaration.[136] In response to a parliamentary question in 1995, the UK Government stated that what is and is not covered in the embargo is left to national interpretation. To the Minister of Trade and Industry, the ban includes, inter alia, 'lethal weapons such as machine guns' and their 'ammunition' and other equipments that could be used for internal repression. All these are sought to be determined on case-by-case bases,[137] as reiterated in 2002.[138] It has to be noted that the ambiguity may cause problems. For instance, as officially reported, 54,415,665 Euros worth 139 licences of defence exports were granted from EU states to the country in 2001. Italy, the UK and Austria were among those which authorised such exports.[139] The details of such defence exports remain secret although it appears that these transfers do not include small arms.

Thus, so far as SALW are concerned, there seems to be no disagreement over their inclusion in the embargoes in question.

The third issue is whether the embargoes embrace the supply of small arms to NSAs and individuals. The embargoes restrict any transfers to the territory of target states in general. The Declaration against Myanmar, for instance, strictly banned any supply, shipment or sale 'to any person or body' in destination.[140] The same thing has been said in the prohibition of arms transfers to Indonesia.[141] In that sense transfer of small arms by a state, to NSAs[142] or individuals who may use arms to abuse human rights, seems to be restricted too.

131 *CCP on Zimbabwe*, above n 126, para 1.
132 *CCP on Burma*, above n 129, No 5(a)(ii).
133 *CCP on FRY*, above n 130, No 1 and 2; see also *CCP on Zimbabwe*, above n 126, Art 2.
134 *CCP on FRY* (96/184/CFSP), 26 February 1996, fn 1.
135 Above, n 125.
136 See, eg *SIPRI*, at < http://projects.sipri.se/expcon/euframe/euchiemb.htm>
137 <http://projects.sipri.se/expcon/euframe/euchiuk.htm>
138 See, eg *UKMIL*, above n 118, at 825.
139 *EU Fourth Annual Report of the EU Code of Conduct*, above n 117 , Annex ii, pp 43 and 25.
140 *Council Reg*, above n 129, Art 1; see also, *CCP on Zimbabwe*, above n 126, No 1; see also, *CCP on FRY*, above n 130, Art 2.
141 *Council Reg* (EC) No 2158/1999, OJ L 265, 13 October 1999, pp 1–7, Art 1(1)(a).
142 See ch 1.

The fourth and the most controversial issue concerns the termination of these sanctions. There are three situations where termination of EU Embargoes may be realised. The first is where embargoes of the SC are lifted; in such cases the EU may terminate its actions in line with the decisions of the UN SC. For example, this happened in lifting the embargo against the FRY in 2001.[143] The second is based on the expiry date of a measure. The embargoes often indicate that they will be enforced for a renewable 12 or 6-month period from the date of their adoption.[144] Afterwards, either they have to be renewed by another CCP or they will not have legal effect. The embargo against Indonesia, for example, expired in January 2000.[145]

The third problematic situation regarding termination arises when the Council takes an indefinite action. This highly depends on a change of circumstances in a target country, concerning improvements in human rights conditions, to be assessed and decided by the EU Council. The question of lifting the arms ban against China is a good case in point. The EU-China Summit of 2004 revealed the political will of the EU 'to continue to work towards lifting the embargo', a positive signal which was welcomed by China.[146] Yet, the latter added that 'political discrimination on this issue was not acceptable and should be immediately removed'. The EU on the other hand 'reaffirmed that work on strengthening the application of the EU Code of Conduct on arms exports was continuing'.[147] The Code's criteria appeared to have been given a priority over the political desire to lift the measure.

Such a split in views and interests not only exist between China and the EU, but amongt EU Member States. Countries such as France, Germany, Italy and Portugal have explicitly supported the move to revise and terminate the 15-year-old embargo. It has been said that the human rights condition in the country 'has improved significantly since 1989'.[148] In contrast, the Nordic states, the Netherlands, Britain and Spain are either against or reluctant to drop the ban, due to continuing concerns of human rights violations in China and the need to uphold the values of the EU Code on arms exports[149]; the US has also been strongly insisting that the EU should sustain the action.[150] EU countries, therefore, are unable to

[143] *CCP on FRY* of 8 October 2001 (2001/719/CFSP), No 3, in accordance with UN SC Res 1367/2001.

[144] See, eg *CCP on Zimbabwe*, above n 126, Art 7; see also *CCP on Burma*, above n 129, Art 7.

[145] *Council Reg*, above n 141, Art 6.

[146] *Joint Statement of the 7th EU-China Summit*, 8 December 2004, para 7.

[147] *Ibid*, sub-para 2.

[148] 'EU Wants Action in China' *Asian Times*, 26 March 2004, at <http://www.atimes.com>; see also, 'EU Split on China arms ban, but "tide turning" towards lift' *Agence France Press*, 8 December 2004, 12.27 pm.

[149] *Ibid*, see both articles; see also *UKMIL*, above n 118, p 827.

[150] *Asian Times*, above n 148.

establish a common position[151] on the matter. What is obvious is that China is still accused of massive violations of civil and political rights.[152] Although the fate of this embargo is uncertain, it indicates the problem of the absence of clear parameters which might help assess changes or improvements in the circumstances of respect for human rights. Once a state is known for committing serious violations of human rights, it seems to be that there is a rebuttable presumption that such violations exist, or may exist, in later times, unless the contrary is proved innocent of these violations.

The last issue touches on the question of the consistency of the EU embargoes. Although the practice has seemed to be generally consistent for many years, it is, however, doubtful whether it applies to all cases of serious violations of human rights in the world. For example, violations of basic human rights in Zimbabwe may not be worse than such abuses in Eritrea. The latter arbitrarily kill, detain and threaten its citizens, including top officials of state and journalists, based on their political beliefs on a large scale; the private press is entirely banned in the country.[153] Yet the country managed to import $355 million worth in weapons in 1997–99 alone. Russia and other eastern European countries and some NATO members have been implicated in such transfers.[154] In the year 2001 too, the UK issued 3[155] and Denmark 2[156] export licences of arms to Eritrea—we don't know whether this includes small arms. Yet Romania refused to grant a licence for SALW export to Eritrea in 2002, which was worth $2 million[157]; the reasons are undisclosed though. The implications of this inconsistency will be examined in subsequent sections.

To sum up, the EU, other than its Joint Action and the Code, has established a model system of arms embargoes in response to breaches, or to prevent violations of human rights (see further p 211); they include small arms in their ambit. Gross and systematic violations of civil and political rights are usually emphasised. In most cases transfers to state agencies and other persons have been proscribed. Instances of such bans have been occurring for many years. Even so, the assessment of situations, the scope of weapons and technologies, questions of termination and compliance continue to cause controversies.

In their common position of 2000, African states expressed their grave concerns on the proliferation of SALW, and they underlined that such a

151 *UKMIL*, above n 118, p 846, para 6.

152 *Human Rights Watch*, World Report 2003, China, at <http://www.hrw.org/wr2k3/asia4.html>

153 *Ibid*, Eritrea, at <http://www.hrw.org/wr2k3/africa4.html>; see also, '*Eritrea, Country Report on Human Rights Practices 2004*, released by the US Bureau of Democracy, Human Rights, and Labor, 28 February 2005.

154 <http://www.fas.org/asmp/profiles/wmeat/WMEAT99-00/10-Table3.pdf>

155 *EU Fourth Annual Report of the EU Code of Conduct*, above n 117, p 36.

156 *Ibid*, p 20.

157 *SAS 2003*, above n 120, p 110.

situation 'jeopardizes the respect for fundamental human rights'.[158] Accordingly, they agreed to ensure 'that the behaviour and conduct of member States and suppliers . . . go beyond narrow national interests'.[159] Most importantly, under part 2(v) of the Declaration, their commitment to promote 'comprehensive solutions to the problem . . . include control and reduction, as well as supply and demand aspects' of the SALW issue. They also called on suppliers to stem their dumping of arms to Africa and co-operate in order to bring about the success of their objectives, as stated in part 2(iii) of the common position.

Further, the Nairobi Protocol on Firearms,[160] in paragraph 4 of the Preamble affirms that, 'promoting the observance of human rights' shall be one of the strategies to arrest the excessive availability of small arms. And so Article 10(a) underlines the obligation of States Parties to establish an effective system of export-import authorisation of SALW.

The ECOWAS Convention took this debate some steps forward. In accordance with Article 6(3)(b), 'transfers shall not be authorised if they are destined to be used: for the violation . . . or infringement of human and peoples' rights and freedoms, or for the purpose of oppression'. It is very ambitious restriction indeed (see chapter ten).

The African approach, in particular ECOWAS's commitment, is a good input to the development of a human rights-based norm on the trade in weapons. Even so most of the efforts lack detailed standards for such restriction and are control-orientated measures. The problem of generality is even worse in the Brasilia Declaration of 2000.[161] Article 4 of the Declaration refers to the unshakable commitment of Latin American and Caribbean States to 'basic norms of international law'. While it is fair to argue that IHRL is included in such basic norms, it is not clear whether the Declaration was intended to embrace human rights norms as part of the initiative taken to fight the proliferation of small arms.

Overall, it has been recognised at the regional level that human rights impacts of small arms transfer should be taken as criteria for arms transactions. The parameter is relatively clear in regional organisations rather than at global level. Apart from the limitation on a case-by-case basis, the practice on embargoes has duly regarded contraventions of these parameters and the prevention of human rights abuse. Threefold problems arise out this practice: first, human rights based criteria are not adequately explicit; for instance, the 'clear risk' parameter is essentially left to domestic interpretation and enforcement; secondly, the chapeau of regional instruments generally talks about 'respect for human rights', and the consequences of non-state abuses and failure to deter such abuses are not

158 *Bamako Declaration*, 2000, pt 1(v).
159 *Ibid*, 2(1).
160 Above, n 48.
161 See p 156.

sufficiently explained in practice; finally, efforts of developing regions do not give a clear picture on the question. Further details may be found in the domestic practices of states and NGOs.

8.3.3 Domestic Efforts

The practice in the US, South Africa, France, Germany and others on the one hand, and China and Russia on the other, with regard to the human rights-based standard, will now be examined.

The US McKinney-Code of Conduct[162] permits transfers of SALW only if a government in destination promotes democracy and the government: (a) 'was chosen by and permits free and fair elections'; (b) 'promotes civilian control of the military and security forces'; (c) 'promotes the rule of law'; and (d) 'promotes the strengthening of political, legislative, and civilian institutions of democracy', as clearly shown in Section 3(a)(1) of the Code.

In particular, Section 3(a)(2) of the Code added that transfers could only be authorised if the recipient state:

> (A) Does not engage in gross violations of internationally recognized human rights, including—(i) extra judicial or arbitrary executions; (ii) disappearances; (iii) torture or severe mistreatment; (iv) prolonged arbitrary imprisonment, (v) systematic official discrimination on the basis of race, ethnicity, religion, gender, national origin, or political affiliation . . .;
> (B) Vigorously investigates, disciplines, and prosecutes those responsible for gross violations of internationally recognised human rights;
> (C) Permits access on a regular basis to political prisoners. . .;
> (D) Promotes the independence of the judiciary and other official bodies that oversee the protection of human rights;
> (E) Does not impede the free functioning of domestic and international human rights organisations.

The requirements seem to be cumulative.

The following features of the US law are of note. The first is that the country's legislation clearly emphasised civil and political rights, including gross violations of the right to life and security. Democratic rights such as fair and free election have also been considered in the criteria. The second is that it has taken into account both the negative and positive human rights obligations of recipient states. The third is that detailed factors have been set out to assess the situation of importing countries. The last one is as shown in Section 3(a) of the Code, the President has to report to Congress the fact that a country meets the requirement of the law prior to the authorisation of an export license. This helps Congress to oversee the application process.

[162] *Code of Conduct on Arms Transfers Act of 1999.*

The US law is also of exceptional importance for two main reasons; first, the Code including the criteria on human rights has been reiterated in the International Arms Sales Code of Conduct Act of 1999, which was intended to lay a base for negotiating a multilateral binding instrument on arms transfer. The President was authorised to do so.[163] Secondly, considerations of these bills particularly of the first one, by the US House of Representatives began in 1993.[164]

Similarly, paragraph 4 of the Preamble of the South African National Conventional Arms Control Act of 2002 underlined that:

> The Republic is a responsible member of the international community and will not trade in conventional arms with states engaged in repression.

Section 15 of the Act has thus set out 'guiding principles and criteria', for export authorisation of arms. The Committee which is entrusted to deal with licences must avoid: '(c) contributing to internal repression, including the systematic violation or suppression of human rights and fundamental freedoms'; and (d) transfers of such weapons 'to governments that systematically violate or suppress such basic rights.[165] While the commitment of the country is strong and clear-enough in respect of violations by states, it appears to be silent on positive obligations and failures.

Several states have, moreover, declared their intent and policy on the subject. For instance, Canada, as a mater of national policy, 'closely controls' transfers of small arms to 'governments that have a persistent record of serious violations of the human rights of their citizens, unless it can be demonstrated that there is no reasonable risk that the goods might be used against the civilian population'.[166] By the same token, the Australian Government adheres to the policy that a transfer is denied 'to governments that seriously violate their citizens' rights unless there is no reasonable risk that the goods might be used against those citizens'.[167] It appears, in principle, that no transfer of small arms should be granted to violators of human rights.

The UK,[168] French[169] and German[170] national policies on the arms trade have incorporated the OSCE and EU criteria for arms exports. The element of 'respect for human rights' has been explicitly adopted. For example, part I(2) of the Policy Principles of Germany establishes that 'the issue of

[163] *US International Arms Sales Code of Conduct* 1999, ss 1262(a), (b), (1), (2); see also *ibid*, s 4.

[164] <http://www.fas.org/asmp/campaigns/code/codehist.html#_ftnref1>

[165] [emphasis added].

[166] <http://first.sipri.org/db/dbf/export_reg_display >

[167] *Ibid.*

[168] *The Consolidated EU and National Arms Export Licensing Criteria* (26 October 2000, Hansard HC Hansard cols 199–203W), Criterion 1(d) and Criterion 2 (a).

[169] *French Policy on Export Controls*, at <http://projects.sipri.se/expcon/db1.htm>

[170] *Policy Principles of the Government of the Federal Republic of Germany for the Export of War Weapons and other Military Equipments*, Berlin, 19 January 2000.

respect for human rights in the countries of destination and end-use is a key factor in deciding whether or not to grant licenses for the export of war weapons and other military equipment'. Also, 'internal repression' and sustained, systematic abuses of human rights' have been emphasised in part I(3) of the Principles. Sub (4) of the same part suggests that factual findings of the EU, European Council, UN, OSCE, other international bodies and international human rights organizations 'will be taken into account', to assess the risks, as will be considered below.

The policy statements, in particular those of Canada and Australia, have asserted two fundamental commitments: to halt arms transfers to repressive regimes and to deny the use of small arms for violations and abuses of human rights. Although phrases such as 'seriously controls' as shown in the Canadian policy and 'must avoid' adopted in the South African legislation, seem not to be strong enough.

In addition, on 15 March 2005 the UK Foreign Secretary called for 'a legally binding international treaty', which will control the sale of small arms, on the basis of 'core principles covering abuse of human rights' (see further 8.3.4).[171] This has lead to the UN sponsored arms trade treaty process and the adoption of GA Resolution 61/89 of 2006 (see further chapter ten).

In contrast, the Russian[172] and Chinese[173] legislation on exports of arms for example have not referred to the term 'human rights' at all. Even so Article 4(1) of the Federal Law of the Russian Federation on exports of arms of 1998 has adopted 'observance of the international commitments of the Russian Federation in the field of control of the exports of military products and dual-purpose goods', as one guiding principle. Russia is also a party to the OSCE and Wassenaar arrangements although China is not.

There are four points that should be noted in the discussion on domestic practice: (1) states generally focus on the terms 'gross', 'serious', 'systematic' and 'persistent' with regard to violations of basic human rights; repression has also been frequently stated. It should be noted, however, that some of the US's law requirements, such as democratic government, fair and free election, are not seen in other states' legislation or policies, as criteria of their own; (2) some states have mentioned both the absence of respect for human rights by governments and their attitude and responses towards abuses; the US law is constructive in that sense; (3) some valuable indicators may be deduced from the practices; particularly important,

[171] 'Straw to Call for Arms Control Treaty' *Guardian* (15 March 2005) 11; see also Hansard HC vol 415 cols 989–90W (19 November 2003).

[172] *Military-Technical Cooperation of the Russian Federation with Foreign States*, Federal Law of the Russian Federation 1998, most of the principles under Art 4(1) talk about countries' national interests.

[173] *People's Republic of China, Regulations on Export Control of Military Items*, Decree No 234, 1997, Art 5 contain only peace and security, self-defence, and non-interference principles as criteria.

inter alia, are the actual conduct of a state, its responses to violations and abuses and the availability and impartiality of institutions of the rule of law; and (4) many major exporter states of small arms have taken strict legal measures; in some, relevant measures have existed for more than a decade. All these practices may have a significant impact on the formation of a rule of law on this question (see 8.3.5). Nonetheless, the degree of commitment, the indicators to be used and the human rights norms involved vary from country-to-country. The position of NGOs and critical opinion will now be considered.

8.3.4 NGOs and Writers

As an initiative of prominent NGOs such as Amnesty International and Oxfam, the FCIAT will be discussed first. Article 3 (b) of the FCIAT[174] put forward:

> A Contracting Party shall not authorise international transfers of arms in circumstances in which it has knowledge or ought reasonably to have knowledge that transfers of arms of the kind under consideration are likely to be: . . . used in the commission of serious violations of human rights.

Certain elements have to be explained in the light of the commentaries and related works on the working Draft. First, serious violations are said to include breaches of the non-derogable provisions of the ICCPR, the Convention against Torture, the European Convention on Human Rights, the American Convention on Human Rights and the African Charter on Human and People's Rights.[175] For instance, violations of 'the right to life and the prohibition on cruel inhuman and degrading treatment—the right most likely to be breached by abuse of small weapons'[176] must be among the appropriate candidates for serious violations.

Secondly, the phrase 'use or likely use' may have two elements; the first one concerns the scope of potential users of small arms for example: (a) by state officials to commit, inter alia, the act of torture, extra-judicial executions and illegal detentions; and/or (b) by individuals to abuse human rights.[177] The second element focuses on the *locus delicti* of the use and likely use of arms in violations/abuses of human rights. As written in paragraph 9 of the commentary on the Draft, the restriction based on human rights 'flows from the obligation not to participate in the international wrongful acts of another State', as enshrined under Article 19 of the ILC Draft Articles on state responsibility.[178] So, as per the comment-

[174] *Draft 2003* (p 83) [emphasis added].
[175] *Ibid*, Commentary, p 5, para 11.
[176] Gillard, above n 123, para 36.
[177] *Ibid*, paras 34 and 35.
[178] Above, n 174.

ary, the phrase under consideration demonstrates the use of arms in a third state's territory.

Finally, the element of 'knowledge' or 'reasonably to have knowledge' is derived from Article 16 of the ILC Draft Articles. Whenever a state transfers SALW, being aware of the use or likely use of them again human rights, it amounts to a breach of international law.[179] For example, Article III of the Genocide Convention prohibits not only the act of genocide, but conspiracy to commit genocide and complicity in genocide. Thus a state which provides weapons for the commission of such a crime could be held responsible for its complicity. This is so if it can be proved that a supplier state did provide arms with 'intent to destroy' a racial or ethnic group, required by Article II of the Convention. Yet 'it is unlikely that states supplying weapons have the intent to' do so, and in effect to be deemed as accomplices in genocide. In spite of the absence of intent to commit such an international crime by a supplier state, however, 'the supply of weapons in circumstances where if it is apparent that they will be used to perpetrate genocide will . . . amount to a violation of international law'.[180]

The FCIAT has generally attracted the attention of NGOs and others. A number of human rights advocates and organisations have been campaigning in support of this initiative. They have been calling on states to ratify the 'Convention' by the year 2006. The October 2003 launch by IANSA, Amnesty International and Oxfam, which was conducted in 67 countries, both among victims and suppliers, implies the significance of, and the widespread support for, the FCIAT. In Cambodia alone, more than 39,000 people have demonstrated in favour of the initiative. The organisers underscored that[181]:

> The Arms Trade Treaty [FCIAT], if widely accepted, will establish a firm and unambiguous international mechanism to prohibit the sale of weapons where there is a clear risk that those weapons will be used for serious abuses.

Brazil's President Lula, as the first head of state to fully support the Draft has declared his 'readiness to play a key role in pushing for an international treaty to control arms'.[182] States have also shown a positive attitude towards such an effort, in an informal discussion carried between NGOs and states on the document.[183] In addition, on 25 February 2004,

[179] Above, n 175.

[180] Gillard, above n 123, para 37; see also above n 11.

[181] *Shattered Lives*, above n 21, p 75; see also 'Charities Campaign Against Arms Trade' *BBC News*, 9 October 2003; see also, Radio Free Europe, *World: Humanitarian Groups Seek Arms Control Treaty for Light Weapons*, Prague, 9 October 2003; see also, 'One Death a Minute: toll of the booming arms trade' *The Independent*, 10 October 2003; see further, at <http://www.iansa.org/control_arms/cambodia.htm>

[182] *Press Release*, Amnesty International, 28 November 2003, at, <http://www.scoop.co.nz/mason/stories/WO0311/S00278.htm>

[183] This has been noted during the NGO training-Lauterpacht Research Centre for International Law, Cambridge, 22 November 2003.

five concerned members of the European Parliament made a written declaration, in support of the FCIAT. They called on Member States to negotiate the Draft at UN level, so as to 'create a clear legal framework for arms transfers based on international human rights standards'.[184] The UK Government gave an indication in 2005 that it backs most of the criteria of the FCIAT, including international human rights.[185] The real reaction of key exporters and importers to this effort remains to be seen, though (see chapter ten).

So this proposed Convention intends to prohibit transfers to countries where there is a risk of the use of small arms in violation of basic IHRL, either by states or others. It will have an important impact on the development of the SALW legal regime and IHRL, as it is intended to codify existing customary law. However, whether the IHRL obligation not to transfer SALW is entirely attached to the wrongful act of another state or is an independent obligation of states is some thing to be clarified later (see 8.3.5, and chapter nine).

Secondly, the ICCAT[186] made IHRL criteria a priority. Article 3 set out the principles: '(A) arms transfers may be conducted only if it can be reasonably demonstrated that the proposed transfer will not be used by the recipient state, . . . to contribute to grave violations of human rights'. Such violations include genocide, extra-judicial executions, enforced disappearances, torture, detentions in violation of human rights standards and other crimes against humanity such as ethnic cleansing; and (B) the same restriction apply to states who failed to take positive measures to ensure respect for human rights. Article 5 reiterated the requirement 'respect for democratic rights'. The details are a duplicate of the US laws on arms exports and thus it is unnecessary to repeat them here (see pp 263–65).

As seen above, the Code is essential because it has adopted a stricter threshold for transfers, addresses both negative obligations and due diligence standards and prohibits arms supplies to states or NSAs (see further p 219).

It is of note, moreover, that some gun-control opponents share the restriction in question. Robert Delfay, who served for many years as a President of the National Shooting Sports Foundation (NSSF) USA and the Sporting Arms and Ammunition Manufacturers Institute (SAAMI) told the workshop of the WFSSA of 2002 that the arms 'industry has no interest in commerce with human rights abusers'.[187] However, he also reflected his

[184] *Written Declaration on Strengthening EU Arms Export Controls and Working towards an International Arms Trade Treaty*, 25 February 2004, p 2.

[185] Jack Straw, above n 171.

[186] *Peace Laureates Code of Conduct*, 1997 [emphasis added].

[187] WFSA International Workshop, 'Export, Import and Brokering of Small Arms and Firearms: Identifying the Problem, Partnership for Solutions' 13–14 June 2002, Naples, p 56.

concerns over restrictions on 'legal civilian commerce',[188] and 'national prohibitions of trade with certain states'.[189] The business interests involved may be in conflict with human rights law limitations on the arms trade.

The views of writers on the problem will now be considered. Inter alios, Frey has written that 'when establishing export control measures, states are bound under human rights . . . law not to participate in internationally wrongful acts, including the serious human rights violations of the recipient state'.[190] She added that arms transfers to states or NSAs in a situation where the 'arms are likely to be used to commit serious violations' of IHRL,[191] should not be authorised. Gillard[192] shares this belief. The appreciation of such a restriction by publicists is of a vital importance, though their understanding on the independent nature of the obligation is contentious, as we shall discuss in a while.

In opposition to this, Kopel thinks 'non-state actors may be oppressed groups attempting to secure their legitimate rights in the face of a tyrannical government and should therefore be entitled to receive arms'.[193] The ICJ and several writers have clearly rejected this assertion (see 6.1.3).

Thus NGOs and writers have established that serious violations and abuses of human rights law provide a strong legal ground for restricting the supply of small arms. They have emphasised the fact that this obligation is an already existing duty of states under international law. There appears however a confusion on the source and level of the obligation, as will be addressed in chapter nine.

In summary, the practice we have seen so far at global, regional and national levels has dominantly supported the human rights-based standard for small arms transfer. Essentially, actual or potential gross violations of the non-derogable ICCPR rights have been emphasised. The practice ranges from binding regional instruments, UN and regional embargoes and domestic legislation to that of diverse political commitments. NGOs and publicists have been trying to codify these rules. Nevertheless, whether we do in fact have a *lex lata* rule needs to be examined.

8.3.5 The IHRL Rule of Transfers

This section will address whether a human rights based rule of transfer has emerged. If the response is in the affirmative, the sources, contents and

188 *Ibid*, p 54.
189 Above, n 187.
190 Frey, 'Small Arms and Light Weapons: The Tools Used to Violate Human Rights' (2004) 3 *Disarmament Forum* 44.
191 *Ibid*, p 40.
192 Above, n 123, para 55.
193 Kopel, 'The UN Small Arms Conference' XXIII *SAIS Review* (Winter/Spring 2003) 319.

problems of the rule must be appropriately identified. The application of IHRL on the whole, and the emergence of a specific customary law of arms control on the issue have to be considered. Emphasis will be given to the latter.

Under conventional IHRL, states are obliged to respect and ensure respect for human rights in their respective jurisdictions. Furthermore, although the territorial application of human rights by a state has usually been emphasised[194] and the collective responsibility of states to ensure respect for IHRL is less clear than IHL obligations,[195] third states have legal rights and some duties, in respect of failure of compliance with certain norms of international human rights by another state.[196] For example, preambular paragraph four of the ICCPR has considered:

> The *obligation* of States under the Charter of the United Nations to *promote universal respect* for, and observance of, human rights and freedoms [emphasis added].[197]

As a minimum, states must refrain from promoting or supporting violations of IHRL. Brownlie, referring to relevant state practice, wrote that, 'a state violates international law if . . . it . . . encourages, or condones', acts such as genocide, murders and disappearances, torture, arbitrary detentions, systematic racial discrimination, or 'consistent pattern of gross violations'[198] of human rights.

More specifically, the Special Rapporteur on human rights referred to the ICCPR and affirmed that the non-derogable fundamental human rights and freedoms such as the right to life imposes an absolute limitation upon a state's freedom to trade in SALW[199] (see p 252).

The quantitative or qualitative restriction on the trade in implements of torture could offer a relevant analogy here. Article 2 of the Torture Convention requires states to prevent the act of torture in their own jurisdiction. The UN Special Rapporteur on torture, in addition, submits that[200]:

194 Joseph, *The International Covenant* (2000), above n 7, p 7, para 1.12.

195 See 7.2.

196 Chazoournes, 'The Collective Responsibility of Sates to Ensure Respect for Humanitarian Principles' in Bloed, Leicht, Nowak and Rosas (eds), *Monitoring Human Rights in Europe: Comparing International Procedures and Mechanisms* (Dordecht, Martinus Nijhoff, 1993) 247–48; for the responses of states see, eg Steiner, 'International Protection of Human Rights' in Evans, *International* Law (Oxford, Oxford University Press, 2003) 758; for *erga omnes* and *jus cogens* norms of international human rights see above, nn 13 and 14.

197 See also, *The Vienna Declaration and Programme of Action on Human Rights 1993* (1994) 1-1 IHRR. 240, para 4; see also White, *The United Nations System: Toward International Justice* (London, Lynne Rienner, 2002) 58–60.

198 Brownlie, *Principles of Public International Law*, 6th edn (Oxford, Oxford University Press, 2003) 537.

199 See also Gillard, above n 123.

200 Broven, *Civil and Political Rights, including the Question of Torture and Detention*, 13 January 2003, p 13, para 35 [clarification added].

> the enactment of legal and other measures to stop the production and trade of equipments specially designed to inflict torture or other cruel, inhuman or degrading treatment is part of this (Art 2) obligation of a general nature to prevent acts of torture.

Indeed, 'international human rights law has up to now mainly addressed the question of circumstances',[201] in which arms or other equipments can be used, other than the tools themselves. In our case, developments of the use of force and firearms have addressed the obligation of states not to use weapons in contravention of human rights obligations (see p 242).

In respect of SALW transfers, moreover, the practices we have gone through condemned arms exports to places and situations where human rights are violated or likely to be violated. Some core protections such as the right to life, security, etc, as embodied in the ICCPR may be interpreted to accommodate such contemporary practice in accordance with Article 31(3)(b) of the VCLT, as discussed in IHL (see p 232).

Besides, such restrictions may arguably be seen in the light of the object and purpose of human rights treaties, as per Article 31(1) of the VCLT; for example, the universal promotion of human rights has been considered as a core object and purpose of the ICCPR. And so denying tools of violations and abuses of basic ICCPR rights, inter alia, of Articles 6 (the right to life), 7 (freedom from torture), and 9 (the right to liberty and security) may well be important considerations in interpreting and applying the Treaty.

So therefore the freedom of action of states regarding arms transfers may be subject to the general norms of international human rights,[202] similar to other cardinal principles of international law (see pp 134–35). This is so not only because of specific human rights treaties, but as a matter of customary law of human rights (see p 239).

201 *Ibid*, pp 2 and 8 (14).

202 McGoldrick, 'Extraterritorial Application of the International Covenant on Civil and Political Rights' in Coomans and Kamminga (eds), *Extraterritorial Application of Human Rights Treaties* (Oxford, Oxford University Press, 2004) 52–53. He meticulously pointed out that 'an extraterritorial application of the ICCPR can arise where the state party takes measures within its own territory but they will have an effect on individuals in the territory of another state. These cases are interesting but not that problematic. Properly understood, the violations of the ICCPR only appear to occur in the territory of another state. In fact, the states parties obligations are clearly grounded in measures it has taken within its own territory'; see also Coomans, 'Some Remarks on the Extraterritorial Application of the International Covenant on Economic, Social and Cultural Rights', in Coomans and Kamminga (eds), *ibid*, p 192; see also Cerone, 'The Application of Regional Human Rights Law beyond Regional Frontiers: the Inter-American Commission on Human Rights and US Activities in Iraq' *ASIL Insight* (October 2005) p 1, at <http://www.asil.org>, he noted that 'it is accepted in principle that states may be bound by human rights treaties with respect to their extraterritorial conduct'; in contrast, see eg Lawson, above n 15, at 104–05. He suggested [though it appears in the context of acts of a state outside its territory] that accountability from extraterritorial operations may arise 'if there is a direct and immediate link between the extraterritorial conduct of a state and the alleged violation of an individual's rights. . . it [direct and immediate link] may be a useful test to delimit the scope of the Contracting states' obligations in the context of extraterritorial situations' [emphasis original].

Due to the territorial limit on states' obligations of IHRL (the European Convention on Human Rights in particular) and the embryonic nature of human rights restrictions on extraterritorial conduct within a state, however, such an assertion does not provide specific restrictions on the arms trade—though it ought to develop in this direction. It is thus desirable to examine the formation or otherwise of a specific customary rule of small arms transfer in the context of human rights.

State practice and *opinion juris*[203] will have to be examined regarding the rule at hand. Has there been sufficient state practice on restricting arms transfers in view of human rights? The first important element here is the consistency and uniformity issue.[204] In the interest of avoiding a duplication of facts, it needs only to be pointed out here that the global, regional and domestic practices we have discussed above, such as the GA resolutions, SC arms embargoes, DC Guidelines, the ECOWAS Convention, OSCE documents, the EU Code, the EU arms embargoes, the Wassenaar guidelines, declaration of African states and a number of domestic legislation and policies have, in general terms, consistently and uniformly[205] promoted IHRL, as criteria for small arms transfer.[206] The core elements of such uniform practice include:

> Denying the use of SALW against human rights norms; (b) real and/or future risks of violations; (c) violations or abuses of fundamental individual human rights including the right to life and security, the protection from torture, cruel and inhuman treatment and forced disappearances of a person; (d) gross, systematic and widespread violations; (e) failure to prevent or stop such grave violations or abuses; (f) restriction of such transfers both to government of states and NSAs; (g) determination on case-by-case basis of such situations and transfers; and (h) although consideration of the elements depend upon particular circumstances, the general practice shows that, the element (d) is a denominator of all, either in actual or potential terms.

This is not to say that the practice is absolutely consistent and uniform as can be indicated as follows. First, the failure of the international community to apply the criteria strictly to all destinations with serious violations and abuses of human rights[207] appears to be evident. Secondly, there is a difference of emphasis on the kinds of human rights that have to be taken into account; some for example focus on democratic government and elections as a criterion whereas the majority of states do not (see 8.3.3). Finally, there are obvious practices that are contrary to the human rights-based prohibition; for example, G-8 Countries are blamed[208] for ignoring

[203] See, eg p 74.
[204] For general consideration of this element, see p 74.
[205] See 5.7; see also p 227 ('IHL').
[206] See pp 250–53; see also, Hansard HC Deb vol 415 col 855W (8 May 2003).
[207] See, eg p 261.
[208] *News Release*, 'A Catalogue of Failures: G 8 Arms Exports and Human Rights Violations' *Amnesty International*, 19 May 2003.

the effects of their arms exports on human rights; in particular, the governments of the US, Russia, France, Britain and Germany often supply 'unparalleled levels of arms' to armed forces and law enforcement agencies, who are engaged in persistent and gross violations of human rights norms; it shall be emphasised that the 'US military aid is currently furnished to more than 30 countries identified by the US itself as having a "poor" human rights record, or worse'; the controversy over arms transfers to Nepal[209] and to Eritrea could also be seen as examples of this. As reiterated in various norms of small arms transfer,[210] however, absolute uniformity of the practice or application of the rule has not been required to establish such a customary rule.

The second element is about the duration[211] of the practice. Among others, GA Resolutions, the DC Guidelines and the OSCE principles and UN arms embargoes since the early 1990s have integrated IHRL as a condition for small arms transfer. These have been reinforced by various regional and domestic measures during the last 5–8 years. The Italian law was adopted in 1990. The practice has therefore existed for a reasonably long duration[212] (see chapter seven).

The last one is the generality[213] of the human rights-based practice. A majority of states have backed human rights criteria for transfers. From the suppliers side, for instance, 16 EU, 50 OSCE, and 33 Wassenaar Member States have been actively involved. Moreover, African states could be mentioned as supporters of these restrictions, as shown for example in the Nairobi Protocol,[214] and the ECOWAS Convention. Besides this, considerable domestic laws and policies have also adopted this rule of transfer.[215] Yet some important states such as China have neither explicitly supported nor objected to the IHRL based criteria for the arms trade. Despite that, the generality aspect of the practice seems to be duly satisfied (see further pp 229–32).

In a word, there seems to be adequate state practice on human rights based restriction of arms transfers. It has to be underlined too that such practice is also the practice of international organisations such as the UN (SC, GA, Human Rights Commission, Disarmament Commission, etc), AU, ECOWAS, EU and OSCE. It is well recognised to date that such organisations play a significant role in the formation of customary law (see further p 138).[216] However, state practice alone is not enough to claim a rule of law.

209 See, eg p 257.
210 See pp 74, 137, 228.
211 See in general, p 76.
212 See pp 137 and 229.
213 See in general, p 75.
214 See 8.3.2.
215 See 8.3.3.
216 See also *Namibia Advisory Opinion, ICJ Repts* 1971, para 22.

Hence the *opinio juris*[217] component of the 'rule' needs to be discussed. The GIAT has for example adopted the term 'shall', relative to restricting arms transfers, in consideration of IHRL. It had been adopted unanimously and can also be considered as an instrument of declaration of relevant norms of international law (see 8.3.1). Although not a legally binding instrument, the OSCE criteria obliges participating states 'to avoid' transfers upon IHRL considerations. The legally binding EUJA considered respect for human rights as a principle for arms transfer. Small arms transactions are totally banned in the ECOWAS Convention. The use of weapons against human rights norms has expressly been codified as a legal standard. The arms embargoes of the EU which also considered international human rights standards are legally binding measures on EU states (see 8.3.2). Most of the political instruments adopted at the regional level have also been envisaged to be adopted in the national legislation and policies of member states (see pp 138*ff*).

Further, the US and South African legislation expressly incorporated the rule at hand (see 8.3.3) mentioning that the US Congress intention is wider in scope. As shown in section 1262(a) of the International Arms Sales Code of Conduct Act of 1999, it has decided and authorised the President to negotiate a multilateral legal instrument, with the objective of prohibiting 'arms transfers to countries that do not observe certain fundamental values of human liberty'. The UK has disclosed its intention to call for a legally binding treaty on arms sales 'to be signed by all the world's big arms exporters' (see p 265). These may affirm not only states' desire to be legally bound by the criteria at issue, but to codify the existing customary international norm. GA Resolution 61/89 (towards an arms trade treaty) furnishes more evidence on the certainty of such an interpretation of the practice. The psychological aspect of the IHRL-based rule relating to the transfer of light weapons appears to be thus reasonably established.

Yet two conflicting views might arise on the formation of human rights based substantive restriction upon the trade in SALW. On the one had, it appears to be that state practice and *opinio juris* requirements have realistically been formed. Publicists and prominent NGOs also support the obligation of states to refrain from arms supply which could be used against IHRL (see 8.3.4).[218]

On the other hand, it may also be argued that as the European Commission on Human Rights in the *Tugar* case[219] has indicated, the obligation to respect and ensure respect for IHRL is a matter left to weapons recipient and user states. Three relevant conclusions of the Commission are of note here. First, it stated that: 'the "adverse conse-

[217] See in general, p 76.

[218] See also pp 229–33 ('IHL').

[219] *Tugar v Italy*, European Commission of Human Rights, First Chamber, Admissibility of Application, 18 October 1995; see also p 218 ('IHL').

quences" of the failure of Italy to regulate arms transfers to Iraq are "too remote" to attract the Italian responsibility',[220] under Article 2 of the European Convention on Human Rights; secondly, it observed that regulating 'transfers of arms . . . by a High Contracting Party' is not 'guaranteed by the Convention'[221]; and finally, it recalled that 'neither the Convention governs the actions of States not Parties to it, nor does it purport to be a means of requiring the Contracting States to impose Convention standards on other States'[222] (see further 7.2.3.4).

Nevertheless, the European Convention on Human Rights, as shown in paragraph 1 of its Preamble, is founded on the Universal Declaration of Human Rights of 1948. Paragraph 2 of the Convention, further, considered that the UDHR 'aims at securing the universal and effective recognition and observance of the rights therein declared'. In the light of this, the Commission could have examined the nature of the EU arms embargo against China, which was in response to the 1989 repression by the latter, as well as the 1991 OSCE criteria for arms transfers which also comprehends human rights. Although the human rights-based rule may not have emerged clearly at the time, the Commission seemed to have failed to look at these aspects of the case. The *erga omnes* character of IHRL in general, and some crucial global protections and obligations of human rights nature in particular, have not been examined either. It therefore missed the opportunity to positively contribute to the controversy over arms transfers.

Moreover, the Commission's analysis does not seem to reflect contemporary international law on arms transfer, due to the following reasons: the first is that the rule at hand has been in a progressive development. Importantly, the transfer in point occurred in the early 1980s, and the case was brought to the attention of the Commission in the early 1990s. Major developments have been attained afterwards. For instance, Italian Law No 185/90 prohibits 'the export of weapons contrary to Italy's international commitments'; this law also 'forbids the export of weapons to countries declared guilty of violations of international conventions on human rights'.[223] The company and others who were involved in such a deal had also been convicted of illicit trafficking in arms.

The second is that, as clearly stipulated under Article 41(2) of the ILC Draft Articles on State Responsibility, 'States are under a duty of abstention', which includes 'not to render aid or assistance',[224] in situations where serious, gross or systematic violations of IHRL, such as genocide,

[220] *Ibid*, p 4 [emphasis added].
[221] *Ibid* [emphasis added].
[222] *Ibid* [emphasis added].
[223] Above n 219, p 2, b (2) [emphasis added].
[224] Crawford, *The International Law Commission's Articles on State Responsibility: Introduction, Text and Commentaries* (Cambridge, Cambridge University Press, 2002) 249, para 4 [emphasis added]; see also ch 9.

torture and racial discrimination occur in weapon recipient state(s). This is due to the peremptory nature of such norms (see 8.1). For these reasons, the European Commission's line of thinking does not appear to be sound. As a result, the use-based rule of IHRL has evolved as custom.

Other comparable restrictions on international transfers of goods strengthen this position. With respect to torture and implements, the GA, in its Resolution 56/143 of 2002 called on all Governments[225]:

> To take appropriate effective legislative, administrative, judicial or other measurers to prevent and prohibit the . . . trade, export and use of equipments that is specifically designed to inflict torture or other cruel, inhuman or degrading treatment.

Here, quantitative and qualitative prohibition has been stipulated. Similar to SALW, however, as shown in the EU efforts, devices such as thumb cuffs, shackle boards, restraint chairs and pepper gas weapons could be used for both legitimate law enforcement deeds and to inflict torture or other cruel or inhuman treatment.[226] Article 9(a) of the European Commission's proposal for a Council's regulation on the trade in such equipment, has proscribed any transfer of such dual-use tools if there are indications that the end-user country commits, or does not deter acts of torture or violations of a similar nature. Article 8 of the Proposal also placed similar restrictions on exports of the equipment in question for purposes of civilian use.

In particular, Article 11(a) provided that transfers of such equipments to law enforcement of a third state shall be denied and prevented, 'if there are indications' that torture or other cruel treatments 'have occurred' during interrogation, or the destination country has not ensured that 'statements obtained through torture . . . shall not be invoked as evidence'. As per sub (b) of Article 11, when authorities are not satisfied that people responsible for such crimes are not held responsible the effect would be refusal of export of such materials. This regulation has been intended to be legally binding, as stated in Article 18 of the Regulation.[227]

Additionally, several states such as the UK, Argentina, Lebanon, Tunisia, the US, Switzerland and Germany, have taken positive action to prevent transfers of equipments of torture. Some countries have also enacted legislation to restrict exports of these devices, 'taking into account human rights' records.[228] The UK has appealed to others to impose

[225] GA Res 56/143/2002, para 11 [emphasis added]; see also the position of the *Special Rapportuer*, above n 200; see also, below n 226, Annex I and Arts 4 and 5.

[226] *Proposal for a Council Regulation Concerning Trade in Certain Equipment and Products which Could be used for Capital Punishment, Torture or other Cruel, Inhuman or Degrading Treatment or Punishment*, Commission of the EC, Brussels, 30 December 2002, (COM(2002)770), Annex II.

[227] See also Steve Wright, 'Civilising the Torture Trade' *Guardian* (13 March 2003).

[228] Above n 200, pp 9–12.

uniform restrictions 'to prevent would-be torturers from procuring such equipment elsewhere'.[229] The US has revealed that export of such tools is denied, under the Lantons-Hyde Amendment to the Export Administration Act (Sec 311, HR-2581), if a foreign government is engaged 'in a consistent pattern of human rights violations'.[230]

The Special Rapporteur on torture has praised all these efforts, in particular the draft Regulation of the EU, which was fully backed by the European Parliament. This was found to be necessary to prevent violations of fundamental human rights.[231] NGOs, particularly Amnesty International, has been significantly strong and active in influencing intergovernmental organizations and states, to take appropriate measures on the problem.[232]

While indications and occurrences of torture could suffice for a refusal of export of implements of torture, the number and magnitude of occurrences is much more emphasised in the trade in small arms issue. In both cases, however, real and possible contraventions of IHRL have been considered as a ground for prohibition.

The second area of analogy is environmental law (see also 6.3). The 1989 Basel Convention on the Control of Trans-boundary Movements of Hazardous Wastes and their Disposal,[233] for example, acknowledged under paragraph 19 to the Preamble: 'the growing international concern about the need for stringent control of transboundary movement of hazardous wastes and other wastes, and of the need as far as possible to reduce such movement to a minimum'. In addition, paragraph 24 of the Preamble underlined the principle that such movement of wastes 'should be permitted only when the transport and the ultimate disposal of such wastes is environmentally sound'.

As indicated under amended Article 4A(1), the 'Convention requires developed countries to prohibit all exports of hazardous wastes to developing countries'.[234] An interesting aspect of this Convention is its adoption of the precautionary principle to this regime. Whenever there is a scientific uncertainty on the consequences of the transfer of hazardous or radioactive wastes, the law requires a full assessment of risk to the environment before any movement or transit of such substances takes

229 *Ibid*, para 21.

230 *Ibid*, para 28.

231 *Ibid*, paras 27 and 34.

232 *Ibid*; see also Amnesty International, *Stopping the Torture Trade*, AI index: ACT/40/002/2001, 26 February 2001.

233 *Basel Convention on the Control of Transboundary Movements of Hazardous Wastes and their Disposal*, 22 March 1989, entered into force 1992.

234 Cook, 'Precedents from the Export and Transport of Endangered Species: CITES and other Trade-related Multilateral Environmental Arrangements: Models for Control of Trade in Small Arms and Light Weapons?' in Dahinden et al (eds), *Small Arms and Light Weapons, Legal Aspects of National and International Regulation* (Geneva, United Nations, vol iv, 2002) 60.

place.[235] Similarly, it is widely adopted in multilateral environmental agreements such as in the preservation of endangered species, that such a precautionary measure has to be taken, whenever there are 'threats of serious or irreversible damages' or uncertainties of risk to the environment, 'by a particular product or type of trade'. Most significantly such a preventive approach continues 'to evolve in response to changing patterns of trade analysis of risk'.[236] It is essential to note here that Article 4(2)(g) of the Basel Convention imposes 'a duty not to import if the waste will not be managed in an environmentally sound manner'.

Hence, environmental law regulates transfers of harmful goods to the environment of a third country. In any case of doubtful circumstances, there should not be a transfer of this type, unless and only if science assures the absence of a risk of so acting. Even so, the risk assessment in the SALW transfers 'could be focused on the social and strategic effects rather than scientific appraisal',[237] which may include human rights.

Finally, it has already been established that states are under the obligation not to encourage violations of humanitarian law (see 7.2.5).

In view of this analogy and the analysis of customary law creation, thus, the content, scope, rationale and problems of the use-based rule of arms control relating to human rights could be summarised in the following way:

(1) As a rule, a transfer of small arms is prohibited when: (a) gross, serious or systematic violations and abuses of human rights exist in a destination country; and/or (b) there is a foreseeable risk of such kind.
(2) The tests and scope of the rule include: (a) actual atrocities by a state, NSAs, or individuals; (b) the use of SALW against human rights; (c) excessive unregulated availability of small arms; (d) the possibility of diversion of end-uses or end-users of small arms transit; (e) lack of responsible reactions to deter violations and abuses; and (f) failure to promote essential institutions of the rule of law.
(3) The rationale of the rule has taken into account the atrocious effects of the use, abuse and availability of weapons on fundamental human rights norms and aims at, inter alia: (a) promoting universal human rights, in accordance with states' existing obligations; (b) preventing violations and abuses through denying the main tools of such deeds; and (c) not aggravating and contributing to existing attacks upon the values in issue.

[235] Cook, at 61.

[236] *Ibid*; see also Kervella, 'Precedents from the Export and Transport of Dangerous Goods', in Dahinden et al (eds), *ibid*, at 47.

[237] Above, n 235; see also Shaw, *International Law*, 5th edn (Cambridge, Cambridge University Press, 2003) 768–77. He emphasised the 'special responsibility of developed states in the process of environmental protection'.

(4) The following problems seem to be apparent. Among others: (a) violations and discriminatory application of the rule by states is not infrequent; (b) fragmented application and decision making has been a reality; (c) the tests/criteria have not been adequately developed—this may lead to variation in emphasis; (d) as shown in the *Tugar* case, furnishing individual remedy on the basis of violations of the rule would be a serious challenge; and (e) the rule and its details are not yet codified at the global level.

While some of the shortcomings have to be left to the progressive development of international law, violations must be considered very seriously (see chapter nine).

8.4 CONCLUSIONS

Fundamental human rights constitute *erga omnes* obligations of states. Certain civil and political rights also qualify as *jus cogens* norms. As part of a state's duty to respect human rights, the use of small arms and related measures against human beings may only be permitted under extreme cases. States have also a positive obligation to deter abuses of such lethal weapons by non-state parties and/or individuals. Despite that, small arms are the principal implements of violations and abuses of human rights. It has also been established to date that an excessive availability of such arms put human rights norms at risk. Consequently, and in the first place, the arms trade ought to be in compliance with general international law of human rights—the law seems to be evolving in this direction; and secondly, it appears to be that a specific rule of custom, which could be termed as the use—based rule of international human rights impose restrictions upon trans-boundary transfers of small arms by states. Every state owes the international community as a whole, the obligation to abstain from contributing to persistent, serious, grave or systematic breaches of human rights. While this rule focuses on supplier states, it should also prohibit any state to be involved in such illegal transaction. The UN arms trade treaty process is believed to affirm the certainty of this finding, and possibly the application of IHRL to the trade in SALW. Notwithstanding the rapid development of this rule, breaches of it and the challenges of codifying it remain a major problem.

PART III

CONCLUSIONS

9

State Responsibility and Arms Transfers: Some Reflections

INTERNATIONAL LAW HAS provided not only the peace and security, non-intervention, IHL and IHRL driven obligations of non-transfer of SALW,[1] but a framework through which states could be held responsible in cases of breaching them.[2] Two matters of nature and scope of this responsibility regime are worthy of note here. First, only states are subject to the responsibility in question, although such violations may also lead to individual criminal liability[3]—the Geneva Conventions for example require states to impose penal sanctions, in order to suppress 'all acts contrary to the provisions'.[4] This aspect is not within the scope of the book. Secondly, the framework at issue deals with 'secondary rules of state responsibility: that it to say, the general conditions under international law for the state to be considered responsible'. The contents of obligations are to be defined under primary rules of international law.[5] In our case these are to be found, inter alia, in the aforementioned rules of arms transfer.

The general notion of the internationally wrongful act of a state, its application to breaches of rules of SALW transfer and the legal consequences that might arise out of it, will need to be assessed.

In principle, as enshrined in Article 1 of the ILC Draft Articles on State Responsibility, 'every internationally wrongful act of a State entails the international responsibility of that State'. This principle has duly been affirmed by the PCIJ in the *Phosphates in Morocco* case,[6] and by the ICJ in

[1] See 5.7, 6.3, 7.2.1, 8.3.5.

[2] *ILC Draft Articles*, 2001, Art 1.

[3] International Military Tribunal, *Trial of the Major War Crimes*, Nuremberg, 1947, I, 255–79; see also ICRC, '*Arms Availability*", below n 52, at 25.

[4] Provost, *International Human Rights and Humanitarian Law* (Cambridge, Cambridge University Press, 2002) 103–09; see, eg *GC. I*, Art 49; see also, Pictet, *The Geneva Conventions of 12 August 1949, Commentary* (Geneva Convention I, ICRC, 1952) 362.

[5] Crawford, *The International Law Commission's Articles on State Responsibility: Introduction, Text and Commentaries* (Cambridge, Cambridge University Press, 2002) 74–75; see also Spinedi, 'International Crimes of State: The Legislative History' in Weiler, Cassese and Spinedi (eds), *International Crimes of State* (Berlin, Walter de Gruyter, 1988) 13–14.

[6] *Phosphates in Morocco*, Preliminary Objection, 1938, *PCIJ*, Series A/BB, No 74, p 10, at p 28.

the *Corfu Channel*, *Nicaragua* and *Legal Consequences* cases,[7] among others. An internationally wrongful act of a state considers, inter alia, the following five circumstances. First, two basic elements need to be fulfilled. Pursuant to Article 2 of the Draft Articles: (a) a conduct that is 'attributable to a state', either commission or omission is required; and (b) the conduct shall constitute 'a breach of international obligation. The law of state responsibility requires only an act or omission, and not an intention, negligence or fault of a state, for the purposes of establishing state responsibility, save certain exceptions such as the case of genocide; also, actual damage is not necessary to establish such responsibility.[8]

Secondly, consistent with Article 3 of the Draft Articles, 'the characterisation of an act of a State as internationally wrongful is governed by international law'. This means that: (a) 'it is independent of its characterization as lawful under the internal law of the State concerned'; and (b) invocation of, or compliance with, internal law could not be an excuse.[9] The PCIJ, in the *Treatment of Polish Nationals* case underlined that, in principle, a state can rely 'as against another state . . ., only on international law and international law obligations'.[10] The ICJ in the *Reparation for Injuries* case has also affirmed that when a state is held responsible 'based on the breach of an international obligation . . . the Member cannot contend that this obligation is governed by municipal law'.[11] An internationally wrongful act could only be established under international law obligations.

Thirdly, Article 12 of the Draft specifies 'what is meant by a breach of an international obligation'. A breach exists when 'a state is *not in conformity with* what is required of it by that obligation, regardless of its *origin* or *character*' [emphasis added]. Three elements deserve clarification: (1) the phrase 'not in conformity with' applies, as has been demonstrated by the ICJ in the *Nicaragua* case, to 'incompatibility with the obligations', and to acts 'contrary to' or 'inconsistent with'[12] a rule in question; the Court in the *Gabcikovo-Nagymaros Project* case also used the expression 'failure to comply with'.[13] As stated in Article 13 of the Draft Articles, 'for responsi-

[7] *Corfu Channel* case, *ICJ Repts* 1949, p 23; *Nicaragua* case, *ICJ Repts* 1986, paras 115 and 186, p 142, para 283 and p 149, para 292, and for *Legal Consequences*, below n 29, para 147; see also Crawford, above n 5, p 77, para 3.

[8] See also Crawford, *ibid*, at 82–85; in particular, see p 84, paras 9 and 10; see also, Brownlie, *System of the Law of Nations-State Responsibility Part I* (Oxford, Oxford University Press, 1983) 189-92.

[9] See also Crawford, above n 5, at 86.

[10] *The Treatment of Polish Nationals and Other Persons of Polish Origin or Speech in the Danzig Territory*, 1932, *PCIJ*, Series A/B, No 44, p 4.

[11] *Reparations for Injuries Suffered in the Service of the United Nations* case, *ICJ Repts* 1949, p 174, at 180; see also *Fisheries* case, p 132.

[12] *Nicaragua* case, *ICJ Repts* 1986, paras 115 and 186.

[13] *Gabcikovo-Nagymaros Project (Hungary/Slovakia)* case, *ICJ Repts* 1997, para 57; see also Crawford, above n 5, at 125.

bility to exist, the breach must occur at a time when the state is bound by the obligation';[14] (2) the term origin is synonymous to sources. An international obligation 'may be established by a customary rule of international law, by a treaty or by a general principle applicable within the international legal order'[15]; and (3) although state responsibility embrace breaches of bilateral obligations or of obligations *erga omnes*, 'obligations imposed on state by peremptory norms . . . may entail a stricter regime of responsibility than that applied to other internationally wrongful acts'.[16] The notion, regardless of the character of obligations, could not mean that every breach is equally treated under the law of state responsibility.

Fourthly, state responsibility could be primary / independent or derivative. The former relies on the principle that 'state responsibility is specific to the state concerned'. Yet an 'internationally wrongful act often results from the collaboration of several states rather than one state acting alone'. Such situations 'may involve independent conduct by several states, each playing its own role' in the breach.[17] The *Corfu Channel* case[18] is a typical example of this kind. Albania's independent responsibility has been established due to its failure to warn the UK of the mines laid by a third state.[19] On the other hand, Article 16 of the ILC Draft addresses aiding or assisting another state, in the commission of an internationally wrongful act by the latter. Such responsibility is to be derived from the conduct of a third state, as an exception to the principle of independent state responsibility.[20]

Finally, circumstances such as consent, self-defence, counter measures, *force-majeure*, distress and necessity may preclude the wrongfulness of a conduct of a state, as set out in the ILC Draft Articles 20–25 respectively. Nevertheless, they 'do not annul or terminate the obligation . . . rather they provide justification or excuse for non-performance'.[21] The ICJ in the *Gabcikovo-Nagymaros* case made it clear that 'even if a state of necessity is found to exist, it is not a ground for the termination of a treaty. It may only be invoked to exonerate a state from its responsibility'.[22] In addition, 'they do not work if doing so conflicts with peremptory norm'. Thus, as the

[14] Crawford, *ibid*, at 131; see also Karl, 'The Time Factor in the Law of State Responsibility', in Spinedi and Simma (eds), *United Nations Codification of State Responsibility* (New York, Oceana, 1987) 95.

[15] Crawford, *ibid*, at 126, paras 3 and 4; see also *Barcelona Traction, Light and Power Company, Limited* (Second Phase) *ICJ Repts* 1970, para 86.

[16] Crawford, *ibid*, p 127, paras 6–7; see also Spinedi, above n 5, at 21–28 and 55–62.

[17] Crawford, *ibid*, p 145, paras 1 and 2; see also Brownlie, above n 8; see also Quigley, 'Complicity in International Law: a New Direction in the Law of State Responsibility' (1986) *BYIL* 77, 90-91.

[18] *Corfu Channel* case, above n 7, at 22.

[19] Crawford, above n 5, at 146.

[20] *Ibid*, pp 148–49, paras 1 and 2.

[21] *Ibid*, p 160, para 2.

[22] Above n 13, p 63, para 101.

Special Rapporteur on State Responsibility has mentioned, these circumstances must only serve as 'a shield not as a sword'.[23]

Article 21 of the Draft Articles states that: 'the wrongfulness of an act of a state is precluded if the act constitutes a lawful measure of self-defence taken in conformity with the Charter of the United Nations.' Undoubtedly, it shall fully comply with Article 2(4) of the Charter.[24] This exception could not preclude responsibility 'in all cases or with respect to all obligations'.[25] It shall not breach, for instance: (a) IHL obligations applicable to both international and internal armed conflicts[26]; (b) non-derogable international human rights obligations[27]; and (c) 'respect for the environment' as one element of the 'principles of necessity and proportionality'.[28] Above all, the ICJ in the *Legal Consequences Advisory Opinion* underlined that 'Israel cannot rely on a right of self-defence or on a state of necessity in order to preclude the wrongfulness of the construction of the wall resulting from the considerations . . .', inter alia, 'breaches by Israel of various of its obligations under the applicable international humanitarian law and human rights instruments'.[29]

Circumstances such as self-defence, the security interest of a state, etc cannot be acceptable grounds, if they are in conflict with IHL obligations and other intransgressible norms of international law. Although the circumstances precluding a state's responsibility have to be determined on case-by-case bases, the general rule here appears to be that they could not justify violations of peremptory rules of international law.

The question is how do these general conditions of an internationally wrongful act, apply to breaches of rules on SALW transfers? Some degree of enquiry on the responsibility of states in the case of failure to respect and ensure respect for IHL standards on SALW import-export may show the nature of the application of the law of state responsibility to breaches of the norms on the arms trade.

Primarily, it is necessary to establish a conduct that might be attributable to a state and the breaches of the obligations therein. As has already been established in chapter seven, failure to deny or prevent transfers of SALW: first, to violator states of IHL, secondly, to destinations where risks of violations are apparent, and/or thirdly, where the destination is flooded by unrestricted weapons, constitutes a breach of customary and/

[23] Crawford, above n 5, p 160, para 1.

[24] *Ibid*, para 2; for Arts 2(4) and 51 see also, 4.2.1.

[25] *Ibid*, at 166, para 3.

[26] *Nuclear Weapons*, ICJ, p 257, para 79; for the position of the ICJ on the limits of the right to self-defence see also p 261; see also, Crawford, above n 5, para 3.

[27] Crawford, *ibid*.

[28] *Nuclear Weapons*, above n 26, p 242, para 30; see also *Multilateral Convention on the Prohibition of Military or any other Hostile Use of Environmental Modification Techniques*, 10 December 1976, 1108 *UNTS*, p 151, Art 1; see also Crawford, *ibid*, p 167, para 4.

[29] See paras 142 and 137; see also *Nicaragua*, above n 12, paras 252, 255 and 256.

or treaty obligations under present-day international law. These could also be described as the use and availability based rules of IHL on transfers.[30] These obligations fully rely on international law.[31]

The problem of invoking such responsibility lies on how to determine a state's breaches. The indicators / tests of the ICRC and the GGE Panel of 1997 might be of help in this regard. Transferring weapons while: (a) there is no respect for IHL; or (b) there is no stability and security in a country of destination; or (c) there is a problem of unregulated diffusion of SALW in destination; or (d) there is lack of capacity to maintain effective control over imported SALW; or (e) there is a possibility of diversion of end-uses or end-users; and / or (f) satisfactory preventative measures are not in place, could be useful tests to determine whether a certain transfer breaches the obligations at hand.[32] These and other indicators might be used in aggregate or otherwise, depending on particular situations. The actual effects, adverse consequences, and clear risks of the use of small arms against norms of humanitarian law all have to be considered when the need arises.

According to Articles 1 and 2 of the Draft Articles of the ILC, hence, 'transfer' and / or 'failure to prevent a transfer' of arms by a state, may constitute a conduct attributable to that state. As discussed earlier: (a) only an act of transfer or failure to stop a transfer, and not motives for doing so are needed; (b) actual atrocities or any other harm, as a result of the use of transferred weapons, are not required[33]; an 'ends test' does not seem to be applicable to breaches of IHL obligations. It has to be emphasised also that states have a primary obligation to ensure respect for IHL.[34] Finally, bearing in mind Article 12 of the Draft Articles, IHL in general and the rules in discussion in particular are obligations *erga omnes*, and thus applicable to every state. As they are intransgressible in character, their breaches are subject to a stringent regime of responsibility.[35]

In the light of the aforesaid wrongful conduct and breaches of the obligations in question, we now turn to address the responsibility of SALW exporting states.

[30] See 7.2.5 for detailed indicators, see 7.2.1.

[31] See 7.3.

[32] See, eg GGE 1997 (p 222), for ICRC (p 225).

[33] See, eg p 371.

[34] See, eg Crawford, above n 5 at p 84, para 9.

[35] See p 285; see in particular Cassese, *International Law*, 2nd edn (Oxford, Oxford University Press, 2005) 244, 263. He underlined that: agreement has now crystallized on the need to distinguish between *two forms or categories of State responsibility*: responsibility for 'ordinary' breaches of international law, and a class of 'aggravated responsibility' for violations of some fundamental general rules that enshrine essential values (such as peace, human rights, self-determination of peoples). . . The emergence in the world community of values (peace, human rights,. . .) deemed of universal significance and not derogable by States in their private transactions has lead many states to believe that gross infringements of such values must perforce require a stronger reaction than those normally taken in response to violations of bilateral legal relations [emphasis original].

The statement of the representative of Kenya to the UN 2001 Conference on Small Arms is an outstanding point to start with. He assumed that:

> Arms-exporting States had a particular responsibility to ensure that small arms and light weapons did not end up in the hands of governments or other actors who violated human rights and international humanitarian law.[36]

As Crawford noted, an existence of a breach 'depends on the precise terms of the obligation, its interpretation and application, taking into account its object and purpose and the facts of the case'.[37] Even then, we could only look at the general application of the elements to the breaches of the rules on transfers, as detail facts of such business are hardly disclosed in state practice.

Questions of attribution and level of responsibility are worth particular attention. In countries where the supply of arms is a direct function of governments, the issue of attribution might be less complex than in those who have fully privatised such a business. The question is whether transfers of arms made by companies and/or individuals of a country, in violation of the norm in discussion, are attributable to a state of that country? In such a case, the law of state responsibility, as stated in Article 8 of the Draft Articles, requires a 'conduct directed or controlled by a state', in order to affirm attribution. The Special Rapporteur of the ILC on State Responsibility for instance considers that the conduct shall be an integral part of a specific operation of a state and not an incidental or peripheral one.[38] Additionally, the Appellate Chamber of the ICTY in the *Tadic* case stated: 'the requirement of international law for the attribution to a State of acts performed by private individuals is that the State exercises control over the individuals. The degree of control may, however, vary according to the factual circumstances of each case'.[39] Therefore, the physical transfers of weapons and authorisation of them, or a failure to regulate and control such transfers by agents of a state among other things might constitute commission or omission respectively, depending on the circumstances of particular cases.

Regarding the level of responsibility, the responsibility of exporter states' is perhaps twofold. First, pursuant to Articles 1 and 2 of the Draft Articles, a supply of weapons in breach of the use and availability based rules entails state responsibility, independent of the responsibility of a recipient state, as it would amount to a breach of an *erga omnes* obligation. The ICJ has supported such a notion of independent state responsibility. Although it was clear that the US was not directly engaged in the atrocities

[36] *UN Conference on the Illicit Trade in Small Arms*, 11 July 2001, para 2.

[37] Crawford, above n 5, at p 125, para 1.

[38] *Ibid*, at 110; see also Aust, *Handbook of International Law* (Cambridge, Cambridge University Press, 2005) 410–11. He noted: 'the organ can be legislative, executive or judicial, or of any other nature, including one carrying out commercial functions'.

[39] *Prosecutor v Tadic*, (Case IT-941 1999) para 117[emphasis original].

committed in the country, the Court has found arming the *contras* in Nicaragua, a breach of the obligation not to encourage violations of IHL, which entails an independent responsibility. Though it was not about weapon transfers, the Court in the *Corfu Channel* case had determined Albania's responsibility for failing to warn the UK, even though the mines were laid by a third state. The responsibility of Albania 'was original and not derived from the wrongfulness of the conduct of a third state'. By implication, Albania's failure was associated with prevention of the wrongful conduct. Hence the collaborative conduct of states at the same time might constitute the original responsibility of each state.[40] In our case, in addition to an importer and/or users of small arms, a supplier state would be a co-perpetrator of such an international wrongful act, provided that the necessary elements of state responsibility were satisfied.

In the *Tugar* case, the European Commission on Human Rights has undermined IHL issues, as has been touched on earlier. Among others, three points had been spelt out for rejecting the case: (1) '[T]here is no immediate relationship between the mere supply, even if not properly regulated, of weapons and the possible 'indiscriminate' use thereof in a third country'. (2) 'the 'adverse consequences' of the failure of Italy to regulate arms transfers to Iraq are 'too remote' to attract the Italian responsibility'; and (3) 'the injuries suffered by the applicant are exclusively attributable to Iraq' and not to Italy, under Article 2 of the European Convention.[41]

Certain problems appear to be evident, concerning the case and its impact on the current state of the norm. First, the Commission did not want to deal with IHL obligations and any responsibility therefrom, probably due to the scope of Article 2 of the European Convention and its limited mandate. Breaches of the right to life within a territory and/or jurisdiction of Member States entails responsibility,[42] as discussed in relation to IHRL above. Secondly, as disclosed by the Commission itself, licence of such exports was secretly given under the wider discretion of the executive, and the company who supplied the mines was found guilty

[40] Crawford, above n 5, at 145–46; see also *Nicaragua*, above n 12, at 137; see also *Corfu Channel*, above n 7, at 22; for independent state responsibility in general see, fns 17–18, p 373; see also Cassese, above n 35, at 245. He went to the extent of saying that: 'current needs have resulted in the possibility for States to be held *accountable for lawful actions*. . .under some treaties on the use of outer space (for example, the 1972 Convention on International Liability for Damages Caused by Space Objects) or on the exploitation of nuclear energy (for example, the 1960 Convention on Third Party Liability of Operators of Nuclear Ships) States are liable to pay compensation, either under international law or within municipal law system (in the form of civil liability) to states or persons injured by their lawful but ultra-hazardous activities' [emphasis original].

[41] *Tugar v Italy* case, p 4, see also, p 218, fn 89.

[42] *European Convention on Human Rights*, 4 November 1950, Arts 1, 2 and 27; see also, *Bankovic and Others v Belgium and 16 Other Contracting States*, 52207/99, ECHR, 12 December 2001, para 75.

of the illegal transfer of arms to Iraq by the Brescia Court in the country. It appears that these facts could make establishing attribution of the conduct to Italy more difficult,[43] if not impossible. In an IHL sense, however, the failure to introduce a proper law might amount to a breach of the obligation to 'ensure respect' for IHL.[44] Lastly, the rules of transfer under discussion might not have been as clear at the time of the supply in question as it stands now.[45] Nonetheless, the *Nicaragua* case was decided in 1986 affirming the validity of the responsibility under discussion[46]; the *Tugar* case could not therefore disprove the view that states are independently responsible for any supply of weapons in breach of IHL-based legal standards.

Secondly, and alternatively, the responsibility of exporter states might arise in the context of derivative state responsibility. Article 16 of the ILC Draft extended state responsibility to those states which grant any material or financial aid and/or assistance to the wrongful act of another state. It reads[47]:

> A state which aids or assists another State in the commission of internationally wrongful act by the latter is internationally responsible for doing so if : (a) that state does so with knowledge of the circumstances of the internationally wrongful act; and (b) the act would be internationally wrongful if committed by that state.

Three key elements of the article are worth explaining. First, this and other related articles 'are exceptions to the principle of independent state responsibility', and 'they only cover certain cases'. Secondly, as the phrase 'by the latter' in the chapeau to Article 16 implies, the acting state is only primarily responsible, and any assisting state will only have 'a supporting role'. This means that the assistance or aid of the latter alone could not constitute a breach of an international obligation. Examples of such situations include, 'facilitating the abduction of persons on foreign soil, or assisting in the destruction of property belonging to nationals of a third state'. The acting state and the assisting one would, in such cases, be incurring primary and derivative responsibility respectively. Care must be taken to distinguish 'the situation of aid and/or assistance from that of co-perpetrators or co-participants in an international wrongful act'. Finally, two elements are required: (1) prior knowledge of the circumstances of the wrongful act; and (2) the act in question shall be a breach, if committed by the assisting state. The requirements are cumulative.[48]

[43] *Tugar* case, above n 41.
[44] See p 200.
[45] *Tugar* case, above n 41.
[46] *Nicaragua* case, above n 12.
[47] Emphasis added; see also Crawford, above n 5, at p 149, para 4.
[48] Crawford, *ibid*, at p 147, para 8, p 148, para 1, p 149, paras 4 and 5; see also Quigley, above n 17, at 78.

Could these elements of derivative state responsibility fit in the transfers of SALW, in the light of breaches of the use and/or availability based rules?

The ICRC claimed that exporter states have moral, political and 'in some cases, legal responsibility to the international community for *the use made of their weapons and ammunition*'. Publicists have reiterated this position. Consistent with this line of thinking concerning state responsibility, selling to, or aiding of, weapons to a country, or facilitating such transactions, being aware of the circumstances of the use of such weapons entails a derivative state responsibility reliant on the wrongful act of an importer state, particularly of the use of relocated weapons, contrary to humanitarian norms. The second requirement is obvious, as any breach of IHL by a destination state is a breach of the same nature if committed by a state that sales or aids arms to the former.[49]

In reality, transfers of SALW in breach of the norm at issue occur as confirmed, for example, by the Sanctions Committee of the SC for Angola.[50] Some also contend, as revealed in the workshop organised by the Government of Switzerland, that countries such as France and Egypt have provided weapons and contributed to the Rwanda Genocide. Countries such as China, France, Iran Iraq, Russia, South Africa and the US have given weapons and other support to Sudan's civil war, in which two million people have died. In the internal conflict in Burundi, states such as China and Bulgaria have contributed through weapons supply. In all these and other cases, governments together with guerrillas have been involved in gross violations of IHL. Arguably, 'these governments are, by their acts of commission, or omission, or by sheer neglect, accessories to the abuses that are being committed'.[51]

Supplier states could be held responsible for the use of their weapons in other jurisdictions. Yet the perception of the ICRC and others, on the notion of derivative responsibility in respect of supplier states, is vague. For example, the reference made to 'some cases'[52] by the ICRC, is not explained. It might only be sensible if attribution and other elements of state responsibility are intended as conditions. Moreover, the limit made to the 'use made of their weapons and ammunition',[53] as a requirement seems to be incomplete or misperceived, in point of law. Three principal

[49] ICRC, *Arms Availability*, p 25, para 2, and pp 21–22 [emphasis added]; see also Gillard, 'What is Legal? What is Illegal? Limitations on Transfers of Small Arms under International Law' (Cambridge, *LRCIL*) 8, para 32; see also Frey, 'The Question of Trade, Carrying and Use of Small Arms and Light Weapons in the Context of Human Rights and Humanitarian Norms': working paper submitted in accordance with Sub-Commission Decision 2001/120, 30 May 2002, pp 18–20, para 73.

[50] See p 110.

[51] Hilterman and Bondi, 'State Responsibility in the Arms Trade and the Protection of Human Rights' *Workshop on Small Arms*, Geneva, 18–20 February 1999, p 1.

[52] See ICRC, *Arms Availability*, 1999.

[53] *Ibid.*

bases have been discussed to demonstrate the problem. First, the nature of the breach involved does not seem to correspond with such a limited approach. As has been reiterated, states are legally obliged not to facilitate, or support, violation of IHL. Also, they have a positive obligation to prevent such atrocities. In this account thus episodes of deaths and other human suffering, contrary to IHL, as a result of the use of supplied arms, are not required to establish the responsibility of a certain state. For that reason, a transfer made under clear risk of violation is sufficient, given that elements of state responsibility are fulfilled.[54]

Secondly, although making a sharp distinction between primary and derivative responsibility appears not to be simple, co-participant states' responsibility of breaches of humanitarian norms ought not to be confused with the derived one. This position has persistently been pursued by the ILC, since the early days of its draft Articles. Crawford has explained that when there exists a substantive rule which prohibits a state 'from providing assistance in the commission of certain wrongful acts by other States or even requiring third States to prevent or repress such acts', such supplies and questions of accountability thereof, could not depend on 'any general principle of derivative responsibility'.[55] Lastly, prevented atrocities, whether due to multilateral efforts or otherwise might not lead to the exoneration of a state's responsibility for its wrongful act, in breach of the use and/or availability based rules. The actual use of arms by recipient states or NSAs, contrary to the norms at issue, could only be one ground for primary responsibility; breaching the rules of IHL applicable to the trade in arms also entails an original state responsibility. Exporter states' responsibility is thus beyond what the ICRC has envisaged.

The focus of the international community on suppliers of SALW does not necessarily show the absence of importer states' responsibility. It is obvious that importing states are responsible for perpetrating wrongful acts such as wilful murders, targeting civilians, etc, in breach of IHL, using small arms. The ICRC stated that 'the primary responsibility of compliance with international humanitarian law falls upon users of weapons'.[56] In addition, they are accountable for any failure to ensure respect for IHL in their territory; this includes violations of IHL by NSAs or civilians, as a result of a failure to effectively regulate the small arms in a country.[57] For example,

[54] See, eg 7.2; see also 7.2.5; see also Crawford, above n 5, p 77, para 3.

[55] Crawford, *ibid*, pp 148–49, para 2, and p 146, para 7; see also Quigley, above n 17, at p 105, para 3, he noted that Art 27 of the Draft Articles of the ILC, which dealt with complicity, did not include co-perpetrators; for the 1978 Draft Articles on State Responsibility see ILC *Year Book*, 1978, vol 2, p 99, Art 27.

[56] *Arms Availability* p 25, para 2.

[57] Gillard, above n 49, para 32; see also, Kalshoven, 'The Undertaking to Respect and Ensure Respect in all Circumstances: from Tiny Seeds to Ripening Fruit (1999) 2 *YBIHL* 10–12; see also Provost, above n 4, at 75–76; see also, *Tugar* case, above n 41, at p 5, paras 6 and 9.

as regards the Darfur crises, the SC underlined that 'the Government of Sudan bears the primary responsibility' to ensure that 'all parties are obliged to respect international humanitarian law'. In view of that, it was ordered to 'fulfil its commitments to disarm the Janjaweed militias'.[58]

Their responsibility must be extended to the importation of such arms itself, independent of the carnage on the ground. Five principal reasons could justify this: (1) although states have the right to import weapons for self-defence, security needs and participating in peacekeeping,[59] however, such a right could not be exercised to the detriment of states' *jus cogens* obligations; (2) the IHL obligations on transfers, along with common Article 1 of the Geneva Conventions obliges states, including importers, to ensure respect for IHL; so importing, or failure to prevent transfer of weapons by a destination state, while risks of use of them against norms of humanitarian nature are evident, amounts to a breach of the rules (see further 7.2.5). As long as the circumstances such as evident risk of use in breach of IHL, widespread violations of IHL and/or unregulated diffusion are established, the importation itself has to be illegal, which could entail the responsibility of the recipient state[60]; (3) the humanitarian law based rules have generally been backed by importer states[61]; (4) as discussed above, actual acts such as genocide and extra-judicial killings need not necessarily occur[62]; and (5) the act of transfer of SALW, in breach of the rules at hand, often involves both a supplier and a recipient state (see 4.1.1).

The GIAT upholds such a line of argument. The principle set out in paragraph 21 asserts that:

> States receiving arms have an equivalent responsibility to seek to ensure that the quantity and level of sophistication of their arms imports are commensurate with their legitimate self defence and security requirements and that they do not contribute to instability and conflict in their regions or in other countries and regions or to illicit trafficking in arms.[63]

Although the principle has not directly referred to IHL, it affirms the notion that recipient states could be held primarily responsible for their importation of weapons, which might imperil *erga omnes* obligations.

As seen above, it seems to be irrational to decline from invoking the answerability of a state, whenever it is engaged in weapon imports, while tensions runs high between ethnic groups and in effect jeopardizes IHL protections.[64] This aspect is not emphasised by the international

[58] Res 1556/2004, Preamble, para 7, operative, para 6.
[59] See *UN PoA* (p 97); see also Mexico's Statement in the SC Debate, 19 January 2004, p 11.
[60] See p 287.
[61] See p 205, fn 45; see also p 211, fn 62.
[62] Above, n 34.
[63] Above, n 41, para 21.
[64] See 7.2; see also GGE 1997, paras 34–37; see also *Tugar* case, above n 41, at 5.

community. The centre of attention is rather on suppliers. It appears to be that this could only be a matter of priority to stem transfers at the main stream, and not of exculpation of recipient states' responsibility regarding illegal SALW imports. Indisputably, determining the illegality or otherwise of certain importation may not be an easy business, as a matter of the problem of judging the facts and circumstances surrounding such activities and not as a matter of law.

What is, then, the ultimate impact of state responsibility relating to breaches of the use and/or availability based rules of small arms transfers? Two possibilities will be discussed with emphasis on supplier states. First, pursuant to Article40 (1) of the ILC Draft Articles, a supplier state could be held responsible for its serious breaches of IHL, as the basic rules of the law of armed conflict are generally accepted as 'intransgressible in character', and therefore have attained *jus cogens* status.[65] A breach is serious in reference to Article 40(2), if 'it involves a gross or systematic failure' to comply with a legal obligation. So, 'a certain order of magnitude of violations' is required. Similarly, the term 'gross' refers to 'the intensity of the violation or its effects; it denotes violations of flagrant nature, amounting to a direct and outright assault on the values protected by the rule'. The term 'systematic' refers to an act or omission 'carried out in an organized and deliberate way'. Factors such as 'intent to violate the norm, the scope and number of individual violations, and the gravity of their consequences for the victims' have to be considered in establishing the seriousness of a violation.[66]

In this account it is clear that every violation of peremptory norms, including IHL, may not constitute a serious breach, as indicated by the ILC. Hypothesis might be of help at this point. State X's authorisation of SALW transfer to state Y, in breach of the use and availability based rules, could only be a serious breach if a minimum of four conditions are fulfilled. First, such transfer shall be an intended violation of IHL in general and/or the norms of transfers in question in particular. Secondly, it shall systematically be conducted; an involvement, inter alia, of security and intelligence institutions might fit in such situations as an example. Thirdly, it must be committed repeatedly; thus incidental transfers might

[65] *Nuclear Weapons*, above n 26, at 257, para 79; see also, 7.2); for the ILC Draft Articles 2001, see also p.120; see also Meron, 'Is there Already a Differentiated Regime?' in Weiler et al (eds), above n 5, at 227–29; see also Bokor-Szego, 'Short Comments on the Concept of Crimes of States and Some Related Notions' in Weiler et al (eds), *ibid*, at 239; see also Ago, 'The Concept of "International Community as a Whole": A Guarantee to the Notion of State Crimes' in Weiler et al (eds), *ibid*, at 252–53.

[66] Crawford, above n 5, p 246, para 3, p 247, paras 7and 8; see also, Quigley, above n 17; see also Meron, *ibid*, at 229; see also Spinedi, 'Convergences and Divergences on the Legal Consequences of International Crimes of States: With Whom Should Lie the Right of Response?' in Weiler et al (eds), above n 5, at 244–45, there is at present a general agreement on the point that contemporary international law makes a distinction between more serious and less serious wrongful acts.

not be enough. Finally, the arms in question have to be used in actual and gross violations of IHL. We cannot generalise that every violation of the use and/or availability based rules result in a serious breach. This test applies to breaches on a case-by-case basis.

If this stringent test of a serious breach has been affirmed positively, in the sprit of the ILC Draft Article 41(1) (2) and (3), the following consequences might follow. First, 'states shall cooperate to bring to an end' the serious breach of arms transfers. Such positive duty to co-operate could be attained under the umbrella of a 'competent international organization, in particular the United Nations'. States are obliged: (a) not to recognise such a breach, or situations created by the breach; and (b) 'not to render aid or assistance in maintaining that situation'.[67] The ICJ in the *Legal Consequences Advisory Opinion* has explicitly avowed these obligations of states in response to the violation of IHL by Israel.[68]

Aside from the law of state responsibility, the Geneva Conventions, particularly of common Article 1, have clearly stipulated such an obligation. States have a duty to act to stop events of violations. However, they do not seem to adopt such a rigorous test as the one set out by the ILC for establishing a universal obligation.[69] The ICJ has also affirmed that, by virtue of the Geneva Convention relative to the Protection of Civilian Persons, all States Parties have an obligation, 'while respecting the UN Charter and international law, to ensure compliance by Israel with international humanitarian law'.[70]

In brief, the problem here is that the conduct of weapon transfers is secretive in nature, and it could be extremely difficult to establish the intent of state officials, as set out in the ILC Draft. Alarmingly, it could generally be a challenge that contemporary transfers are mostly profit driven in contrast with other gross violations of IHL. Yet, it shall be borne in mind that intent to transgress the rules is what is required rather than a desire to commit mass murder or similar catastrophes. All the same, establishing state responsibility, within the context of serious breaches, appears to be too difficult to achieve.

Secondly, even if breaches of the rules on transfers have not constituted a serious breach, in the sense of Article 41 of the ILC draft on state responsibility, state X is obliged to comply with twofold obligations: (1) according to Article 30(a) and (b) of the Draft Articles, it shall cease, not repeat, and give guarantee of non-repetition of arms transfers.[71] As stated

[67] Crawford, *ibid*, at 249–50; see also Cassese, 'Critical Remarks on the Application of the Concept of Crimes of States to Humanitarian Law' in Weiler et al (eds), above n 5, at 232.

[68] Para 159.

[69] Pictet (1958), *Commentary: IV Geneva Convention Relative to War*, Geneva, p. 16; see also Pictet (1952), above n 4, at 136; see also Quigley, above n 17, at 91.

[70] *Legal Consequences* (n 68).

[71] See also, Crawford, above n 5, at 196–200; see also McCaffrey, 'Lex Lata or the Continuum of State Responsibility' in Weiler et al (eds), above n 5, at 242; here what is

in Article 48(1)(a) and (b) of the Draft, either an injured state or other legally interested states are entitled and obliged to claim this, as the breach involves universal duties and corresponding rights[72]; and (2) state X has to make reparation, as shown in Articles 31(1) and (2) and 42 of the Draft Articles, for the damages it has brought about, on state Y, or on other injured states. Even so, who is an injured state has to be determined objectively. Y is injured, in the sense of the obligation in question, 'if it is specifically affected' by a violation of IHL-based rules of transfers. Here, 'particular adverse effects' of the transfers of weapons by state X has to be established. For instance, state X's provision of weapons to fighters in state Y, might be used in massacres of civilians, in the territory of the latter. State Y is, in such cases an injured state. Thus, state X would be under an obligation to repair the damage, either material or moral; the latter includes loss of life or other impacts of war. Equally, state Y is legally entitled to be compensated for the injury it has particularly suffered. This is only the case if the latter brings a legal claim.[73] It should be mentioned that, if the wrongdoer sustains its international wrongful act, state Y could even have resort, as pointed out in Article 49 of the Draft Articles, to a lawful countermeasure, to stop the wrongful act and induce performance of the obligation.[74]

Finally, both primary and derivative kinds of state responsibility result in legal consequences. The above rules apply in both cases, depending on the circumstances of particular breaches. However, an 'assisting state will only be responsible to the extent that its own conduct has caused or contributed to the internationally wrongful act', a matter which shall be left to a competent dispute settlement body.[75]

In summary, the rules of IHL on SALW transfers and the Articles on state responsibility have made it clear that violations of all the rules on arms transfer (though the vigour and clarity of the rules vary) entail state responsibility, when attribution is attested. Both exporters and importers of small arms might therefore incur responsibility. Cassese admits (despite some criticisms) that the ILC Draft Articles consider such notion of state responsibility:

> involved is not two separate fields,. . ., but a continuum of responsibility which entails less serious consequences at one end, and more serious ones at the other. All violations of international law, no matter how serious they are, have at least the potential, either because of their gravity, or because of their cumulative effect, of weakening the international legal order.

[72] Crawford, above n 5, at 276–8; see also *Legal Consequences*, above n 68; see also, Cassese, 'Critical Remarks', above n 67.

[73] Crawford, above n 5, at 201–06, 255–60; see also, *Factory at Chorzow* case (Jurisdiction), 1927, *PCIJ*, Series A, No 9, p 21; see also *PCIJ* (Judgment) p 47.

[74] Crawford, above n 5, at 281; see also White, and Abas, 'Counter Measures and Sanctions' in Evans, *International Law* (Oxford, Oxford University Press, 2003) 505*ff*.

[75] *Ibid*, p 148, para 1; see also Quigley, above n 17, at 125–27; see also McCaffrey, above n 71.

> Violations of community obligations (such as a sporadic disregard for a human right, or the *delivery of arms* by a state to insurgents fighting in another country) are put on a par with very serious breaches of such obligations (such as massacres, large-scale torture, aggression, and so on). In other words, any breach of community obligation, whatever its gravity, can trigger the same legal reaction.[76]

The responsibility of suppliers or those who facilitate such transactions could be primary or derivative. It seems to be clear from the nature and scope of the obligation at issue, however, that such a breach is unlikely to be unoriginal; such breaches could be considered as serious breaches, and therefore all states assume an obligation to stem them, subject to the strict criteria of state responsibility. However, IHL imposes a duty on states without a need for such a test. An additional difficulty is that the difference between a serious and a non-serious breach seems to be a matter of emphasis, as regards breaches of universal norms; and a state that is found responsible is under an obligation to cease and not repeat the breach, and to repair the damage it might have caused. This has to be done in a lawful manner under international law. It is the responsibility of states to consider the features of a particular rule which has been breached in addition to the factual circumstances of such a breach.

[76] Above n 35, at 271.

10

Findings and Recommendations

PRESENTLY, SMALL ARMS are responsible for millions of deaths, instability, violence, crime, and refugee flows across the world. Therefore their use, misuse, proliferation and unrestricted international circulation, primarily by states, has raised serious legal concerns of an international nature. This chapter will highlight some findings and recommendations, derived from the core issues examined in the book.

As seen in Part I, the following points are worth highlighting concerning the definition of small arms. While there is not yet a settled definition of SALW, the trend of the world community seems to be in favour of a wider definition, which comprises the salient features of small arms, such as suitability, lightness, accessibility, versatility of use, and their distinction from *lex specialis* arms control regimes. Accordingly, small arms include machetes, revolvers, automatic firearms, shoulder-fired launchers and missiles, ammunition, explosives, and all parts and components of such weapons.

In view of (a) the need to minimise duplication of efforts, (b) the nature of the weapons, and (c) to be able to regulate armaments in a more suitable legal framework, therefore, weapons and their components such as incendiaries, booby traps, laser blinding devices, MCW (eg battle tanks and fighter aeroplanes) and nuclear or other sensitive materials, are not SALW.

One of the controversies over definition is that some states and publicists wish to restrict the definition of small arms only to those weapons designed for military specification, while many others adopt a general approach, which embraces 'military' and 'civilian' weapons, with certain exclusions. The core criticism of the latter approach is that it threatens the 'civilian' possession and legal use of small arms. Despite this, the restrictive approach seems to disregard at least four problems. First, military weapons such as AK-47 have been excessively dispersed and are not only in the hands of militaries, but NSAs, criminals and law abiding civilians. Secondly, 'civilian weapons' are also in use in illegal or undesirable armed conflict and in violation of other norms of international law. Thirdly, some 'civilian weapons' are easily convertible to military type arms. And lastly, adopting a broad definition does not necessarily pose a threat to the lawful use of firearms.

Although the focus should be on regulating semi and fully automatic machine guns, due to the extent of the danger they could entail, a comprehensive approach has to be preferred and so adopted, to place all small arms within the reach of international law.

The second controversy relates to overlaps among SALW and other *lex specalis* arms control regimes. Mainly, weapons addressed in other frameworks, in particular the UN Inhumane Weapons Convention of 1980, and the UN Conventional Weapons Register of 1995, are not considered as SALW, though not without exceptions. For example, as discussed in chapter two, anti-personnel landmines are small arms; besides, even if man-portable air defence systems (MANAPADs) and light artillery have recently been *exceptionally* included in the scope of the UN Register of conventional weapons,[1] this does not suggest that they are disqualified from being considered light weapons. Two reasons could be given for this: first, they fulfil the features of SALW, and secondly, as the Register is only a transparency measure which does not involve any substantive legal restriction, the small arms regime may best regulate the use and transfers of such weapons, as seen in chapter six. When a question of overlap arises, the features of the weapon in question, and the contents of the regulations placed on it, including potential limitations will have to be considered.

However, the UN arms trade treaty process (GA Resolution 61/89/2006) concerns all conventional weapons, small, light and major or strategic armaments. Due to the peculiar features of SALW albeit the treaty needs to include and define these weapons as one cluster of conventional weapons; we shall come back to other aspects of this development below.

Whereas definition is important, it should be neither a priority, nor a blockade, to tackle the most essential challenges attached to the arms trade and their proliferation (see 2.2.5).

One of the challenges of the small arms issue seems to be the question of substantive restriction on their manufacturing. Three findings should be emphasised here. The first is that although there were some endeavours to limit the manufacture of small arms during the League era, and there are also some concerns and efforts in this direction at the moment, there appears to be *no* international legal norm, in spite of the continuing manufacture of SALW, which is fuelling the proliferation and illegal trafficking of small arms globally. Sadly, the UN is far behind the League of Nations' era on the problem.

However, as is shown in the ECOWAS Moratorium and domestic laws (see 3.5), there are some emerging norms, which restrict the small arms manufacture, especially 'military type' weapons, by states and authorised industries. As indicated in the UN PoA of 2001, regional and national

[1] *Statement by the President of the Security Council*, 17 February 2005, p 2.

measures, there appears to be a general consensus upon the need to strictly control manufacturing of small arms. Such regulatory measures may well be useful as a means of imposing substantive restrictions, or facilitate such measures, on small arms manufacture.

The second finding is that, in the absence of real commitment to limit manufacturing of small arms by producing states, the excessive availability and accumulation of these arms is most likely to persist as an international problem. Goldblat noted for example, 'Transfers of conventional weapons cannot be prevented or even significantly limited as long as their manufacture remains un-limited'.[2] Indeed, it could be difficult to stem the appetite of recipients and dealers of small arms to involve themselves in the illicit-trafficking and grey market deals of such arms, without having reasonable *restraints* and international *standards* on their manufacture. In addition, it does not seem plausible to ignore the question of manufacture of small arms, while embarking upon micro disarmament,[3] collection and destruction of surplus weapons,[4] as remedies for the crisis of small arms proliferation and its adverse consequences. Even so, states have legitimate rights to manufacture weapons for legal end-uses.

Finally the following standards need to be considered in future efforts of the international community, to respond to the challenge of small arms proliferation; (a) manufacturing of small arms should be permitted merely for *legal* uses; (b) states shall manufacture SALW, especially the most lethal and dispersed ones, *only* for self-defence, security and participation in peacekeeping uses and functions, consistent with international law obligations; (c) such restrictions should include bilateral treaties on licensed-production by states; (d) lessons have to be learnt from analogous dual-use items, particularly of the manufacture of narcotic drugs and their substantive restrictions; (e) to promote a greater transparency and ensure the compliance of states with the restrictions, there should be an international body that can oversee the process; and (f) the attention given to licence, reporting and record-keeping of manufacturing activities needs to be strengthened.

Certainly, all this could be reduced to rhetoric without political will and greater co-operation among states. Further research is therefore essential to set out realistic standards for such reductions and limitations.

The second key challenge, as examined in Part II, pertains to *substantive* restrictions on international small arms trade and transfer. Now, as detailed analysis and conclusions have been provided in each chapter, we shall concentrate on some central and general findings and possible suggestions.

[2] Goldblat, *Arms Control: A Guide to Negotiations and Agreements* (London, Sage Publications, 1994) 187.

[3] *Report of the SG on Small Arms*, 7 February 2005, paras 28–29.

[4] See, eg HC Hansard vol 419 cols 955-56W (25 March 2004).

The major findings are the following.

(1) The pervasive belief that we have *no* international legal norms on arms transfer is either old-fashioned or flawed. The international order has acquired relevant general international law norms, inter alia, non-intervention, humanitarian law and peace and security, and particular customary rules of international law (arms control law) relating to such norms—the latter includes fundamental human rights based restrictions. The arms trade is therefore subject to such primary legal restrictions. However, the norms relating to non-intervention and IHL are more concrete and clearer than the rest, when we talk of specific rules of transfer. Deducing peace and security and IHRL based norms seemed to have been fairly controversial. For example, while there are significant developments in IHRL regarding the regulation of the transfer of small arms as implements of violations and abuses, the evolution of specific norms appears to be in a progressive development. Yet international law does not accept arms transfer to areas of violations/abuses of human rights. Consequently, a state shall not engage itself in transfers of small arms, whenever there is *actual or apparent risk of their use* in civil and inter-state conflicts, international terrorism, gross violations of the law of armed conflict and human rights; transfers of weapons to the territory of a state without the consent and knowledge of the latter is also an intervention to sovereignty, and may amount to aggression as well in the appropriate circumstances. Arms supply to governments in purely civil war situations may well be illegal intervention and so prohibited.

Lora Lumpe wrote in respect of norms on transfers that 'in addition to reminding states of their current international law obligations, there is a need to develop or strengthen laws or norms against certain [kinds of] state practice'.[5] Further, Professor Laurance, referring to the UN PoA, in particular to the link between illicit transfers of small arms and their humanitarian and peace and security consequences, and the commitment of states 'to strengthen or develop norms and measures', commented that 'given this shared assessment of the problem and its consequences, it will be difficult for states to behave contrary to this norm'.[6] The latter refers to the commitment of states he mentioned earlier.

Even so Nicholas Marsh believes 'the one case where international law intrudes on the exports of small arms is in the case of states or organisations that are subjects of arms embargoes'.[7] Those who

[5] Lumpe, *Running Guns: the Global Black Market in Small Arms* (London, Zed Books, 2000) 227.

[6] Laurance, 'Shaping Global Public Policy on Small Arms: After the UN Conference' 9(1) *The Brown Journal of World Affairs* (Spring 2002) 195.

[7] Marsh, 'Two Sides of the Same Coin? The Legal and Illegal Trade in Small Arms', *ibid*, at 218.

support such a position rely upon the argument that the responses of the international community are essentially *soft law* and not legally binding.

As dealt with in Part II, however, the measures of states and organisations are more than soft law. Some recent developments reinforce the latter argument. The 2004 SAS unveils, 'as of December 2003, Brazil, Cambodia, Costa Rica, Finland, Macedonia, Mali, and the Netherlands had pledged their support for a treaty to control the arms trade'.[8] It has also attracted the express support of thirteen states, during the July 2005 UN BMS on small arms.[9] The reason why this is particularly important is that the Treaty's (FCIAT) substantive restrictions are clearly founded on states' existing international law obligations.

In addition to supporting the FCIAT, the UK government reiterated such legal obligations, in various occasions. In response to a parliamentary question in 2004, the Secretary of State for Trade and Industry expounds:

> The UK has one of the strictest and most transparent arms export licensing systems in the world. All export licence applications are rigorously assessed on a case-by-case basis against the Consolidated EU and National Arms Export Licensing Criteria. . .Criterion 1 specifically addresses respect for the UK's international commitments and international obligations.[10]

The transformation of the ECOWAS Moratorium into a Convention in July 2006[11] is also evidence of codifying existing norms that limit the transfers of small arms. Articles 3 and 6 have entirely banned transfers of small arms into, or from, Member States if: (i) their 'authorization violates' international law, inter alia, humanitarian law, the duty of non-intervention, the prohibition of the use of force; and (ii) 'the arms are destined to be used' for the violations of humanitarian and human rights norms, to exacerbate internal and regional conflicts and tensions, and to conduct and encourage terrorist acts—there is no exception on such and similar cases.

This instrument is permanent and would be legally binding, subject to ratification. Appropriate implementation, verification, dispute

[8] GIIS, *Small Arms Survey 2004: Rights at Risk* (Oxford, Oxford University Press) 133.

[9] *Press Release*, 'Thirteen More Governments Announce Support For Arms Trade Treaty, *Control Arms*, 15 July, 2005, it was said that Benin, Colombia, Germany, Ghana, Guinea, the Netherlands, Norway, Senegal, Sierra Leone, Spain, Turkey, Uganda, and the Vatican gave support to the Draft.

[10] HC Hansard vol 420 col 66W (19 April 2004); see also *The Export Controls Act 2002*, entered into force in May 2004, the Act explicitly refers to the Consolidated Criteria.

[11] *ECOWAS Conention on Small Arms and Light Weapons, their Ammunition and Other Related Materials*, 14 June 2006, signed by Heads of State and Government of Member States; see also Griffiths, 'Focus on Small Arms and Light Weapons at the UN' *Ploughshares Monitor* (Winter 2004) 2.

resolution, reporting and institutional arrangements have been set out in Chapter VI of the Convention. As per Article 28 of the latter, an Independent Panel of Experts has to be established to help monitor compliance of Member States with their obligations under the Convention. Its scope is incredibly broad: on top of transfers of SALW, issues of brokerage, civilian possession, regional and national register of weapons, among other things, are all contained therein.

Such a move is gaining wide-ranging support from states and international organisations. For instance, the UN SC's statement of 17 February 2005 assured that:

> The Security Council renews the support given to the plan of ECOWAS to strengthen the moratorium . . ., to replace it with a *mandatory convention* . . .and calls upon all States and organisations in a position to support this endeavour.[12]

Additionally, The UN High-level Panel on Threats, Challenges and Change of 2004, highlighted that 'a comprehensive approach to the small arms problem emerged in the late 1990s and seeks to create international action to *limit their production and spread*'.[13]

All these concerted efforts by the international community have lead to the adoption of GA Resolution 61/89 of December 2006 entitled: '[T]owards an arms trade treaty: establishing common international standards for the import, export and transfer of conventional arms'[14] which also enjoyed an overwhelming majority vote of governments in the UN GA's First Committee. Some of the key reasons for, and decisions of, the Resolution are now briefly explained. The GA, recalling its resolutions on arms transfers, inter alia, 46/36 of 1991 and 51/45 of 1996 (see chapter five), 'guided by the purposes and principles' of the UN Charter, reaffirming its 'respect for international law, including international human rights law and international humanitarian law, and the Charter', and acknowledging 'the absence of common standards' on the trade in 'conventional arms' as 'contributory factor' to conflict, terrorism, instability, the displacement of people and 'the growing support across all regions for concluding a legally binding instrument' on import-export of arms, as clearly stated in preambular paragraphs 1, 2, 7, 9 and 10 respectively, has requested the Secretary-General to: (i) 'seek the views of Member States on the feasibility, scope and draft parameters for a comprehensive, legally binding instrument establishing common international standards for

[12] *Statement by the President of the SC*, 7 February 2005, para 11 [emphasis added].

[13] *A More Secure Order: our Shared Responsibility*, Report of the Secretary-General's High-level Panel on Threats, Challenges and Change, 2004, para 96 [emphasis added].

[14] The Assembly endorsed a draft Resolution of the First Committee (UN Doc A/C.1/61/L.55) by a recorded vote of 153 in favour, one against and 24 abstentions.

the import, export and transfer of conventional arms' and report to the Assembly in late 2007; and (ii) 'establish a group of governmental Experts' to carry out a study on the issue including 'draft parameters' for the treaty, beginning 2008, to be reported to, and considered by, the Assembly in the same year.

Some preliminary comments are made here. First, unlike the UNPoA, the process covers any arms transfer, whether licit or illicit, sale or aid, etc. Secondly, it's intended to be legally binding, and the authoritative preambles of Resolution 61/89 seem to have given a green light to consider international law norms including peace and security, human rights, humanitarian law, sovereignty and non-intervention. The issue of human rights would be very delicate in this project.

Thirdly, the vote of 153 developing and developed states in favour of this initiative provides a very strong case to argue in favour of the emergence of rules of transfer. Albeit the US voted against, countries such as Russia, China, Belarus, Israel and Iran abstained. This means that only one major exporter of arms rejected the decision. This action is neither understandable nor acceptable in the eyes of domestic laws of the US. The 1999 Code of Conduct demands similar multilateral action on the problem.[15] Whether those who abstained are acquiescing or otherwise to the practice will have to be seen further in the forthcoming sessions of the Assembly.

Fourthly, despite the fact that the background of the Resolution largely relates to SALW, the treaty will cover all conventional armaments, with the possible exclusion of certain weapons—further comments will be made later. And lastly, this arms trade treaty project which appears to codify or extend existing laws (custom or treaty) to arms transactions would face a real challenge of global application unless the US and a few other significant states embrace the process. The wish of greater majority of states, IGOs and NGOs must prevail though.

So the legal norms on transfer do not appeared to be utopian. The use of small arms against the fundamental values mentioned earlier, the excessive accumulation, the capacity and commitment of a state to prevent the misuse and diversion of end-use and end-users of weapons, shall be among the general tests to authorise or otherwise their transfer. Hence in principle, the freedom of action for states regarding small arms transfer is restrictive.

Undoubtedly such a conclusion and prohibitions recognise certain exceptions: the import-export of small arms for self-defence, security,

[15] See Stohl, 'UN to Consider Arms Trade Treaty—US Opposes', *Centre for Defence Information*, 16 November 2006.

and peacekeeping uses, the maintenance of public order in special international entities, and whenever states agree to do so by treaty or domestic legislation, without contravening international law, appears to be permitted, subject to scrutiny of the circumstances of individual cases of such transfers. Thus, a distinction has to be made between licit and illicit transfers of small arms.

(2) The definition of the illicit trade in SALW shall include any sale or aid of such tools by states, in contravention of the aforementioned rules on arms transfer. The perception that an illicit transfer is all about covert black market sales does not seem justifiable under international law. A transfer of small arms is only legal if it fully complies with relevant international legal norms and the laws of supplier and recipient states (see 4.1.1). For this reason, the UN PoA on the 'Illicit Trade in Small Arms and Light Weapons, In All Its Aspects', shall incorporate state-to-state and state-to-NSA arms transfers, whenever conducted contrary to international and / or domestic laws and regulations.

(3) Even so violations of these norms by states are real problems. Breaches of mandatory arms embargoes of the UN and regional organisations, global, regional, and even national norms are not rare. Such contraventions may be caused intentionally or due to lack of awareness of their obligations. Indeed, the pressure from gun industries and lobbyists on states and international organisations, the gun culture in some societies, and the absence of adequate legal research on the subject, may obscure an appreciation of the rules in question.

(4) Moreover, the reality of lack of detailed criteria required for the application of these legal norms has to be acknowledged. Although it differs from rule to rule, the standards are not sufficiently crystallised to ensure uniform application and compliance of states with the rules and norms of the arms trade. This is particularly true regarding humanitarian law and human rights based restrictions, on the trade in small arms. For example, the factors needed to determine would-be violations and changes in circumstances have to be developed further.

(5) By the same token, implementation of the rules, such as arms embargoes, global and regional guidelines, and domestic requirements are full of loopholes; to mention just a few, the absence of a global institutional framework (eg a register of small arms, the UN Atomic Energy Agency-like verification framework, etc), the UN SC's non-uniform measures and lenient responses to any violations of its embargoes, the ineffectiveness of the EU to overcome the discriminatory application of the rules by Member States, and the fact that importing states, African countries for example, have not yet taken institutional and practical measures to put in force such norms.

(6) This is not to deny developments in implementation at global and regional levels; for instance, introducing monitoring panels and sanc-

tions committees—to observe the implementation of SC arms embargoes and to carry out investigations on alleged violations, the PoA's requirement of national implementation reports to the UN Disarmament Commission, the well organised and integrated institutions of ECOWAS that deal with the importation and exportation of arms, and the EU and US measures of transparency of arms exports, are indeed positive phenomena in the control of small arms transfer.

Relying on these findings, therefore, the following recommendations may help build up the small arms transfers' international law regime.

(1) In order to clarify the norms on transfers and overcome the shortcomings therein, endeavours of codification, either in the form of a convention or GA resolution, should be made a priority. This may follow the UN route, or the Mines Convention kind of process, in which like-minded states and NGOs may take an active part in achieving its success.[16]

It is worth noting that the UN High-level Panel on Threats, in its Report to the Secretary-General underlined that:

> Member States should expedite and conclude negotiations on *legally binding* agreements on the marking and tracing, as well as the brokering and *transfer*, of small arms and light weapons.[17]

Regrettably, the UN Secretary-General's report entitled 'Larger Freedom: towards development, security and human rights' of 21 March 2005 confined its recommendations to codifying norms on brokerage and marking and tracing of small arms[18]; no explanation was given for such restrictive calls on Member States. Yet during the British presidency, the EU has called 'for negotiations to begin, within the UN PoA process, on global principles for the control of transfers of SALW'.[19]

As considered earlier, several states expressly supported the UN High-level Panel and EU's view, though a few governments are concerned with matters other than SALW transfers. The UN small arms Review Conference of June 2006, which was meant to reinforce the UN PoA, did not reach a substantive conclusion at all.[20] Taking into account GA Resolution 61/89, and gaining lessons from the

[16] *A More Secure Order*, above n 13, para 95; see also Brem, 'Restricting the Illicit Trade in and the Misuse of Small Arms and Light Weapons: What can we Learn from Ottawa?' paper delivered at the 42nd Annual ISA Convention, Chicago, 25 February 2001, pp 7–8.

[17] Above, n 13[emphasis added].

[18] See para 120.

[19] Statement by Ambassador Freeman (UK), on behalf of the European Union, *Thematic Debate Intervention on Import/Export Control and Illicit Brokering*, BMS, 14 July 2005, para 3.

[20] UN Press Release, 'Secretary-General Disappointed Small Arms Conference Ended without Agreement, But Says Global Community Committed to Action Plan to Curtail Illicit Trade' 10 July 2006.

ECOWAS practice, therefore, it's vital to combine the arms trade treaty process with that of the UN PoA. This will enable the international community to tackle both sides of the arms trade, the 'licit' and 'illicit' transactions and associated problems. This approach is also resource/ cost effective.

Concern may be expressed about the distinction between SALW and strategic armaments. Both have differences and similarities (see chapter two). Provided that this is reflected in the treaty and SALW are clearly dealt with as one group of conventional weapons, there is no reason why both cannot be addressed in one treaty regime. Yet a careful emphasis needs to be made to address the most pressing challenge of human security.

Furthermore, while the approach adopted in the 2003 draft FCIAT is a good model in codifying the rules, efforts have to embrace both the *demand* and *supply* aspects of the problem,[21] of course with emphasis on the latter. The ECOWAS Convention has adopted this approach. The treaty/resolution must also encompass an implementation framework, most importantly, a global register of SALW transfers. It is essential to mention that the functions of the International Narcotics Control Board[22] and the UN Commission on Narcotic Drugs,[23] in enforcing the 1961 Single Convention on Narcotic Drugs, could provide valuable lessons to the small arms regime.

Relevant regional norms, treaties and other instruments have to be welcomed and encouraged. Regional organisations, such as the EU have to come up with more clear and legally binding instruments on the arms trade.

Bearing in mind all this, it is most likely that the standards established in this work will either be incorporated into a global arms trade treaty or serve as strong basis for it.

(2) Lessons from other fields of international law, inter alia, the controls and limits on the movement of industrial wastes, narcotic drugs and nuclear materials have to be learnt for the small arms transfers' regime. It should be emphasised that the common feature of such regimes of control is that they have embraced, not only the actual harm of the movement of the goods, but the *precautionary* and *preventive* measures, which have to be taken to avoid or minimise the risks.

[21] Scott, 'The UN Conference on the Illicit Trade of Small Arms and Light Weapons: An Exercise in Futility?' (2003) 31 *GA.J.INT'L and COMP.L.* 713.

[22] *1961 Single Convention on Narcotic Drugs*, Art 1(1)(a), as enshrined in Art 9(4), 'the Board, in cooperation with Governments,. . . shall endeavour to limit the. . ., manufacture, and illicit trafficking in and use of, drugs'.

[23] *Ibid*, Arts 5 and 9, as shown in Art 8, one of the functions of the Commission is to 'make recommendations for the implementation of the aims and provisions of this Convention, including programmes of scientific research'.

Since peremptory norms and *erga omnes* obligations of states, relating to peace and security, IHL and IHRL, have been targeted by the unrestricted flows and use of small arms, a preventive approach to the problem appears to be particularly desirable.

(3) States have to be reminded of their obligations and responsibilities regarding the arms trade. Their legal advisors have professional and moral responsibility to appreciate and explain the rules to their respective governments. Moreover, NGOs, including the ICRC, have to take a clear and firm stance on the legal standards in question—so that they will be able to maximise their influence on the codification and progressive development of the rules on SALW transfers.

(4) As an effective way of addressing global concerns, in particular in arms control issues, strong co-operation[24] among states is vital to tackle the challenge of unrestricted arms transfers.

(5) The primary rules established in this book alone cannot solve small arms' unrestrained international transfers. On the one hand, attention should be paid to tightening and standardising the regulation of dealers,[25] and marking and tracing[26] of SALW, parallel to the efforts underway to clarify and enforce relevant primary obligations—these will help control the *supply* side of the issue. On the other hand, disarmament, collection and destruction of small arms, in particular in post-conflict and peace-building UN, regional and national engagements[27] help drain the *demand* for arms imports.

In brief, though this work has dealt with the substantive obligations aspect of the small arms trade, it has to be urged that the international community should exert a multifaceted effort to arrest the illegal circulation and use of these deadly weapons with their atrocious consequences.

[24] See, eg UN PoA 2001, para 32; see also Bull, *The Control of the Arms Race: Disarmament and Arms Control in the Missile Age*, 2nd edn (Frederick A Praeger, New York, 1965) xxxv.

[25] GA Res 58/241/2003, 'The Illicit Trade in SALW in All Its Aspects', para 11.

[26] eg, *Report of the Group of Governmental Experts established Pursuant to General Assembly Resolution 56/24 V of Dec. 2001*, 'The Illicit Trade in Small Arms' 2003, para 98.

[27] In *Larger Freedom*, above n 18.

Bibliography

Books and Articles

A Project of the Graduate Institute of International Studies (GIIS), *Small Arms Survey 2002: Counting the Human Cost* (Oxford, Oxford University Press).

——, *Small Arms Survey 2003: Development Denied* (Oxford, Oxford University Press).

——, *Small Arms Survey 2004: Rights at Risk* (Oxford, Oxford University Press).

——, *Small Arms Survey 2005: Weapons at War* (Oxford, Oxford University Press).

Academician General Yuriy Kirshin, 'Conventional Arms Transfers During the Soviet Period' in I Anthony (ed), *Russia and the Arms Trade* (Oxford, Oxford University Press, 1998) 49.

Ago, 'The Concept of "International Community as a Whole": A Guarantee to the Notion of State Crimes' in Weiler et al, 252–53.

'Addressing Small Arms in the Caucasus, Tougher Controls on UK Exports Needed' *Update* (No 31, January 2003) 2.

D Akande and S Williams, 'International Adjudication on National Security Issues: What Role for the WTO?' (2003) 43 *VJIL* 366.

M Akehurst, 'Custom as a Source of International Law' 53 (1974–75) 47 British Ybk Intl L 1.

P Allott, *The Health of Nations: Society and Law beyond the State* (Cambridge, Cambridge University Press, 2002).

Amnesty International, 'Arms Flows and International Law: the G8 must also Obey the Rules' *The Terror Trade Times* (Issue No 3, 2002).

——, 'Failed UN Small Arms Conference' *The Terror Trade Times* (Issue No 3, 2002).

——, *A Catalogue of Failures: G8 Arms Exports and Human Rights Violations*, 19 May, 2003 (AI Index: IOR 30/003/2003).

K Annan, 'Small Arms, Big Problems' *International Herald Tribune* (10 July 2001).

I Anthony, 'Causation and the Arms Trade, with Reference to Small Arms' in Dhanapala et al (eds), *Small Arms Control Old Weapons, New Issues* (Aldershot, Ashgate Publishing, 1999) 78.

——, 'Illicit Arms Transfers', in I Anthony (ed), *Russia and the Arms Trade* (Oxford, Oxford University Press, 1998) 157.

——, 'Decision Making Procedure for Export Controls: relevance to small arms', in Dahinden et al, *Small Arms and Light Weapons: Legal Aspects of National and International Regulation* (Geneva, United Nations, 2002)

AC Arend and RJ Beck, *International Law and the Use of Force* (London and New York, Routledge, 2001).

B Arts, M Noortmann, and B Reinalda, *Non-State Actors in International Law* (Gateshead, Athenaeum Press, 2001).

A Aust, *Handbook of International Law* (Cambridge, Cambridge University Press, 2005).

MA Bellesiles, *Arming America: the Origins of a National Gun Culture* (New York, Random House, 2000).

I Berkol, 'Marking and Tracing Small Arms and Light Weapons, Improving Transparency and Control', *Special Issue 2002*, at < http://www.grip.org-pub-rap-rgo2-hs1_alg.pdf>

G Best, *Humanity in Warfare*, New York, Columbia University Press, New York, 1980).

——, *War and Law Since 1945* (London, Clarendon Press, 1994).

A Bloed, L Leicht, M Nowak and A Rosas (eds), *Monitoring Human Rights in Europe: Comparing International Procedures and Mechanisms* (Dordecht, Martinus Nijhoff, 1993).

LP Bloomfield, 'Small Arms and Light Weapons: US Policy and Views' (2001) 6(2) *Electronic Journal of the US Department of State* No 1.

E Blunt, 'Child Recruitment was War Crime' *BBC News*, 1 June 2004.

W Boese, 'Wassenaar Members Adopt Small Arms Initiatives', *Arms Control Today* (January/February 2003).

L Boisson de Chazoournes, 'The Collective Responsibility of Sates to Ensure Respect for Humanitarian Principles', in A Bloed, L Leicht, M Nowak and A Rosas, *Monitoring Human Rights in Europe: Comparing International Procedures and Mechanisms* (Dordecht, Martinus Nijhoff, 1993) 247.

H Bokor-Szego, 'Short Comments on the Concept of Crimes of States and Some Related Notions' in Weiler, Cassese and Spinedi, *International Crimes of State* (Berlin, Walter de Gruyter, 1988) 239.

S Bosco, L Braucher and B Kessler, *Encyclopedia Britannica Ready Reference* (Deluxe edn, CD-Rom, 2003).

J Boutwell and M Klare, 'A Scourge of Small Arms' *Scientific American* (2000) at <http://www.pugwash.org/reports/pim/pim21.htm>

——, 'Small Arms and Light Weapons: Controlling the Real Instruments of War', *Arms Control Today* (August/September 1998).

——, *Light Weapons and Civil Conflicts: Controlling the Tools of Violence* (New York & Oxford, Rowman & Littlefield Publishers, 1999).

J Boutwell, M Klare and LW Reed (eds), *Lethal Commerce: the Global Trade in Small Arms and Light Weapons* (Cambridge, Mass, American Academy of Arts and Sciences, 1995).

K Boyle and S Simonsen, 'Human Security, Human Rights an Disarmament', (2004) 3 *Disarmament Forum* 5.

S Brem, 'Restricting the Illicit Trade in and the Misuse of Small Arms and Light Weapons: What can we Learn from Ottawa?', paper delivered at the 42nd Annual ISA Convention, Chicago, 25 February 2001.

H Briggs, 'The International Court of Justice Lives up to its Name' (1987) 81 *AJIL* 78.

O Bring, 'Regulating Conventional Weapons in the Future—Humanitarian Law or Arms Control?' (1987) 24 (3) *Journal of Peace Research* 275.

F Brockway and F Mullally, *Death Pays a Dividend* (London, Victor Gollancz, 1944).

J Brown, *Arms Control Issues for the Twenty-First Century* (New Mexico, Sandia, 2000).

I Brownlie, *Principles of Public International Law*, 5th edn (Oxford, Clarendon Press, 1998).

——, *Principles of Public International Law*, 6th edn (Oxford, Oxford University Press, 2003).

——, 1983, *System of the Law of Nations-State Responsibility, Part I* (Oxford, Oxford University Press, 1983).

M Brzoska, 'Design and Implementation of Arms Embargoes and Travel and Aviation Related Sanctions', *Result of the Bonn Process*, 2001, p 32, at <http://www.bicc.de/events/unsanc/2000/pdf/booklet/chapter_2.pdf>

H Bull, *The Control of the Arms Race: Disarmament and Arms Control in the Missile Age*, 2nd edn (New York, Frederick A Praeger, 1965).

A Burnett, 'International Organisations' at <http://www.asil.org/resource/intorg1.htm>

A Buzuev, *Transnational Corporations and Militarism* (Moscow, Progress Publishers, 1985).

A Carter, *Success and Failure in Arms Control Negotiations* (Oxford, Oxford University Press, 1989).

A Cassese, 'The Martens Clause: Half a Loaf or Simply Pie in the Sky?' (2000) 11 *EJIL* 187.

——, *International Law* (Oxford, Oxford University Press, 2001).

——, *International Law*, 2nd edn (Oxford, Oxford University Press, 2005).

____, 'Critical Remarks on the Application of the Concept of Crimes of States to Humanitarian Law' in Weiler, Cassese and Spinedi (eds), *International Crimes of State* (Berlin, Walter de Gruyter, 1988) 233.

Centre for Humanitarian Dialogue, 'Rebel Groups and Weapons: Limiting the Damage' *Hd Bulletin: Small Arms and Human Security* (No 3, June 2004) 1.

J Cerone, 'The Application of Regional Human Rights Law Beyond Regional Frontiers: the Inter-American Commission on Human Rights and US Activities in Iraq' *ASIL Insight* (October 2005) at <http://www.asil.org>

J Charney, 'Universal International Law' (1993) 87 *AJIL* 543.

J Charney and JRV Prescott, 'Resolving Cross-Strait Relations Between China and Taiwan' (2000) 94 *AJIL* 453.

Chi Chi Sileo, 'Gun Control War Targets Our Worst Nightmares' *10* (23) *Insight* (June 1994) 12–15

B Collier, *Arms and the Men: The Arms Trade and Governments* (London, Hamish Hamilton, 1980).

J Collier, *The Settlement of Disputes in International Law: Institutions and Procedures* (Oxford, Oxford University Press, 2000).

K Cook, 'Precedents from the Export and Transport of Endangered Species: CITES and other Trade-related Multilateral Environmental Arrangements: Models for Control of Trade in Small Arms and Light Weapons?' in E Dahinden et al, *Small Arms and Light Weapons: Legal Aspects of National and International Regulation*, (Geneva, United Nations, vol iv, 2002) 59.

D Cortright, G Lopez, and L Gerber, 'Sanctions sans Commitment: An Assessment of UN Arms Embargoes', *Fourth Freedom Forum*, April 2002, p 11, at <http://www.fourthfreedom.org/pdf/ArmsEmbargoes.pdf>

F Coomans and MT Kamminga (eds), *Extraterritorial Application of Human Rights Treaties* (Oxford, Intersentia, 2004).

F Coomans, 'Some Remarks on the Extraterritorial Application of the International Covenant on Economic, Social and cultural Rights, in F Coomans and MT

Kamminga, *Extraterritorial Application of Human Rights Treaties* (Oxford, Intersentia, 2004) 183.

Countries Agree to Negotiate on Explosive Remnants of War, *Arms Control Today* (Jan–Feb / 2003)

Court Clears US Gun Makers, *BBC News*, 15 May 2003.

P Craig and GD de Burca, *EU Law: Text, Cases and Materials*, 3rd edn (Oxford, Oxford University Press, 2003).

J Crawford, 'The Criteria for Statehood in International Law' [1976] *British Ybk Intl L* 93.

——, *The Creation of States in International Law* (Oxford, Oxford University Press, 1979).

——, *The International Law Commission's Articles on State Responsibility: Introduction, Text and Commentaries* (Cambridge, Cambridge University Press, 2002).

W Cukier, D Lochhead, J Susla and A Kooistra, 'Emerging Global Norms in the Regulation of Civilian Possession on Small Arms': draft for review, *SAFER-Net,* July 2003.

W Cukier, A Sarkar and T Quigley, 'Firearms Regulation: International Jurisprudence' (2000) 6 *Canada Criminal Law Review* 99.

A D'Amato, 'Trashing Customary International Law' (1987) 81 *AJIL* 102.

E Dahinden, J Dahlitz and N Fischer, *Small Arms and Light Weapons: Legal Aspects of National and International Regulation*, Geneva, United Nations, vol iv, 2002).

D Dahinden, 'Meeting the Challenges of Small Arms Proliferation: Example of the OSCE Document', in E Dahinden, J Dahlitz and N Fischer (eds), *Small Arms and Light Weapons: Legal Aspects of National and International Regulation* (Geneva, United Nations, vol iv, 2002) 1.

J Dahlitz and D Dicke, *The International Law of Arms Control and Disarmament: Proceedings of the Symposium, Geneva, 28 February–March 1991* (New York, United Nations, 1991).

J Dhanapala, AM Donwaki, S Rana and L Lumpe, *Small Arms Control Old Weapons, New Issues* (Aldershot, Ashgate Publishing, 1999)

LA De Alba, 'A Regional Perspective on the Problem of Small Arms and Light Weapons' (2002) 2 *Disarmament Forum* 49.

J De Arechage, 'The Work and the Jurisprudence of the International Court of Justice 1947–1986' [1987] *British Ybk Intl L* 1.

BP Dean, 'Self-Determination and the US Support of Insurgents: A Policy-Analysis Model' *Military Law Review* vol 122 (Fall / 1988) 149.

E Denza, 'The Relationship between International and National Law' in Evans, *International Law* (Oxford, Oxford University Press, 2003) 415

J Dhanapala, 'Multilateral Cooperation on Small Arms and Light Weapons: From Crisis to Collective Responsibility' 9(1) *The Brown Journal of World Affairs* (Spring 2002) 161.

J Dhanapala, S Rana and L Lumpe, *Small Arms Control: Old Weapons, New Issues* (Aldershot, Ashgate Publishing, 1999)

M Dixon and R McCorquodale, *Cases and Materials on International Law,* 3rd edn (London, Blackstone Press, 2000).

K Doehring, 'Self-determination' in Simma et al (eds), *The Charter of the United Nations: A Commentary,* 2nd edn (Oxford, Oxford University Press, vol I, 2002) 47.

MW Doyle, 'Liberalism and World Politics' (1986) 80 *American Political Science Review* 1151.

S Dragani, 'Interrelationship between Illicit Trafficking in Small Arms, Drug Trafficking, and Terrorist Groups: African and European Issues' in Alves and Cippollone (eds), *Curbing Illicit Trafficking in Small Arms and Sensitive Technologies: an Action Oriented Agenda* (New York, United Nations, 1998) 77.

DW Drezner, 'How Smart are Smart Sanctions?' (2003) 5 *International Studies Review* 107.

E Duarte, 'Chemical and Biological Agents' in Alves and Cippollone (eds), *Curbing Illicit Trafficking in Small Arms and Sensitive Technologies: an Action Oriented Agenda* (New York, United Nations, 1998) 233.

P Eavis, 'Analysis: Arms Trade—A question that won't go away for Labour—is it ethical to sell arms to aountries at aar?' *The Independent* (London, 28 May 2002).

——, 'SALW in the Horn of Africa and the Great Lakes Region: Challenges and Ways Forward' 9(1)*The Brown Journal of World Affairs* (Spring 2002) 251.

N Elaraby, 'Practical Problems with Multilateral Arms Control Treaties' in Dahlitz and Dicke (eds), *The International Law of Arms Control and Disarmament, Proceedings of the Symposium, Geneva, 28 February–2 March 1991* (New York, United Nations, 1991).

VH Ezell, 'UN Confab OKs Global curb On Small Arms' *National Defence* (October 2001), at <http://www.nationaldefensemagazine.org/article.cfm?Id=618>

——, 'Small Arms: Dominating Conflicts in the Early Twenty-First Century' 9(1) *The Brown Journal of World Affairs* (Spring 2002) 305.

R Falk, 'Nuclear Weapons, International Law and the World Court, A Historic Encounter' (1997) 9 *AJIL* 66.

S Faltas, and WC Paes, 'The Problem of Small Arms in Developing Countries: the Current International Debate and Recommendations for Development Cooperation, in Particular Technical Cooperation' *Division* (No 43/2001) Deutsche Gesellschaft fur: Germany.

T Farer, 'Drawing the Right Line' (1987) 81 *AJIL* 113.

D Feldman, 'The Place of Arms Control and Disarmament in the System of International Law', in Dahlitz and Dicke (eds), *The International Law of Arms Control and Disarmament*: *Proceedings of the Symposium, Geneva, 28 February–March 1991* (New York, United Nations, 1991).

CG Fenwick, 'When is there a Threat to the Peace? – Rhodesia' 61 *AJIL* (1967) 753.

Final Chance to Strengthen Export Control Bill' *Update* (No 29/Spring/2002) 4.

N Fischer, 'Outcome of the UN Process: the Legal Character of the UN Programme of Action' in E Dahinden, J Dahlitz and N Fischer (eds), *Small Arms and Light Weapons: Legal Aspects of National and International Regulation*, Geneva, United Nations, vol iv, 2002) 159.

N Florquin, and E Berman, *Arms And Aimless: Armed Groups, Guns, and Human Security in the ECOWAS Region* (Geneva, Small Arms Survey, 2005).

T Franck, 'Some Observations on the ICJ's Procedural and Substantive Innovations' (1987) 81 *AJIL* 116.

J Freedson, 'The Impact of Conflict on Children: the Role of Small Arms' (2002) 3 *Disarmament Forum* 37.

B Frey, 'Small Arms and Light Weapons: The Tools Used to Violate Human Rights' (2004) 3 *Disarmament Forum* 37.

J Frowein and N Krisch, 'Action with Respect to Threats to the Peace, Breaches of the Peace, and Acts of Aggression' in Simma et al (eds), *The Charter of The United Nations: A Commentary*, 2nd edn (Oxford, Oxford University Press, vol I, 2002) 701.

T Gabelnick, 'Conventional Arms Control in the Asia-Pacific Region: The Case for a Supply-Side Regime on International Law' *Federation of American Scientists* (October 2001).

——, 'Small Arms: U.S., "rogues" hold out' 57 *Bulletin of the Atomic Scientists* (September / October 2001) 18.

Galtung, *There are Alternatives: Four Roads to Peace and Security* (Nottingham, Spokesman Books, 1984) 124–31.

TD Gill, 'Legal and some Political Limitations on the Powers of the UN Security Council to Exercise its Enforcement Powers under Chapter VII of the Charter' (1995) *Netherlands Yearbook of International Law.*

E Gillard, 'What is Legal? What is Illegal?' in L Lumpe (ed), *Running Guns: The Global Black Market in Small Arms* (London, Zed Books, 2000) 27.

——, 'International Humanitarian Law and Extraterritorial State Conduct' in Coomans and Kamminga (eds), *Extraterritorial Application of Human Rights Treaties* (Oxford, Intersentia, 2004) 25.

W Glaberson, 'Suit against Gun Makers is Dismissed on Technical Grounds' *New York Times* (27 July, 2003).

J Goldblat, *Arms Control: A Guide to Negotiations and Agreements* (London, Sage Publications, 1994).

NJ Goldring, 'Overcoming Domestic Obstacles to Light Weapons Control', in J Brown, *Arms Control Issues for the Twenty-First Century* (New Mexico, Sandia, 2000) 195.

V Gowlland-Debbas, 'The Functions of the United Nations Security Council in the International Legal System' in M Byers (ed),*The Role of Law in International Politics: Essays in International Relations and International Law* (Oxford, Oxford University Press, 2000) 293.

C Gray, *International Law and the Use of Force*, 2nd edn (Oxford, Oxford University Press, 2004).

LC Green, *The Contemporary Law of Armed Conflict*, 2nd edn (Manchester, Manchester University Press, 2000).

C Greenwood, 'The International Tribunal for former Yugoslavia' 69 *Intl Affairs* 4 (October 1993) 641.

——, 'The Development of International Humanitarian Law by the International Criminal Tribunal for the Former Yugoslavia' in JA Frowein and R Wolfrum (eds), *Max Planck Year Book of United Nations Law* (London, Kluwer Law International, vol ii, 1998).

L Griffiths, 'Focus on Small Arms and Light Weapons at the UN' *Ploughshares Monitor* (Winter / 2004) 2.

AT Hadley, *The Nation's Safety and Arms Control* (New York, The Viking Press, 1961).

P Herby, 'Arms Availability and the Situation of Civilians in Armed Conflict' *International Review of the Red Cross* (30 September 1999, No 835) 669.

——, 'Arms Transfers, Humanitarian Assistance, and Humanitarian Law', in Boutwell and Klare (eds), *Light Weapons and Civil Conflicts: Controlling the Tools of Violence* (Boston, Rowman & Littlefield Publications 1999) 197.

——, 'Humanitarian Implications of Small Arms Proliferation and Proposed Codes of Conduct: Arms Availability—A Matter of Urgent Humanitarian Concern' in Dahinden et al (eds), *Small Arms and Light Weapons: Legal Aspects of National and International Regulation* (Geneva, United Nations, vol iv, 2002).

R HIGGINS, 'Derogations Under Human Rights Treaties', 48 *British Ybk Int L* (1976–77) 281.

J HILTERMAN and L BONDI, 'State Responsibility in the Arms Trade and the Protection of Human Rights' *Workshop on Small Arms*, Geneva, 18–20 Feruary 1999.

K HOMAN, 'The OSCE and Cooperative Security: Conventional Arms Control in Europe' in J Brown, *Arms Control Issues for the Twenty-First Century* (New Mexico, Sandia, 2000) 175.

M HUDSON, 'Some Thoughts about Recognition: Confidential Memorandum of the UN Secretary-General' (1950) 44 *AJIL* 548.

ICRC, *Arms Availability and the Situation of Civilians in Armed Conflict*: a study presented by the ICRC, 1 June 1999, ICRC Publication 1999, Ref 0734.

P INGRAM and I DAVIS (Oxford Research Group), 'The Subsidy Trap: British Government Financial Support for Arms Exporters and the Defence Industry', *Report Summary*, 3 July 2001, at <http://www.saferworld.co.uk>

International Security Information Service (ISIS), 'Qualitative Arms Control and International Humanitarian Law Applicable to Armed Conflict', *Policy Paper*, No 1, July 2001, at <http://www.isisuk.demon.co.uk>

Iran-Palestine Weapons Link 'likely' *BBC News*, 5 February 2002.

Iran to Halt Nuclear Enrichment' *BBC News*, 22 November 2004.

ISN Security Watch, 'EU Maintains Arms Embargo on China', 14 June 2005, at <www.isn.ethz.ch>

D JACKMAN, 'Small Arms and Security in Iraq' *Ploughshares Monitor* (2003) 1.

N JASENTULIYANA, 'The Process of Achieving Effective Arms Control Law' in Dahlitz and Dicke (eds), *The International Law of Arms Control and Disarmament: Proceedings of the Symposium, Geneva, 28 February–March 1991* (New York, United Nations, 1991) 179.

K JOSEPH, 'OSCE and NATO Take Aim at Small Arms' *BASIC Reports: Newsletter on International Security Policy* (No 73, 17 January 2000) 1.

S JOSEPH, J SCHULTZ and M CASTAN, *The International Covenant on Civil and Political Rights: Cases, Materials, and Commentaries* (Oxford, Oxford University Press, 2000).

——, *The International Covenant on Civil and Political Rights: Cases, Materials, and Commentary*, 2nd edn (Oxford, Oxford University Press, 2004).

E JOWITT, *The Dictionary of English Law* (London, Sweet and Maxwell, 1959).

H KABAALIOGU, 'The Obligations to "Respect" and "Ensure" the Right to Life' in B Ramcharan, *The Right to Life in International Law* (Dordecht, Martinus Nijhoff, 1985).

F KALSHOVEN, 'The Undertaking to Respect and Ensure Respect in all Circumstances: from Tiny Seeds to Ripening Fruit' (1999) 2 *Year Book of International Humanitarian Law*.

W KARL, 'The Time Factor in the Law of State Responsibility' in Spinedi and Simma (eds), *United Nations Codification of State Responsibility*, (New York, Oceana, 1987) 95.

A KARP, 'Small Arms—The New Major Weapons' in J Boutwell, *Lethal Commerce: the Global Trade in Small Arms and Light Weapons* (Cambridge, Mass, American Academy of Arts and Sciences, 1995) 17.
——, 'Arming Ethic Conflict' *Arms Control Today* (September 1999).
——, 'Uncertain Prognosis' 5 *Bulletin of the Atomic Scientists* (January–February 1999).
——, 'Small Arms: Back to the Future' 9(1) *The Brown Journal of World Affairs* (Spring 2002) 179.
T KARTHA, 'Controlling the Black and Gray Markets in Small Arms in South Asia' in Boutwell and Klare (eds), *Light Weapons and Civil Conflicts: Controlling the Tools of Violence* (Oxford, Rowman & Littlefield Publishers, 1999) 49.
O KERVELLA, 'Precedents from the Export and Transport of Dangerous Goods' in Dahinden et al (eds), *Small Arms and Light Weapons: Legal Aspects of National and International Regulation*, (Geneva, United Nations, vol iv, 2002) 41.
MSA KHAN, 'Linkages between Arms Trafficking and the Drug Trade in South Asia' in Dhanapala, Rana and Lumpe (eds), *Small Arms Control: Old Weapons, New Issues* (Aldershot, Ashgate Publishing, 1999) 243.
FL KIRGIS, 'The Security Council's First Fifty Years (1995) 89 *AJIL* (1995) 506.
Y KISS, *The Defence Industry in East-central Europe: Restructuring and Conversion* (Oxford, Oxford University Press, 1997).
M KLARE, 'The Global Trade in Light Weapons and the International System in the Post-Cold War Era' in Boutwell et al (eds), *Lethal Commerce: the Global Trade in Small Arms and Light Weapons* (Cambridge, Mass, American Academy of Arts and Sciences, 1995) 31.
——, 'An Overview of the Global Trade in Small Arms and Light Weapons' in Dhanapala, Rana and Lumpe (eds), *Small Arms Control: Old Weapons, New Issues* (Aldershot, Ashgate Publishing, 1999) 3.
——, 'The Kalashnikov Age' 55 *Bulletin of the Atomic Scientists* (January/February1999).
DB KOPEL, 'The UN Small Arms Conference' XXIII *SAIS Review* (Winter/Spring 2003) 319.
S KOPTE and P WILKE, 'Researching Surplus Weapons: Guidelines, Methods and Topics', Bonn International Centre for Conversion *Brief 3* (16 April 2002) 1.
M KOSKENNIEMI, 'The Police in the Temple. Order, Justice and the UN: a Dialectical View' (1995) 6 *EJIL* 325.
S KOULIK, and R KOKOSKI, *Conventional Arms Control: Perspective on Verification* (Oxford, Oxford University Press, 1994).
N KRISCH and J FROWEIN, 'Articles 2(5), 39–43, Introduction to Chapter VII' in Simma et al (eds), *The Charter of The United Nations: A Commentary*, 2nd edn (Oxford, Oxford University Press, vol I, 2002) 137, 701.
E KYTOMAKI and V YANKEY-WAYNE, *Implementing the United Nations Programmed of Action on Small Arms and Light Weapons: Analysis of Report Submitted by States in 2003* (Geneva, United Nations, 2004).
P LANSU, 'Light Weapons—The Questions of International Regulation and the Role of both Global and Regional Institutions' a contribution to a major study 'Towards a more Effective and Legitimate Global Multilateral System' (School of Sociology, Politics and Anthropology of the La Trobe University, November 1998).

R Lawson, 'Life After Bankovic: on the Extraterritorial Application of the European Convention on Human Rights' in Coomans and Kamminga (eds), *Extra-territorial Application of Human Rights Treaties* (Oxford, Intersentia, 2004) 83.

EJ Laurance, 'Shaping Global Public Policy on Small Arms: After the UN Conference' 9(1) *The Brown Journal of World Affairs* (Spring 2002) 193, 195.

B Lombard, 'Small Arms and Light Weapons: a Neglected Issue, a Renewed Focus' *Disarmament Diplomacy* (No 49, August 2000), at <http://www.acronym.org.uk/dd/dd49/index.htm>

C Lootty de Paiva Dias, 'Harmonizing Laws for the Prevention of Illicit Firearms Transfers: Analysis of the Firearms Control Laws of Greater MECOSUR Countries and their Compatibility with OAS-CICAD's Model Regulations, Rio de Janeiro, November 2002, at <http://www.desarme.org/publique/media/mercosur_legislation.pdf>

Lord Cullen, *The Pubic Inquiry into the Shooting at Dunblane Primary School*, 13 March 1996, at <http://www.archive.official-documents.co.uk/document/scottish/dunblane/dunblane.htm>

L Lovelace, 'Is there a Question of Taiwan in International Law?' 4 *Harvard Asian Quarterly* (Summer 2000), at <http://www.taiwandocuments.org/haq1.htm>

EC Luck, 'Choosing Words Carefully: Arms Embargoes and the UN SC', Final Report, *First-expert seminar*, BICC, Bonn, 21–23 January 1999, p 3, at <http://www.bicc.de/events/unsanc/1999/pdf/luck.pdf>

L Lumpe, 'The Leader of the Pack', 55 *Bulletin of the Atomic Scientists* (January/February 1999).

MS McDougal and M Reisman, 'Rhodesia and the United Nations: The Lawfulness of International Concern' (1962) 62 *AJIL* 3.

D McGoldrick, 'Extraterritorial Application of the International Covenant on Civil and Political Rights' in Coomans, and Kamminga (eds), *Extraterritorial Application of Human Rights Treaties* (Oxford, Intersentia, 2004) 41.

L Maresca and S Maslen, 'History and Negotiation of the Ottawa Treaty in L Maresca and S Maslen (eds), *The Banning of Anti-Personnel Landmines: the Legal Contribution of the International Committee of the Red Cross*, (Cambridge, Cambridge University Press, 2000).

B Mariani and A Urquhart, 'Transparency and Accountability in European Arms Export Controls: Towards Common Standards and Best Practice', December 2000, at <http://www.saferworld.co.uk/pubtrans.htm>

N Marsh, 'Two Sides of the Same Coin?' 9(1) *The Brown Journal of World Affairs* (Spring 2002) 217.

B Martenczuk, 'The Security Council, the International Court and Judicial Review: what Lessons from Lockerbie?' (1999) 10 *EJIL* 517.

RJ Mathews and LH McCormack, 'The Influence of Humanitarian Principles in the Negotiation of Arms Control Treaties' *International Review of the Red Cross* No 834 (1999) 331.

L Mathiak and L Lumpe, 'Government Gun-Running to Guerrillas', in Lumpe, *Running Guns: the Global Black Market in Small Arms* (London, Zed Books, 2000) 55.

T Meron, 'The Geneva Conventions as Customary Law' (1987) 81 *AJIL* 348.

——, 'Is there already a Differentiated Regime of State Responsibility in the Geneva Conventions?' in JH Weiler, A Cassese and M Spinedi (eds), *International Crimes of State* (Berlin, Walter de Gruyter, 1988) 225.

T MERON, 'The Humanisation of Humanitarian Law' (2000) 94 *AJIL* 240.

——, 'The Martens Clause, Principles of Humanity, and Dictates of Public Conscience' (2000) 94 *AJIL* 78–89.

D MILLER and W CUKIER, 'Regulation of Civilian Possession of Small and Light Weapons', *Biting the Bullet: Briefing 16*, at <http://www.international-alert.org/pdf/ pubsec/BB_Briefing161.pdf>

F MORRISON, 'Legal Issues in the Nicaragua Opinion' (1987) 81 *AJIL* 161.

J MOUZOS, 'International Traffic in Small Arms: an Australian Perspective' Australian Institute of Criminology, *Trends and Issues in Crime and Criminal Justice* (Canberra, No 104, February 1999).

Trends and Issues (No 104, February 1999) 1.

M MUBIALA, 'The ECOWAS Moratorium on Small Arms in West Africa' (2000) 3 *Year Book of International Humanitarian Law* 245.

RL NAY, *Firearms Regulations in Various Foreign Countries* Law Library of Congress, Washington DC 20540, 1990).

RT NAYLOR, 'The Structure and Operation of the Modern Arms Black Market' in Boutwell et al (eds), *Lethal Commerce: the Global Market in Small Arms and Light Weapons* (Cambridge, Mass, American Academy of Arts and Sciences, 1995) 44.

E NEWSOM, 'Small Arms Use and Proliferation: Strategies for a Global Dilemma', 1999, at <http://www.iansa.org/documents/gov/sept_99/newsom.htm>

P NOEL-BACKER, *The Private Manufacturer of Armaments* (London, Victor Gollancz, vol I, 1936).

G NOLTE, 'Article 2(7)' in Simma et al (eds), *The Charter of The United Nations: A Commentary*, 2nd edn (Oxford, Oxford University Press, vol I, 2002) 148.

L NORRIS, 'Arms Embargoes: Making Sanctions Smarter' *Ploughshares Monitor* (March (2000), at <http://www.ploughshaResca/content/MONITOR/monm00g.html>

G O'CALLAGHHAN, M CROWLEY and K MILLER, 'NATO and Small Arms: From Words to Deeds' *Basic Research Report 2000*, 4 October 2000, British American Security Information Council, at <http://www.basicint.org/pubs/Research/2000from_words.htm>

I OSTERDAHL, *Threat to the Peace: the Interpretation by the Security Council of Article 39 of the UN Charter* (Uppsala, Iustus Forlag, vol 13, 1998).

Oxfam and Amnesty International, 'Shattered Lives: The Case for Tough International Arms Control', AI Index: ACT 30/001/2003.

PP PAN, 'China Puts Threat to Taiwan into Law' *The Washington Post* (14 March 2005) A01.

S PEGG, 'Defacto States in the International System', Institute of International Relations' University of British Colombia, *Working Paper* (No 21, February 1998).

M PETER, 'The Kurdish Crisis and Allied Intervention in the Aftermath of the Second Gulf War' (1991) 2 *EJIL* 114.

D PETRASEK, 'Moving Forward on the Development of Minimum Humanitarian Standards' (1998) 92 *AJIL* 561.

BN PHILIP, *The Private Manufacturer of Armaments* (London, Victor Gollancz, vol 1, 1936).

JS PICTET, *The Geneva Conventions of 12 August 1949, Commentary* (Geneva Convention I, ICRC, 1952).

——, *Commentary: IV Geneva Convention Relative to the Protection of Civilian Persons in Time of War* (Geneva, ICRC, 1958).

B Pirseyedi, *The Small Arms Problem in Central Asia: Features and Implications* (Geneva, United Nations Publication, 2000).

R Provost, *International Human Rights and Humanitarian Law* (Cambridge, Cambridge University Press, 2002).

J Quigley, 'Complicity in International Law: a New Direction in the Law of State Responsibility' (1986) 57 *British Ybk Intl L* 77.

M Ragazzi, *The Concept of International Obligations Erga Omnes* (Oxford / New York, Oxford University Press, 1997).

S Rana, 'The Role of State' in Alves and Cippollone (eds), *Curbing Illicit Trafficking in Small Arms and Sensitive Technologies: an Action Oriented Agenda* (New York, United Nations, 1998) 117

A Randelzhofer, 'Introduction, and Articles 2, 2(4), 51' in Simma et al (eds), *The Charter of The United Nations: A Commentary*, 2nd edn (Oxford, Oxford University Press, vol I, 2002) 112.

J Rehman, *International Human Rights Law: A Practical Approach* (England, Pearson Education, 2003).

M Renner, 'Arms Control Orphans' 55 *Bulletin of the Atomic Scientists* (January / February 1999).

J Rissanen, 'NGO Perspectives: NGOs the small arms issue' (2002) 1 *Disarmament Forum* 37.

A Roberts and R Guelff (eds), *Documents on the Laws of War*, 3rd edn (Oxford, Oxford University Press, 2001).

Ronzitti, 'Problems of Arms Control Treaty Interpretation' in Dahlitz and Dicke (eds), *The International Law of Arms Control and Disarmament: Proceedings of the Symposium, Geneva, 28 February–March 1991* (New York, United Nations, 1991).

LJ Ruben, 'The Role of Arms Manufacturers and Traffickers' in Alves and Cippollone (eds), *Curbing Illicit Trafficking in Small Arms and Sensitive Technologies: an Action Oriented Agenda* (New York / Geneva, United Nations, 1998) 93.

Y Sandoz, C Swinarski and B Zimmermann, *Commentary on the Protocol Additional to the Geneva Conventions of 12 August 1949* (Geneva, ICRC, Martinus Nijhoff, 1987).

M Scheinin, 'Extraterritorial Effect of the International Covenant on Civil and Political Rights' in Coomans and Kamminga (eds), *Extraterritorial Application of Human Rights Treaties* (Oxford, Intersentia, 2004) 73.

D Schindler and J Toman, *The Law of Armed Conflicts* (Geneva, Martinus Nijhoff, 1988).

HL Schloemann and S Ohlhoff, '"Constitutionalization" and Dispute Settlement in the WTO: National Security as an Issue of Competence' (1999) 93 *AJIL*. 431.

M Schroeder and R Stohl, 'Controlling the Most Dangerous Weapons' *The San Diego Union-Tribune* (11 November 2004).

M Schroeder, 'Raising the Bar: The Campaign for an International Arms Trade Treaty' *FAS Public Interest Report* (Spring 2004) 5.

——, 'Of Red Parakeets and Dragon Fire: The Nonproliferation Case for Maintaining the EU Arms Embargo on China', 22 March 2005, at <www.fas.org / asmp / library / articles / Parakeets.html>

B Scott, 'The UN Conference on the Illicit Trade of Small Arms and Light Weapons: An Exercise in Futility?' (2003) 31 *GAJINT'L & COPM.L.* 681.

JB Scott, *The Hague Conventions and Declarations of 1899 and 1907*, 3rd edn (Oxford, Oxford University Press, 1918).

Security Research and Information Centre (SIRC), 'Implementing the Nairobi Declaration to Tackle Small Arms in the Great Lakes Region and the Horn of Africa' *Progress* (No 1, May 2002).

M Shaw, 'The International Status of National Liberation Movements' (1983) 5 *Liverpool Law Review* 19.

——, *International Law*, 4th edn (Cambridge, Cambridge University Press, 1997).

——, *International Law*, 5th edn (Cambridge, Cambridge University Press, 2003).

J Shen, 'Sovereignty, Statehood, Self-determination, and the Issue of Taiwan' (2000) 15 *AmUInT'l LRev* 1102.

B Simma, H Mosler, A Randelzhofer, C Tomuschat and R Wolfrum, *The Charter of The United Nations: A Commentary*, 2nd edn (Oxford, Oxford University Press, vol 1, 2002).

J Singh, 'National, Regional, and Global Measures for Controlling Light Weapons' in Dhanapala, Donwaki, Rana and Lumpe (eds), *Small Arms Control: Old Weapons, New Issues* (Aldershot, Ashgate, 1999) 279.

RP Singh, *Arms Procurement Decision Making: China, India, Israel, Japan, South Korea and Thailand* (Oxford, Oxford University Press, vol 1, 1998).

SIPRI, 'Sources and Methods of Arms Transfers Project', 15 January 2003, at <http://www.sipri.org/contents/armstrad/index.html>

——, *Transfers and License Production of Major Conventional Weapons: Exports to Taiwan, Sorted by Suppliers. Deals with Deliveries or Orders made 1993–2003*, at <http://projects.sipri.se/armstrade/tai_imports93-2002.pdf>

B Sloan, 'General Assembly Resolutions Revisited (Forty Years Later)' (1987) *British Ybk Intl L* 39.

Small Arms Working Group (SAWG), 'Norms on Arms Transfers' 2002, at <http://www.fas.org.asmp/campaigns/smallarms/sawg/1pagers/norms2002.html>

——, 'Seek a Broad and Comprehensive Agenda for 2001 Conference' 2001, at <http://fas.org/asmp/campaigns/smallarms/sawg/2001onepager.htm>

Small Arms, Light Weapons: Mass destruction, *The Hindu*, Nov. 04, 2001, at <www.hindu.com>

C Smith, 'Light Weapons—the Forgotten Dimension of the International Arms Trade' (1998) *Brassey's Defence Year Book* 282.

GM Sociola, 'Illicit Trafficking in Delivery System Technologies and Components: an Assessment' in Alves and Cippollone (eds), *Curbing Illicit Trafficking in Small Arms and Sensitive Technologies: an Action Oriented Agenda* (New York, United Nations, 1998) 23.

M Spinedi and B Simma (eds), *United Nations Codification of State Responsibility* (New York, Oceana, 1987).

HJ Steiner, 'International Protection of Human Rights' in Evans, *International Law* (Oxford, Oxford University Press, 2003) 757.

Stockholm International Peace Research Institute (SIPRI), *The Law of War and Dubious Weapons*, Stockholm, Almqvist & Wiksell Internationa, 1976).

R Stohl, 'UN to Consider Arms Trade Treaty—US Opposes' *Center for Defense Information*, 16 November 2006.

K Suter, *An International Law of Guerrilla Warfare* (New York, St Martin's Press, 1984).

The Colombia Electronic Encyclopedia, 2000, *Small Arms*, at <http://www.infoplease.com/ce6/sci/A0845576.html>

The ICRC and Various Issues related to the Use of Certain Weapons, Statement made at the UN GA, 55th session, 2000 (Official Statement No 840, 31-12-2000) p. 1084

The NGO Committee on Disarmament, Peace and Security, 'Are Disarmament Efforts a Waste?' xxvi (2003) (3) *Disarmament Times*, at <http://www.igc.org/disarm>

D Thompson, *The Oxford English Dictionary* (Oxford, Oxford University Press, 1996).

R Ticehurst, 'The Martens Clause and the Laws of Armed Conflict' *International Review of the Red Cross* (No 317, 30 April 1997) 125.

C Tomuschat, 'Articles 2(3), 19, 33' in Simma et al (eds), *The Charter of The United Nations: A Commentary* (Oxford, Oxford University Press, vol I, 2002) 10.

P Towle, *Arms Control and East-West Relations*, (London, Croom Helm, 1983).

I Traynor, 'The International Dealers in Death' *Guardian*, Special Report: The Arms Trade (9 July 2001), at <http://www.guardian.co.uk/armstrade/story/0,10674,519661,00.html>

UKMIL (2002)73 *British Ybk Int L* 831.

UN Commission on Crime Prevention and Criminal Justice, *United Nations International Study on Firearm Regulation* (New York, United Nations, 1998).

UN Officials Examine Banned Weapons Cargo That Arrived in Liberal, *UN News Service*, 3 Nov, 2003

GH Utter, *Encyclopedia of Gun Control and Gun Rights* (Arizona, Oryx Press, 2000).

D Vagts, 'The Hague Conventions and Arms Control (2000) 94 *AJIL* 31.

C Warbrick, 'States and Recognition in International Law' in Evans, *International Law* (Oxford, Oxford University Press, 2003) 205.

ND White and and A Abas, 'Counter Measures and Sanctions', in Evans, *International Law* (Oxford, Oxford University Press, 2003) 505.

N White, *The United Nations System: Toward International Justice* (London, Lynne Rienner: London, 2002).

——, 'The Will and Authority of the Security Council' (2004) 17 *Leiden Journal of International Law* 645.

G William, M Robert and W Camilla, 'Stray Bullets: The Impact of Small Arms Misuse in Central America', *Small Arms Survey: Occasional Paper* (No 5/Oct/2002).

P Williams, 'Drugs and Guns', 55 *Bulletin of the Atomic Scientists* (Jan–Feb/1999).

R Wolfrum and H Zockler, 'Commentary on Preamble, Articles 1, 18, 55 (a) (b), 56', in World Policy Institute, 'The WTO and the Globalisation of the Arms Industries', 9 December 1999, at <http://www.iansa.org/documents/research/1999/dec_99/wto_arms.htm>

C Wyatt, 'Small Arms and Light Weapons: Light and Lethal' (July/2001) 57 *The World Today* 13.

ZW Yihdego, 'Irresponsible Arms Transfers and Humanitarian Norms: Principles of Humanity and Public Conscience Perspective' (2006) 3 *Australasia Journal of Human Security* 29–42.

——, 'The Role of Security Council Arms Embargoes in Stemming Destabilising Transfers of Small Arms and Light Weapons (SALW): Recent Developments and Challenges' (2007) 54 (1) *Netherlands International Law Review* 115–32.

J Zaleski, 'Precedents from the Export and Transport of War Materials: an Overview of the Multilateral Arms Regulation and Disarmament' in Dahinden, Dahlitz and Fischer (eds), *Small Arms and Light Weapons: Legal Aspects of National and International Regulation* (Geneva, United Nations, vol iv, 2002) 33.

League of Nations and UN Materials

A Call to Control Trade to and in Africa, UN SC (19 November 1998) UN Doc Supp No S/RES/1209/1998.

A More Secure Order: our shared responsibility, Report of the Secretary-General's High-level Panel on Threats, Challenges and Change, 2004.

Analogies Between the Problem of the Traffic in Narcotic Drugs and that of the Trade in and Manufacture of Arms, League of Nations, *Official No* Conf. D.159, Geneva, 4 May 1933.

K Annan, 'If Effectiveness of the UN Arms Register is Strengthened, It Can Serve as Significant Early Warning Mechanism', 30 Aug 2002, at <http://www.un.org/News/Press/docs/2002/sgsm8355.Dochtm>

Basic Principles on the Use of Force and Firearms by Law Enforcement Officials, Adopted by the 8th UN Congress on the Prevention of Crime and Treatment of Offenders, Havana, Cuba, 27 August–7 September 1990.

Chairman's Summary, UN Doc Supp No A/CONF.192 BMS/2003/1, 18 July 2003.

China and UN Register of Conventional Weapons, at <http://www.nti.org/db/china/rocaorg.htm>

Civil and Political Rights, Including the Question of Torture and Detention, Report by Theo van Broven, Special Rapportuer on Torture, UN Doc Doc No E/CN.4/2003/69, 13 January 2003.

Code of Conduct for Law Enforcement Officials, 1979, GA Res 34/169, Annex 34, UN Doc Supp No A/34/46.

Comments by the Delegation of the Russian Federation on the Chairman's working paper entitled 'Draft Programme of Action to Prevent, Combat and Eradicate the Illicit Trade in Small Arms and Light Weapons in All Its Aspects' (A/CONF.192/PC/L.4/Rev 1), 10 April 2001, UN Doc SuppNo A/CONF.192/PC/52, Annex.

Comments of the European Union on the Chairman's revised Draft Programme of Action on Small Arms (A/CONF.192/PC/L.4/Rev 1), 2 March 2001, UN Doc Doc No A/CONF.192/PC/32, Annex.

Committee for the Regulation of the Trade in, and Private and State Manufacture of, Arms and Implements of War, Report on Progress of Work, Geneva, 12 Nov, 1932, League of Nations Doc *Official No* Conf.D.145

Committee for the Regulation of the Trade in, and Private and State Manufacture of, Arms and Implements of War, 23 July 1934, League of Nations Doc No.Conf.D./C.G.171, Geneva, Annex. B, *Draft Articles*

Committee of Experts on Al-Qaeda, established pursuant to SC Res1333/2000, UN Doc Doc No S/2002/101, 5 February, 2002, Annex. iv.

Country Statements on Small Arms, UN GA First Committee, October–November, 2001, at <http://www.reachingcriticalwill.org/1com/2001state/stateindex.html#week1>, <http://www.reachingcriticalwill.org/1com/2001state/state

index.html#week2> and <http://www.reachingcriticalwill.org/1com/2001 state/stateindex.html#week3>

Declaration concerning Firearms, Ammunition and Other Related Materials in the Southern African Development Community, 20 March 2001, UN Doc Supp No A/CONF.192/PC/35, Annex.

Declaration of Principles on Interim Self-Government Arrangements, Report of the Secretary General on the Palestine problem, 11 Oct. 1993, UN Doc Supp No A/48/486, S/26560, Annex.

Draft Programme of Action to Prevent, Combat and Eradicate the Illicit Trade in Small Arms and Light Weapons in All Its Aspects, Working Paper by the Chairman of the Preparatory Committee, UN Doc Supp No A/CONF.192/PC/L.4/Rev.1, 12 Feb, 2001.

Draft Proposal Submitted by Argentina for document A/CONF.192/PC/L.4/Rev.1, 6 April 2001, UN Doc Supp No A/CONF.192/PC/45, Annex.

Draft Proposals submitted by Cuba on Sections I, II and III, document, 2 May 2001 (A/CONF.192/PC/L.4/Rev.1), 10 April 2001, UN Doc Supp No A/CONF.192/PC/47, Annex.

Drafting Proposals submitted by the European Union on document A/CONF. 192/PC/L.4/Rev.1, 29 March 2001, UN Doc Supp No A/CONF.192/PC/40, Annex.

Elements for Consideration in the Substantive Preparation for the 2001 Conference on the Illicit Trade in Small Arms and Light Weapons in All Its Aspects, submitted by the European Union on 2 March 2000, UN Doc Supp No A/CONF.192/PC/6.

EU Programme for Preventing and Combating Illicit Trafficking in Conventional Arms, EU Code of Conduct on Arms Exports, Submitted by Portugal on behalf of the EU, 13 March 2000, UN Doc Supp No A/CONF.192/PC/3, Annexes I and II.

European Union-Canada Statement adopted at the European Union-Canada Summit in Ottawa on 16 December 1999, 11 July 2000, UN Doc Supp No A/CONF.192/PC/11, Annex.

B Frey, 'The Question of Trade, Carrying and Use of Small Arms and Light Weapons in the Context of Human Rights and Humanitarian Norms': *Working Paper* submitted in accordance with Sub-Commission decision 2001/120, UN Doc Supp No E/CN.4/Sub.2/2002/39, 30 May, 2002

GA Res 1514 (XV): Declaration on the Granting of Independence to Colonial Countries and Peoples of 1960.

GA Res 181(II) (A+B)/1947: Future Government of Palestine.

GA Res 1889 (XVII): Question of Southern Rhodesia.

GA Res 2625 (XXV): Declaration on Principles of International law Concerning Friendly Relations and Cooperation among States.

GA Res 2758 (XXVI)/1971: Restoration of the Lawful Rights of the Peoples Republic of China in the United Nations.

GA Res 3236 (XXIX)/1974: Question of Palestine.

GA Res 3237 (XXIX)/1974: Observer Status for the Palestine Liberation Organisation

GA Res 3314 (XXIX): Definition of Aggression.

GA Res 39/11/1984: The Declaration on the Right of People's to Peace.

GA Res 40/3/ 1985: The Proclamation of the International Year of Peace.

GA Res 46/36 L/1991: Transparency in Armaments (UN Doc Supp No A/RES/46/36 L/1991, Annex—UN Register of Major Conventional Arms).

GA Res 46/36/1991: General and Complete Disarmament: International Arms Transfers.
GA Res 48/75 H/1993: Measures to Curb the Illicit Transfer and Use of Conventional Weapons.
GA Res 49/75 M /1994: General and complete Disarmament Measures to curb the illicit transfer and use of Conventional Arms.
GA Res 49/75G/1994: General and Complete Disarmament: Assistance to States for Curbing the Illicit Traffic in Small Arms and Collecting them.
GA Res 50/70B/1995: General and Complete Disarmament: Small Arms.
GA Res 50/72 D/1995: Review of the Implementation of the Rrecommendations and Decisions adopted by the General Assembly at its 10th Special Session: Report of the Disarmament Commission.
GA Res 52/38 J / 1997: General and Complete Disarmament: Small Arms.
GA Res/ 53/77 E /1998: General and Complete Disarmament: Small Arms.
GA Res 53/79 A/1998: Review of the Implementation of the Recommendations and Decisions Adopted by the General Assembly at its 10th Special Session: Report of the Disarmament Commission.
GA Res 54/54 V/1999: General and Complete Disarmament: Small Arms.
GA Res 55/2/2000: UN Millennium Declaration.
GA Res 57/27/2003: Measures to Eliminate International Terrorism.
GA Res 58/55/2003: Promotion at the regional level in the Organization for Security and Cooperation in Europe of the United Nations Programme of Action on the Illicit Trade in Small Arms and Light Weapons in All Its Aspects.
GA Res 59/144/2004: The Role of Diamonds in Fuelling Conflict: Breaking the Link between the Illicit Transaction of Rough Diamonds and Armed Conflict as a Contribution to Prevention and Settlement of Conflicts.
GA Res 59/157/2004: International Cooperation in the Fight Against Transnational Organized Crime: Assistance to States in Capacity-building with a view to Facilitating the Implementation of the United Nations Convention against Transnational Organized Crime and the Protocols thereto.
GA Res 59/66/ 2004: National Legislation on Transfer of Arms, Military Equipment and Dual-use Goods and Technology.
GA Res 59/85/2004: The Illicit Trade in Small Arms and Light Weapons in All Its Aspects.
GA Res 59/86/ 2004: The Illicit Trade in Small Arms and Light Weapons in All Its Aspects.
Good-For-Thought Paper, Contribution to the Realization of an International Plan of Action in the context of the 2001 Conference: Marking, Identification, and Control of Small Arms and Light Weapons, by France and Switzerland, 17 March 2000, UN Doc Supp No A/CONF.192/PC/7, Annex.
Guidelines for International Arms Transfers in the context of General Assembly Resolution 46/36 H of 6 Dec. 1991, 1996, Report of the Disarmament Commission, UN Doc Supp No A/51/42, Annex I.
Guidelines for International Arms Transfers, UN Disarmament Commission, Substantive Session, 22 April–7 May 1996, New York, UN Doc Supp No 42(A/51/42), 1996, Annex. 1.
Guidelines on Conventional Arms Control/Limitation and Disarmament, with Particular

Emphasis on Consideration of Peace in the context of General Assembly resolution 51/45 N, 1999, UN Doc Supp No A/54/42, Annex III.

Guidelines on Conventional Arms Control/Limitation and Disarmament, with particular emphasis on Consolidation of Peace in the context of Resolution 51/45 N, 1999, UN Disarmament Commission, UN Doc Supp No 42(A/54/52), 1999, Annex. III

Interpretative Statement on Section II, paragraph 4, of the draft Programme of Action (A/CONF.192/PC/L.4/Rev.1), working paper submitted by Switzerland, 3 April 2001, UN Doc Supp No A/CONF.192/PC/42, Annex.

Larger Freedom: Towards Development, Security and Human Rights, UN Secretary General's Report of 21 March 2005, UN Doc Supp No A/59/2005.

Latter dated 23 Feb 2000 from the Permanent Representative of Algeria addressed to the Under-Secretary-General for Disarmament Affairs, 25 February 2000, UN Doc Supp No A/CONF.192/PC/2.

Letter dated 16 March 2001 from the Permanent Representative of Namibia to the United Nations addressed to the Under-Secretary-General for Disarmament Affairs, transmitting the text of the Declaration concerning Firearms, Ammunition and Other Related materials in the Southern African Development Community, UN Doc Supp No A/CONF.192/PC/35.

Letter dated 23 February 2000 from the Permanent Representative of Algeria addressed to the Under-Secretary-General for Disarmament Affairs, UN Doc Supp No A/CONF. 192/PC/2.

Memorandum by the US Delegate, No 2, League of Nations, Doc NoConf.D./C.G.171, 1933, Geneva, Annex. A.

Millennium Summit, Part—IV, 'Freedom from Fear', Kofi Annan, 2000, at <http://www.un.org/millennium/sg/report/ch3.pdf>

Monitoring Group on Al-Qaeda, established pursuant to SC Res 1363/200, UN Doc Supp NoS/2002/101, 5 Feb. 2002, Annex. V.

Monitoring Group on Somalia, established pursuant to SC Res 1519/2003.

National Control of the Manufacture of and Trade in Arms, League of Nations, Doc *Official No* Conf.D.184, Geneva, 14 April 1938.

Note verbal dated 1 March 2000 from the Permanent Mission of France to the united Nations and note verbal dated 2 march 2000 from the Permanent observer Mission of Switzerland to the United nations transmitting the 'Food-for-thought paper' entitled 'Contribution to the realization of an international plan of action in the context of the 2001 Conference: marking, identification, and control of small arms and light weapons', UN Doc Supp No A/CONF.192/PC/7, 17 March 2000.

Note verbal dated 2 March 2001 from the Permanent Mission of Sweden to the United Nations addressed to the Department of Disarmament Affairs of the Secretariat, transmitting the Comments of the European Union on the Chairman's revised Draft Programme of Action on Small Arms (A/CONF.192/PC/L.4/Rev.1), UN Doc Supp No A/CONF.192/PC/32.

Note verbal dated 28 June 2000 from the Permanent Mission of Portugal to the United Nations addressed to the Secretariat of the Preparatory Committee, UN Doc Supp No A/CONF.192/PC/10.

Note verbal dated 28 March 2001 from the Permanent Mission of Sweden to the United Nations addressed to the Secretariat of the Preparatory Committee, transmitting, on behalf of the European Union, drafting proposals on the revised Draft Programme of Action, UN Doc Supp No A/CONF. 192/PC/40, 29 March 2001.

Note verbal dated 29 June 2000 from the Permanent Mission of Portugal to the UN addressed to the Secretariat of the Preparatory Committee, UN Doc Supp NoA/CONF.192/PC/11, Annex.

Note verbal dated 29 June 2000 from the Permanent mission of Portugal to the United Nations addressed to the Secretariat of the Preparatory Committee, UN Doc A/CONF.192/PC/11, 11 July 2000.

Note verbal dated 3 April 2001 from the Permanent Mission of Cuba to the United Nations addressed to the United Nations Secretariat, transmitting drafting proposals on the revised draft Programme of Action (A/CONF.192/PC/L.4/Rev.1), UN Doc Supp No A/CONF.192/PC/47, 2 May 2001.

Note verbal dated 3 April 2001 from the Permanent Mission of the Russian Federation to the united Nations addressed to the Chairman of the Preparatory Committee, transmitting drafting proposal on the revised draft Programme of Action (A/CONF.192/PC/L.4/Rev.1), UN Doc Supp A/CONF.192/PC/52, 10 April 2001

Note verbal dated 30 March 2001 from the Permanent Mission of Argentina to the United Nations addressed to the Secretariat of the Preparatory Committee, transmitting dragging proposals on the revised draft Programme of Action (A/CONF.192/PC/L.4/Rev.1), UN Doc Supp No A/CONF.192 PC/45.

Note verbal dated 30 March 2001 from the Permanent Observer Mission of Switzerland to the UN addressed to the Secretariat of the Preparatory Committee, transmitting working paper on the revised draft Programme of Action, UN Doc Supp No A/CONF.192/PC/42, Annex. II

Note verbal dated 30 March 2001 from the Permanent Observer Mission of Switzerland to the United Nations addressed to the Secretariat of the Preparatory Committee, transmitting working paper on the revised draft Programme of Action (A/CONF.192/PC/L/Rev.1), UN Doc Supp No A/CONF.192/PC/42, 3 April 2001.

Note verbal dated 30 March 2001 from the Permanent Observer Mission of Switzerland to the United Nations addressed to the Secretariat of the Preparatory Committee, transmitting, on behalf of Mexico, Switzerland and the United States of America, a working paper on the revised draft Programme of Action (A/CONF.192/PC/L.4/Rev.1), UN Doc Supp No A/CONF.1922/PC/43, 3 April 2001.

Note verbal dated 6 July 2000 from the Permanent Mission of the United States of America to the United Nations addressed to the Secretariat of the Preparatory Committee, UN Doc Supp No A/CONF.192/PC/12.

OSCE Measures on Small Arms, UN Doc Supp A/RES/58/55, 17 December 2003.

Panel of Experts on Angola/UNITA, established pursuant to SC Res 1295/2000.

Press Release, *SC Condemns Madrid Terrorist Bombings,* SC/8022 (SC Res 1530, 11 March 2004).

Programme of Action to Prevent Combat and Eradicate the Illicit Trade in Small Arms and Light Weapons in All its Aspects (PoA), UN Doc Supp No A/CONF.192/15, 2001.

Progress Report of Barbara Frey, Sub-Commission on the Promotion and Protection of Human Rights, UN Doc Supp No E/CN.4/Sub.2/2004/37, 21 June 2004.

Proliferation of Small Arms and Light Wweapons and Mercenary Aactivities: Threat to Peace and Security in West Africa, Declaration of the UN SC, 'UN Doc Supp S/RES/1467/2003, 18 March 2003.

Proposal Submitted by Brazil for document A/CONF.192/PC/L.4/Rev.1, 6 April 2001, UN Doc Supp No A/CONF.192/PC/46, Annex.

Report of a Consultative Meeting of Experts on the Feasibility of Undertaking a Study for Restricting the Manufacture and Trade of Small Arms to Manufacturers and Dealers Authorised by States, 6 July 1999, UN Doc Supp No A/54/160, Annex.

Report of Group of Governmental Experts on Ammunitions and Explosives, UN Doc Supp No A/54/155, *Disarmament study series No 28* (1999), p 90.

Report of the Biennial Meeting of States on the Implementation of the PoA on Illicit Small Arms and Light Weapons, 17–21 July 2003, UN Doc Supp No A/CONF. 192/BMS/2003/1, Annex. 'Chairman's Summary'.

Report of the Economic and Social Council, the Third Committee of the GA, Draft Res XVII/1982, UN Doc Supp No A/37/745.

Report of the Group of Government Experts established pursuant to General Assembly resolution 54/54 V/1999 (Feasibility of Restricting the Legal Trade in Small Arms), 12 March 2001, entitled 'Small Arms', UN Doc Supp No A/CONF.192/PC/33.

Report of the Group of Government Experts established pursuant to General Assembly Resolution 56/24 V of 24 December 2001, entitled 'The Illicit Trade in Small Arms and Light Weapons in All Its Aspects' (Group of Governmental Experts on Marking and Tracing) UN Doc Supp No A/58/138, 11 July 2003.

Report of the Group of Governmental Experts established pursuant to General Assembly Resolution 54/54 V of 15 December 1999 entitled 'Small Arms', UN Doc Supp No A/CONF.192/PC/33, 12 March, 2001.

Report of the Group of Governmental Experts established pursuant to GA Resolution 54/54 V of 15 December 1999, entitled 'Small Arms', 12 March 2001, UN Doc Supp No A/CONF.192/PC/33.

Report of the Group of Governmental Experts on Small Arms (Reviewing Panel), UN Doc A/45/258, 1999, 3 August 1999, *Disarmament Study Series No 28* (1999) p 69.

Report of the Group of Governmental Experts on Small Arms, 27 Aug 1997 (UN Doc Supp No A/52/298) *Disarmament Study Series No 28*, United Nations Publication, p 11.

Report of the Group of Governmental Experts on Small Arms, UN Doc Supp A/54/258, 1999, *Disarmament Study Series No 28* (1999), United Nations Publication, p 43.

Report of the Monitoring Group on Al-Qaeda, UN Doc Supp No S/2003/1070, 2 Dec. 2003

Report of the Monitoring Group on Al-Qaeda, UN Doc Supp S/2002/65, 14 June 2002.

Report of the Monitoring Group on Somalia, UN Doc Supp No SC/8169, 17 August 2004.

Report of the Panel of Experts on UNITA, UN Doc Supp No S/2000/203, 10 March 2000.

Report of the Preparatory Committee for the United Nations Conference on the Illicit Trade in Small Arms and Light Weapons in Its All Aspects, 21 March 2000, UN Doc Supp No A/CONF.192/PC/9.

Report of the Sanctions Committee of the SC on Angola, UN Doc Supp NoS/2000/1225, 21 December 2000, Annex.

Report of the Sanctions Committee on Al-Qaeda, UN Doc Supp No S/2003/1070, Annex.

Report of the Secretary General to the Security Council on Small Arms, 20 Sep. 2002, UN Doc Supp No S/2002/1053, 20 September 2002.

Report of the Secretary General, Small Arms, UN Doc Supp No S/2002/1053, 20 September 2002.
Report of the SG on Small Arms, UN Doc Supp S/2005/69, 7 February 2005.
Report of the UN Conference on the Illicit Trade in Small Arms and Light Weapons in All Its Aspects, UN Doc Supp No A/CONF.192/15, 9–20 July 2001, New York.
Report of the UN First Biennial Meeting of States to Consider the Implementation of the Programme of Action to Prevent, Combat and Eradicate the Illicit Trade in Small Arms and Light Weapons in All Its Aspects, UN Doc Supp No A/CONF.192?BMS/2003/1, 18 July 2003.
Res 59/74/2004: Assistance to States for Curbing the Illicit Traffic in Small Arms and collecting them.
Review of the Recommendations and Decisions Adopted by the GA: Report of the Disarmament Commission in the Context of GA Resolution 51/45 N, 9 June 1999, UN Doc Supp NoA/51/182.Rev.1.
SC Res 217/1965: Question Concerning the Situation in Southern Rhodesia.
SC Res 221/1966: Question Concerning the Situation in Southern Rhodesia.
SC Res 240/1967: The Situation in the Middle East.
SC Res 242/1967: The situation in the Middle East.
SC Res 338/1973: Cease-Fire in the Middle East.
SC Res 417/1977: South Africa.
SC Res 418/1977: South Africa.
SC Res 661/1990: Iraq-Kuwait.
SC Res 687/1991: Iraq-Kuwait.
SC Res 688/1991: Iraq.
SC Res 713/1991: Socialist Federal Rep of Yugoslavia.
SC Res 724/1991: Socialist Federal Rep of Yugoslavia.
SC Res 733/1992: Somalia.
SC Res 748/1992: Libyan Arab Jamahiriya.
SC Res 827/1993: Tribunal (Former Yugoslavia).
SC Res 841/1993: Haiti.
SC Res 853/1993: Armenia-Azerbaijan.
SC Res 864/1993: Angola.
SC Res 917/1994: on Sanctions for Restoration of Democracy and Return of the Legitimately Elected President to Haiti.
SC Res 924/1994: on the Situation in Yemen.
SC Res 929/1994: on Establishment of a Temporary Multinational Operation for Humanitarian Purposes in Rwanda until the Deployment of the Expanded UN Assistance Mission for Rwanda.
SC Res 940/1994: on Authorization to Form a Multinational Force under Unified Command and Control to Restore the Legitimately Elected President and Authorities of the Government of Haiti and Extension of the Mandate of the UN Mission in Haiti.
SC Res 1072/1996: The Situation in Burundi.
SC Res 1076/1996: The Situation in Afghanistan.
SC Res 1101/1997: The Situation in Albania.
SC Res 1132/1997: The Situation in Sierra Leone.
SC Res 1161/1998: on the Situation Concerning Rwanda [to establish Commission of Inquiry on Rwanda].

SC Res 1189/1998: on the International Terrorism.
SC Res 1214/1998: on the Situation in Afghanistan.
SC Res 1160/1998: on the Letters from the United Kingdom (S/1998/223) and the United States. (S/1998/272) [the Federal Republic of Yugoslavia/Kosovo].
SC Res 1261/1999, 1314/2000, 1379/2001, and 1460/2003 on Children and Armed Conflict.
SC Res 1227/1999: on the situation between Eritrea and Ethiopia.
SC Res 1267/1999: on the situation in Afghanistan.
SC Res 1269/1999: on the Responsibility of the Security Council in the Maintenance of International Peace and Security [International Terrorism].
SC Res 1270/1999: on the Situation in Sierra Leone.
SC Res 1373/2001: Threats to International Peace and Security caused by Terrorist Acts.
SC Res 1377/2001: Threats to International Peace and Security caused by Terrorist Acts [Declaration on International Terrorism].
SC Res 1397/2002: The Situation in the Middle East, Including the Palestinian Question.
SC Res 1467/2003: Proliferation of Small Arms and Light Weapons and Mercenary Activities: Threats to Peace and Security in West Africa.
SC Res 1515/2003: The Situation in the Middle East, Including the Palestinian Question.
SC Res 1516/2003: Threats to International Peace and Security caused by Terrorist Acts [terrorist attacks in Istanbul].
SC Res 1519/2003: The Situation in Somalia.
SC Res 1555/2004: The Situation concerning the Democratic Republic of the Congo.
SC Res 1556/2004: Report of the Secretary-General on the Sudan.
SC Res 1558/2004: The Situation in Somalia.
SC Res 1572/2004: The situation in Côte d'Ivoire.
Security Council, *Agenda: Small Arms*, UN Doc Supp No S/PV.4048, 24 September 1999.
TP SEETHARAM, Indian Minister, *Statement in the First Biennial Meeting of States on the Implementation of the PoA of 2001*, 7–11 July 2003, New York.
Small Arms and Light Weapons in Central America: Implementing the UN Programme of Action's Aspects for Control and regulation of Arms Transfers, Recommended Actions for National and Regional Implementation, Approved by Consensus, Arias Foundation, 5 December, 2001, San Jose, Costa Rica, at <http://disarmament.un.org/cab/SALW-orgs.html>
Statement by the President of the SC on Small Arms, UN Doc Supp No S/prst/1999/28, 24 September 1999.
Statement by the President of the Security Council, UN Doc Supp No S/PRST/2005/7, 17 February 2005.
Statement of U Kyaw Tint Swe, Permanent Representative of the Union of Myanmar to the UN, UN Doc Supp NoA/CONF.192?BMS/2003/1, 18 July 2003.
Supervision of the Private Manufacturers of Arms and Ammunitions and of Implements of War, League of Nations, Doc A.92.1926.IX, Res of 21 September, 1926.
Document to an Agenda for Peace: Position Paper of the Secretary-General on the Occasion of the 50th Anniversary of the UN, 3 Jan, 1995, UN Doc Supp No A/50/60-S/1995/1.

Tehran Conference on Human Rights, Res XXIII, 12 May, 1968, 'Human Rights in Armed Conflicts' (A/CONF.32/41).

The 10th Anniversary of the UN Register of Conventional Arms, Symposium, 15 October 2002, New York.

The Coming in to Being of the UN Register, Ambassador Wagenmakers Hendrik's speech (founding father) at <http://disarmament.un.org/cab/reg-10thanniv.html>

The Humanitarian Challenge of Small Arms Proliferation, presented to the First PrepCom—2001 UN Conference on Small Arms, by the Delegation of the Republic of Mali—on behalf of the Eminent Person Group, New York, 28 February–3 March, 2000.

UN Deputy Secretary General, *Speech—UN Conference on Small Arms*, New York, 9 July 2001.

UN Doc Supp No S/PV.392, 24 December 1948.

UN Economic and Social Council Res1986/10, *the Use of Force by Officials of a State*.

UN HRC Comment on the US, UN Doc CCPR/C.79/Add.50, (1995).

UN Press Release, *Secretary General Deeply Moved at Death of President Arafat*, 11/11/2004, UN Doc SG/SM/9585, PAL/2016.

UN Press Release, UN Doc GA/9866, 31 May 2001.

UN Press Release, 'Secretary-General Disappointed Small Arms Conference Ended without Agreement, But Says Global Community Committed to Action Plan to Curtail Illicit Trade', UN Doc SG/SM/10558 DC/3038, 10 July 2006.

UN SC's Debate on Small Arms, UN Doc Supp 7984/29 January 2004.

UN SC's Debate on Small Arms, UN Doc S/PV. 4048, 24 September 1999.

United States Comprehensive Initiative on Small Arms and Illicit Trafficking, 14 July 2000, UN Doc Supp No A/CONF.192/PC/12, Annex.

United States—European Union Statement of Common Principles on Small Arms and Light Weapons, Washington DC, 17 December 1999, submitted on 11 July, 2000, UN Doc Supp No A/CONF.192/PC/10, Annex i.

Working Paper on Elements for a Framework for Cooperation and Action on Illicit Trade in Small Arms and Light Weapons in All its Aspects, submitted by South Africa, 2 March, 2000, UN Doc Supp No A/CONF.192/PC/5.

Working Paper submitted by Mexico, Switzerland and the United States, amendments on document A/CONF.192/PC/L.4/Rev.1, 3 April 2001, UN Doc Supp No A/CONF.192/PC/43, Annex.

Working Paper submitted by the People's Republic of China transmitting preliminary views on the Final Document of the United Nations 2001 Conference on the Illicit Trade in Small Arms and Light Weapons in all its Aspects, UN Doc Supp No A/CONF.192/PC/13, 18 July, 2000.

JR Bolton, United States Press Briefing on Small Arms Conference, 9 July 2001, UN headquarters, New York.

Regional Materials

Annual Report on the Implementation of the EU Joint Action, *OJEC*, No 2001/C216/01, 1 August 2001.

Bamako Declaration: an African Common Position on the Illicit Proliferation, Circulation and Trafficking of Small Arms and Light Weapons, Bamako, Mali, 30 September–1 October 2000.

Best Practice Guidelines for Export of Small Arms and Light Weapons, Wassenaar, Plenary of 11–12 December 2002.

Brasilia Declaration on the Illicit Trade in Small Arms and Light Weapons, The Latin American and Caribbean States, Brasilia, 24 November 2000.

Canada-EU Statement, 'Small Arms and Anti- Personnel Landmines', at <http://www.iansa.org/documents/gov/gov6.htm>

Conference on Strengthening Export Controls on Small Arms and Light Weapons, Lancaster House, London, 14–15 January 2003: fact sheet.

Council Joint Action on the European Union's Contribution on Combating the Destabilising Accumulation and Spread of Small Arms and Light Weapons and Repealing Joint Action 1999/34/CFsP, 12 July 2002, *OJEC, No 2002/589/CFSP*, 19 July 2002.

ECOWAS, *Code of Conduct for the Implementation of the Moratorium on the Importation, Exportation and Manufacture of Light Weapons*, Lome, 10 December 1999, *UNIDIR, 2002/2*.

Elements for Export Controls of Man-portable Air Defence Systems (MANPADS), agreed at the 2003 Plenary <http://www.wassenaar.org/2003Plenary/MANPADS_2003.htm>

EU Code of Conduct on Arms Exports, Council of Europe, May 1998.

EU Council Regulation No 1334/2000 of 22 June 2000, *on the Control of Exports of Dual-use Items and Technology, OJEC (OJ) L 159*, 30 June, 2000, p 1 (as amended by Council Regulation (EC) No 149/2003 of 27 January 2003.

EU Joint Action on Small Arms of 17 December 1998, (1999/34/CFSP), *OJEC, 15/1/999, L/9/1*.

Fifth Annual Report According to Operative Provision 8 of the European Code of Conduct on Arms Transfers, OJEU No 2003/C 320/01, 31 December 2003, p 1.

First Continental Meeting of African Experts on Small Arms and Light Weapons, Report of the Meeting of Experts, OAU Doc SALW/RPT/EXP (I), Addis Ababa, Ethiopia, May 2000.

Implementing the UN PoA: Strengthening Export Controls, Chairman's Summary, Lancaster House Conference, 14–15 January, 2003.

OAU Resolution on Apartheid and Racial Discrimination (CM/Res 142 (X)).

OAU Resolution on Southern Rhodesia, (CM/Res 78 (VII)).

OAU Resolution on Territories under Portégées Domination (CM/Res 137 (X)).

OSCE Decision based on the Interim Report on Nagorno-Karabakh, Committee of Senior Officials, *Journal No 2*, Annex 1, Seventh Committee Meeting, Prague, 27–28 February, 1992.

OSCE Document on Small Arms and Light Weapons (FSC. JOUR/314), Vienna, 24 November 2000.

OSCE Charter for European Security, Istanbul, November 1999.

*OSCE*Decision No 6/99 (FSC.DEC/6/99), 16 November 1999.

OSEC Document on Small Arms and Light Weapons, Forum for Security Co-operation, Adopted at the 308th Plenary Meeting, Vienna, 24 November 2000.

Principles Governing Conventional Arms Transfers, OSCE, 49 Plenary Meeting, Vienna, 25 November, 1993, *FSC/Journal No 49*.

Second Annual Report—on the Implementation of the EU Joint Action of 12 July 2002, OJEC, No 2002/C 330/01.

Second Annual Report: On the Implementation of the EU Joint Action of 12 July 2002 on the European Union Contribution to Combating the Destabilizing Accumulation and Spread of Small Arms and Light Weapons (2002/589/CFSP) *OJEC,* C 330/01, 31December 2002.

South Africa Regional Action Programme on Light Arms and Illicit Arms Trafficking, May 1998, Seminar summary, at <http://www.saferworld.co.uk/pubsouth.htm>

Statement by HE Ambassador John Freeman, Head of the UK delegation to the Biennial Meeting of States [BMS] on behalf of the European Union, *Thematic Debate Intervention: Import/Export Control and Illicit Brokering,* 14 July, 2005.

Tackling Illicit Trafficking in Conventional Arms: Strengthening Collective Efforts by EU and Associate Countries, Executive Summary, April 1999, at <http://www.saferworld.co.uk/pubtrafficking.htm>

Tackling Light Weapons Proliferation: Issues and Priorities for the EU, Executive April 1999, at <http://www.saferworld.co.uk/pubtackling.htm>

The WASSENAAR Arrangement on Export Controls for Conventional Arms and Dual-Use Goods and Technologies, Initial Elements, Plenary of 11–12 July 1996, at <http://www.wassenaar.org/docs/IE96.html>

Third Annual Report on the Implementation of the EU Joint Action, Council of the EU Doc 13657/03, Brussels, 6 November 2003, Annex.

Wassennar Best Practice Guidelines for Export of Small Arms and Light Weapons, Plenary of 11–12 December 2002.

Weapons Trade: OSCE 1999 Small Arms Division', 269th Plenary Meeting, Decision No 6/99, 16 November, 1999, *FSC Journal No 275.*

West African Arms Moratorium, Abuja, 31 Oct. 1998, at <http://www.nisat.org/west%20africa/african.htm>

West African Small Arms Moratorium, High-level Consultations on the Modalities for the Implementation of PCASED, *Workshop Report, UNIDIR, 2002/2,* United Nations: Geneva.

Domestic Laws and Materials

Annual Firearms Manufacturing and Export Report, Year 2001, (AMER), at <http://www.atf.gov/firearms/stats/afmer/afmer2001.pdf>

Arias Foundation, *'Comparative Analysis: Central American Legislation on Issues Related to the Possession and Carrying of Firearms',* at <http://disarmament.un.org/cab/SALW-orgs.html>

Austria—*Legal Gazette I* No 57 of June 2001 (EU Code incorporated in to the law of the country).

Canadian Firearms Act, 1995.

Code of Conduct on Arms Transfers Act of 1999, HR 2269 IH, 106th Congress, First Session, 17 June 1999.

Criteria to be Used in Considering Conventional Arms Export License Applications', Statement by the Secretary of State for Foreign and Commonwealth Affairs, 28 July 1997, at <http://projects.sipri.se/expcon/natexpcon/uk/ukcriteria.html>

Explanatory Memorandum for an Agreement to Facilitate the Restructuring and Operation of the European Defence Industry, Geoff Hoon, Secretary of State for Defence, 2 November 2001, at <http://www.mod.uk/issues/edi/>

Federal Law of the Russian Federation adopted by the State Duma, 3 July 1998.

France, Decree No 234, 22 October 1997.

France, Legislative Decree, 18 April 1939.

French Decree No 95-589 of 6 May 1995.

French Policy on Export Controls for Conventional Arms and Dual Use Goods and Technologies, Information Provided by France to the WASSENAAR Agreement on Export Control, at <http://projects.sipri.se/expcon/natexpcon/France/frenchpolicy.htm>

Guidelines for National Unification of One China, adopted by the National Unification Council, Third Meeting, 23 February 1991, and by the Executive Yuan Council (Cabinet), 2223rd Meeting, 14 March 1991.

Hansard HC vol 415 col 855W (8 May 2003).

Hansard HC vol 413 col 74W (12 May 2003).

Hansard HC vol 413 cols 29-30WS (18 November 2003).

Hansard HC vol 413, cols 989-90W (19 November 2003).

Hansard HC vol 413 col 855W (8 May 2003).

Hansard HC vol 419, cols 955-56W (25 March 2004).

Indian Arms Act, No 54, 1959.

Jamaica Firearms Act: Acts 1 of 1967/ 29 of 1973/38 of 1973/ 8 of 1974 S.19/ 17 of 1974/ 1 of 1983 S. 10/12 of 1985.

Law of the Republic of China on the Control of Firearms, Twentieth Session of the Standing Committee of the Eighth National People's Congress, Presidential Order No 72, July 5, 1996.

National Firearms Act, 1936 (NFA), U.S.C. 26.

National Report of The People's Republic of China on the Implementation of the UN SALW Programme of Action, Ministry of Foreign Affairs, 7 July, 2003.

Order in Council Fixing the Mode of Weaponries, Weapons and Ammunition, French, Order in Council of 18 April 1939.

Palestinian Legislative Council, *Basic Law Draft Resolution*, Third Reading, Passed 2 October, 1997, signed by Arafat on 30 May 2002.

People's Republic of China, Regulations on Export Control of Military Items, Decree No 234, 22 October 1997, effective from 1 January 1998.

PRC White Paper—*The One China Principle and the Taiwan Issue*, the Taiwan Affairs Office and the Information Office of the State Council, 21 February 2000, at <http://www.taiwandocuments.org/white.htm>

President Lee's (ROC), *Deutsce Welle Interview*, 9 July 1999, at <http://www.taiwanheadlines.gov.tw/state/1.htm>

Presidential Decree No 1953, 1 December 2000 to Form the Russian Federation Committee for Military–Technical Cooperation with Foreign States.

Presidential Edict No 1953, 1 December 2000, a Statute on Commission on Questions of the Federation's Military–Technical Cooperation with Foreign States.

Quadripartite Committee: *Strategic Export Control—Annual Report for 2002* (HC 390, 18 May 2004).

Report on Armament Exports to Parliament from France, 2001, p 14, para 1, at <http://www.defense.gouv.fr/english/files/d163/pdf/2.pdf>

Taipei Update, 29 February, 2000, at <http://www.roc-taiwan.org/dc/press/20000315/2000031502.html>

The Arms Export Control Act, 1976 (AECA), 22 U.S.C. 2778.

The Constitution of the Republic of China, Adopted by the National Assembly, 25 December 1946, Promulgated by the National Government on 1 January, 1947.

The Gun Control Act, 1968 (GCA), as amended 18 U.S.C. Chapter 44.

The National Firearms Act, 1988 (NFA), 26 U.S.C. Chapter 53

UK Firearms Act, 1968, Ch. 27, *Public General Acts and Measures*, 1968, Part. I, p 611, London: HMSO.

UK Export Controls Act 2002, Chapter 28

Understanding Canadian Firearms Law, a Guide to Key Information in the Firearms Act, Regulations and, Support Material, Revised March 2001, at <http://www.cfc-ccaf.gc.ca/en/owners_users/guide/default.asp>

US *Code of Federal Regulations,1974*, 22 U.S.

US Department of State, 'Can Small Arms and Light Weapons Be Controlled?', 2 June, 2001, at <http://usinfo.state.gov/topical/pol/arms/stories/01060243.htm>

NGOs and other Sources

Amnesty, BASIC, Christian Aid, Oxfam, Saferworld and World Development Movement, 'Final Analysis: Code of Conduct of the Arms Trade', at<http://www.basicint.org/WT/armsexp/EUcode-final.htm#Introduction>

Curbing Small Arms Proliferation in South Eastern Europe, Saferworld and Partner Seminars, May–June, 2001, at <http://www.saferworld.co.uk/SeminarSouthEastEurope.PDF>

ICRC Report to the BMS to Consider the implementation of the UN PoA to Prevent Combat and Eradicate the Illicit Trade in Small Arms and Light Weapons in all its Aspects, New York, 7–11 July 2003.

J Jackson, private discussion on the WTO Law v. the Arms Trade, Gorgetwon Law Centre, Washington DC, 24 October 2006.

Letter from Colombia, 'Effect of a Ban Carrying Firearms on Homicide Rates in two Colombia Cities', at <http://www.iansa.org/documents/research/2000/colombia.pdf>

Meeting of Eminent Persons Group with NGOs in Support of a successful UN Conference on the Illicit Trade in Small Arms and Light Weapons, Naval & Military Club, London, 18 June 2001, chair's report, at <http://www.geocities.com/eminentpersonsgroup/un2.html>

Model Convention on the Registration of Arms Brokers and the Suspension of Unlicensed Arms Brokering, The Fund for Peace, prepared for the UN Conference on the Illicit Trade in Small Arms, 2001 at <http://www.fundforpeace.org/publications/reports/model_convention.pdf>

NGO Press Release, 'Government's Weak Arms Law Proposals could allow UK Brokers to Supply Iraq, through the Back Door,' 30 January 2003, at <http://saferworld.co.uk/PR300103.htm>

Nobel Peace Laureates' International Code of Conduct on Arms Transfer, 29 May 1997, New York, at <http://www.basicint.org/WT/armsexp/INTLcode.htm>

Press Release, 'Central and Eastern Europe remains Important Source and Transit Route for Arms', *Saferworld*, 2 July 2002, at <http://www.saferworld.co.uk/BeastPr.htm>

Press Release, 'Thirteen More Governments Announce Support for Arms Trade Treaty', *Control Arms*, 14 July2005 10: am GMT.

Report of the Conference on Contemporary Problems of the Law of Armed Conflict, Carnegie Endowment for International Peace, Geneva 15–20 September 1969 (1971), 'the law of Armed Conflicts', New York.

Res XXVIII of the XXth International Red Cross Conference, Vienna, 1965

Reviewing Legal Aspects of Substitution Treatment at International Level, at <http//:eldd.emcdda.org>

M ROCARD, former Prime Minister of France and Co-chair of the Eminent Persons Group, 'The Scourge of Small Arms: Who Supplies, Who Dies?' speech, Kennedy Political Union at American University, Washington DC, 28 February, 2000.

E ROWE, Chairman Manufacturers Advisory Group (WFSSA), 'Report on Firearms Industry Efforts to Fight Illicit Trafficking in Firearms', *UN BMS*, 7–11 July 2003, New York.

Russia to give Palestinian Police 45 APCS, 16 September, 1994, at <http://csf.colorado.edu/dfax/matn/matn9409.htm#T-0047>

The Draft Framework Convention on International Transfers, NGO Working Draft of 21 December 2003.

K TIDSWELL, representative of Sport Shooter Association of Australia (member of WFSA), 'Definition, Reliable Facts and Human Rights Concerns', *First Biennial Meeting of States on Small Arms*, 7–11 July 2003, New York.

D VIVEASH, 'Small Arms after the United Nations Conference: The way forward', *Report on the Public Engagement Roundtable*, Parliament Hill, Ottawa, 25–26 March, 2002.

C WARBRICK, *private discussion on issues relating to small arms trade vis-à-vis international law*, 4 October 2003.

Treaties

The Protocol on Explosive Remnants of War (Protocol V) to the 1980 CCW, 28 November 2003.

1912 International Opium Convention (the Hague Convention).

1925 Convention (drugs).

1949 Geneva Convention I for the Amelioration of the Condition of Wounded, Sick and Shipwrecked members of The Armed Forces in the Field.

1949 Geneva Convention III Relative to the Treatment of Prisoners of War.

1949 Geneva Convention IV Relative to the Protection of Civilian Persons in Time of War.

1977 Geneva Protocol I Additional to the Geneva Convention of 12 August 1949, and Related to the Protection for Victims of International Armed Conflict.

1977 Geneva Protocol II Additional to the Geneva Convention Relating to the Protection of Victims of Non-International Armed Conflicts.

A Proposed Global Convention Prohibiting the International Transfer of Military Small Arms and Light Weapons to Non-state Actors, Canadian Discussion Paper, Canadian Mission to the UN, New York, December 1998.

A Proposed Global Convention Prohibiting the International Transfer of Military Small Arms and Light Weapons to Non-State Actors, Canadian Mission to the UN, New York, December 1998, discussion paper.

Anti Ballistic Missile Treaty (ABM), 26 May 1972.

Australia–US Agreement on Uranium Transfers, 31 July 2001, at <http://www.aph.gov.au/house/committee/jsct/nst/treaties/taiw_nia.pdf>

Biological and Toxin Weapons Convention, 1972.

Canada-US Exchange of Letters of 24 February 1993, 'Non-proliferation assurance to Canadian uranium retransferred from the US to Taiwan', at <http://www.lexum.umontreal.ca/ca_us/en/cts.1993.05.en.html>

Convention for the Control of the Trade in Arms and Ammunition, and Protocol, Signed at Saint-Germain-en-Laye, 10 September 1919.

Convention on Prohibitions or Restrictions on the Use of Certain Conventional Weapons which may be Deemed to be Excessively Injurious or to Have Indiscriminate Effects, 1980.

Convention on Psychotropic Substances, New York, 1971.

Convention on the Physical Protection of Nuclear Material, entered into force 8 February 1987.

Convention on the Prohibition of the Development, Production and Stockpiling of Bacteriological (Biological) and Toxin Weapons and on their Destruction, 1975.

Convention on the Prohibition of the Development, Production, Stockpiling and Use of Chemical Weapons and on Their Destruction (CWC), 1993.

Convention on the Prohibition of the Use, Stockpiling, Production and Transfer of Anti-Personnel Mines and on their Destruction, 1997.

Conventional Arms Forces in Europe Treaty (CFC), 1991.

Declaration Renouncing the Use, in Time of War, of Certain Explosive Projectiles, St Petersburg, 29 November/11 December 1868.

Draft Convention for the Control of the International Trade in Arm, Munitions and Implements of War, League of Nations, *Official No* C.758.M.258.1924.IX.

Draft Convention with regard to the Supervision of The Private Manufacture and Publicity of the Manufacture of Arms and Ammunition and of Implements of War, League of Nations, Doc *Official No* C.393.1929.IX, Geneva, 29 August 1929.

Draft Convention with regard to the Suppression of Private Manufacturer, League of Nations, *Official No* C.393.1929.IX (C.F.A./39(i)), Geneva, 29 August 1929.

Geneva Gas Protocol, 1925.

Inter-American Convention Against the Illicit Manufacturing of and Trafficking in Firearms, Ammunition, Explosives, and Other Related Materials, 1997.

Inter-American Convention on Transparency in Conventional Weapons Acquisition. (Resolution adopted at the first plenary session, held on 7 June 1999).

International Convention for Limiting the Manufacture and regulating the Distribution of Narcotic Drugs, 1931.

International Convention for the Suppression of the Financing of Terrorism, GA Res 54/109/2000, Annex.

International Covenant on Civil and Political Rights, 1966.

International Covenant on Economic, Social and Cultural Rights, 1966.

Protocol Against the Illicit Manufacturing of and Trafficking in Firearms, Their Parts and Components and Ammunition, Supplementing the UN Convention Against Transnational Organised Crime, UN Doc Supp No A/Res/55/255, 31 May 2001.

Protocol on the Control of Firearms, Ammunition and Other related Materials in the Southern African Development Community (SADC) Region, Blantyre, Malawi, 14 August 2001.

Rome Statute of the International Criminal Court, 1998.

Single Convention on Narcotic Drugs, New York, 1961, as amended by the Protocol of 25 March 1972. *Statute of the International Court of Justice*, 1945.

The 1980 UN Convention on the Prohibitions or Restrictions on the Use of Certain Conventional Weapons Which May be Deemed to be Excessively Injurious or to Have Indiscriminate Effects, entered into force on 2 December 1983.

The Nairobi Protocol for the Prevention, Control and Reduction of Small Arms and Light Weapons in the Great Lakes Region and the Horn of Africa, 21 April 2004.

The Treaty on Conventional Arms Forces in Europe, Paris, 19 November 1990.

Treaty Banning Nuclear Weapons Tests in the Atmosphere, in Outer Space and Under Water, 5 August 1963, USA-UK-USSR.

Treaty on the Non-Proliferation of Nuclear Weapons, 1968.

United Nations Convention Against Trans-national Organised Crime, UN GA Res A/55/255, 15 November 2000, Annex I.

Universal Declaration of Human Rights, GA Res 217 A (iii), 1948.

Vienna Convention on the Law of Treaties, 1969.

The African Charter on Human and Peoples' Rights, 1982.

American Convention on Human Rights, 1978.

Selected Websites

http://disarmament.un.org/cab/salw-tracingexperts.html
http://disarmament.un.org:8080/cab/smallarms/
http://europa.eu.int/comm/external_relations/cfsp/doc/small_arms_en.pdf
http://hrw.org/english/docs/2001/07/19/global312.htm
http://pawss.hampshire.edu/topics/smallarms/
http://pawss.hampshire.edu/topics/smallarms/bibliography.html
http://projects.sipri.se/armstrade/atmethods.html
http://sand.miis.edu/projects/guide.htm
http://sand.miis.edu/research/Biblio/biblio_SALW.html
http://sitemaker.umich.edu/ipe/small_arms_forum_draft_resolution
http://tri.army.mil/LC/CS/csi/satoc.htm
http://usinfo.org/usia/usinfo.state.gov/topical/pol/arms/smllarm/homepage.htm
http://www.101guns.com/
http://www.armscontrol.org/
http://www.basicint.org/WT/smallarms/main.htm
http://www.bicc.de/
http://www.bits.de/projects/smallarms.htm
http://www.caat.org.uk/about.php
http://www.caat.org.uk/information/issues/small-arms-issue.php
http://www.cdi.org/issues/armstrade/sm_arms.html
http://www.cdi.org/program/index.cfm?programid=23
http://www.controlarms.org/

http://www.csd.bg/en/euro/arms.php
http://www.dfait-maeci.gc.ca/arms/convweap3-en.asp
http://www.dfat.gov.au/security/small_arms.html
http://www.dfid.gov.uk/pubs/files/smallarmslightweapons04-06.pdf
http://www.encyclopedia.com/html/s1/smallarm.asp
http://www.eureka.lk/sapint/event_smallarms.html
http://www.fas.org/asmp/campaigns/smallarms/sawg.htm
http://www.fas.org/asmp/profiles/smallarmship_db.htm
http://www.fcnl.org/issues/arm/sup/small_arms_backgd.htm
http://www.fcnl.org/issues/issue.php?issue_id=46
http://www.fco.gov.uk/
http://www.fco.gov.uk/servlet/Front?pagename=OpenMarket/Xcelerate/ShowPage&c=Page&cid=1007029393987
http://www.globalissues.org/Geopolitics/ArmsTrade/SmallArms.asp
http://www.globalpolicy.org/security/smallarms/salwindx.htm
http://www.grip.org/bdg/g1899.html
http://www.guncontrol.ca/Content/Temp/small_arms.htm
http://www.hdcentre.org/?aid=61
http://www.humansecuritybulletin.info/archive/en_v1i3/inthenews_2.htm
http://www.iansa.org/
http://www.iansa.org/documents/2001/index
http://www.iansa.org/documents/regional/regindex.htm
http://www.icrc.org/
http://www.idrc.ca/en/ev-26230-201-1-DO_TOPIC.html
http://www.ippnw-students.org/smallarms.html
http://www.isn.ethz.ch/news/dossier/small_arms/editorial/
http://www.itrcweb.org/gd_SMART.asp
http://www.mena-small-arms.org/
http://www.mofa.go.jp/policy/un/disarmament/weapon/
http://www.nato.int/
http://www.nato.int/docu/handbook/2001/hb060204.htm
http://www.nisat.org/
http://www.nra.org.uk/
http://www.nra.org/
http://www.osce.org/fsc/13087.html
http://www.osce.org/fsc/13087.html
http://www.oxfam.org/eng/policy_pape_smallarms.htm
http://www.ploughshaResca/content/CONTROL%20WEAPONS/UNSmallArmsConf.htm
http://www.pna.gov.ps/
http://www.prio.no/page/Project_detail/Research_details/9244/37800.html
http://www.psr.org/home.cfm?id=pressroom19
http://www.research.ryerson.ca/SAFER-Net/
http://www.rmcs.cranfield.ac.uk/symposia/SA2005
http://www.saligad.org/declarations/declarations.html
http://www.sfu.ca/casr/101sm-spec.htm
http://www.smallarms.org.uk/
http://www.smallarmsnet.org/

http: / / www.smallarmssurvey.org /
http: / / www.state.gov / t / pm / wra / c3670.htm
http: / / www.un.org / Depts / dpa / ngo / history.html
http: / / www.una-uk.org /
http: / / www.undp.org / bcpr / smallarms /
http: / / www.unicef.org.uk / unicefuk / policies / policy_detail.asp?policy=5
http: / / www.unicef.org / emerg / index_smallarms.html
http: / / www.unidir.ch / bdd / fiche-ouvrage.php?ref_ouvrage=0-7546-2076-X-en
http: / / www.unidir.ch / bdd / focus-search.php?onglet=5
http: / / www.unidir.org / bdd / fiche-article-fr.php?ref_article=889
http: / / www.useu.be / SUMMIT / arms1200.html
http: / / www.washingtonpost.com / wp-dyn / world / issues / smallarms /
http: / / www.wassenaar.org /
http: / / www.wassenaar.org / docs / criteria.html# paper
http: / / www.wcc-coe.org / wcc / what / international / brazilfinal.html
http: / / www.who.int / topics / small_arms / en /
http: / / www.who.int / violence_injury_prevention / resources / res19 / en /
http: / / www.worldrevolution.org / guide / smallarms
http: / / www.worldrevolution.org / guidepage / smallarms / literature
http: / / www.fas.org / asmp / library / article.html
http: / / www.heckler-koch.de / html / index.html
http: / / disarmament2.un.org / cab / register.html
http: / / disarmament.un.org:8080 / vote.nsf
http: / / www.unodc.org / unodc / en / drug_and_crime_conventions.html
http: / / www.un.org / documents / scReshtm

Index